Alleviating Economic Distress

Alleviating Economic Distress

Evaluating a Federal Effort

Raymond H. Milkman
Christopher Bladen
Beverly Lyford
Howard L. Walton

Foreword by Carl Albert

Lexington Books
D.C. Heath and Company
Lexington, Massachusetts
Toronto   London

To our spouses, lovers,
and other good friends;
also to our parents

Contents

List of Figures

List of Tables

Foreword

The growth and increasing prosperity enjoyed by this nation in the 1950s and 60s were not shared by all areas or all citizens. Residents of some areas of rural America numbered among those who profited only marginally from the country's expanding economy. In every region poverty pockets remain, where inhabitants struggle to eke out a living, and the opportunities and conveniences taken for granted by most Americans are virtually unknown.

Balanced national growth is necessary to improve living conditions in these depressed areas and to break the cycle of deterioration. Unless the growth that occurs during this decade is channeled to insure the economic development of these areas, out-migration of the "fittest" will continue, and those left behind will be trapped in that cycle.

Many of the programs administered by the federal government have some impact on economic development. However, in recognition of the extreme needs of certain areas, Congress has created special programs to stimulate and accelerate their economic development. One of the most substantial programs in this category is administered by the Economic Development Administration (EDA), whose mission is to stimulate development in all regions of the country experiencing economic distress. Since its creation in August 1965, EDA has expended almost two billion dollars for this purpose.

To equip EDA to accomplish its mission, Congress furnished the agency with a unique mix of program tools. Public works grants and loans are available for developing a depressed community's infrastructure; business development loans and loan guarantees can be made to aid private industries that locate or expand in an underdeveloped area; and technical assistance can be furnished to any public or private group or individual working in the field of economic development. In addition, EDA has funds to support planning activities in single counties or multicounty districts, as well as research related to economic development.

When Congress passes legislation creating an agency, it has an obligation to see that the agency's performance is evaluated after a sufficient amount of time has elapsed. This is particularly true in the case of an agency such as EDA, whose program involves considerable experimentation. The agency itself also has an obligation to examine its efforts and attempt to increase its effectiveness. Without rigorous evaluations, Congress and agency administrators have no basis for recommending program modifications or for measuring success.

Despite the importance of evaluation activities both to Congress and agencies themselves, few federal agencies have established ongoing evaluation systems. EDA is an exception. In recognition of the value of evaluation efforts and in response to a request by the White House, EDA officials initiated an expanded and intensified evaluation effort in January 1970. Since that time, more than

750 projects have been evaluated by in-house analysts and private consultants. These evaluations have allowed for project comparisons, as well as examination of total programs, such as the Indian and urban programs. The evaluation function is now an integral part of EDA's program. The analyses conducted to date have been instructive not only to program administrators and Congress, but to the Office of Management and Budget as well.

The evaluation findings to date show that EDA public works projects lead to the location in a distressed area of one job for each $2,300 of agency investment. Certainly this figure will vary over time and there are no data from similar programs to make comparisons, but overall it indicates a reasonably effective program.

Job location is just one of the output measures that has been used to evaluate EDA's programs. The impact of the program on the economy and institutional structure of the grant recipient community are also considered. The fostering of institutions is particularly important, because they provide development expertise at the local level. Evaluations, to date, have shown that EDA has been instrumental in creating lasting economic development institutions at the local level.

EDA's evaluation system has not, however, been limited to providing data demonstrating the agency's effectiveness. Shortcomings have also been identified. Among these is the lack of adequate integration of federal activities affecting economic development, particularly with respect to training funds. The somewhat unrealistic view of EDA growth centers has also been pointed out through the agency's evaluation efforts, as has the need for more specific job placement and advancement objectives for EDA-funded projects related to training.

More important than the number of projects evaluated or results obtained, however, is the fact that program analysis has been established as an ongoing effort at EDA. Not only does this ongoing evaluation system furnish data indicating the level of agency effectiveness; it also provides Congress and agency policy-makers with insights into the reasons for the program's successes and failures. The latter seems to me a particularly valuable function for government agencies, and I would encourage more agencies to engage in the types of evaluation activities described in this book.

Carl Albert

Speaker of the House of
Representatives

United States Congress

Preface

It is extremely difficult to write a book about program evaluation that will satisfy both the theoretician and the practitioner. Those who are theoretically oriented are interested in rigorous analytic models that allow for analysis of cost and benefit data over appropriate time horizons. They are interested in assurances that appropriate discount rates and efficacious experimental design are implemented.

Alleviating Economic Distress will not completely satisfy this group of individuals, for our emphasis was on devising a practical approach to program evaluation—one that could be implemented and was easily understood by decision makers. As a result, our approach to conducting evaluations was usually to start at the project level, to get our hands dirty through in-depth interviews with project applicants (typically local economic development groups) and direct project beneficiaries (typically medium-sized corporations). It was at this level that the problems of attributing benefits were solved rather than through application of mathematical models. Programs were then analyzed through compilations of project data and through application of appropriate supporting research.

One of our major goals as evaluators was to see the recommendations generated by analyses implemented by decision makers in the operating divisions of the agency. For this reason, substantial emphasis was placed on the presentation of results. All studies culminated with a briefing or seminar, where findings, conclusions, and recommendations were presented to top agency officials. While we realized some success in having valid recommendations implemented, our "batting average" could have been considerably higher.

One factor we believe contributed to our disappointing impact in this area was the program analysis group's position in the agency's organizational structure. We feel that the organizational position of a program evaluation group in the bureaucracy, or in a private concern, is of prime importance. In many cases, significant changes cannot be brought about by collective bargaining; they must be decreed. Decrees, almost by definition, have optimal results if they come from positions of power. If high level decision makers expect evaluation to serve as a tool for improving program effectiveness, evaluation staffs must report directly to them.

There are two major sections in *Alleviating Economic Distress*. The first places the evaluation of the Economic Development Administration's (EDA) programs in context through an historical analysis of agency activities. The second part describes the evaluation approach that was developed and presents the results of its implementation. Three chapters in the latter section are directed to the question of growth centers and their role in economic development for distressed areas. Theoreticians will probably find Chapter 9 most to their liking, for an analytical growth center identification system is presented there. Although the approach taken is rather elementary, it has the advantage of being easy to implement. Program analyses relating to EDA activities on Indian reservations and projects concerned with training are also discussed in the second section.

What is presented here is clearly no more than a beginning. A movement toward developing more sophisticated methodologies is needed in the field of program evaluation. However, new approaches must entail reasonable implementation costs and should be developed for use by the decision maker rather than for journal publication. We hope that this documentation of our efforts at one government agency will stimulate those working in the program evaluation field to develop additional tools to meet their needs. Although each analyst conducting research of this nature must design an approach to fit his particular problem, the material presented here should provide a basis on which to structure an evaluation system, as well as guide in its implementation. In a sense, then, *Alleviating Economic Distress* can be viewed as a case study which should be of help not only to those involved in evaluating economic development programs, but to all who are working in the field of social program analysis.

Raymond H. Milkman, Christopher Bladen,
Beverly Lyford, Howard L. Walton

Washington, D.C., March 1972

Acknowledgments

No one can summarize thousands of pages of analysis with claims to final authority. The analysis of Economic Development Administration (EDA) programs was far too vast to report it all—all the economically distressed areas with all their problems, all the experiences of the people who designed programs, and all the insights gained by the hundreds of analysts involved in conducting program evaluation. This book presents four individuals' views of the Economic Development Administration and the process and results of program evaluation within this agency. It would not, however, have been possible without the help of countless friends and colleagues.

The first of these is the present Assistant Secretary of Commerce for Economic Development, Robert A. Podesta. As administrator of EDA, he decided to make evaluation an ongoing part of EDA activities; without his support and encouragement, the effort would not have been undertaken. Secondly, we thank George T. Karras, director of EDA's Office of Public Works, who taught us what stimulating economic development is all about. Mr. Karras was often a sharp critic of our work but never failed to participate in and encourage the evaluation process.

Much of the methodology used in conducting the evaluations of EDA activities was conceived by Barry M. Kibel, consultant to EDA. Other contributors to methodology development included Harold A. Hovey, William H. Oldach, Wilbur A. Steger, and Harold W. Williams. Other notable contributors to the evaluation effort from outside government were Peter B. Davis, Padraic P. Frucht, Norman H. Jones, Jr., Roy Littlejohn, Joseph W. Noah, and Richard C. Reagan. Present and former EDA personnel who made substantial contributions were Louise LeB. Adamson, J. Theodore Anagnoson, Raymond V. Arnaudo, Dolphine S. Bass, Daryl M. Bladen, Jason Benderly, Mary Helen Blume, Peggy B. Burke, J. Michael Cavanaugh, Patricia A. Christian, Laurence H. Clark, Margaret M. (Bee) Corkery, Kenneth L. Deavers, Henry L. Eskew, John C. Flory, Steven Frank, Harry Gildea, Thomas R. Herrick, Kathleen Hoag, Katherine D. Hoagland, Lillian L. Jackson, Neil G. Macey, Howard L. Magnas, Samuel R. Rosenblatt, Frederick A. Ricci, Michael M. Samordic, C. James Sample, Patricia E. Simpich, Craig C. Singer, Anthony J. Sulvetta, and Mary A. Toborg.

Herbert S. Becker provided leadership and was responsible for the general administration of the effort.

We are especially grateful to Patricia D. Beander for assisting in the preparation of the final manuscript.

The authors prepared this book as individuals and not as official representatives of the Economic Development Administration. Therefore, its contents should not be construed as reflecting the official policy or viewpoint of that agency.

Raymond H. Milkman, Christopher Bladen,
Beverly Lyford, Howard L. Walton

**Part I:
The Evolution of
Economic Development
Administration Policies**

1

Economic Development Programs Preceding EDA

The foundation for federal legislation providing aid to economically depressed areas was laid in the decade before the creation of the Economic Development Administration (EDA). Debate, compromise, coalition building, experimentation, success and failure all played roles in shaping the agency that exists today. However, although congressional guidance cannot be discounted, the primary influence in preparing the EDA legislation was the experience acquired from the operations of the Area Redevelopment Administration (ARA). Other influences included the concepts embodied in the Appalachian Regional Development Act and public and congressional reaction to the Public Works Acceleration Act (APW).

Creation of an Agency

The Area Redevelopment Administration was established in May 1961, with the stated goal of implementing an effective program to alleviate conditions of substantial and persistent unemployment and underemployment in certain economically distressed areas. This action represented a climax to seven years of heated debate on the subject, during which time two similar programs had been rejected by presidential vetoes.

Regarded as an experimental program to give legislative support to the declarations of the Full Employment Act of 1946, ARA succeeded in creating jobs and generating income in depressed areas throughout the county. However, despite its accomplishments, the ambitious undertaking was plagued from the outset with a variety of problems. Conceived as an organ for encouraging private enterprise to locate in depressed areas and armed with such tools as business loan funds and public facility grants, ARA emerged as an enthusiastic organization trying to administer a broadly defined and inadequately funded program. It was further handicapped by the national economy, which, by operating considerably below capacity, produced a climate particularly unfavorable to the expansion or establishment of business.

As implemented by ARA, area redevelopment focused on creating jobs in depressed areas. Congressional pressures to designate eligible areas and expend funds played havoc with any notions of planning entertained by program administrators. For the most part, experience dictated policy. Projects were analyzed by top agency officials at project review meetings. As each element

3

requisite to project approval was isolated, a guideline was issued declaring an agency policy to require that element in future projects.

One example of this procedure was the "bird in hand" policy adopted in the first year of the agency's existence. This decision to require that any public works grant or loan be directly linked to a business venture represented an interpretation of the legislation by ARA administrators and grew out of a concern to preserve reason in the project selection process. Without a requirement of this type, there was no logical basis for choosing among the hundreds of project applicants competing for ARA's limited public works funds. The effect of this decision was twofold: to demonstrate the demand for public facilities funds; and to indicate to congressmen and local communities that ARA had a broader commitment than funding public works facilities in depressed communities.

The difficulties of ARA can in large part be attributed to the agency's image, which was tarnished by mistakes and unrealized expectations. An overenthusiastic staff filled early reports and news releases with inflated figures concerning job creation and unemployment reduction, and the General Accounting Office publicly accused ARA of claiming false results. Accompanying this criticism were cries of impracticality and political motivation in the selection of projects.

Also joining in the fray were advocates of regional and growth center approaches to economic development, who attacked the ARA program as artificial. Even elements of organized labor, previously overwhelmingly in support of the ARA concept, criticized the agency for allegedly assisting in business relocations. ARA was further discredited by its mistakes in encouraging local businessmen to expand. Although ARA intentions were good in such cases, the results were often devastating: to the individuals whose enterprises failed, to local communities, and to ARA's image as a redevelopment agency.

ARA's effectiveness in creating jobs and lowering the incidence of unemployment was further impaired by funding problems. During most of the period covered by ARA operations, more than 1,000 counties were eligible for assistance. However, the agency's four-year appropriation was only $551.9 million, or just over $550,000 per county. Actual obligations were even lower, totaling $352.3 million, or approximately $352,000 per county.

Other funding problems also hindered agency operations. The total public facility grant authorization of $75 million was requested and appropriated during the first two years of operation. However, ARA obligated only $41.5 million, or 55 percent, of this amount. (Primarily because of a shortage of acceptable project applications, the newly created agency experienced difficulty in obligating its resources during the first year of operations; less than 4 percent of the $40 million public facility grant appropriation was expended. During the 1963 fiscal year, this problem was remedied, and approximately $34 million of the $35 million public facility grant appropriation was obligated.)

Public Works Acceleration Act

In September of 1962, Congress passed the Public Works Acceleration (APW) Act. This act, which was legislated as a counterrecessionary measure to generate temporary employment, stipulated that one-third of its $900 million authorization be allocated for public works projects in ARA-designated areas. Other areas eligible for APW funding were approximately 300 labor market areas that had exhibited substantial unemployment for at least nine of the preceding twelve months. Under ARA criteria, counties could not become eligible for agency assistance unless they had experienced substantial unemployment for considerably longer periods of time, ranging from two to four years.

ARA administered the APW program and, with the help of the Community Facilities Administration and the Public Health Service, expended approximately $851 million in APW funds in less than two years. During that period, the program afforded temporary relief to unemployed residents of depressed areas and provided infrastructure facilities for hundreds of underdeveloped communities. However, the APW legislation required no evidence of local planning to award a grant or loan. Although the absence of such a requirement expedited the processing of project applications, it also resulted in criticism that the program had minimal ties to concepts of area redevelopment.

By January of 1963, less than five months after the APW legislation was enacted, the response to the program had been so great that states and communities were discouraged from filing further project applications. Applicants for public facility grants could still seek ARA funds, but even that resource was exhausted by the end of June. In light of this situation, a bill to increase the ARA authorization and provide additional public facility grant funds was introduced in Congress during the spring of 1963. After being defeated in the House by a five-vote margin, the bill was passed by the Senate on June 26 and returned to the House for reconsideration. Congress adjourned without taking further action, thus depriving ARA of public facility grant funds during the 1964 and 1965 fiscal years.

Decision to Replace ARA

Beset with these and other troubles, the Area Redevelopment Administration was sacrificed for reasons of political expediency. While accepting ARA's premise that economically lagging areas could be stimulated through such tools as public works funds and technical assistance, the administration and a majority of the nation's legislators affirmed the necessity of divesting the program of the ARA image through the creation of a new agency. However, ARA and APW experience had resulted in the approval of 9,866 projects, the creation of an estimated 117,000 permanent jobs, and the generation of approximately 210,000 man-years of short-term employment. In addition, more than 25,000 community leaders had served on local economic development committees. As a result, even those advocating the discontinuance of ARA recognized that valuable lessons had been learned.

Lessons Learned from ARA/APW Experience

Among the insights gained through ARA and APW experience was a recognition of the overwhelming demand for public works funds at the local level. Sponsors of the original depressed areas legislation had pictured economically distressed communities as possessing a basic infrastructure, but not putting it to full use. Thus, they assumed that residents would primarily be interested in establishing and attracting new businesses as a means of promoting economic development. This assumption might have been valid for the legislation's original targets—northeastern and mid-Atlantic communities suffering from the problems of coal, textiles, and other declining industries. However, it did not hold for the southern agricultural areas included to acquire more widespread support for the ARA bill. The response to ARA and APW programs not only showed that such communities lacked a basic infrastructure, but also indicated that industries were reluctant to locate in areas lacking public works and development facilities.

In recognition of this demand, framers of the EDA legislation increased emphasis on public works and renamed the bill accordingly, calling it the "Public Works and Economic Development Act of 1965." This step not only replied to the demonstrated needs of local communities, but also allowed the measure to be introduced through the Senate Public Works Committee. It was anticipated that this committee would be more agreeable to the provisions for expanded funds for each of the program tools than would the Banking and Currency Committee, which had not been particularly successful in acquiring funds for ARA.

ARA experience with local, area, and state level planning was also instrumental in shaping the EDA legislation. Overall Economic Development Programs (OEDPs) composed under ARA never attained the sophistication advocated by professional planners. The majority of these documents, which describe an area's economic problems and needs and propose solutions, failed to evolve as viable blueprints for alleviating economic distress. The lack of funds for hiring full-time economic development staffs resulted in inadequate planning and inefficient programs at the local, area, and state levels. Most communities were unable to prepare meaningful OEDPs and implement plans effectively with part-time, volunteer workers. Nonetheless, ARA administrators maintained the OEDPs were a spur to economic development because the necessity of preparing such documents forced local leaders to meet and discuss plans for their area. To combat these problems and increase the quality of local planning, the EDA legislation continued the requirement for OEDPs and provided planning and operating funds for nonfederal planning groups.

Several provisions of the EDA legislation stemmed from dissatisfaction with the results of ARA's approach to area redevelopment on a county basis. The assumption that the county represented the only basic unit through which economic development could be achieved was disproved as a result of ARA/APW experience. Although ARA administrators experimented with some regional and multicounty planning, framers of the EDA legislation devised a significantly broader geographic approach to economic development. One component of this approach involved the establishment of regional commissions for dealing with economic problems on a multistate basis. This particular strategy evolved from ideas explored in ARA technical assistance studies and from the provisions of the Appalachian Regional Development Act, which established a regional commission to coordinate economic development in Appalachia.

The regional approach was accompanied by legislative prescriptions for a multicounty district program similar to that employed in France and the United Kingdom. Reflecting the belief that certain areas could not mount effective attacks on unemployment and low income on their own, this program encouraged the pooling of talents and resources to achieve common aims. The act stipulated that financial provisions for the district program be withheld for a period of one year after EDA began operations. It was expected that this interval would be devoted to planning.

Included in the legislation was a capability to designate growth centers in economic development districts, a provision inserted partially to answer criticism directed at ARA by economists and planners in other agencies. The growth center concept also reflected European influence and the search for an alternative to urban migration.

Several basic assumptions underlay this strategy. The first was that the provision of jobs, income, and local services in growth centers would benefit not only these centers, but residents of the surrounding areas as well. A second assumption was that accelerating and increasing the growth and prosperity of such centers would encourage residents of nearby depressed areas to seek work in the growth center instead of migrating to other areas. An additional assumption was that it would be less expensive to provide benefits to the target population (i.e., the unemployed and underemployed residents of depressed areas) through investments in growth centers than by funding projects in less developed areas.

ARA and APW experience underlined a number of additional deficiencies in the enabling legislation. The requirement forcing ARA to administer its programs through delegate federal agencies hampered operations and resulted in extra work for ARA personnel. The delegate agencies proved incapable of processing loans and grants at the speed necessary in a program such as ARA's, and at least one agency attempted to acquire ARA funds for its own use. Determined to spare EDA the inefficiency and overwork that resulted from this procedure, ARA administrators pressured Congress to remove the delegate agency requirement and allow EDA to operate independently.

As a result of the efforts of these ARA officials and certain congressmen, administration of the EDA program is primarily an in-house operation. Although EDA's Office of Technical Assistance has considerable interaction with the Department of Labor in relation to training activities, the Business Development Program is the only agency program that receives administrative assistance from another agency. In this case, the Small Business Administration (SBA) retained a small portion of the responsibilities it held under ARA. This entails investigating new business ventures that apply for business loans and supplying EDA with the information obtained.

Job training under the ARA program contributed significantly to the reduction of unemployment in depressed areas. Approximately 70 percent of the 45,000 jobless workers trained with ARA assistance were placed in the jobs for which they were trained. The success of ARA's job training program was partially responsible for the passage of the Manpower Development and Training Act of 1965. This act set aside special funds for use in training residents of ARA- or EDA-designated areas. The act stipulated that EDA was to assume responsibility for stimulating and reviewing applications for the expenditure of these funds.

Another problem that arose under ARA involved the percentage of local funds necessary before a grant could be approved. The ARA Act required only that the applicant contribute to project cost "in proportion to its ability" to pay. Lacking legislative stipulations as to how to determine "ability," agency officials experimented with several policies, including a complicated formula established by the Community Facilities Administration for determining the optimal amount for each applicant. Another policy implemented under ARA identified the local share as the part of the project cost that could be financed by user charges. However, political pressure—applied by constituents to congressmen and transferred to agency officials—often proved the ultimate factor in specifying a local contribution, and no ARA policy prevailed. As a result of APW success with legislation requiring specific percentages, a similar requirement was incorporated in the EDA legislation.

A final case in which ARA experience dictated EDA legislation relates to the criteria established for determining eligibility for agency funds. ARA's legislation provided specific guidelines only in relation to substantial and persistent unemployment. To be eligible for ARA funds under these criteria, an area had to have an unemployment rate of 6 percent or more for the most recent calendar year for which statistics were available; have averaged 6 percent or more unemployment for one of the time periods specified below; and meet one of three conditions: (1) have experienced unemployment 50 percent above the national average for three of the preceding four calendar years; (2) have experienced unemployment 75 percent above the national average for two of the preceding three calendar years; or (3) have experienced unemployment 100 percent above the national average for one of the preceding two calendar years.

In addition, the ARA Act empowered the Secretary of Commerce to designate as redevelopment areas those areas (including Indian reservations) "which he determines are among the highest in numbers of percentages of low-income families." Although the legislation directed the Secretary to prescribe detailed standards for designating areas on this basis, and indicated a few factors that should be considered in establishing such standards, it did not dictate specific criteria.

With the aid of data provided by the Departments of Agriculture, Labor, and Interior, ARA administrators developed such criteria. These included specific standards for designating areas on the basis of median family income, percentages of low production farms in the area, and median farm family income. The ARA criteria were used as a basis for preparing the EDA legislation, which specifies standards for determining area eligibility. In addition to the unemployment measures cited in the ARA Act, the standards originally set by the EDA legislation permit designation of the following places:

1. Areas with median family incomes not exceeding 40 percent of the national median
2. Indian reservations manifesting the greatest degree of economic distress
3. Areas designated by ARA (subject to yearly review on the basis of EDA criteria)
4. The one area that most nearly qualifies for designation in states which otherwise would have no designated areas

Places where economic changes have caused or threaten to cause substantial unemployment can also become eligible for EDA aid. Under the ARA legislation, the Secretary of Commerce had no authority to designate places where such changes threatened to result in high unemployment. To eliminate this inadequacy, the framers of the EDA legislation inserted provisions giving the Secretary power to respond to requests from such areas and declare them eligible for EDA aid. In addition, the Secretary of Commerce was given authority to make public works grants to those areas that had substantial unemployment during the preceding calendar year as determined by the Secretary of Labor on the basis of average annual unemployment statistics.

Figure 1-1 identifies places eligible for EDA aid as of July 1971. Most of these areas meet the criteria described above. However, some have been designated on the basis of criteria legislated since passage of the original EDA Act. These criteria are discussed in the following chapters.

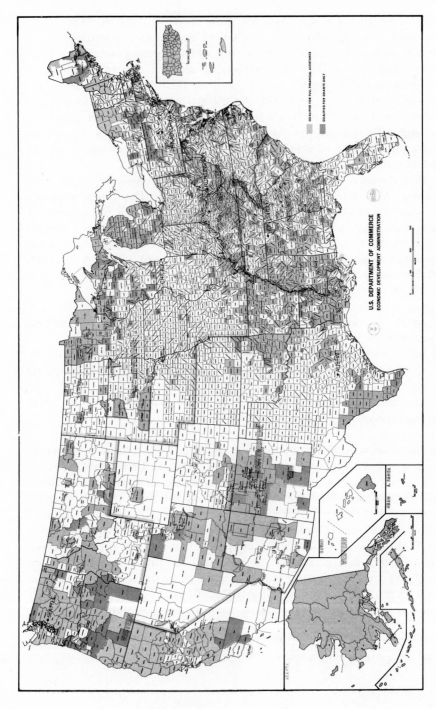

Figure 1-1. EDA Qualified Areas, July 31, 1971

2 Creation of the Economic Development Administration

Despite ARA's difficulties in maintaining a good public image, its success in creating jobs and generating income convinced Congress and the administration that the mission of permanently alleviating conditions of substantial and persistent unemployment and underemployment in economically distressed areas and regions was a feasible one. Indeed, the appeal of a comprehensive program of federal assistance to provide jobs and higher incomes for persons residing in areas where jobs were scarce and incomes low increased during ARA's tenure. The results of ARA assistance supported the program's premise that federal aid could be employed to effect economic viability in lagging areas.

Expanded Mission

While reaffirming the original ARA mission, the framers of EDA's legislation also emphasized the related goal of stemming migration from the nation's depressed areas. Those involved in structuring the EDA program recognized the endless cycle of economic distress that plagues many areas of the country. This cycle is caused by the fact that an area with a declining economic base cannot finance the public improvements necessary to attract new industry. As a result, the young people and more aggressive members of the labor force who are unable to secure local employment and are concerned about careers are forced to leave the area. Prospective employers thus find the area lacking not only in public facilities, but also stripped of the most important ingredient for rehabilitation—the availability of a high-quality labor force. The EDA legislation was designed to help local residents break this crippling cycle.

The framers of the EDA legislation also stressed the need to encourage expanded economic growth in the natural growth centers of depressed regions and areas. Accelerating the creation of employment opportunities in or near such centers was believed the most effective and timely approach to providing jobs for residents of neighboring depressed areas. The growth center strategy outlined in the legislation was included as one specific means of extending the benefits of natural growth centers to redevelopment area residents.

Those preparing the EDA legislation recognized one major deficiency in the ARA program: no particular importance had been attached to stimulating meaningful, long-range economic planning by residents of distressed areas. To remedy this situation, a clause requiring the use of such planning in conjunction with EDA financial and technical assistance was inserted in the act's statement of purpose.

In addition, the legislators provided for grants to organizations with planning responsibilities under Title III of the act and specifically discussed the use of regional commission funds for planning purposes in Title V. These provisions identified EDA's responsibility to stimulate planning at local, district, state, and regional levels as one strategy for achieving its mission.

Interpreting the EDA Legislation

The EDA legislation states that the agency's mission is "to provide grants for public works and development facilities, other financial assistance and the planning and coordination needed to alleviate conditions of substantial and persistent unemployment and underemployment in economically distressed areas and regions." However, responsibility for establishing priorities is left to agency administrators.

The act's general nature invites a variety of interpretations. It gives no indication whether the federal government has accepted responsibility for the revitalization of all distressed areas or only a limited number. Is an area with greater need to be assisted before an area with more potential? Are the creation of jobs and generation of income the most important measures of the agency's success? How much emphasis is to be placed on the stimulation and development of long-term planning and problem solving capabilities at the local level? Although several area development strategies are outlined in the act, no explanation is given as to the relative importance of each.

In short, Congress structured the EDA legislation to allow agency policy makers to determine program direction. The act also provided EDA administrators with the flexibility to respond to local development problems on an individual basis.

The interrelated tasks of defining EDA goals and priorities posed problems for agency policy makers. The nature and causes of chronic depression and unemployment in certain areas of the nation had not been satisfactorily identified when EDA began operations. Although ARA's research program was responsible for some pioneering in this field, data describing economic conditions on a regional or area basis were far from adequate.

Even had this information been available, there was no widespread agreement on solutions to economic problems. While one school of thought argued that the provision of job opportunities and the generation of increased income were the most important ingredients in building viable economies in depressed areas, another contended that development assistance alone could not produce self-sustaining growth. This group emphasized the necessity of involving local residents in such development activities as the identification of needs, the establishment of priorities, and the formulation of an approach for addressing priorities.

Efforts to set goals and assign priorities were further complicated by the diversity of the economic problems confronting the nation's depressed areas. In operational terms, economic development obviously entailed different activities in different places. For instance, an area designated for EDA assistance on the basis of a low median family income would not necessarily benefit from the generation of new job opportunities. If the jobs offered salaries no higher than those already earned and were not filled by workers seeking to supplement family incomes, residents of the area would still suffer the discomforts associated with a low standard of living. In such a case, training projects to upgrade the skills of the local work force and loan assistance to better paying industries would appear more appropriate.

On the other hand, in areas designated on the basis of substantial unemployment, the creation of jobs at any salary level would partially alleviate the employment problem.

EDA policy makers agreed that the agency's overall mission was to assist areas of substantial and persistent unemployment and underemployment to achieve lasting economic gains through the establishment of stable, diversified local economies. The difficulty lay in identifying goals and priorities that would be relevant to the various situations likely to be encountered by the agency; obtaining agency-wide commitment to those goals and priorities; and insuring that EDA resources were applied in conjunction with them. The easiest course to follow would clearly have been to set broad goals, never identify agency-wide priorities, and evaluate each proposed project in terms of the individual needs of the area involved.

Although EDA has functioned as an operating agency for more than six years and has expended approximately $1.7 billion in federal funds, the approach to achieving the agency's mission is still a subject of discussion. Each administrator has struggled to determine precisely what constitutes economic development, which strategies would be most effective in improving the economies of depressed areas, and what priorities should be enforced. The fact that few agency-wide policies have been established testifies to the complex nature of such problems and the lack of unanimity among those responsible for solutions. Pragmatically, the director and staff members of each program office have set priorities and used their own judgment in determining the exact nature of EDA's mission.

Furnishing Program Tools

Arming the agency to accomplish its mission required more skill in developing policies and procedures to successfully implement traditional programs than in introducing new concepts. The consensus among those connected with the ARA program was that, except for the lack of planning funds, the tools furnished to the agency were suitable and sufficient for accomplishing its mission. It was commonly believed that ARA's problems stemmed from the manner in which the tools were applied and the low level of funding.

As a consequence, the basic tools furnished to EDA were substantially the same as those provided in the ARA legislation. Public works grants and loans were continued as a means of improving the social and economic overhead of communities and regions. Business loans were again provided to aid businesses creating employment in designated areas. Technical assistance grants were retained as aids in identifying development opportunities in economically distressed counties and towns, and funds were provided to support economic research. In addition, the EDA legislation introduced planning and administrative grants to finance full-time planners at the local level.

Public Works Grants and Loans

Introduced as a supplementary inducement to acquire congressional approval of the ARA legislation, the Public Works Program of grants and loans emerged under EDA as the major tool for stimulating economic development in depressed areas. Never has the annual percentage of public works expenditures fallen below 60 percent of EDA's total obligations, and, in the first year of operation, public works outlays accounted for 73 percent of the agency's $302 million obligation.

As ARA and APW experience resoundingly demonstrated, business loans and technical assistance are not sufficient tools for waging a fight against economic problems. Unless a community or area possesses the basic infrastructure to support economic activity, efforts to establish or expand businesses and educate residents to make the best use of available resources have small impact. Adequate water and sewer systems, industrial and commercial provisions, health centers, and transportation systems are among the facilities necessary if economic development is to occur. EDA public works grants and loans are used to help communities develop this infrastructure.

Business Loans

The legislators and interest groups who campaigned in the 1950s for a federal program to aid depressed areas perceived the major handicap to such areas as the unavailability of credit for establishing or expanding businesses. In accordance with this view, more than 50 percent of the funds authorized by the Area Redevelopment Act were earmarked for loans to industrial and commercial enterprises in designated areas. Although ARA operations revealed the grassroots belief that a lack of public facilities and not the unavailability of credit was the major deterrent to area development, the Business Loan Program continued to be regarded as an essential feature of the effort to transform lagging areas into viable economic units.

The EDA legislation not only dictated a substantially increased program of loans, but also removed the constraints precluding loans to sizable corporations. The Area Redevelopment Act allowed the agency to extend loan assistance to a business only if such aid were not otherwise available from private lenders or other federal agencies on reasonable terms. Thus, multimillion dollar enterprises that could have contributed significantly to the economies of depressed area were excluded from participation in ARA's Business Loan Program because they could have obtained financial aid from other sources. Without the inducement of a long-term, low-interest loan, few such companies elected to locate in designated areas.

EDA was spared this limitation through the inclusion of a clause that allows the Secretary of Commerce to make loans if the aid is not otherwise available "on terms which, in his opinion, will permit the accomplishment of the project." Therefore, if a firm's location in a depressed area as opposed to another site is contingent on receipt of an EDA loan, the Secretary can approve such aid.

Technical Assistance

EDA's Technical Assistance Program is regarded by many as the most flexible tool furnished any federal agency. Unlike the public works and business development loans and grants, technical assistance can be provided to any area that exhibits substantial need. In addition, the legislation places few limitations on the types of projects that can be implemented with technical assistance funds. Feasibility studies, management assistance, and reports evaluating and recommending resource usage are all outputs of the Technical Assistance Program, which enables communities and organizations to overcome specific economic development problems.

Under ARA, technical assistance assumed a supporting role with respect to the agency's other program tools. Technical assistance funds were often used to finance background studies to help ARA officials decide whether to furnish public works or business loan aid. Of all the categories of studies supported by ARA technical assistance grants, those studies initiated to develop regional action programs received the highest level of funding. Projects involving central city action programs, tourism and recreation, and mineral industries and ore processing also received a substantial percentage of the $16.1 million expended by ARA under its technical assistance provisions. In addition, ARA technical assistance funds financed the studies that recommended the formation of an Appalachian Regional Commission, and defrayed some of the expenses incurred by groups establishing training schools for minority unemployed and underemployed in a number of cities.

The unique value of a program of this type did not go unheeded by ARA administrators, congressmen, or Bureau of the Budget (BOB)[a] representatives. The EDA legislation contained an expanded discussion of technical assistance and provided a substantially increased authorization for technical assistance, research, and information services.

Planning and Administrative Grants

The framers of the Public Works and Economic Development Act of 1965 were cognizant of the problems encountered by ARA as a result of inadequate planning at local, county, and state levels. In most instances, planning was limited to preparation of the Overall Economic Development Programs (OEDPs) required for designation, and these documents were weak in several respects. Written by local residents who often viewed the documents as just another paperwork requirement of the federal government, the OEDPs prepared under ARA lacked sophistication and were frequently disregarded during the process of developing projects. In addition, the OEDPs dealt with county problems and resources, while ARA funded projects through towns. These shortcomings handicapped ARA administrators and forced them to employ an individual project approach that decreased the program's effectiveness and drew criticism from Congress.

The ARA administrators, BOB personnel, and congressmen involved in preparing the EDA legislation recognized that these shortcomings did not indicate a lack of interest or intelligence on the part of state and local planners. The major problem was insufficient funds. Planners were left to their own devices to finance economic development organizations, and, at the local and county levels, this resulted in part-time volunteer workers whose effectiveness was hindered by the absence of a full-time staff to direct and coordinate their efforts. The situation at the state level was somewhat improved in that the use of part-time volunteers was not necessary. However, in most states, the funds allocated for economic development efforts were far from adequate to establish an effective planning organization.

In response to these difficulties, those drafting the EDA legislation included provisions authorizing grants-in-aid to defray up to 75 percent of the staff and administrative expenses of appropriate public or private non-profit state, area, district, or local organizations. It was anticipated that these planning grants would allow local and district groups to hire full-time planners to organize the local effort, study the broader aspects of economic development, and propose projects conforming to the area's OEDP. In addition, it was expected that the

[a]Renamed the Office of Management and Budget in 1970.

grant program would make it possible for state planning organizations to increase the scope of their activities in the field of economic development.

Economic Research Funds

The remaining program tool supplied to EDA was funds for economic research. The Economic Research Program dictated by the EDA legislation represented a continuation and expansion of the ARA practice of funding studies considered valuable to those working in the field of economic development. Among the subjects designated for investigation were the causes of unemployment, under-employment, underdevelopment and chronic depression in various areas and regions, and the formulation and implementation of national, state, and local programs to raise income levels and solve other related problems. In addition, research funds were to be used to assist in providing the personnel necessary to conduct such national, state, and local programs.

Training Provisions

As previously noted, another tool used by ARA to stimulate area redevelopment emerged from the legislative debates in a somewhat altered form. Instead of allotting agency funds for training unemployed or underemployed residents of designated areas, Congress and the administration chose to limit EDA training funds to the annual appropriation provided by the Manpower Development and Training Act of 1962 (MDTA). Thus, EDA was given responsibility for stimulating, reviewing, and recommending applications for the expenditure of the MDTA funds. However, the Department of Labor controlled the funds, and EDA lacked the authority to see that its recommendations were followed.

This arrangement has never been completely satisfactory from EDA's point of view. Without direct access to training funds, agency officials cannot insure that funds are allocated to training projects directly related to EDA grants or loans. In addition, although $22 million has been appropriated each year for use in training residents of EDA-designated areas, the agency staff has often experienced difficulty in communicating its recommendations for use of this money to the Department of Labor. The MDTA legislation requires only that special funds be set aside for job training programs in designated areas of economic distress; no minimum amount is mentioned. Therefore, the Department of Labor can legally justify furnishing only a small portion of the $22 million appropriation to fund EDA-associated projects.

Applying the Tools

As inheritors of the ARA/APW legacy and recipients of a broadly stated mission, the first EDA administrators shouldered a sizable burden. The infant agency was obligated to expand a year's appropriation in eight months, despite the concurrent responsibilities of recruiting a staff, organizing the program, and establishing assistance priorities. On the positive side, however, were the existence of a holdover staff of ARA employees, the lessons learned from ARA experience, the optimism and enthusiasm of the new officials, and the possession of a proven set of program tools.

3

Initial Program Implementation: September 1965 to September 1966

The EDA legislation was signed into law on August 26, 1965, and Eugene P. Foley was appointed Assistant Secretary of Commerce and Director of Economic Development in September. The following three months were devoted to acquiring a qualified group of individuals to assume leadership responsibilities in the new agency. The majority of those recruited were economists or lawyers with experience in the business and academic communities. These professionals were widely regarded as an exceptionally talented group.

In addition to staffing efforts, the EDA administrators quickly became involved in soliciting project applications from designated areas. Although the ARA/APW project backlog was publicized as a rationale for rejecting applications, a substantial number of the holdovers failed to meet EDA criteria. As a result, the lack of feasible project applications was a major problem confronting EDA administrators in the fall of 1965.

Acquisition of Project Applications

The strategy devised for obtaining project applications was based on the theory that the more applications acquired, the better the chances of obligating the full appropriation and of selecting successful projects. This strategy also enabled EDA administrators to cite impressive demand statistics to Congress and the Bureau of the Budget (BOB) in attempting to acquire funds for the next fiscal year.

In mid-November, a conference was held in Washington for briefing field coordinators on their role in EDA's operation. At this meeting, EDA administrators stressed the need for aggressive project solicitation and the importance of local planning. Following this orientation conference, the field coordinators returned to EDA-designated areas with the goal of stimulating as many project applications as possible. Ironically, this approach necessitated a policy of disregarding local OEDPs, as there was insufficient time for examining every project in terms of its relation to the plans contained in an OEDP.

Organizing the Program

While field coordinators (currently referred to as Economic Development Representatives—EDRs) worked to spark local interest in the EDA program and

19

assisted in the preparation of OEDPs and project applications, EDA personnel in Washington concentrated on organizing the program, developing a project scoring methodology, and establishing agency priorities. As noted, the enabling legislation did not dictate approaches to these tasks, allowing EDA officials to make decisions in such areas.

When ARA was created, all decision-making power was lodged in the headquarters staff in Washington. This staff included legal and technical specialists to answer questions and solve problems stemming from the experiences of field representatives. ARA administrators believed a direct link between the field personnel and the Washington decision makers would reduce the possibilities for misinterpretation and, therefore, refrained from establishing intermediate levels of authority.

Under ARA, the personnel situated in the Washington headquarters were organized in geographic units. Those assigned to a particular division were responsible for the use of all program tools within the area overseen by that division. For example, the chief of the Northeast Division coordinated all public works, business development, technical assistance, and other ARA activities in the region represented by that division. As a result, if a town in his area applied for a high risk business loan, he could suggest and fund a technical assistance study to determine a more feasible undertaking. ARA officials suggested that this coordinated use of program tools increased their effectiveness in alleviating the problems of depressed areas.

ARA's centralized structure drew considerable criticism from members of Congress, who charged the program was too Washington-oriented to be responsive to the actual needs of local areas. Although ARA administrators resisted pressure to decentralize, sentiment for increasing field input to the decision-making process prevailed in the EDA organization. Impressed with the concept underlying ARA's experience with an experimental service office in Huntington, West Virginia, Assistant Secretary Foley decided to staff field offices in different areas of the country. Each office was responsible for coordinating and supervising EDA activities for the region in which it was located. This served to diffuse decision-making responsibilities and increase interaction between EDA personnel and residents of depressed areas.

Congress also acted to insure that the EDA organization was less centralized than that of its predecessor. The Development District Program was legislated not only to improve planning and projects by combining the efforts of two or more redevelopment areas, but also to give local citizens more voice in determining priorities. It is also possible to view the regional commission provisions as a further means of decentralization.

Primarily an innovator, Foley has been criticized on the grounds that he devoted too little time to organizing his staff. A large number of his recruits reported directly to him, as did the directors of each of the program tool offices. According to some staff members, this loosely structured organization resulted in considerable confusion and a lack of coordination between the various offices and divisions. However, Foley was among those responsible for reordering the organization of the Washington headquarters staff.

Citing the institutional biases of certain ARA holdovers and the nature of the new legislation as reasons for a change in structure, EDA officials established the program tools as line functions. All public works projects were administered by one office; all business loans were handled by another; and EDA technical assistance efforts were grouped under the jurisdiction of a third unit. Staff members of each of the three offices were expected to coordinate projects with staff members of the other offices.

In addition to establishing EDA field offices and organizing the Washington staff, Assistant Secretary Foley appointed a task force in February 1966, to develop and recommend an approach for implementing the District Program outlined in the EDA legislation. In conjunction with the establishment of this group, the Assistant Secretary also invited the governors of thirteen states in the Ozarks, Northeastern, and Upper Great Lakes areas to submit recommendations on the establishment of three regions. The recommendations were to provide statements concerning the need for designation and the initial boundaries of the economic development region. At the same time the Assistant Secretary was issuing his invitation, the Office of Regional Economic Development was formally established and given responsibility for administering EDA's contributions to this regional development program.

Project Funding

During this early period in EDA's history, considerable emphasis was placed on developing an effective system for evaluating project applications. Efforts toward this end were initiated before the close of 1965. These initial endeavors were important because they indicated the potential value of analysis techniques in preparing an EDA project selection methodology. Planners, operating officials, and program analysts were all engaged in these activities. Because these groups were particularly concerned with developing a scoring system and selection criteria to represent the agency's stated objectives, their efforts also emphasized the importance of articulating priorities.

Unfortunately, the time constraints governing evaluation of the hundreds of projects being submitted through the field coordinators prevented EDA administrators from coming to grips with the priority problem during the first year of operation. The pressure to expend the appropriation before June 30 overshadowed other considerations, although the importance of planning and funding projects that provided direct aid to the unemployed and underemployed were continually stressed.

Despite the absence of specific agency guidelines, surprisingly uniform selection criteria evolved. Throughout the agency, decision makers favored projects from those areas closest to de-designation and from areas evincing the most severe economic depression. No conscious decision was made to support projects from such areas, but hindsight suggests several explanations for the high incidence of such choices. These include the belief that assisting the least depressed areas would effect their rapid de-designation, thus freeing the agency to concentrate on the more needy areas. Political pressure to produce immediate, visible results has also been given as a reason for the choice of such projects, which often were the best planned and promised the greatest success. As for the preponderance of aid to extremely depressed areas, it has been suggested that this trend was a reflection of an agency-wide recognition of the political necessity of selecting justifiable projects.

Public Works Projects

The type of projects funded through EDA's program tools during the first year of operations followed in the pattern established under ARA. As anticipated from responses to the APW Act, requests for funds to construct water and sewer systems to serve industrial parks significantly outnumbered applications for other types of public works projects. Combined with allocations for waste and sewage treatment, funds expended for water and sewer systems during the 1966 and 1967 fiscal years composed approximately 60 percent of the Office of Public Works budget. Grants and loans for developing harbor facilities in depressed areas also ranked high on the list of public works expenditures, as did funds for tourism and road construction projects. Statistics for this period suggest that public works assistance was heavily focused on the least populous areas.

Business Loan Projects

The Business Loan Program directors recognized the difficulties incurred by ARA as a result of its lending policies and attempted to avoid similar problems by emphasizing the importance of experienced management, proven industry, and a practical debt ceiling. In addition to establishing the advisability of dealing with experienced management and established businesses, the ARA background provided information on specific industries. For example, the unfortunate results of loans to wood products industries and certain tourism efforts led EDA to be particularly careful in dealing with such enterprises. Concurrently, the success of ARA loans to small steel mills utilizing a continuous casting process paved the way for EDA assistance to similar projects. During fiscal year 1966, EDA's Office of Business Loans made loans primarily to manufacturers, including producers of wrought iron and wood products, a manufacturer of glass containers for medicines and cosmetics, a steel products firm, and an electronic parts manufacturer.

Technical Assistance Projects

Under EDA, technical assistance continued to serve as a device for funding experimental studies and for answering specific questions posed by communities and economic development organizations. The latter type of assistance, often referred to as informational projects, predominated during the first two years of EDA's existence. Local communities and organizations requested feasibility studies, particularly for tourism and recreation projects; aid in determining optimal locations for factories and industrial parks; and advice on which management techniques to apply in particular situations. Another widely requested type of assistance involved determining new uses for resources no longer in demand.

Before funding such studies, EDA officials examined the circumstances surrounding each request to determine if there were a reasonable chance of obtaining favorable results and if those in a position to act on the results of the study were likely to do so. In a number of instances, a feasibility study was performed to facilitate a decision on funding a public works project or awarding a business loan. This practice also represented a continuance of ARA procedures. It was also during this period that the first technical assistance grants to support institutions were funded.

Planning Grant Projects

EDA's Planning Grant Program was inaugurated in the spring of 1966, and by the end of June, eleven grants worth $574,000 had been awarded. During this period, emphasis was placed on aiding the infant District Program, a trend that has continued to the present. No attempt was made to solicit grants from single areas; a policy of responding to unusual needs as they arose was established in dealing with these units.

Another practice instituted during the first year of the Planning Grant Program involved awarding grants to state groups to secure their aid in forming districts and writing OEDPs. These policies were applied by program administrators with relatively few modifications during the first eighteen months of the program's operation. Even in this early stage of the program, it was recognized that one of the most important benefits of planning grant funds was the increased capability of communities to mobilize to determine problems and outline goals.

Economic Research Projects

When EDA was created, few major university economics departments specialized in the study of subnational economics. Moreover, as previously noted, data describing economic conditions on a regional or areal basis were far from adequate. EDA's Economic Research Program addressed both these deficiencies. Several broad problem areas were identified during the first year of operations, and research funds were made available for analyses related to those areas. These actions were taken not only to increase the data base as a first step toward identifying effective measures to stimulate local, areal, and regional economic development, but also to attract the attention of competent specialists to the field of subnational economics.

Guidance was sought from the academic community, and within the predetermined broad problem areas, university researchers were given latitude to investigate topics of special promise or interest. One premise underlying the policy of awarding contracts to university scholars was that the knowledge obtained by such individuals would be disseminated through the academic community. In addition, it was expected that such research projects would occasionally result in the introduction of new courses in the field of economic development. EDA's Office of Economic Research also awarded research contracts to public and private groups interested in economic development.

In an attempt to interest more students in the problems of economic development at local, areal, and regional levels, the Office of Economic Research established a student interm program during the first year of the agency's existence. This program, which was launched in the summer of 1966, was designed to familiarize college students with the economic development problems facing communities and to give the students first-hand experience in dealing with local organizations. Another objective of the program was to involve educational institutions and other federal, state, and private agencies in similar undertakings.

EDA and Urban Development

While cognizant of the necessity of expending the fiscal year 1966 appropriation of $332.4 million by June 30, EDA administrators, particularly Assistant Secretary Foley, viewed the program as innovative in nature and accordingly sought avenues of experimentation. As early as December 1965, Foley met with minority leaders in Oakland, California, to discuss their problems and consider ways in which EDA could assist them. After a number of follow-up conferences with the mayor, representatives of the business and financial communities, and other interested persons, a decision was reached to concentrate and coordinate EDA resources in the Oakland area in an all-out effort to reduce the city's unemployment problems. Technical assistance funds played an important role in plans for the Oakland experiment, and members of the Office of Technical Assistance staff were leaders in the field work involved.

The significant feature of this program was the introduction of employment plans to insure that the jobs created reached the unemployed and under-employed. This approach was conceived in February 1966 on the basis of on-site observations by EDA personnel. Developed in conjunction with Oakland officials and interested citizens, these documents were addressed to employers receiving EDA business loans or leasing or acquiring property developed by an EDA public works grant. The employment plan required employers to specify the ways in which they proposed to provide maximum employment opportunities for the long-term unemployed residing in Oakland, including training where needed.

An integral component of this approach to solving Oakland's problems was the creation of an Employment Review Board. Composed of representatives of Oakland's most severely depressed neighborhoods, labor, management, and EDA, this seven-member panel was responsible for reviewing plans and advising EDA as to their quality. Once plans were approved, employers were required to submit monthly reports to the review board, which notified EDA of the degree to which actual practices conformed to the original plan. Failure of the employer to comply with the plan was considered a default and justification for withdrawal of EDA funds.

At the time of its inception, the Oakland project was envisioned not only as an experimental attempt to directly link EDA-stimulated jobs with an area's unemployed population, but as a model for future EDA and other federal agency involvement in selected areas of the nation's urban centers. During this period, EDA's legislation precluded the agency from designating most cities. The only way for EDA to assist nondesignated urban core areas was through the Technical Assistance Program, which could fund projects for any area demonstrating substantial need. However, technical assistance disbursements in the first year of operations totalled only $6.9 million, of which approximately $1.9 million was expended to aid urban areas. Thus, urban involvement constituted only a small portion of the overall economic development program administered by the agency.

The Assistant Secretary and other top EDA officials contended that the concentrated poverty areas located in major cities should be eligible for EDA assistance. They persistently lobbied for the authority to enter more cities and requested additional funds for activities in these metropolitan areas. Although the requests were denied during this period, EDA's role in American cities continued to be the subject of numerous debates among agency personnel, congressmen, BOB representatives, and other individuals concerned with the crises of urbanization.

Organizing the District Program

The Task Force on Economic Development Districts appointed by the Assistant Secretary in the spring of 1966 spent several months discussing such topics as regional commission administration of the program and gubernatorial authority without reaching any concrete decisions. Pressure to expend the appropriated funds obscured other considerations, and the new fiscal year with its funds for the district program was only a month away when Foley delegated authority for organizing the program to William J. Nagle, who was designated as his special assistant.

The situation confronting Nagle and his staff necessitated prompt action. Not only was the establishment of organization guidelines essential, but preliminary recognition of districts and economic development centers also required immediate attention. Responses to the Assistant Secretary's request for district boundary proposals had provided more potential districts than could conceivably be funded during the 1967 fiscal year. In determining which districts to assist, EDA officials considered the percentage of district population living in redevelopment areas; per capita income in the district; percentage of families with annual incomes under $3,000; trading area and transportation patterns; and existence of a well-located economic development center.

A decision to organize and administer the program from Washington was reached shortly after the appointment of Nagle as program director. This decision reflected the fear that state or local level administrators would be subject to gubernatorial control and program direction. The feeling was that governors might not devote enough effort to involving the unemployed and underemployed residents in planning for the district. Nonetheless, in administering the program from Washington, EDA administrators worked closely with these elected officials, emphasizing the need to involve the unemployed and underemployed in planning for the district. EDA personnel also stressed the importance of minimizing state involvement after district boundaries were designated. If an established group of developers or planners existed within the district boundaries, EDA sought to use that group as a basis for the district organization.

By September of 1966, sixty-seven districts had been authorized for establishment, and a number of these newly formed entities had been designated as recipients of EDA-funded planning grants. Program officers in Washington assisted these state and local units in organizing district boards of directors, incorporating as official organizations, and applying for EDA planning and administrative grants. Aid was also provided in evaluating the qualifications of prospective district directors and other district staff members, as well as in advising the staff on how to be effective in directing a development organization.

During this early period of development, the need for haste in organizing districts often resulted in less representation for unemployed and minority groups than Washington leadership desired. However, the agency succeeded in resisting pressure to require that all district board members be local officials; as a result of EDA efforts, only 51 percent of a board's membership must be local officeholders.

Formation of Regional Commissions

Gubernatorial responses and EDA efforts resulted in the designation of three economic development regions during the 1966 fiscal year: the Ozarks Economic Development Region; the Upper Great Lakes Economic Development Region; and the New England Economic Development Region. The EDA legislation dictates that regional designation be followed by requesting the governor of each state comprising that unit to appoint one individual to serve as a member of a regional commission. This commission is headed by a federal cochairman appointed by the President. In addition, a state cochairman is elected by the commission members.

At the close of the 1966 fiscal year, a federal cochairman had been appointed for one commission, and similar procedures were being followed in organizing the other two. In addition, EDA had supplied all three commissions with funds to cover administrative costs and finance technical assistance studies. The Office of Regional Economic Development had authorized the expenditure of $932,000 for fifteen research projects related to regional development planning. Three of these projects provided economic data on the newly designated regions. Activities during this period also included discussions on the future designation of other regions.

Activities during the Summer of 1966

In June of 1966, with only a small percentage of the appropriated funds unobligated, agency officials were free to consider matters not directly related to approving and funding projects. Ross D. Davis was appointed to the position of EDA Administrator and given responsibility for handling staffing and organizational responsibilities. This allowed Assistant Secretary Foley to direct his attention to establishing policies, identifying priorities, and developing innovative approaches to the problems of economically depressed areas.

It was during this period that plans for a six-week seminar on regional economic development were formalized and implemented. This meeting, which combined the expertise of social science scholars with that of development planners and administrators, contributed to a redirection of the energies and efforts of individuals working in the field of regional economic development. Essentially, this involved concentrating on the depressed sections of a region instead of the entire area. Data collection and planning that had formerly been accomplished on a regional basis were narrowed to reflect the problems of the region's depressed areas.

Other activities engaged in by EDA during the summer and fall of 1966 included further development of guidelines for use in project evaluation and work on an agency-wide planning, programming, and budgeting system. In addition, the first in a series of steps designed to decentralize EDA's Public Works Program occurred on July 1, at which point area office personnel were given responsibility for preliminary processing of public works projects.

Efforts to establish meaningful project selection criteria received particular emphasis during this period. The Assistant Secretary requested that all pending public works projects be ranked separately by area office personnel, officials in the Washington Office of Public Works, and a group of EDA economists. When this had been accomplished, the three groups met in Washington and compared rankings.

The economists had ranked projects according to the estimated EDA investment per job and the degree of distress in the area, while the other two groups had employed a variety of criteria. For this reason, the project rankings differed. However, a joint meeting resulted in a consensus on project rankings. The outcome of this effort was a marked increased in emphasis on two project selection criteria: the estimated EDA investment per job; and the hardship suffered by the area.

4

Program Maturation: October 1966 to January 1969

In September of 1966, Assistant Secretary of Commerce Foley resigned his position, leaving the year-old agency leaderless. The gap was quickly filled. In mid-October, Ross Davis, the recently appointed EDA Administrator, was sworn in as Assistant Secretary and immediately turned his attention to those problems he considered most pressing.

Eugene Foley had been concerned with using EDA tools in the nation's cities, experimenting with techniques and projects, and encouraging local long-term planning. The new appointee shared his predecessor's enthusiasm for local planning and experimentation. However, Davis was convinced that top priority should be given to developing agency guidelines and reorganizing the EDA staff. In articulating the reasons for this emphasis, he specified the necessity of assuring Congress that EDA was an intellectually honest agency, applying relevant criteria to evaluate project applications. He also expressed the need to increase EDA's impact.

Reorganizing the EDA Staff

The new Assistant Secretary restructured EDA with the goal of creating a chain of communication that would enable him to determine if his directives were being observed at all levels of operation. This reorganization, which took place in December of 1966, established four major areas of responsibility, covering all EDA functions.

Deputy Assistant Secretaries were appointed to head each of these areas, which included: (1) responsibility for assisting the Assistant Secretary in all matters affecting EDA, as well as for coordinating all EDA field activities to provide uniform operating policies in EDA area and field offices; (2) responsibility for overseeing all EDA public works, business loans, and technical assistance projects to assure maximum resource coordination; (3) responsibility for recommending policies and procedures for coordinating EDA's programs with those of other federal, state, and local agencies; and (4) responsibility for planning for regions, districts, redevelopment areas, and other areas of substantial need. It was anticipated that this reorganization would increase the efficiency and effectiveness of EDA operations.

Other Modifications

It was during this period that Assistant Secretary Davis met with the administrators of the agency's Business Loan Program to discuss his decision to rename the program. Explaining that the program should be viewed as a means of building the private sector of the economy and not simply as an instrument for processing loans, he announced that the program would subsequently be referred to as the Business Development Program.

Early in 1967, the EDA organizational structure was further amended by the introduction of a new position. The Assistant Secretary announced the appointment of a program manager to oversee activities in the Oakland area. This action was precipitated by the need for a Washington level authority to advise the Assistant Secretary on the details of the Oakland project and to make day-to-day decisions. Envisioned as the agency-wide focal point for information on activity in Oakland, the program manager reported directly to the Assistant Secretary and was charged with reviewing and recommending every application submitted in regard to Oakland. The program manager was also responsible for coordinating EDA efforts in Oakland with those of other agencies.

The concept was subsequently refined and formalized, and program managers were appointed for the Watts section of Los Angeles, the stockyards area in Chicago, the Brooklyn Navy Yard, the Mexican-American border area, Puerto Rico and the Virgin Islands, EDA-designated Indian reservations, and Alaska. Although the efforts of these officials were handicapped in some instances by insufficient cooperation within the agency, the concept gained widespread acceptance and approval. The program managers became particularly effective in expediting the processing and approval of projects connected with their areas of responsibility.

Need to Identify Agency Guidelines

The second phase of the effort to increase EDA's impact entailed the identification of agency guidelines. Although former Assistant Secretary Foley had established a group to study and recommend policies, no directives had been issued, and no agency-wide strategy for allocating funds had been employed. As a consequence, there was no consistent rationale for selecting or rejecting applications that met the very general criteria of the act. Without such a rationale, it was difficult to overcome pressure from applicants and their congressmen to approve certain projects. This tenuous position caused Congress to view the program with considerable skepticism and disfavor.

The need for specific policies was also emphasized by the fact that 110 of the 364 projects funded during the first year of operation were located in areas that were declared ineligible after the annual designation review. The majority of the

110 projects had not progressed beyond the planning stage when this designation review was held. Therefore, it was obvious that their impact had been minimal, and that EDA assistance had played little or no role in effecting the de-designation of such areas. A result of the natural inclination to select the most promising projects, this occurrence was regarded by agency administrators as one that could have been avoided with proper planning and the identification of guidelines.

In addition, despite the abundance of rhetoric on the subject of EDA's mission, no consensus had been reached. Generating jobs and raising incomes in depressed areas, developing local capabilities to plan for economic growth, and providing residents of lagging areas with the economic benefits enjoyed by those in other sections of the country were among the mission definitions offered by various staff members. Assistant Secretary Davis contended that this ambiguity had to be resolved before the program could achieve total effectiveness. He also emphasized the necessity of accomplishing these tasks in as short a time as possible to maximize their effects on fiscal year (FY) 1967 expenditures.

Worst First Policy

Rationale and Reaction

After conferring with the Deputy Assistant Secretary for Economic Development Planning, Robert M. Rawner, and other members of the staff, Davis announced the selection of a funding strategy in December of 1966. This strategy, which the Assistant Secretary envisioned as an interim measure, called for giving first consideration to the "worst areas—those with the highest unemployment rates and lowest family incomes."[1] It was to be applied in conjunction with EDA efforts to improve the capabilities of communities, districts, and areas in the preparation and implementation of plans for local economic development. The new strategy also gave priority to projects that promised to have a clear and direct impact on unemployed and underemployed residents of depressed areas.

Davis outlined a system whereby areas experiencing the worst problems in each of the seven categories on which designation is based would receive top priority for EDA aid. These categories cover areas with substantial unemployment, persistent unemployment, substantially decreasing populations, low median family incomes, and sudden rises (or threatened sudden rises) in unemployment. The remaining two categories are economically depressed Indian reservations and areas that qualify on the basis of the "one redevelopment area per state" regulation. This legislative requirement stipulates that in states in which no areas meet the act's designation criteria, that area which comes closest to meeting the criteria shall be designated as a redevelopment area.

To determine the order or priority within the categories, agency officials were to compute the "job gap" in each eligible area. This measurement was identified as the number of jobs that would have to be created to lower the rate of unemployment or raise the median family income to that level necessary to remove an area from eligibility for EDA assistance. The "job gaps" were then to be used to set target budgets to indicate how much the agency would consider investing in an area during a specific time period.

In explaining the chosen strategy to his staff, Assistant Secretary Davis identified EDA's mission as one of changing "the statistics to bring the unemployment figures in the lagging areas down closer to the national rate."[2] However, the fact that he alluded to other goals in the same meeting forecast the difficulties he would experience in obtaining agreement on one specific mission.

While the "worst first" strategy satisfied Congress and furnished EDA personnel with a more rational approach for allocating funds, economists and others within EDA were quick to spot possible weaknesses. The major complaint voiced by critics emphasized the futility of funding areas with extremely limited potential for economic development. The advice of these strategists was to fund projects and locations with a tradeoff between area distress and project cost/benefit ratios. Opponents of worst first also submitted that the policy was in direct contrast to the principle of the District Program legislated by Congress. They contended that it eliminated the growth center approach to economic development, assumed that all areas were independently capable of economic transformation, and precluded area and regional planning.

Another argument against the policy was the one-sidedness of the criteria established for defining the worst areas. Critics maintained that judging areas solely on the percentage of unemployment and level of median income overlooked absolute numbers of unemployment. Others suggested that such indicators as labor force participation might be better measures of need than unemployment.

Worst First Policy's Impact on EDA Operations

As noted previously, the worst first strategy was successful in that it allowed EDA administrators to convince Congress that theirs was not a "pork barrel" agency. The policy also was partially responsible for a deviation from the previous year's funding strategy, which favored projects that promised the greatest results and led to the funding of a substantial number of projects in areas that would have improved economically without EDA assistance. In addition, the worst first strategy provided agency officials with an acceptable rationale for rejecting projects.

Unfortunately, in many cases, the policy applied differed substantially from the theoretical concept advocated by the Assistant Secretary. The system Davis envisaged contained provisions for considering the merits of projects from severely depressed areas and rejecting them if the chances of success were minimal. The procedures that developed ranged from almost automatic acceptance of projects from such areas to the more prevalent practice of camouflaging disregard for the policy with lip service to its principles and a few "show" projects from severely depressed communities.

The worst first policy's impact on the Public Works Program was limited to a temporary emphasis on funding projects from such areas. Statistics for the 1967 fiscal year indicate a 32 percent reduction in the average cost per project, which allowed an increase in the number of projects funded. This decline in average cost was largely attributed to the smaller scope of projects submitted by communities with the greatest degree of economic distress. Three factors led to the gradual relaxation of this policy: (1) the inability of depressed communities to contribute their proportion of project costs; (2) the stringency of administrative regulations such as those concerning compliance with civil rights measures; and (3) a general feeling that a substantial number of the worst first areas lacked the initiative and resources to take advantage of EDA projects.

The worst first policy found few advocates in the Business Development Program. As an argument against the application of this criterion, James T. Sharkey and his staff produced findings that loan funds could not be better used in the most severely depressed areas. They argued that the Business Development Program was not suited to the policy because such factors as reasonable assurance of repayment must be considered in allocating loan funds. Their contention was that the program would quickly be riddled with unpaid loans and either die completely or evolve as a grant program if the worst first policy were applied.

The problem was resolved when the Assistant Secretary met with Sharkey and other officials in the Office of Business Development and explained that loan applicants from the neediest areas should not be awarded loans automatically. Only when all other factors were equal or when the aid promised unusual benefits to the target population or the area's economy were the neediest areas to be given priority in awarding loans.

The worst first policy also had limited appeal for the economists administering the Office of Technical Assistance, who regarded it as inefficient and retrogressive. John H. Nixon and his assistants contended that the needs of the most depressed areas were obvious; no technical assistance studies were necessary to determine local problems. As a result, lip service and a small number of studies for severely depressed areas were the only manifestations of the worst first strategy. Efforts to aid local and regional organizations formulate plans continued to receive considerable attention, as did projects aimed at developing and improving the human resources of particular localities.

Priorities for awarding EDA planning and administrative grants were not measurably altered as a result of the worst first policy. Groups involved in the organization of development districts and the preparation of OEDPs continued to receive a majority of the agency's planning grant funds. Although the Office of District and Area Planning awarded some planning grants to individual areas exhibiting unusual need, this practice did not indicate adherence to the worst first strategy. Rather, it represented an extension of an earlier posture, which was originally adopted because no better allocation formula had been developed.

Although figures cited at the conclusion of the 1967 fiscal year revealed a considerable redirection of funds in the months following the worst first pronouncement, the trend did not carry over into FY 1968. Seriously depressed areas continued to receive EDA attention, but operating officials allocated funds with little or no regard for the policy, and its proponents gradually lowered their voices.

Preparation of Area Policy Papers

The December 1966 memorandum that announced the selection of the worst first policy also described a new approach to planning for economic development. Concerned with EDA's tendency toward project-by-project spending, Assistant Secretary Davis proposed a system that would result in programmed funding and, at the same time, inform administrators of the field coordinators' activities and the problems of specific localities. Under this system, field coordinators and area office personnel were to prepare plans (later referred to as Area Policy Papers) that contained a simplified analysis of an area, proposed an EDA program to eliminate the existing problems, provided a cost estimate for the proposed activities, and outlined the expected results. These papers were to be reviewed and approved by EDA personnel in Washington.

Davis anticipated that the use of the Area Policy Papers would provide continuity of effort, as projects could be identified and funds earmarked at least a year in advance. Such documents with their descriptions of area potential were viewed as essential to the success of the worst first policy, which called for EDA funding in an area only if achievement of project goals appeared possible. The Assistant Secretary also believed that the identification of goals and priorities in specific areas would increase the effectiveness of EDA field coordinators and facilitate evaluation of the agency's performance. It was expected that field coordinators would work with local residents in composing these documents and, in the process, aid in the establishment of a local capability to plan, coordinate, and implement an economic development program.

The policy papers developed during the following year failed to accomplish the desired results. There were a number of reasons for the lack of success. These included the fact that the field coordinators were neither interested nor numerous enough to perform their roles and the reluctance of Washington staff members to go into the field and assist the coordinators in composing the documents. The plans eventually had to be prepared in Washington by the Washington staff. As a result, the documents consisted primarily of descriptions and were short on analysis and evaluation; they reflected no real feeling for the problems confronting local residents. These shortcomings made the papers of little use, and EDA administrators called for the development of a new system to achieve the goals of the Area Policy Paper program.

Efforts to Stimulate Community Involvement

In his December 1966 memorandum announcing the worst first policy and the decision to prepare individual strategy plans for all designated areas, Assistant Secretary Davis stated that one of the agency's strategies would be to emphasize "a process for economic development."[3] On July 1, 1967, the Office of Public Works moved to implement this strategy through the institution of a new procedure for developing and processing projects. Convinced that economic development responsibilities entailed more than funding isolated projects, Office Director George T. Karras and his staff sought an approach that would directly relate public works projects to broader programs of economic development. The primary objective of the procedure was to stimulate and enhance the economic development process in depressed communities.

EDA officials describe the economic development process as the efforts of a community to achieve its economic potential. These efforts include a perception of the need for a conscious attempt to achieve this potential, and the organization and perseverance necessary to sustain such an attempt. The mission to foster and ameliorate this process is regarded by some as the factor that differentiates EDA's program from those of other federal and state agencies involved in funding public works projects. It is through the stimulation of this long-term process that EDA extends its impact beyond the actual jobs created or incomes increased.

The processing procedure introduced in 1967 emphasizes community participation in planning and implementing economic development activities. Among the features of this procedure is a preapplication conference, which is attended by the project applicant and community leaders, as well as the Economic Development Representative (EDR)[a] for the area, personnel from the area office, and interested county, district, and state representatives. Regarded by many as the most significant step in the development of public works projects, the conference serves to introduce the potential applicant to EDA application forms, requirements, and the technical aspects of submitting an acceptable application.

The preapplication conference also provides an opportunity for a formal discussion of the status of the economic development process in the community.

---

[a]Formerly referred to as a field coordinator.

This discussion touches on such issues as the borrowing capacity of the community; the relationship of the proposed project to the area's OEDP; and the involvement of the management, labor, academic, and religious sectors of the community in sustained planning and problem solving related to economic development. The community's responsibility and need to focus on those who are unemployed or underemployed is also considered. Advice and encouragement are offered by EDA personnel as a means of stimulating the process. It is this assistance that gives credence to EDA's role as an economic development agency, and not simply an organization for disbursing funds.

Moreover, EDA's assistance in this capacity is not limited to offering advice and encouragement. If a proposed project lacks potential or fails to concur with established requirements or priorities, the applicant is immediately apprised of the decision, and the EDR works with the community leaders to develop alternative projects. In instances where EDA funding is inappropriate, the EDR directs the applicant to that federal or state agency best suited to meet the community's needs.

EDA's Urban Development Policy

During the period between October 1966 and January 1969, EDA policy makers continued to debate the agency's urban role. The Oakland experiment suffered a number of setbacks, and without the impetus supplied by Foley's enthusiasm, efforts to salvage the project lacked the vigor that had characterized previous activities in that area.

An Urban Projects Division was established in the Office of Technical Assistance in December of 1966, and the number of EDA dollars applied in urban areas increased every year. However, the absence of pressure to introduce legislation that would allow EDA to enter more cities illustrated the reluctance of Davis and various other agency officials to substantially expand EDA's urban activities. Among their arguments against such expansion was the lack of proof that the agency's tools were relevant to the economic problems of cities, particularly the larger urban complexes. While convinced that the agency was applying its tools effectively and efficiently in rural areas, and skeptical of EDA's potential to have a significant impact on urban problems, these agency policy makers were reluctant to divert funds to what they felt might be a less effective use. They appeared ready to expand urban assistance activities only if the agency received a budget increase.

Nevertheless, those who favored increased aid to the poverty pockets located in the nation's major cities persevered in their arguments, and were successful in some instances. For example, in 1967, legislation was passed that allowed EDA to provide public works and industrial/commercial loans to urban units designated by the Office of Equal Opportunity (OEO) as special impact areas.[4] In addition, EDA's Office of Technical Assistance became increasingly involved in urban development. This included encouraging and funding the establishment of inner city private business development organizations, and recruiting and training individuals to work in center city areas.

Assistance was also provided to individuals applying for loan funds in connection with establishing businesses in such areas, and funds were furnished for feasibility studies to interest outside industry in locating branch plants in urban centers. Moreover, business counseling was provided to firms considering moves to eligible urban areas, and emphasis was placed on aiding minority entrepreneurs located in inner city neighborhoods. It was also during this period that the Office of Technical Assistance cooperated with the Model Cities Administration by awarding grants to several officially designated model cities. However, despite such activities, the opposition to a substantial increase in urban expenditures remained, and no final decision on the extent of EDA's urban involvement was made during the second Assistant Secretary's tenure.

Preparation of District OEDPs

EDA statutes require the submission and approval of an Overall Economic Development Program (OEDP) before a development district can be officially designated. Until such designation is accomplished, a district's growth centers are not eligible to receive EDA public works, business development, and technical assistance funds. In addition, a district's redevelopment areas cannot take advantage of the 10-percent bonus grants available for projects in redevelopment areas participating in the program of a designated district. (Planning grants are available earlier for use in preparing OEDPs.)

Because of the OEDP requirement, considerable effort was directed toward preparing these documents during the first year of operation. (For the District Program, this was fiscal year 1967.) In a number of instances, EDA District Program personnel assisted local district staff members in these endeavors, which attempted to identify the economic problems of a district and outline a plan for solving them.

EDA District Program personnel were also involved in evaluating the OEDPs received from districts and determining whether to approve the plans or require their revision. Unfortunately, the process of preparing and approving an OEDP was a slow one. Under the system devised by the program administrators, approximately one year was required to complete the procedures and declare a district eligible to receive the full spectrum of EDA assistance. However, despite this lengthy time factor, twenty-two districts had been designated at the conclusion of the 1967 fiscal year. In addition, a firmer position had been adopted in respect to the composition of district boards of directors. In fact, in their zeal to insure the participation of local unemployed and minority groups,

EDA District Program personnel occasionally antagonized the local power structure, and were accused of neglecting those with the means and knowledge to provide beneficial assistance in the economic struggle.

Other Developments during Fiscal Year 1967

In December of 1966, Assistant Secretary Davis announced the designation of two new regions. These were the Coastal Plains Region in the eastern section of Georgia, North Carolina, and South Carolina, and the Four Corners Region, which includes counties in Arizona, Colorado, New Mexico, and Utah. By August 1967, federal cochairmen had been appointed to head regional commissions for both areas. These commissions began to function shortly thereafter, bringing the number of operating commissions to five.

At the recommendation of Jonathan Lindley, Deputy Assistant Secretary for Policy Coordination, a Policy Planning Board was established in May 1967 to assist the Assistant Secretary in the formulation of EDA policies. This board was composed of the four Deputy Assistant Secretaries, the Chief Counsel, the Director of the Office of Program Analysis and Economic Research, and the Director of the Office of Administration.[b] The Policy Planning Board's primary function consisted of reviewing and commenting on proposed policy statements before submission to Davis. As part of the review process, board members were expected to prepare position papers on proposed policies and compose draft Economic Development Orders (MEDOs). In addition, board members were to provide staff assistance to Lindley to aid him in performing studies and surveys necessary for preparing policy statements.

Effects of Time

As the agency aged, EDA personnel became more adept at evaluating projects and allocating funds in a relatively short period of time. Increased attention was given to area OEDPs, and emphasis on funding projects that would directly aid unemployed or underemployed area residents was continued. In accordance with the general feeling that economic development remained an incompletely understood process, the program offices funded a number of experimental projects, i.e., projects that introduced innovative approaches to stimulating economic development.

---

[b]EDA's Office of Administration was renamed the Office of Administration and Program Analysis in November 1968, when the program analysis function was transferred. At the same time, the Office of Program Analysis and Economic Research became the Office of Economic Research.

Altered Scope of Business Development Program

By 1968, with interest rates increasing, borrowers had begun to seek sources with more favorable lending terms. As a result, previously disinterested corporations became aware of EDA's loan program and began to take advantage of its lower interest rates (2 percent below the private rate) and longer repayment periods. For the most part, these corporations were considerably larger than former loan applicants. This circumstance combined with the termination of aid to such traditionally depressed areas as Carbondale, Illinois, and Wilkes-Barre, Pennsylvania, which had historically received substantial amounts of ARA and EDA loan assistance, to alter the scope of the Business Development Program.

Although the previous emphasis on creating permanent jobs was continued, fiscal year 1968 witnessed a definite shift in policy in EDA's Business Development Program. Not only were more sizable corporations funded, but the dollar value of individual loans was increased. This was coupled with a decrease in the percentage of total project cost represented by EDA loans. For example, in fiscal year 1966, EDA loans consisted of approximately 50 percent of the total costs of the projects funded, a figure which dropped to 33 percent in fiscal year 1968 with the implementation of the new policies. These policy changes led to a decrease in the EDA investment per job.

In conjunction with the increase in individual loan size, the directors of the program emphasized the selection of projects with private industry backing and managers who possessed the capital necessary for success. Loans to businesses connected with a district program also increased during this period, as did loans to businesses run by minority entrepreneurs.

Institutional Projects

As the Technical Assistance Program matured, institutional projects began to acquire considerable support and, after two years of operation, outnumbered informational projects. In attempting to establish permanent sources of competent technical assistance, institutional projects provide funds to economic development centers at universities, organizations attempting to provide economic development planning, and other groups with similar functions. During the final year of the second Assistant Secretary's tenure, projects of this type were increasingly linked with inner city development, particularly in relation to blacks and other minority groups.

Among the efforts instituted by the Office of Technical Assistance were grants to national business development organizations and trade associations. With EDA's support, these groups work to stimulate the development of business and industry and help create meaningful jobs, usually in central city areas. The activities of the business development groups include loan packaging, franchise and dealership assistance, contractor bonding, contract procurement, technical assistance, business training, and various special projects. The activities of the trade associations include publications, technical assistance to members, national interaction with other trade associations, and conventions and seminars.

Increase in Aid to Indians

EDA's Planning Grant Program, which was organizationally separated into district grants and single area grants during the 1968 fiscal year, was marked by a substantial increase in district planning grant expenditures. Another policy shift during FY 1968 involved a 50 percent increase in the total number of single area grants with a similar decrease in the dollar value of individual grants. These policies continued into fiscal year 1969 with a notable exception in the area of aid to Indian reservations. Funds directed toward these poverty pockets increased to more than 55 percent of the total single area grant expenditures, a trend that continued in fiscal year 1970.

Research Trends

When EDA was established, a major problem confronting officials of the agency's Office of Economic Research was the lack of sufficient county data. This deficiency was also recognized by Congress and personnel of the General Accounting Office, who requested that more current estimates of county income and employment be developed. In fiscal year 1967, the Office of Economic Research assumed the initiative in this area by supplying the Office of Business Economics with funds for the purpose of accelerating that agency's efforts to develop such estimates.

It was also during fiscal year 1967 that Assistant Secretary Davis agreed to use EDA research funds to sponsor a study on federal program coordination. The study was undertaken in response to a recommendation by the National Public Advisory Committee on Regional Economic Development, which was created to advise the Secretary of Commerce on the EDA program.

During the 1968 fiscal year, Davis instructed personnel in the Office of Economic Research to place more emphasis on studies directly related to the EDA program. The more general research efforts that characterized earlier operations were to be cut back and eventually eliminated. However, several of these studies were continued because they had become highly specific and applicable to EDA activities with the passage of time. Among the studies initiated under the new policy were an evaluation of EDA's Business Loan Program and the development of alternatives to urban renewal and urban job creation.

The Public Works and Economic Development Act of 1965 required that the Secretary of Commerce establish an independent study board to investigate the effects of government procurement, scientific, technical, and other related policies on regional economic development. The group created as a result of this requirement worked closely with EDA research personnel in accomplishing its task. The board's report, which was published in December 1967, stated that "adjusting government purchasing patterns would not provide the stimulus needed to cure all regional economic ills."[5] The board also concluded that major diversion of government procurement and science programs might bring undesirable side effects.

Evaluation Efforts

Another significant change in the scope of EDA's research activities took place in fiscal year 1969 with the initiation of an accelerated effort to evaluate EDA's programs. The Office of Technical Assistance had undertaken evaluation studies of the Technical Assistance Program in fiscal year 1967 and an examination of thirteen EDA business loans was initiated in FY 1968, but the other agency programs had not been analyzed formally to determine their effectiveness. Several private consulting firms were awarded contracts to develop methodologies for evaluating each of the agency's program tools, and plans for future activities were the subject of considerable discussion.

Expansion of the District Program

As previously noted, the District Program with its growth center strategy gained prominence during the period following EDA's first year of operation. By the close of fiscal year 1968, 101 districts had been formed, and project approvals in districts had increased from 8.5 percent of EDA's total resource allocations in fiscal year 1967 to 36.3 percent in fiscal year 1969. A significant portion of this amount was expended in towns and cities designated as growth centers, based on the theory that these entities were best equipped to use EDA assistance and would provide employment opportunities for residents of the surrounding area.

The growth center approach reflects European influence and, while viewed rather skeptically by some agency officials, received the full support of Thomas S. Francis and his subordinates in the Office of Development Organizations. However, despite this support, it was not until December 1966—almost six months after the District Program was initiated—that the first growth center was designated. Moreover, sixteen of the twenty-three towns identified as EDA growth centers during the 1967 fiscal year were not designated until June 1967. Thus, the growth center concept had little or no influence on EDA operations until the agency had been in existence for almost two years.

Positive Action Programs

In fiscal year (FY) 1967 when EDA began funding projects in growth centers, there was no agency policy regarding a center's obligation to nearby redevelopment areas. Determined to insure that the unemployed and poorly paid residents of depressed areas derived the benefits of EDA expenditures in growth centers, administrators of EDA's District and Public Works Programs developed the Positive Action Program approach. This approach, which was formalized in September 1968, was designed to make certain that a growth center community would accept its responsibility to less developed areas.

The Positive Action Program policy called for members of the power structure of each proposed center to meet with representatives of the surrounding depressed areas and explain the ways in which they would assist residents of the deprived regions. These intentions, which ranged from giving special attention to hiring depressed area inhabitants to providing such areas with transportation facilities, were expressed in document form for EDA's approval. In addition to these original plans, designated growth centers were required to submit supplementary material with each new request for project funds, explaining the relation of the proposed project to their efforts to improve the economies of the depressed areas.

Regional Commission Programs

In FY 1968, an Executive Order from the White House authorized the Secretary of Commerce to transfer responsibility for coordinating regional commission activities from EDA to a special assistant for regional economic coordination, who would report directly to the secretary. This action was partially a response to the complaints of the federal cochairmen that EDA officials were not interested in the program. It also reflected concern that the individual to whom the cochairmen reported was too far beneath them in rank to have much effect on their activities.

However, except for temporarily appeasing the federal cochairmen, the reorganization had little impact. The Assistant Secretary for Economic Development retained responsibility for delegating commission funds, and neither the new special assistant nor the federal cochairmen had sufficient leverage to acquire the full cooperation of the governors of states composing the commissions.

Despite administrative problems, the regional commissions continued to expand activities. In FY 1968, the commissions began to develop projects and submit applications for supplementary grant money to the EDA Office of Public Works. Since that time, the commissions have cooperated with various economic development districts in structuring and funding projects; and, in some cases, commission members have worked closely with EDA area office personnel to plan and implement multistate projects. Regional commission planning has also been used by governors whose staffs are not equipped to plan for the state's long-range development.

Efforts to Develop an Improved Planning System

In June 1968, EDA policy makers initiated efforts to develop an improved planning system. This action was taken with the knowledge that a new President would be elected in five months, an event almost certain to result in the appointment of a new Assistant Secretary for Economic Development. Cognizant of the inadequacies of the existing Area Policy Papers and mindful of their own problems in acquiring a working knowledge of EDA's programs and aims, Davis and his staff deemed it important to present the future Assistant Secretary with as effective and complete an organization as possible. The Resource Planning and Management System that evolved from this effort represented an attempt to improve and expand the earlier Area Policy Paper Program.

The new Action Programs were prepared by EDA Washington staff personnel, field office workers, Economic Development Representatives, state agency representatives, and local residents. These were essentially blueprints to help areas solve their problems. They included plans, possibilities, long-term goals, short-term goals, strategies, and specific three-year programs. In addition to specifying EDA's role in a particular locality, the documents outlined areas in which other federal agencies could lend assistance.

To insure the use of these plans, each area's Economic Development Representative was required to submit a monthly progress report to EDA administrators. The three-year programs were to be keyed into the agency's internal program and budgeting system, and the Washington Review Committee was established to evaluate completed Action Programs. When the new Assistant Secretary was appointed in February 1969, a substantial number of Action Programs were in various stages of development, and the Resource Planning and Management System was explained and recommended by the outgoing administration.

5

The Republican Tenure: February 1969 to September 1971

The new Assistant Secretary for Economic Development, Robert A. Podesta, differed from his predecessors in that he had no previous experience in directing a federal government program. Acknowledging his inexperience in administering a program like EDA's, he assigned top priority to acquiring a working knowledge of the agency, its tools, and its mission. In conferring with outgoing Assistant Secretary Davis, Podesta placed particular emphasis on learning the capabilities of his inherited staff.

Consideration of Two Proposals

During the first six months of his tenure, the new appointee's activities also included consideration of two proposals initiated by his predecessor: the Resource Planning and Management System and a plan for restructuring the organization. The Resource Planning and Management System was in the final stages of development when the change of administration occurred, and by June 1969, the Washington Review Committee had recommended seventy-five Action Programs for approval by the Assistant Secretary.

Although a number of these documents have been used by area offices, districts, and local workers, no official agency decision was ever rendered. Numerous explanations for this inaction have been advanced, ranging from claims that the Action Programs were not relevant because they did not present a true picture of area conditions to charges that too much authority was lodged with Washington officials and not enough at the local level. Podesta himself emphasized EDA's role in motivating local leaders and outside concerns to work for economic development, asserting that the Action Programs were not primary motivating factors.

The other action proposed to Podesta soon after his appointment involved reorganizing the agency staff. Experience had revealed certain shortcomings in the organization of program tools as line functions. Theoretically, the staff members of each of the program tool offices were to coordinate projects with staff members of the other offices. This practice was expected to result in a program approach to the problems of depressed communities and eliminate the funding of isolated projects with no ties to broader development programs. However, no framework was developed to structure such coordination. As a result, EDA personnel in each program office suffered from a tendency to become immersed in the operations of their particular program and neglect coordination with other offices.

The coordination problem led a substantial number of EDA officials to agree that a better organizational structure could be devised. The plan, which was proposed in the spring of 1969 after several months of deliberation, called for organizing the program tools as staff functions at the disposal of various offices. Among these were an office for rural areas, another for urban areas, and a third for districts and growth centers. A number of special area (e.g., Indian reservations and Puerto Rico) offices were also included. This arrangement was expected to be instituted in conjunction with continued efforts to decentralize EDA's organizational structure.

Among the arguments advanced by the plan's proponents was the beneficial effect the altered structure would have on the agency's capability to focus on the individual problems of different types of economically depressed areas. It was also contended that this approach would allow the agency to design blueprints for the economic development of areas over a multiyear period, thus substituting a program approach for single project planning. Uppermost in the thinking of some was the urgent need of the center sections of the nation's major cities. Such advocates of the reorganization envisioned the consolidation of EDA's activities in cities under one division as a step toward increased and more effective efforts in these pockets of concentrated economic depression.

Assistant Secretary Podesta agreed that the reorganization might facilitate implementation of EDA's policy to offer a coordinated program of aid to depressed areas. However, he decided to postpone a final decision until he had acquired more experience with the existing organization and Congress had made a decision on the agency's future.

Preparing for Congressional Hearings

The new administration's orientation period was complicated by the impending expiration of the agency's authorization. Because of the June 30, 1970 expiration date, the learning process necessarily included an appraisal of EDA's operations and consideration of the agency's position on such issues as urban involvement and implementation of the growth center strategy. Relying heavily on the expertise of EDA's veteran staff, Podesta and his staff prepared to face Congress and the Bureau of the Budget in the forthcoming debate over the agency's future.

Efforts to Improve Existing Activities

Faced with the possibility that EDA's charter might not be renewed and convinced that major policy issues could only be decided at higher levels,

Assistant Secretary Podesta concentrated on improving existing activities during his first year at EDA. Emphasis was placed on selecting good projects, improving the quality of business loans, and increasing the business community's involvement in economic development activities. During the last months of 1969, EDA staff members began to work with congressional leaders to develop legislative amendments that would improve the agency's program. However, no drastic shifts in emphasis were announced, and the assistance channeled to the Mississippi areas devastated by Hurricane Camille represented the only major funding alteration.

The philosophy underlying these policies, which were perpetuated during the second year of Podesta's term, was that if the agency invested the available resources effectively, Congress and BOB would recognize EDA's potential contribution to efforts to achieve more balanced national growth and expand its mandate and appropriation. This posture placed responsibility for substantially altering the program outside the agency and freed EDA personnel to concentrate on the current program.

The value of such a practice is clear. For example, since an in-house decision to increase involvement in urban areas would be relatively meaningless unless additional funds were provided, extensive deliberation on the subject would consume valuable time without substantially affecting aid to the cities. Policies during fiscal years 1969 and 1970 called for this time to be devoted to identifying more effective ways of applying the funds available for use in urban areas and to assisting area and district planners involved in urban economic development.

Expanded Evaluation Program

As one means of preparing for the congressional hearings, agency administrators ordered the acceleration and expansion of the evaluation effort initiated by the preceding administration. This decision, which was made in December 1969, also reflected (1) the fact that enough time elapsed to accurately analyze the impact of a significant number of projects and (2) a request from BOB, stimulated by a directive from the White House, to undertake expanded evaluation activities. It was expected that these activities would provide some indication of EDA's success in creating jobs, generating increased income, and stimulating the economic development process in the nation's depressed areas.

Private contractors implemented the evaluation methodologies developed previously to weigh the impact of each of the agency's program tools. The contractors also joined with EDA personnel in conducting in-depth case studies of various EDA-designated areas. The intent of these studies was to acquire a valid perception of EDA's overall impact in a given area. As explained in the chapter entitled "Evaluation Approach," emphasis was placed on identifying EDA investment per job created, the percentage of jobs that were taken by members of the target population, and EDA projects' impact on local development activities.

EDA's Contributions in Urban Areas

While advocating that less time be allotted to in-house discussion on EDA's role in the cities, agency administrators were eager to inform Congress and BOB of EDA's unique contributions in urban areas. A special study was structured as part of the program evaluation to report on EDA's impact in five major urban areas. During this period, most EDA officials agreed that if the agency's charter were renewed, it would only be a matter of time until EDA expenditures in urban areas matched the agency's aid to rural America.

The basis for this consensus lay in a political phenomenon: the power structure of Congress had shifted since 1965, and urban representatives were demanding increased assistance. In November 1969, Congress passed legislation directed toward extending EDA's urban program. The EDA Act was amended to allow the agency to designate any OEO Special Impact Area that submitted an acceptable OEDP. Such areas would then be eligible for EDA public works grants.

Continuation of Policies

During fiscal years 1969 and 1970, operations in the agency's program tool offices continued in established patterns, reflecting Assistant Secretary Podesta's decision to perpetuate previous policies. However, in-house planning activities declined, as did vocal emphasis on directing EDA-provided benefits to the unemployed and underemployed. The period was also characterized by efforts to increase communication between EDA and residents of depressed areas and improve procedures for dispensing aid.

Both the Office of Development Organizations (District Program) and the Office of Public Works continued to decentralize operations during the 1969 and 1970 fiscal years. This trend, which was directed toward increasing local participation in the EDA program, was reflected in the Office of Public Works by changes in staffing levels and program responsibility. The office trimmed its Washington staff by more than twenty employees, while substantially increasing public works personnel in regional offices.[a]

In addition, administrators in the Office of Public Works delegated substantial authority to the regional office directors and their staffs. Where staffing and experience permit, regional office personnel now handle the development and processing of public works projects from receipt of the initial forms to a final

[a]Formerly referred to as area offices.

recommendation. In most instances, a positive recommendation by the regional office is tantamount to final approval.

Changes in the Office of Development Organizations also reflected a continuation of the decentralization philosophy. The period was marked by increased delegation of authority to regional offices, and economic development districts were consistently encouraged to shoulder the major burden of responsibility for planning and project implementation. Moreover, a number of EDA officials continued to advocate the ultimate independence of these entities.

Notable among FY 1969 and 1970 efforts to improve EDA aid distribution was the development of the two-stage OEDP for designating economic development districts. Since the District Program's inception, EDA personnel had sought to decrease the time required for preparing and processing OEDPs prior to designation of districts. However, no real progress was made toward achieving this objective until the two-stage OEDP was introduced in the final months of 1968. Use of this formula reduced the time required for district designation from one year under the previous formula to from three to five months.

Conceived with the dual purpose of accelerating the designation process and increasing the amount of local input to the planning process, the two-stage OEDP was welcomed by Washington EDA personnel, district staff members, regional office employees, and district board members. The first stage of this document consists primarily of a statistical portrait of the district, its resources, and problems. It is prepared by the district organization and its planning staff with assistance from EDA. With the acceptance of this portion of the OEDP, the district is automatically designated, and its redevelopment areas can take advantage of the 10 percent bonus on grants to designated counties in economic development districts.

It is at this point that regional offices assume responsibility for assisting in the further development of the district, including preparation of the second stage of the OEDP. This stage of the OEDP reports on the further development of the district. Preparing it involves organizing special-purpose citizens' committees to insure that the district's program reflects local needs and desires; interesting district residents in the problems of their area; stimulating a planned approach to problem solving; and marshaling local citizens to take action on such aspects of economic development as industrial promotion, tourism, and education. EDA personnel place particular emphasis on the importance of involving the local unemployed, low-salaried workers, and members of minority groups in these discussions.

It was also during this period that other federal and state agencies recognized the value of development districts as basic planning vehicles. This recognition, which was encouraged by EDA personnel, was evidenced by the support given to district projects. For example, by January 1970, the Department of Housing and Urban Development (HUD) was funding projects in seventeen EDA-designated districts, and the Department of Health, Education and Welfare (HEW) was involved in comprehensive health planning and implementation efforts in twelve districts. A number of these projects entailed a considerable amount of interagency coordination, much of which was handled by district staff members.

The major shift in policy in the District Program during fiscal years 1969 and 1970 was the expected progression from emphasis on OEDP preparation to emphasis on implementation of programs. Districts that received funds to hire staffs and write OEDPs in 1966 and 1967 began using EDA grants to implement the plans developed in those OEDPs. In addition, considerable attention was devoted to formulating a plan for decreasing EDA planning and administrative support to the oldest and stablest districts.

Use of Public Works Appropriations

Fiscal year 1969 was characterized by an increase in public works funds to growth centers and development districts. In addition, there was a shift in policy concerning the types of public works projects funded. In the years since EDA's inception, a small number of projects with less traditional ties to economic development had been proposed locally and supported by Karras and his staff in the agency's Office of Public Works. These included an educational television station, a cultural center, and other projects designed to enhance the quality of life by means other than directly creating jobs, raising incomes, or providing services such as water and sewer lines. Projects of this type were usually located in EDA-designated growth centers.

Proponents of a broad definition of economic development consider projects of this type important elements in stimulating economic growth. Members of this school of thought argue that such facilities as libraries and cultural centers influence industrial location decisions. They assert that when other factors are equal, ultimate industrial location decisions are based on the amenities a town has to offer. This approach is opposed by supporters of a more narrow definition of economic development, who assign top priority to the direct creation of job opportunities.

With the change in agency leadership during fiscal year 1969, the latter viewpoint temporarily gained ascendancy. Amenity-oriented projects were discouraged, and public works officials were instructed to stimulate and fund time-proven projects directly related to job creation. Given EDA's limited resources, the Assistant Secretary deemed it more appropriate to fund projects with proven job creation capabilities than to risk failures by experimenting with demonstration projects of unknown potential.

Although this decision was viewed as particularly significant by administrators of the Public Works Program, the actual number of projects affected was small. For the most part, the types of projects supported with public works grants and loans remained relatively constant during the period between

February 1969 and September 1971. Water and sewage systems, industrial parks, health facilities, and public buildings continued to be regarded as essential to the development of viable economies, and the economically deprived areas of the nation continued to exhibit substantial need for these basic facilities. The construction of skill centers to train and educate the unemployed and underemployed residents of an area received particular emphasis. Approximately seventy such centers had been designated as recipients of EDA public works funds by September 1971, and in many cases the agency's Technical Assistance Program provided supplementary funds for instructional costs and equipment.

Shifts in Emphasis

Assistant Secretary Podesta devoted considerable attention to revitalizing the agency's Development Loan Program. Although policies initiated during his predecessor's administration had included emphasizing loans to sizable corporations, progress in this direction failed to satisfy the new administrator. In addition to stressing the importance of dealing with large corporations, he called for increasing the size of the loan program and consideration of more effective methods for attracting multimillion dollar companies to the nation's depressed areas. Emphasis was also placed on acquainting large corporations with the financial incentives offered by the program and decreasing the time required to process loans.

Two organizational modifications instituted during the 1970 fiscal year indicated a change in the agency's policy with regard to Indians. These actions involved the transfer of the Office of the Special Assistant for Indian Affairs from the organization under the Deputy Assistant Secretary (DAS) for Policy Coordination to a position directly beneath the DAS for Economic Development and the placement of Indian affairs officers in three area offices. The changes were evidence of agency officials' intention to place increased emphasis on providing employment opportunities and higher wages to the unemployed and underemployed residents of designated Indian reservations.

EDA Technical Assistance in Fiscal Year 1970

Under the third Assistant Secretary for Economic Development, the agency's Technical Assistance Program began to be articulated somewhat differently. Prior to fiscal year 1970, technical assistance was regarded as a place-oriented program like public works and business development. However, at the urging of program directors Arnold H. Leibowitz and Israel M. Baill, Podesta decided to change its image to that of a program related to human resources. It was also agreed that Office of Technical Assistance officials should take advantage of the program's flexibility to emphasize the possibilities of using technical assistance grants to finance demonstration projects and innovative proposals.

Leibowitz, Baill, and their staff were not in a position to immediately realign the program on the basis of these decisions. Although personnel in the Office of Technical Assistance began to consider such projects as demonstration programs to test industrial processes, President Nixon and his advisers were the first to take advantage of the new articulation. Recognizing the tremendous flexibility of the program, they increasingly called upon it to meet Presidential initiatives. These included aid to the Office of Minority Business Enterprise (OMBE), the Interagency Economic Adjustment Committee, and the Trade Adjustment Assistance Program. While the Office of Technical Assistance had previously established a practice of coordinating with other agencies, this marked the first time a substantial portion of EDA's technical assistance funds had been used to support such agencies' programs.

In addition to supporting Presidential initiatives, EDA's Technical Assistance Program continued to provide aid directed toward inner city development, funded feasibility studies, helped foster the establishment of training centers, and supported efforts to help inexperienced local government officials attract and retain industry. Feasibility studies on the development of industrial parks were favored by administrators in the Office of Technical Assistance during the period, as that type of project had been particularly successful in the past. The Technical Assistance Program's role in establishing training centers was also emphasized. These facilities were actively needed because a number of business loan and public works projects had been completed, and the local unemployed and underemployed had to be trained to fill the jobs created.

During FY 1970, a new policy was introduced in regard to funding institutional projects. These projects, which are designed to establish permanent, competent sources of technical assistance, had been emphasized by personnel in the Office of Technical Assistance since EDA's second year of operations. The new policy called for reasonable assurance before project approval that if EDA withdrew its support after a certain period, the organization would possess the independent means to continue.

The Office of Technical Assistance also continued the practice of coordinating projects with other agencies. For example, during FY 1970, the office funded a project to assist in the development of minority-owned shopping centers. This project, which was developed in cooperation with the Office of Minority Business Enterprise, also received funds from the Small Business Administration and involved dealings with local representatives of HUD.

Evolution of Regional Commission Program

With the change of administration in January 1969, Maurice H. Stans was appointed Secretary of Commerce, and new federal cochairmen were named to head the five regional commissions. Incoming Secretary Stans showed considerable interest in the Regional Commission Program and worked closely with the federal cochairmen in planning future activities, estimating budget figures, and evaluating methods of strengthening the program.

In November 1969 the Public Works and Economic Development Act was amended to expand the authority of the commissions to provide funds for technical and planning assistance, including demonstration projects, and to authorize "first dollar" grants. The latter provision permits a commission to use its funds for all or any portion of the basic federal grant for any project authorized by a grant-in-aid program without sufficient funds to cover the project's cost.

Concurrently, the new administration moved to rationalize the relationships between the regional commissions and EDA. This move culminated in the issuance of departmental orders on April 1, 1970, which clearly identify the independent authority of the regional commissions and the relationships with the Secretary of Commerce and his Special Assistant for Regional Economic Coordination. Under the new orders, regional commission appropriations are allocated to the Secretary of Commerce. The Secretary's Special Assistant administers the distribution of these funds to the commissions on the basis of financial plans submitted to the Secretary by the commissions. However, the Special Assistant continues to coordinate commission activities with EDA operations. This includes tracing the progress of commission projects moving through EDA funding channels.

Evaluation Results

The accelerated evaluation program initiated in January of 1970 was completed during the summer of the same year. The results, which are presented in detail in the following chapters, were primarily positive, indicating that, within the limitations imposed by low funding levels, EDA had demonstrated competence in solving economic development problems. Agency projects were judged to have alleviated economic distress in many areas at a reasonable cost to the government.

However, while praising the innovative approaches applied in some instances, the evaluators noted a number of deficiencies. Prime among these was the lack of control to insure timely provision of training in connection with EDA projects. Training funds, which are obtained through the Department of Labor, play an important role in reinforcing public works and business loan assistance.

One-Year Extension of EDA Program

By June 1970, it was apparent that neither the administration nor the Congress was prepared to propose a new program; further consideration of EDA and its relation to other government programs was deemed necessary. To insure that economically depressed areas would continue to receive federal assistance while the program was being considered, Congress voted to extend the Public Works and Economic Development Act for one year. The decision was approved by the President on July 6, 1970.

During the twelve-month period between passage of the amendment that extended EDA's authorization and June 1971, Podesta and his staff continued in the pattern followed in the preceding eighteen months. No major redirection of program funding was initiated, and emphasis was placed on improving existing activities. In addition, the Assistant Secretary and his staff continued their efforts to develop a legislative program that would increase the agency's effectivness.

Increasing Program Effectiveness and Scope

In mid-July of 1970, EDA opened a regional office in Philadelphia. The significance of this action was twofold. In March 1969, President Nixon asked Congress for reorganizational authority to allow him to introduce changes aimed at improving the delivery of government services to the public. Upon receipt of this authority, he announced a program designed to concentrate federal agency activities in ten regional centers across the nation. Since Philadelphia is one of these centers, the consolidation of EDA's Wilkes-Barre and Portland regional offices there represented the agency's first step toward complying with the President's program.

As of September 1971, EDA had relocated its Duluth regional office in Chicago, which is one of the ten centers designated by the President. Moreover, plans were being finalized for the combination of the Huntington and Huntsville regional offices in Atlanta, and the creation of a new region to be served by a regional office in Denver. The new region was to be composed of states formerly under the jurisdiction of the regional offices in Austin and Chicago. Both Atlanta and Denver are among the regional centers named by the President.

The opening of the regional office in Philadelphia was also significant because it marked the institution of a new organizational structure within a regional office. This structure, which came to be known as the "Philadelphia Plan" within the agency, was developed to accomplish two major objectives: to make field financial and engineering operations more efficient; and to provide greater emphasis on a balanced program rather than individual project promotion. This was accomplished by grouping technical specialists in a single division and by establishing closer coordination between regional office program division personnel and Economic Development Representatives in evaluating local economic problems and developing approaches to their solution.

This approach was consistent with the reorganization proposal considered when the Assistant Secretary first assumed leadership of the agency. That proposal, which called for organizing by entity programs (e.g., urban program, Indian program, etc.) instead of program tools, was also designed to substitute an affirmative program approach for single project development. The new structure was also similar to that proposed in the reorganization in that technical personnel were separated from those concerned with program development, enabling the latter group to concentrate on helping design and implement balanced development programs.

By September 1971, initial problems had been resolved, and the new structure had resulted in such an increase in efficiency that it had been introduced in EDA's regional offices in Huntington and Austin. In addition, agency officials were proceeding with plans to implement the organizational structure in the new regional offices in Atlanta and Denver.

As part of the agency's continuing effort to improve existing activities, Assistant Secretary Podesta established the Office of Development Lending in August 1970. This unit, which was originally staffed by personnel from the Office of Business Development, was assigned responsibility for involving large private corporations in EDA activities and solving development problems through the coordinated application of the agency's various tools. Acquainting corporations with the benefits of EDA's Business Development Program and encouraging them to open branches in designated areas were primary functions of this office.

Soon after the Office of Development Lending was established, its functions were expanded to include assistance to minority entrepreneurs. Working closely with OMBE, personnel in this office used the communications network they had built with private industry and banking establishments to help minority businessmen gain entrance to the nation's complex economic system. This office also assisted minority enterprises in acquiring EDA funds and in negotiating complicated business transactions.

By late 1971, the need for the types of projects and activities undertaken by the Office of Development Lending had been demonstrated. Since that Office had been established primarily to determine if such a need existed, its purpose had been served. As a result, preparations were made to transfer the personnel and functions of the Office of Development Lending to EDA's Office of Business Development in early 1972.

By fiscal year 1971, the student intern program initiated by EDA's Research Program had spread from the southern states to the Midwest, West, and New England. In addition, the number of students participating in the EDA-funded portion of the program annually had increased from 19 to 250, and the agency's support had grown from $71,000 in FY 1967 to $318,000. Moreover, the program had resulted in the preparation of approximately 280 reports for use by local organizations. Even more impressive than the increased scope of the program was the assumption of cost by state agencies. In FY 1971, the State of North Carolina funded all but a small part of that state's student intern program, and a trend toward state funding appeared in Georgia, Texas, and Virginia.

Shifts in Policy Concerning Indians

Perhaps the most significant shift in policy during the first six months of fiscal year 1971 involved EDA assistance to residents of designated Indian reservations. In 1969, Congress amended the Public Works and Economic Development Act of 1965 to allow EDA to make 100 percent public works grants in connection with projects on designated Indian reservations. However, the agency did not adopt such a policy until October 1970. At that time, Podesta announced at an EDA/OEO seminar on economic development planning that EDA-designated reservations would no longer be required to furnish 20 percent of public works project costs. Under the new policy, the agency would be capable of providing grants to cover the entire costs of public works projects on Indian reservations. In instituting this policy, EDA responded to a long-standing complaint by Indian leaders that the 20-percent requirement prevented reservations from acquiring projects that could provide badly needed jobs.[b]

Another policy shift affecting EDA's assistance to Indian reservations occurred during the summer of 1971. Prior to that time, a significant number of public works projects on Indian reservations were never completed. Such situations were a result of cost overruns during the period between project approval and the actual letting of bids for project construction. Regional office practice was to compensate for such overruns by persuading tribes to identify deductible alternates, i.e., project features that could be eliminated. Such features could then be dropped from project specifications, and the project could be completed within the limits of the original grant or loan amount. This approach was not successful, as manifested by the incidence of incomplete projects. Tribes were usually unwilling to modify project plans; moreover, they lacked the resources to complete the projects with local funds.

When EDA officials in Washington belatedly learned of the incomplete projects in the summer of 1971, immediate action was taken to remedy the problem. Through discussions with EDA Deputy Assistant Secretary for Economic Development Charles A. Fagan, III and his staff, regional office personnel agreed to fund cost overruns for projects on Indian reservations rather than continue the past practice. The adoption of this policy insured that EDA would provide the additional funding necessary to complete Indian reservation projects according to originally approved specifications.

Interaction with Other Agencies

During the period between July 1970 and September 1971, agency policy makers continued to emphasize the importance of coordination with other federal and state agencies. Among those agencies that received EDA support for

[b]The Economic Development Order stating this policy became effective January 15, 1971.

their programs were the Office of Minority Business Enterprise, the Bureau of Domestic Commerce (BDC), the Farmers Home Administration (FHA), and the Federal Water Quality Administration (FWQA). This support included assistance to organizations designated as OMBE affiliates, aid to BDC's Trade Adjustment Assistance Program, and cooperation with FHA in coordinating development activities with housing programs.

The agency's assistance to OMBE was perhaps the most substantial of these efforts. When OMBE was created in March 1969, EDA was already engaged in efforts to assist minority entrepreneurs, and provided both advice and financial help to the new agency, which had no grant-in-aid or loan funds of its own. EDA's support of OMBE's efforts increased in fiscal year 1971, when $3.5 million in technical assistance funds were used to finance OMBE affiliates in approximately twenty cities. These affiliates are local organizations that provide general information, assistance in loan packaging, and postloan and other business counseling to minority entrepreneurs.

The period between July 1970 and September 1971 was also marked by increased emphasis on coordinating with the five regional commissions. In mid-July 1970, a directive was issued advising agency personnel to notify federal cochairmen of EDA project activity within regional commission boundaries or projects of national or regional significance. This notification was to be accomplished during the early phases of project development, and the federal cochairmen were to reciprocate by providing similar information concerning projects being developed by the commissions or under their auspices.

EDA also continued to play a major role in the SODA Demonstration Project. This effort, which was proposed by the Southern Oklahoma Development Association (SODA) in December 1968, represents a local organization's attempt to obtain assistance from federal and state agency personnel in designing and implementing a comprehensive development program. In proposing the project, SODA identified a series of local, state, and federal actions that would lead to the formulation of a development plan for the ten-county district, as well as a priority ranking of needed projects. In addition to accelerating the socioeconomic growth of south central Oklahoma, it was expected that the SODA project would serve as a model for other nonmetropolitan areas that suffer from the lack of a coordinated approach to development by federal, state, and local units of government.

By January 1971, eight federal government departments and the Office of Equal Opportunity had signed a Memorandum of Agreement, pledging to identify their technical assistance capabilities that might be of use to SODA in its development efforts. In addition, SODA had specified the area's needs by functional category, stated the functions and responsibilities of those involved in the project, provided a schedule of the project's phases, and obtained responses to its Specific Development Needs Report from the various federal participants in the project. (Responses from state agencies were delayed by a gubernatorial change, resulting personnel modifications, and the February 1971 creation of a Department of Community Affairs and Planning at the state level.)

Between January and September 1971, SODA completed a multiyear program design for mobilizing state and federal capabilities, and using them to develop the ten-county district. During this period, EDA's role as the lead agency in the SODA project included having agency staff members meet periodically with SODA personnel and board members to discuss the project's progress and report on federal responses. At the end of August 1971, agency officials involved in the SODA project reported that the evaluation of the first phase of the project (i.e., the program design phase) was underway and that EDA was responsible for insuring its completion by the end of October. Implementation of SODA's work program was scheduled to begin in January 1972.

In October 1970, EDA's Office of Development Organizations completed a survey to calculate the amount of funding by other federal agencies, state agencies, and local residents in 100 economic development districts. The study revealed that EDA's $4.5 million planning grant assistance to the 100 districts in FY 1971 was being complemented by $4.7 million from other federal agencies, $3.6 million in local funds, and $1.5 million in state funds.

Of the 100 districts surveyed, only 32 were operating on EDA planning grant funds alone. Eighteen were funded by one other federal agency; 25 were funded by two other agencies; 22 were securing assistance from three other agencies; and 3 were receiving funds from four other agencies.

National Public Advisory Committee Recommendations

It was also during October 1970 that the National Public Advisory Committee on Regional Economic Development met to review EDA activities. The committee was briefed both orally and in writing on EDA's basic operations and on the agency's progress. As a result of this meeting, the committee reached several tentative conclusions about the EDA program, and these were formally presented to Secretary Stans in January 1971. These conclusions, which the committee chairman prefaced by emphasizing the limited background on which they were based, included a recommendation that Congress "broaden and make specific the power of EDA to coordinate all economic planning in the country."[1] The committee also concluded that EDA's technical assistance and planning grant authorizations should be expanded and emphasized, and indicated approval of the agency's growth center strategy.

Responses to Evaluation Results

The activities during FY 1971 also included consideration of ways to correct the program deficiencies noted in the preceding spring's evaluation efforts, and the design of new studies to answer questions raised by the analyses. These studies included evaluations of EDA's Selected Indian Reservation Program, the agency's training activities, and national organizations receiving EDA technical assistance funds. In addition, an in-house evaluation team was formed to evaluate the agency's growth center strategy. Emphasis was placed on determining the impact of this strategy on migration trends and the usefulness of Positive Action Programs.

During this period, both the Office of Public Works and the Office of Business Development took steps to remedy problems noted in the evaluation studies. In the Office of Public Works, this consisted of considering modifications in project application forms. Administrators of the Business Development Program concentrated on decreasing the time required to process a loan. By the end of January 1971, efforts toward this end had resulted in a decision to process loans in Washington, thereby freeing regional office business development personnel to work with EDRs in promoting EDA's loan program and assisting potential loan recipients to prepare applications. This procedure, which was implemented in April 1971, had cut the time between loan application and approval from 190 days to approximately 100 days by September.

Another improvement in agency operations that was partially attributable to the results of the evaluation program involved manpower training. During the 1969 and 1970 fiscal years, EDA administrators had experienced difficulties in obtaining training funds from the Department of Labor for use in connection with EDA projects. In November 1970, with the results of the evaluation indicating the importance of training and the continuing reluctance of the Labor Department to make training funds available, Podesta met with Assistant Secretary of Labor Malcom R. Lovell, Jr. to discuss the situation.

As a result of that meeting, an agreement was reached whereby the Department of Labor would set aside $12 million in funds to support training programs related to EDA-funded projects. Although this amount was considerably less than the $22 million specified in the Manpower Development and Training Act for use in training residents of EDA-designated areas, it represented a step forward. For the first time, EDA was able to insure that a specific portion of the $22 million would be used to support training programs connected with agency projects. A similar agreement was reached for fiscal year 1972.

EDA's Urban Activities

Funds for the Urban Program represented a slightly larger percentage of the agency's budget in FY 1971, and budget proposals for ensuing years contained additional increases. Faced with the prospect of an expanded urban program in the near future, agency policy makers concentrated on developing a more effective strategy for urban development. Two OEO special impact areas—the Midwest Impact Area in Chicago and the Lower East Side Impact Area in New York—were designated during the fall of 1970, and agency officials decided to implement coordinated development programs in both places. Their intention was that EDA activities in these areas would serve as models for future aid to urban centers.

By September 1971, Richmond, California, the South Central Los Angeles Special Impact Area, the South Bronx Special Impact Area, and the inner-city area of Kansas City, Missouri, had also been designated under the Special Impact Areas Program. These areas were to be included in the agency's demonstration program, which was directed toward creating jobs, increasing incomes, and stimulating minority entrepreneurship and employment in a limited number of urban areas.

In May 1971, the Assistant Secretary established a policy of major significance for agency activities in such urban areas. This policy, which was based on a recommendation from Deputy Assistant Secretary for Policy Coordination Richard L. Sinnott, set the grant rate for all nonrevenue generating projects in urban special impact areas at 80 percent. Prior to this time, special impact areas were subject to grant rate procedures established primarily for rural counties. These procedures involve determining the percentage of project cost funded by EDA according to such factors as an area's unemployment rate or out-migration rate. For most urban special impact areas, no accurate data exist for these categories. Moreover, the kinds of problems faced by residents of the nation's central city areas are often not reflected in such statistics.

The new policy solved these problems by stipulating that public works grant rates in urban special impact areas would no longer be based on such statistics. Rather, with the exception of revenue generating projects, public works grants in such areas would be for 80 percent of total project cost. For revenue generating projects, the grant rate would be that percentage of total project cost that would not be covered by the income generated.

A Broader Concept of Economic Development

During his second year as director of EDA's program, Assistant Secretary Podesta not only gave impetus to the allocation of funds on an entity program basis,[c] but also began to direct agency personnel to view project development as a direct response to local problems. He had reached the conclusion that traditional projects which aim at directly creating jobs through the location of industry cannot fully meet the development needs of some communities.

Several factors contributed to this change of philosophy. One was EDA's

---

[c]Prior to fiscal year 1970, EDA appropriations were allocated solely on the basis of program tools. At that time, a decision was made to present a budget based on entity programs to the Secretary of Commerce and OMB. Thus, subsequent budget proposals identify a specific amount for projects in urban areas (or districts, Indian reservations, etc.) as well as a breakdown of urban area funding by program tool.

experience in attempting to stimulate economic development in such inner-city areas as Watts in Los Angeles and parts of Washington, D.C., where traditional public works and business loan projects were insufficient to meet development needs. As a result, the agency experimented with alternative approaches to development, such as approving public works funds:

1. To build a multipurpose service center and a day care center along with shell commercial buildings on an industrial park in Watts.
2. To construct a community health center and a minority-owned and -operated hotel in Washington, D.C.

On-site observations of earlier experimental projects also led the Assistant Secretary to broaden his concept of economic development. The results of such projects as the construction of an indoor theatre for the Oregon Shakespearean Festival convinced him that unconventional projects could have a significant effect on an area's development. Podesta also recognized that projects like the Shakespearean theatre, a cultural center, or a downtown parking garage could effect results much more quickly than a traditional project. The former can be completed and enhance a community's attractiveness to private industry, attract tourists, or revitalize local businesses within a year, while an industrial park project usually entails time not only for developing the park itself but also for industrial prospecting and plant construction. Thus, jobs do not result until at least a year following the park's completion.

These insights, gained from the Assistant Secretary's involvement in EDA's efforts in all parts of the country, led him to encourage projects designed to enhance the quality of life and provide communities with important development facilities other than those which directly create jobs and immediately raise incomes. He became particularly interested in the idea of locating such development facility projects in EDA-designated growth centers, where they could accelerate the growth of an already expanding economy.

EDA Legislative Proposal

Throughout the period between June and December 1970, Podesta and his staff continued their efforts to develop a legislative program that would increase the agency's effectiveness. Congress and the administration were engaged in similar endeavors. The House Subcommittee on Economic Development initiated an evaluation and investigation of EDA to improve its ability to prepare new legislation for the agency. The administration, whose concern was focused not on EDA individually, but on the broad range of federal programs related to the country's economy, concentrated on developing substantive measures to execute a national growth policy.

Through its sponsorship of a national growth conference in the spring of 1970 and agency personnel's staff work for the Domestic Affairs Council in the area of rural development, EDA contributed to the administration's efforts. The national growth conference was an outgrowth of studies initiated by EDA's Office of Economic Research during the first two years of the agency's operations. When the President cited the need to "redirect" the nation's growth in the 1970 State of the Union Message,[2] Dr. Samuel M. Rosenblatt and other officials in EDA's research office recognized the relevance of such a policy to work on regional growth centers that had been supported by agency research funds.

Subsequently, a decision was made to have the researchers who had been working in this area describe their findings to an assemblage of EDA officials, White House staff representatives, members of the Council of Economic Advisers, and staff personnel from the various regional commissions. The political problems associated with using regional growth centers to implement a national growth strategy was one of the topics discussed at this conference.

During the spring and summer of 1970, agency personnel also assisted the House Subcommittee staff in collecting data on the results of EDA projects. Major emphasis, however, was placed on internal efforts to prepare a legislative proposal. These efforts were directed by EDA Chief Counsel William W. Blunt and Kenneth L. Deavers, director of EDA's Office of Planning and Program Support.

In mid-December, the in-house proposal was completed and delivered to Secretary Stans for submission to the Office of Management and Budget. It represented a departure from the existing legislation in a number of areas. Among the most significant changes were the inclusion of appropriations for training and assistance to disaster areas, increased credit assistance, a higher population limit for growth centers (500,000) and a provision reducing the number of redevelopment areas required to form an economic development district from two to one.

In addition, the proposed designation criteria provided for a slightly different group of redevelopment areas. The change in these criteria included designation of places with median family incomes less than 50 percent of the national median (40 percent under the original Act), designation of areas with a significant decline in per capita employment over a ten-year period, and a specific ruling against designating areas demonstrating net migration over a ten-year period. Another meaningful departure from the existing legislation was a provision allowing the agency to fund public works and business development projects of direct benefit to growth centers. Under the original act, projects were required either to have some impact on redevelopment areas or to benefit a multicounty district.

Prevailing Tendency

The development of legislative proposals, improvement of existing programs, and increased emphasis on interagency coordination were all means by which agency administrators prepared for the future. However, these activities involved no major shifts in policy. The prevailing tendency among EDA's high-level officials in the fall of 1971—as during the preceding months—was to continue in established patterns until actions by Congress or the administration dictated or facilitated major policy changes.

**Part II:
Evaluation of Economic
Development
Administration Activities**

6 Evaluation Approach

Introduction

Evaluation of the effects of any activity can take two forms: (1) pre- and post-observations on the relevant variables can be observed and significant differences determined; or (2) post-observations can be collected on the relevant variables and compared with the results of similar activities. Basically, the first technique determines the effects of an activity without comparing it to other similar activities, while the second technique relies on comparisons. Note that the first technique cannot be used if the decision to evaluate an activity is made after the activity has originated. This is particularly relevant to government programs because evaluation is not usually considered an integral part of the program.

Within these two approaches to evaluation, there exist a myriad of problems. Numerous questions arise.

—At what point in time should the pre- and post-observations be taken?
—How are the relevant variables determined?
—What methods should be used to determine significant differences?
—Are the differences due to other influences?
—What methods should be used to compare results from similar activities?

A simple example will show the complexity of problems that can exist in evaluating the impact of a given activity. Consider the case of determining the effectiveness of a course in calculus. One approach would be to decide what specific subject matter students should master, and administer pre-course and post-course tests. However, in isolation, test scores for any given class would not be useful. Comparison with some norm would be necessary. Perhaps, giving the same tests to a sufficient number of people in the same circumstances would provide this norm. The course could then be called effective if the class performed better than the norm.

The question of attributing success then comes into play. Was it a superior text or an outstanding teacher that made the course effective? Maybe the students were generally brighter than the pupils on which the norm was based. Isolating the factors that "cause" success is almost impossible. Other problems arise when the question of retention is considered. One course might appear effective only because the post-course test was administered to the class at the end of the semester. If a similar test were applied one year after completion of the course, other classes might look better. Perhaps the method of instruction, lecture or program, affects retention.

There are numerous other problems associated with this example, and they are all typical of those that arise in trying to evaluate the effectiveness of any activity. The same types of problems are encountered in the evaluation of the impact of regional economic development programs.

Framework for Evaluation of EDA Programs

Chapter 2 describes EDA's program tools. Essentially, the purpose of these tools is to alleviate conditions of substantial and persistent unemployment and underemployment in economically distressed areas and regions. In the past, counties have been designated as distressed if they met the following criteria.[a]

1. *Unemployment*: the unemployment rate was 6 percent or more, in the most recent calendar year; had averaged 6 percent or more for one of the time periods specified below; and the annual average rate has been at least: *(a)* 50 percent above the national average for three of the preceding four calendar years, *(b)* 75 percent above the national average for two of the preceding three calendar years, or *(c)* 100 percent above the national average for one of the preceding two calendar years.
2. *Population Loss*: the population loss had been 25 percent or more between the 1950 and 1960 census periods, and median family income had been between 40 and 50 percent of the national median.
3. *Income*: median family income had been less than 40 percent of the national median.
4. *Sudden Rise in Unemployment*: the unemployment rate was 50 percent or more above the national average due to the closing of a major source of employment.[1]

Within these designated areas, EDA uses public works grants and loans, business loans, planning grants, and technical assistance grants to help promote economic improvement.

One conceivable approach to evaluating the effects of EDA's programs would be to monitor changes in the measures that are used to designate areas. If significant changes were found to occur, then EDA might consider its program to be successful. However, this approach involves many difficulties.

[a]These criteria have been revised for fiscal years 1972 and 1973, but for the purposes of this chapter, the original criteria are appropriate. This is so because the programs evaluated were conceived under the original criteria.

1. Data on median family income on a county basis are only available every ten years. Therefore, a decade would pass before certain programs could be evaluated.
2. Determination of significant changes in these measures is difficult. The unemployment rate in a given county may decrease over a period of years, but the question is what change must occur for it to be significant.
3. Assuming that a significant change occurs, the problem of attribution arises. Since EDA's programs, in many cases, only indirectly affect the unemployment rate, there is no way of determining whether EDA is the cause of these changes.

EDA does not use per capita income as a measure for designation. However, because this indicator is available annually, it is normally used as a surrogate for median family income.[2] Monitoring changes in this indicator might be another reasonable way to evaluate EDA's programs. However, this too is subject to the problems of determining significant changes, and then attributing them to the EDA program.

Attributing changes in the primary measures of per capita income and migration rate to EDA programs is further complicated if the time factor is considered. In any given county, changes in these primary measures represent a long-term phenomenon. It may take as long as ten years for these changes to occur. Therefore, evaluation of a program could not be performed until ten years after the program was initiated; not because the data are not available, but because expected changes take that long to occur.

Possible Evaluation

Leading Indicator Approach

To avoid waiting for long periods of time to elapse before evaluation procedures are initiated, a leading indicator approach might be considered. This approach is currently being employed by the National Bureau of Economic Research to predict changes in the national economy. For example, the industrial production index is used as a leading indicator.

Theoretically, analogous leading indicators for the primary measures of unemployment or income could be developed at the regional level. Changes in these measures could then be tied to the impact of EDA's programs. However, attempts to develop these leading indicators at the regional level are difficult because of the lack of data. Very few variables are observed at this level or are observed more often than by the decennial census. Some variables for which bi-monthly data are available are listed below:

1. Total county unemployment and employment
2. State unemployment
3. Percent of county employment in manufacturing
4. Percent of county employment in agriculture
5. F.W. Dodge construction data: number of nonresidential and manufacturing projects; total floor space of nonresidential and manufacturing projects; value of nonresidential projects; value of manufacturing projects; and total value of construction projects

Attempts to determine leading indicators of county unemployment rates from this list are described in *Decision Making Aids for Measuring and Predicting Economic Change in EDA Designated Areas*, DECISION Studies Group, August 1970. The basic conclusion of this study was that the possible leading indicators of unemployment were not significantly predictive. Only when unemployment rates of prior periods were inserted in the equations did reasonable predictors result.

Even if the conclusions of this study were more encouraging, tying the impact of EDA projects to changes in the leading indicators would be difficult. Relations between EDA projects and certain elements of the Dodge construction data would probably exist. However, the relations between projects and other variables, such as unemployment for the state containing the county, would be difficult to estimate.

Secondary Measure Approach

Another approach, similar to the leading indicator method, is to link changes in the primary measures of unemployment and per capita income to a set of secondary measures.[3] These secondary measures may not have any significant time relationship to the primary measures, but it is expected that they can be tied to the impact of EDA's projects more closely.

These secondary indicators can be thought of as falling into three general categories: economic, social, and political, as shown in table 6-1. The indicators in table 6-1 have been chosen because: (1) there is available data on them at the regional level; and (2) they are partially supported by the literature on regional economics. The following outline discusses these secondary indicators in some detail. For each indicator, a short justification is given, followed by a suggested measure(s).

1. *Change in Residentiary Employment*
   Residentiary employment, usually referred to as non-basic employment, is the total employment in the following sectors:

Table 6–1

Secondary Indicators of Economic Development

Economic Indicators	Social Indicators	Political Indicators
Change in Residentiary Employment	Regional Class Structure	Political Participation
Index of Growth Industries	Educational Profile	
Degree of Economic Concentration		
Change in Labor Force Participation Rate		
Loan Potential of Financial Institutions		
Government Fiscal Effort		
Government Investment Effort		

a) Contract construction
b) Public utilities
c) Eating and drinking establishments
d) Finance, insurance, and real estate
e) Lodging places
f) Other retail trade
g) Business and repair services
h) Amusements
i) Private households
j) Educational, medical, and professional services
k) Public administration

Due to the relatively slow growth of manufacturing over the past decade, changes in residential employment should influence regional economic development.

Measure(s): The percentage increase of employment in the residentiary sector over a ten-year time period.

2. *Index of Growth Industries*

The nation's industries are usually broken down into thirty-two primary sectors. Over the past decade, some of these have experienced significant growth; they are referred to as "growth industries."

Measure(s): An index of relative growth, derived by comparing the regional rates of growth in the thirty-two industrial sectors with national rates in the same sectors.

3. *Degree of Economic Concentration*
A diversified industrial mix provides the opportunity for a region to more easily shift resources from industry to industry. This allows the region to react to fluctuations in demand, and avoid situations like that presently confronting residents of Seattle.

Measure(s): An index of employment concentration, based on the distribution of regional employment in the thirty-two industrial sectors.

4. *Manufacturing Productivity*
Regions with the highest growth rates in manufacturing productivity will be able to attract new firms, and thereby enhance economic growth.

Measure(s): The ratio of value added in manufacturing to man-hours worked in manufacturing.

5. *Manufacturing Investment*
Capital investment in manufacturing is considered one of the most basic contributors to economic development. Less developed regions are notable because of their low level of capital formation.

Measure(s): The ratio of new capital expenditures to value added in manufacturing.

6. *Change in the Labor Force Participation Rate*
The labor force participation rate is the number of employed and unemployed persons compared to the adult population. Past studies have shown that variations in this indicator account for a significant portion of the per capita income differences among states (e.g., states with low labor force participation rates tend to have low per capita incomes).

Measure(s): Ratio of the number of people employed and unemployed to the total population.

7. *Loan Potential of Financial Institutions*
The amount of loan money available in local banks indicates, to some degree, the ability of local groups and firms to obtain funds for development projects.

Measure(s): *a)* Total demand, time, and savings deposits.
b) Changes in total demand, time, and savings deposits.

8. *Government Fiscal Effort*
Local governments must be able to raise revenue for the provision of public services if development is to occur. Historically, property taxes have been the main source of this revenue.

Measure(s): *a)* Total per capita government revenue
b) Ratio of property taxes to total revenue

9. *Government Investment Effort*
Since many local governments cannot finance all needed social investment through their tax base, they rely on local citizens to assume debt through

such instruments as bonds. Willingness of local citizens to contract debt is an indication of a positive attitude toward development.

Measure(s): The ratio of total local government debt to total local government revenue.

10. *Political Participation*

The degree of local political involvement is an indication of community awareness and involvement. The hypothesis is that citizen participation in politics furthers economic development.

Measure(s): *a)* The percentage of eligible voters voting in presidential elections.

b) The change in voter turn-out over four-year periods.

11. *Regional Class Structure*

The distribution of income can affect the rate of economic development in many regions. For example, the defeat of local bond issues may be due to a feeling of powerlessness on the part of low-income citizens.

Measure(s): *a)* The ratio of families earning more than $10,000 to families earning less than $3,000.

b) The percent of white collar employment.

c) The percent of non-white population.

12. *Educational Profile*

It is well documented that education and income are closely related. Median school years completed is a good measure for the level of educational achievement. However, it cannot be aggregated from county data to provide a measure for a whole region. Thus, the following measures are used.

Measure(s): *a)* The percentage of persons twenty-one years of age and over who completed less than five years of school.

b) The percentage of persons twenty-one years of age and over who have completed high school.

Project-Oriented Approach

Because of all the problems inherent in attributing changes in primary and secondary measures to EDA project impact, and because of the lack of empirical relationships between primary and secondary indicators, EDA in its initial evaluation attempts chose a project-oriented approach. The focus was on the project: estimating its costs and benefits.

Definition of Project Benefits

EDA adopted a set of general project impact measures which were applied, with varying emphasis, to all types of EDA projects—public works grants, business loans, planning grants, and technical assistance grants. In addition, other measures were applied to projects with specialized objectives. Examples of the specialized projects are training projects, such as grants to construct skill centers, and growth center projects, where the emphasis is on aiding depressed area residents through funding projects in nearby "growing" urban places.

Table 6-2 illustrates the different types of evaluation criteria which were initially applied by EDA to assess the impact of its projects. Discussion of the general criteria appears in the following sections. Discussion of the special criteria employed for program-oriented evaluations is presented in the methodology sections of the chapters that present the results of those evaluations. Data sources are identified later in this chapter.

As shown in table 6-2, EDA has developed special criteria for evaluating the Selected Indian Reservation Program. At present, the methodology for applying these criteria is in the pilot-test stage. However, if the methodology proves useful, EDA will consider employing it to evaluate a broader range of its programs.

Job Location. The Public Works and Economic Development Act of 1965 states that the agency is "to alleviate conditions of substantial and persistent unemployment and underemployment in economically distressed areas and regions." One way EDA has attempted to achieve this has been through encouraging private enterprise to expand or locate in depressed communities and thereby create jobs for the local residents. This is primarily accomplished through the agency's Public Works and Business Loan Programs.

The number of local jobs created and the EDA dollars invested per job created are used to measure the agency's effectiveness in these efforts. In each case, an attempt is made to clearly distinguish between the jobs created as a result of the EDA project, and those that would have been created even if the EDA project had not been funded. Only the jobs attributable to the EDA project are counted.

Table 6-2
Project Evaluation Criteria

General Criteria	• Job Location
	• Economic Structure
	• Private Investment
	• Development Process
	• Service
Special Criteria for	• Economic Development Groups in Urban Areas
	• Skill Centers
	• Planning Grant Program
	• Growth Center Program
	• Selected Indian Reservation Program

The job location criterion includes saved, new, and discounted future jobs directly attributable to EDA funding:

1. A *saved job* is a job which existed in an area but would have been eliminated without the EDA project.
2. A *new job* is a job which did not exist previously and was generated or made possible as a direct consequence of an EDA project.
3. A *discounted future job* is a job not yet existing but with reasonable certainty of being generated within one year or less. Because it is an expected job, it is discounted by an appropriate risk factor, varying from 0 to 100 percent.[b]

Jobs created by other investments dependent upon the EDA investment are also counted. An example of this is the employment created because a firm establishes or expands operations to supply an EDA-assisted firm.

When feasible, estimates of indirect jobs are also calculated using factors developed from the E.J. Ullman and M.F. Dacey paper "The Minimum Requirements Approach to the Urban Economic Base," published in the *Proceedings of the 1960 IGU Symposium*. The basic premise in using this multiplier is that the jobs created by the agency lead to the generation of additional jobs in service industries as a result of increased spending within the local economy. The procedure used to calculate these indirect employment effects involves multiplying the number of direct jobs by a factor that varies according to the population of the community in which the project is located. Table 6-3 presents the factors that are used.[c]

Total job impact is the sum of the direct and indirect jobs. However, this measure does not compensate for differences in wage scale and length of the work week, nor take into account the effects of seasonal employment. When this is judged necessary, the income earned by the direct job holders is divided by $6,500 (the average annual manufacturing wage in 1968) to obtain a measure called "direct job equivalents."

The indirect job multiplier is applied to direct job equivalents. Total job equivalents is the sum of direct and indirect job equivalents. A measure of effectiveness for a given EDA project is then calculated by dividing the EDA investment by the total number of job equivalents. This gives investment per job ratios that can be used to compare projects.

---

[b](1) 100 percent of specified impact is credited if plant or expansion is completed and hiring has begun; (2) 75 percent of specified impact is credited if plant or expansion is completed but hiring has not begun; (3) 50 percent of specified impact is credited if plant or expansion is under construction and completion is expected within one year; (4) 25 percent of specified impact is credited if plant or expansion is not under construction but completion is expected within a year; (5) No impact is credited if none of the above apply.

[c]A detailed explanation of how these factors were derived from the Ullman-Dacey paper is given in Appendix B, "Estimation of Indirect Jobs."

Table 6-3

Factors Used to Calculate Indirect Employment Effects of EDA Projects

Population	Number of Indirect Jobs Per Direct Job[a]
Over 1,000,000	1.3
800,000 to 1,000,000	1.2
300,000 to 800,000	1.0
100,000 to 300,000	0.8
25,000 to 100,000	0.7
15,000 to 25,000	0.6
10,000 to 15,000	0.5
5,000 to 10,000	0.4
Under 5,000	0.3

[a]Note[b], appendix B. explains how the above data was derived.

Economic Structure. A simple count of the absolute number of jobs created in a region provides an incomplete picture of a project's impact. The purpose of the economic structure criterion is to help alleviate this problem by analyzing the quality of the jobs created by the EDA project. This involves examining jobs to determine their contribution to the local economy's growth and stability. This includes a determination of the degree to which the jobs are held by area residents and by the low-income or unemployed workers of the area. Since this criterion is linked to the location of jobs, it is most relevant to the evaluation of the Business Loan and Public Works Programs.

For the evaluation of public works projects and business development loans, the eight factors enumerated below were selected as representative of the range of impact on the economic structure of communities. Each factor was assigned three quality levels. Then, weights from zero to twenty were determined for each factor and quality level. This was accomplished through the use of "Pairwise Comparison Forms," completed by agency officials. These forms required each factor to be compared with every other factor to determine the relative importance attached to each. Using the weights established on the basis of the responses contained on the forms, it is possible to compute a total score for each project by summing the scores for each of the eight factors. The factors and the weights used are described below.

Stability of New Employment. This factor is used to evaluate the stability of the firms that locate as a result of EDA projects. Where more than one employing activity is involved, the dominant activity is evaluated. If no one activity is dominant, an average is used.

Quality Level	**Weight**
The employing activity is a new company, not affiliated with a larger parent company.	0

Quality Level	Weight
The new employing activity is an established company that does not meet the qualifications of the following quality level.	5
The new employment is likely to be sustained at present or higher levels because the employing activity is a government agency, a quasi-public agency (such as a hospital or educational institution), or a top-rated company with a stable or growth history and a superior credit rating.	10

Potential Growth of Employing Activity. This factor is designed to evaluate the growth potential of the new employing activities by comparing the growth of the particular industry over the most recent five-year period for which figures are available with the growth in national employment.

Quality Level	Weight
The employing activity has grown in employment less than the national employment growth (or has declined) in the past five years.	0
The employing activity has grown in employment at the national average for employment growth (plus or minus 10 percent) over the past five years.	5
The employing activity has grown in employment faster than the national employment growth in the past five years.	10

Employment Diversification. This factor is used to evaluate the extent to which the EDA-generated jobs diversify the employment opportunities in the area and make the area less vulnerable to severe employment loss because of cyclical changes in one industry.

Quality Level	Weight
More than 50 percent of the new jobs created as a result of the EDA project are in or are closely dependent upon the primary employment classification in the area.	0
More than 50 percent of the new jobs created as a result of the EDA project are in industrial or other classifications which have previously existed in the area but which are not the leading employment classification.	2
More than 50 percent of the new jobs created as a result of the EDA project are in industrial or other classifications which have not previously existed in the area.	5

Previous Employment Status of New Employees. This factor is used to evaluate the extent to which the new jobs go to individuals who previously experienced economic distress as a result of unemployment or underemployment.

Quality Level	Weight
Less than 1/3 of the new employees were either previously unemployed, earned less than $3,000 in the year preceding the start of current employment, or came from a family falling within the Office of Economic Opportunity income poverty guidelines. (These guidelines are presented in table 6-4)	0
From 1/3 to 2/3 of the new employees were either previously unemployed, earned less than $3,000 in the year preceding the start of current employment, or came from a family falling within the OEO income poverty guidelines.	10
More than 2/3 of the new employees were either previously unemployed, earned less than $3,000 in the year preceding the start of current employment, or came from a family falling within the OEO income poverty guidelines.	20

Head-of-Household Employment. This factor is designed to evaluate the extent to which the jobs credited to the project have gone to heads of households; that is, the principal wage earners of families.

Quality Level	Weight
Less than 1/3 of the new employees are the principal wage earners of their families.	0

Table 6–4
OEO Income Poverty Guidelines: November 1971

Number in Household	Nonfarm Income under	Farm Income under
1	$2,000	$1,700
2	$2,600	$2,100
3	$3,300	$2,800
4	$4,000	$3,400
5	$4,700	$4,000
6	$5,300	$4,500
7	$5,900	$5,000
More	add $600 per person	add $500 per person

Source: "OEO Income Poverty Guidelines (Revised)," OEO Instruction 6004–1c, Washington, D.C.: Office of Economic Opportunity, November 19, 1971, p. 3

Quality Level	Weight

From 1/3 to 2/3 of the new employees are the principal wage earners of their families. 7

More than 2/3 of the new employees are the principal wage earners of their families. 15

Previous Residence of the Work Force. This factor is designed to evaluate the extent to which the new jobs went to individuals who came into the area from other areas eligible for EDA assistance.

Quality Level	Weight

Less than 1/3 of the new employees previously lived in the area or in an area which was eligible for EDA assistance at the time the project was approved. 0

From 1/2 to 2/3 of the new employees previously lived in the area or in an area which was eligible for EDA assistance at the time the project was approved. 7

More than 2/3 of the new employees previously lived in the area or in an area which was eligible for EDA assistance at the time the project was approved. 15

Utilization of Underutilized Resources. This factor is designed to evaluate the extent to which the new jobs serve to foster greater utilization of underutilized local resources (such as wood, scenary, human resources). Underutilized resources are identified in the area OEDP.

Quality Level	Weight

New jobs created as a result of the EDA project do not result in increased utilization of underutilized local resources. 0

New jobs created as a result of the EDA project meet criteria in the OEDP for utilization of underutilized resources, but receive less than first priority. 7

New jobs created as a result of the EDA project meet first priority in OEDP for utilization of underutilized local resources. 15

Contribution of New Jobs to Economic Base. This factor is designed to evaluate the contribution which the new jobs make to strengthening the economic base of the area. The evaluation is accomplished by estimating the percentage of the output of goods or services exported out of the area. Where an industry produces goods which are shipped to another industry in the area for further processing prior to export out of the area for ultimate consumption, the output is considered as export. Where an industry (such as a hotel) provides services in the area to individuals who come from outside the area, such services are also considered as exports.

Quality Level	Weight
The new employing activities export less than 40 percent of the output of their goods and services outside the area in which the project is located. If the employing activities export less than 40 percent of their output from the area, the relevance of the stability and growth characteristics of the firm is reduced. Accordingly, scores for these factors are both lowered one grade.	0
The new employing activities export 40 to 70 percent of the output of their goods and services outside the area in which the project is located.	5
The new employing activities export 71 to 100 percent of the output of their goods and services outside the area in which the project is located.	10

Private Investment. As one means of evaluating the Business Loan and Public Works Programs, the amount of private capital investment per agency dollar obligated is computed. This is done whenever the data are available.

In the case of the Business Loan Program, this private capital investment consists of the private capital that helps finance the original project, and the private capital invested in firms that locate in the area to service the EDA-assisted firm. In the case of the Public Works Program, the private capital investment consists of the private investment in firms that locate in the area or increase operations as a direct result of agency-financed projects.

Development Process. Certain human attitudes and activities at work in a community have an influence on the ability of that community to realize its full economic potential. This human force, which can mobilize available resources in order to develop the local economy, can be thought of as constituting an economic development process. For the purpose of evaluation, the development process has been described by ten factors, and an attempt is made to measure changes in these factors as a result of EDA projects.

Each factor was assigned five quality levels, and, as in the case of economic structure impact, weights were derived from comparisons of factors by agency officials. The results indicated that all ten factors were of equal importance. The level of these factors are determined at two points in time: before application to the agency; and at the time of the evaluation. This allows for determining changes in the economic development process. Attributing changes in the process to the agency project is then accomplished by asking community representatives about the dependence of economic development in their community on the project.

The five quality levels for each of the ten factors are presented below.

Local Government's Attitude. The quality levels for this factor are as follows.

1. The local government is actually opposed to any development projects.
2. The local government is indifferent to development projects, although not opposed to them.
3. The local government is willing to support community development projects if pushed hard enough but seldom, if ever, takes the leadership.
4. The local government takes some leadership in pressing for the more important development projects.
5. The local government takes considerable leadership in pressing for implementation of a wide range of development projects.

Attitude of Lending Institutions. In measuring the attitude of local lending institutions, the following quality levels are applied.

1. Lending institutions are generally hostile to all forms of development financing.
2. While lending institutions are not openly hostile to development financing, they generally do not make money available for such purposes.
3. Lending institutions make money available for development financing to some favored borrowers or in connection with a few gilt-edged projects.
4. Lending institutions make money available for development projects on a reasonable basis.
5. Lending institutions take leadership in promoting and stimulating development projects and participate aggressively in their financing.

Attitude of Dominant Economic Group. The quality levels for measuring the attitude of the dominant economic group are as follows.

1. The dominant economic group sees development as a threat to its interests and opposes development projects.
2. Although not opposed to development projects, the dominant economic group is indifferent or contemptuous regarding development projects.

3. Some members of the dominant economic group are willing to go along with the development process, and their efforts balance the indifference or opposition of others.
4. Most members of the dominant economic group will cooperate in achieving development projects.
5. Key members of the dominant economic group are taking leadership in helping to plan and carry out a broad development program.

Cooperation of Community Organizations. The cooperation of community organizations is measured by using the following quality levels.

1. Community institutions are generally unconcerned and unaware of community development activities and projects.
2. Community institutions are vaguely concerned about development, but they are uninformed and take no part in the process.
3. Community institutions are informed and interested in the development process but their contribution is minimal.
4. Community institutions are interested and informed about development projects, and they are taking effective action to support them.
5. Community institutions are enthusiastic about development; they participate in sponsoring many projects; and take leadership on occasion.

Effectiveness of Community Planning Efforts. The following quality levels are used to measure the effectiveness of community planning efforts.

1. There is either no organized planning going on in the area, or if there is, the "plan" simply exists on paper, and is ignored.
2. Planning activities, if they exist, are generally limited to routine zoning, building ordinances, etc.
3. There is relatively effective planning of the traditional variety (physical planning) and there is a full-time planning staff (or its equivalent in voluntary activities by the local planning commission).
4. In addition to relatively effective physical planning, a start has been made on broader planning (capital budgets, manpower, health, etc.).
5. Planning activities are well-supported locally, cover a wide range of subjects, and plans are influential and effective in guiding local development.

Effectiveness of Local Development Organization. The following quality levels are used to evaluate this factor.

1. There is no local development organization.
2. There is a local development organization on paper, but it accomplishes very little.

3. There is a functioning local development organization, but it is not effective because it does not have a full-time executive.
4. There is a local development organization functioning with a full-time executive.
5. There is a local development organization functioning; it has a full-time executive; and there is considerable community support for the organization and participation in its projects.

Borrowing and Financing Capacity. An area's borrowing and financing capacity is measured on the basis of the following quality levels.

1. The area:
   a) levies tax rates which, compared to other jurisdictions in the state, do not require residents to make an equitable contribution to local development, and
   b) collects revenues for public services (such as water and sewer) in ways and amounts which are inadequate to finance a reasonable level of services; and
   c) has shown a consistent unwillingness to support bond issues for community development.
2. Two of the above are true.
3. One of the above is true.
4. The local people are about average in their willingness to finance local improvements.
5. The local people are above average in their willingness to finance local improvements, and they show an unusual capacity to raise money in support of local development projects.

Cooperation with Neighboring Communities. The following quality levels are used to judge cooperation with neighboring communities.

1. The area does not participate in the district program.
2. The area is a part of the district program, but inactive.
3. The area is a part of the district program, but plays only a small and minor role.
4. The area is a part of the district program and plays an active role.
5. The area takes an effective leadership role in the district organization.

Effectiveness in Using State and Other Federal Development Programs. The quality levels for measuring this factor are as follows.

1. There are virtually no other state and federal programs operating locally, and there is no effort under way to start some.

2. There are virtually no other state and federal programs locally, but action to start programs has begun.
3. There are a few other state and federal programs operating locally, but they have limited effectiveness.
4. The area is making use of available state and federal programs.
5. The area is making outstanding use of available state and federal programs.

Concern for Poor and Minority Groups. Concern for poor and minority groups is rated according to the following quality levels.

1. The area's leadership is actually hostile to programs which will benefit poor and minority groups.
2. While not actually hostile to programs for the benefit of poor and minority groups, the area's leadership is indifferent to their needs.
3. The area's leadership pays lip service to the needs of programs which will benefit members of poor and minority groups, but actually accomplishes only a bare minimum.
4. The bulk of the area's programs benefit more established groups, but the area's leadership is concerned about programs which will benefit members of poor and minority groups, and has had some success in establishing such programs.
5. Most of the development programs are planned for the benefit of members of poor and minority groups.

Service. One possible impact of an EDA public works project is the provision of a service to the poor in the local community. For example, a water system may service a new industry, and also provide running water to an area that previously had to use outside wells. Some projects were in fact approved solely on the basis of their anticipated service impact. The purpose of the service impact evaluation, therefore, is to identify the extent to which the project is providing a new or improved service to poor households in the community.

A service grade is derived on the basis of a scheme that considers the number of poor households being served, the percentage of the project output received by poor households, and the percentage of the total number of poor households in the community that is being served. The specific grade assignment scheme is illustrated in table 6-5.

Definition of Project Costs

One measure of project effectiveness used by EDA is the ratio of EDA's investment to the number of jobs attributable to the project. However, this

Table 6–5
Scheme for Grading Service Impact

Poor Households Served	Impact of Service				
	New and Important	Improved and Important	Not Important	No Service	Negative Service
If over 750 and 75% of total output or 75% of poor households	A	B	C	None	F
If 500–750 and 50–74% of total output or 50–74% of poor households	B	C	D	None	F
If 250–499 and 25–49% of total output or 25–49% of poor households	C	D	E	None	F
If less than 250 and less than 25% of total output or less than 25% of poor households	D	E	None	None	F

measure does not reflect the true cost to the government of a project investment. Opportunity costs, overhead, and pay backs are not included. For this reason, in the case of business loan and public works projects, true costs to the government of the total portfolio of funded projects have been calculated.

Costs are defined as the difference between total disbursements and total receipts. Disbursements include direct and indirect administrative costs and the opportunity cost of foregoing alternative investments. Receipts are the principal and interest payments accruing from public works loans and business loans.

Opportunity costs are the economic benefits foregone because money was not alternatively invested. For a grant program with no financial return, the opportunity cost is the absolute gain from another investment. For a loan program, this cost is the difference between received income and income from an alternative mode of investment. EDA uses a 10 percent opportunity rate of interest, as suggested by the Office of Management and Budget.

The direct costs of administering EDA are part of the total cost of each program tool. These include activities prior to project approval, during construction, and after completion of the project. Administrative costs are assigned to each program based on estimates of the amount of time each office spends on the given program. The costs associated with EDA's Business Loan and Public Works Programs are presented in chapter 7.

Program-Oriented Approach

Development of Pilot Methodology

EDA often funds sets of projects in a given geographic area. For example, numerous areas have received in sequence a planning grant to determine and assign priorities to area needs, a public works grant to develop an industrial area, and finally a business loan to attract a firm to the industrial park. Evaluating these projects individually can be misleading in terms of attributing benefits. For this reason, more recent EDA evaluations have attempted to focus on the impact of programs on a total geographic area. A pilot methodology has been developed and tested for EDA's Selected Indian Reservation Program.[d] This methodology is discussed below. Modifications to this methodology should prove useful for evaluating programs in other types of geographic areas (counties, districts, etc.).

Evaluation Criteria

Figure 6-1 shows the hierarchy of criteria used to evaluate EDA projects associated with the Selected Indian Reservation Program. Many of the criteria already discussed are applied to the evaluation of these projects. In addition, certain discount and bonus schemes have been introduced. Basically, the evaluation system produces two scores: one reflecting income impact per EDA dollar cost; and a second reflecting the development potential of the project per EDA dollar cost.

The income score is derived directly from the realized job and income impact attributable to the project or set of related projects. Each source of income change attributable to the project is identified. The income derived from these sources is modified on the basis of the stability of the employing activity in question, the extent of Indian entrepreneurship, the degree of difficulty associated with economic development on the particular reservation, the level of private investment generated, and by the indirect income spun off as a result of the direct income impact. The bonus and discount system utilized to handle these modifications is explained below. The adjusted income impact is then related to the level of EDA cost in the project to produce a final income score.

The development potential score for a project expresses its traceable impact upon: (1) the infrastructure of the reservation; (2) tribal borrowing power; (3) tribal leadership as related to economic development; (4) skill levels of tribal members; and (5) knowledge of development opportunities on the reservation. Based on the level of impact, a score ranging from 0 to 100 is obtained. This score is adjusted to account for the degree of difficulty associated with economic development on the particular reservation. A final potential score is then obtained by relating the adjusted score to the level of EDA cost.

[d]For a complete description of EDA's Selected Indian Reservation Program, see chapter 11.

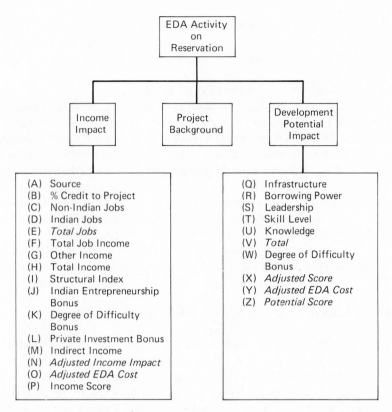

Figure 6-1. Framework for Evaluation of EDA Projects in Selected Indian Reservation Program

Income Impact (Refer to Figure 6-1). (A) is the source of the generated jobs and/or impact, that is, the income generating activity. Only sources that could not have realized this impact without the EDA project are included.

(B) is the percentage of that impact which is assigned to the project. For example, a business loan may be given 50 percent credit for the impact realized and a public works project may be given the other 50 percent credit. The assignment of percentages is based on the premise that EDA projects will be credited only if their contribution is considered to be necessary for subsequent income generated. In cases where more than one EDA project is deemed critical, the 100 percent credit is divided in proportion to each project's contribution.

(C) is the actual number of project-related jobs taken by non-Indians.

(D) is the actual number of project-related jobs going to Indians (not necessarily to tribal members).

(E) is the total number of jobs credited to the project, the sum of (C) and (D).

(F) is the job income associated with the jobs in (E).

(G) is other income accruing to the reservation from the project. This includes fees for mineral extraction and for testing, rents, increased sales, and similar items.

(H) is the total income, the sum of (F) and (G).

(I) is a structural index used to assess the stability of the firm or enterprise which was the source of the generated income. The most stable activities are given full credit for income generated, under the assumption that the identified income flow will continue for several years. The annual income flows for less stable activities are proportionately reduced to reflect their relative instability.

1. 100 percent of the income is credited to stable firms in growth industries.
2. 80 percent of the income is credited to stable firms in nongrowth or cyclical industries.
3. 75 percent of the income is credited to new firms in growth industries.
4. 50 percent of the income is credited to new firms in nongrowth or cyclical industries.

(J) is a bonus for Indian entrepreneurship. It is applied as follows:

1. 25 percent bonus for a venture which is tribally owned or controlled; up to 25 percent for partial, but noncontrolling tribal ownership; and
2. 10 percent bonus for a venture which is owned or controlled by an individual tribal member or group of members; up to 10 percent for partial, but not controlling ownership by a tribal member.

(K) is a degree of difficulty bonus which reflects the relative difficulty of achieving economic development successes on the various reservations. Among the factors which reflect the degree of difficulty are isolation from markets, climatic conditions, resource deficiencies, transportation deficiencies, manpower deficiencies, lack of community amenities, and relations with neighboring non-Indian communities. The reservations are grouped according to their degree of difficulty as reflected by these factors. Three groupings have been established, with the most difficult group receiving a 10 percent bonus, the middle group a 5 percent bonus, and the least difficult no bonus.

(L) is a bonus for private investment in economic development ventures. It is assigned on the basis on the ratio of private (nongovernment or nontribal) to EDA investment as follows:

1. 0 percent for a ratio of less than 0.5;
2. 5 percent for a ratio from 0.5 to 0.99;
3. 10 percent for a ratio from 1.0 to 1.49;
4. 15 percent for a ratio from 1.5 to 1.99; and
5. 20 percent for a ratio of 2.0 or over.

(M) accounts for the multiplier effect of the income generated. Some of the income derived from the various sources attributable to EDA will be respent on the reservation and help support additional individuals and families. Hence, it should be included as part of the realized income impact. The service economy of each reservation is evaluated during field visits. As a result, indirect income multipliers are determined and applied to the direct income identified. These multipliers are:

1. 0 percent if the shopping opportunities on the reservation are insufficient to meet the daily needs of the residents;
2. 15 percent if the shopping opportunities on the reservation are sufficient to meet the daily needs of the reservation residents, but durable goods are generally unavailable; and
3. 30 percent if the shopping opportunities are more than sufficient to meet the daily needs of the reservation residents, and durable goods such as clothing and smaller appliances are available.

(N) is the adjusted income impact. It is the gain (or loss) from total income resulting from the above described discounts and bonuses.

(O) is the adjusted EDA cost of the project. This figure is equal to the full amount of EDA grants plus 25 percent of the total amount of EDA loans. (It has been determined that the actual cost to the agency for loans approximates 25 percent of initial outlay after repayment and accounting for defaults and administrative and opportunity costs.)

(P) is the final income score. This is equal to the adjusted income impact (N) expressed as a percentage of the adjusted EDA cost (O).

Development Potential Impact. The impact of each project (or related projects) on the development potential of the reservation in question is gauged by assessing its effects on five factors. These factors are weighted to reflect their relative importance, utilizing weights derived during a group working session involving key EDA operating personnel and evaluators. Projects are awarded points for each factor up to the maximum defined by the weight assignment. The sum of the five weight assignments totals 100, so a project with maximum impact on development potential can conceivably receive 100 points. The rationale for assigning points follows.

(Q) is infrastructure (25 points). A full 25 points is accrued by a project which results in a major change in infrastructure such as to make the area more attractive to industry and/or other economic ventures. A minor change in infrastructure is assigned a value up to 10 points. A major change is defined as one which provides an infrastructure component essential to development, while a minor change is one which is contributory but not essential to development. These two benchmark values serve as guides in assessing infrastructure points.

(R) is borrowing power (15 points). Points for this factor are assigned with the following descriptions as guidelines:

1. 15 points if the project allows the tribe to secure funding for most development projects;
2. 10 points if the project allows the tribe to secure funding for some development projects, but financing is still a limitation; and
3. 5 points if the project results in a discernible improvement in the tribe's ability to secure development financing, but the inability to finance development is still a major drawback.

(S) represents leadership (35 points). Three areas in which an EDA project can contribute to reservation leadership have been isolated and are utilized to assess this factor. These are higher level of positive development-oriented action, greater continuity of leadership, and improved attitude toward the development process. For each project, the evaluators determine as best as possible the contribution generated from the project in each of these areas with respect to tribal leadership. On the basis of a group consensus, a point value up to a possible 35 points is assigned.

(T) is skill level (10 points). Points for this factor are assigned with the following as benchmarks:

1. Ten points if the project has made a material and significant contribution to the quality of the labor force and/or the quality of managers, or has materially and significantly increased the capacity of the reservation to train effective workers and managers;
2. Seven points if the contribution of the project to the improvement in the present or prospective quality of the labor force, including management, is directly evident, but not significant; and
3. Three points if the contribution of the project to the improvement of the present or prospective quality of the labor force, including management, is evident, but only indirectly through related experience rather than specific training.

(U) is knowledge (15 points). The assessment of the project contribution to tribal knowledge is assessed with the following as a guide:

1. fifteen points if the project results in a breakthrough in the potential utilization of previously unused or severely underutilized resources;
2. ten points if the project materially increases the know-how of the tribe on how to take full advantage of its resources; and
3. five points if the project defines an efficient, feasible manner in which the tribe can utilize its known resources.

After completing the assignments for any project, the points given are compared against all previously assessed projects. As needed, adjustments are made in the point assignments made to the current or previously assessed projects. In this way, a consistent set of point assignments emerges.

(V) is the total development potential points accumulated by the project. It is the sum of the previous five items.

(W) is the degree of difficulty bonus and is the same as (K) above.

(X) is the adjusted development potential score which is the total of the accumulated points plus the degree of difficulty bonus.

(Y) is the adjusted EDA cost and is the same as (O).

(Z) is the final potential score which is the number of adjusted development potential points per $100,000 of adjusted EDA cost.

Evaluation Process and Problems

Description of the Evaluation Process

During the last two years, EDA has evaluated approximately 600 projects. The evaluation process can be generally described by the flow chart shown in figure 6-2. This section will describe the major parts of the process, and discuss some of the problems in performing each step.

The selection of criteria is a crucial step in the development of methodology. Ideally, criteria should be developed by studying the stated objectives of a program. However, in practice, objectives are usually stated so loosely that it is difficult to agree on evaluation criteria. Nevertheless, agreement on evaluation criteria is essential if the results of the analysis are to be used by operating officials to improve project impact. In some cases, total studies can be negated by the claim that the wrong evaluation criteria were used.

One method that has been tried to obtain agreement on criteria is pair-wise comparison; this method was described in some detail in the discussion on the economic structure evaluation criterion. Basically, this approach requires concerned agency officials and experts to weight the importance of different evaluation criteria. From the individual scores, a consensus weighting system is derived. This allows each person to have an influence on the criteria to be used for evaluation.

Selecting a representative sample of projects is another major area of concern. Again, evaluation studies can be negated if the projects evaluated are not typical. Choosing a homogeneous sample is extremely difficult since there may be substantial variations in project objectives, operational time, and even agency policies in effect at the time of project approval. Currently, EDA project evaluations are hampered by the size of available homogeneous samples. Sometimes, this prevents developing general results, and reduces an evaluation to a series of case studies. However, this condition will improve as the number of approved projects increases.

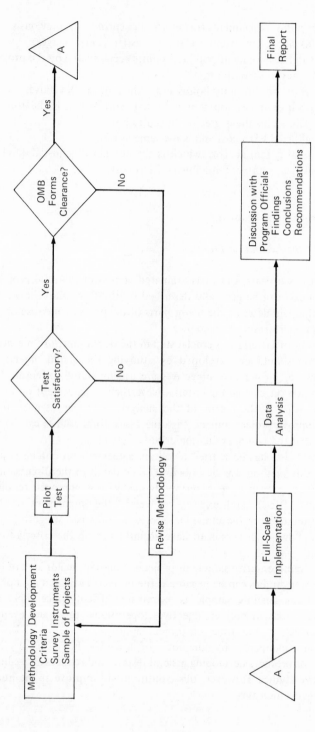

Figure 6–2. Typical Evaluation Process

Availability of data is another problem faced by evaluators. National, state, county, and local population data are frequently limited or out of date. For example, it is frequently not known how many people are unemployed in a given area. The unemployment rates normally reported are not completely accurate because they do not count many persons who have become frustrated in trying to find a job and are no longer actively seeking work. Underemployment is also difficult to define, and accurate statistics are unavailable.

Income data are also lacking in some situations. This is particularly true with regard to the incomes of American Indians. The inaccuracy of the data that are available and the absence of other information have handicapped EDA's efforts to analyze project impact on reservations.

Data on migration are also difficult to obtain. The Census Bureau can provide rough estimates, but only every ten years. The Social Security 1 percent sample, although timely, is restricted by disclosure and size problems.

Discussion of results with program officials is an important part of the evaluation process. The purpose of evaluation is to help achieve a better allocation of resources. This can be accomplished only if evaluation conclusions are communicated to program officials in a meaningful way. However, the concept of evaluation implies examining and judging another's work, with the possibility of finding imperfections. Because of this, there is an inherent tendency for the evaluator to be perceived as a threat.

Instead of the program officer and evaluator working together within the framework of common goals, the two frequently appear as antagonists. Unless a common ground can be established and maintained between the program officer and the evaluator, the possibility that the evaluation will have an impact is small. Conclusions and recommendations resulting from the analysis will be better received and more likely to be implemented if liaison has been maintained between the two functions.

Development of Questionnaires

The development of questionnaires consists of four stages:

1. definition of the objectives of the evaluation;
2. translation of these objectives into broad questions to be answered;
3. translation of these broad questions into subquestions; and
4. translation of the subquestions into precise data requirements.

Figures 6-3, 6-4, and 6-5 provide examples of the stages in the development of questionnaires for the evaluation of economic development groups.

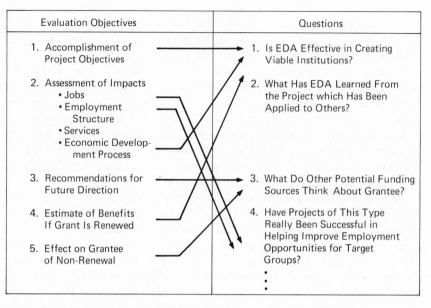

Evaluation Objectives	Questions
1. Accomplishment of Project Objectives	1. Is EDA Effective in Creating Viable Institutions?
2. Assessment of Impacts • Jobs • Employment Structure • Services • Economic Development Process	2. What Has EDA Learned From the Project which Has Been Applied to Others?
3. Recommendations for Future Direction	3. What Do Other Potential Funding Sources Think About Grantee?
4. Estimate of Benefits If Grant Is Renewed	4. Have Projects of This Type Really Been Successful in Helping Improve Employment Opportunities for Target Groups?
5. Effect on Grantee of Non-Renewal	

Figure 6–3. Translation of Evaluation Objectives into Questions (Evaluation of an Economic Development Group)

Pilot Test

After the survey instruments have been developed, the next step is to conduct a pilot test of the evaluation methodology. A first step in preparing for the pilot test is to conduct a thorough training session. At the training session, the objectives of the project are discussed and interviewing procedures are described. Questionnaires are distributed and described in detail. Members of the field teams become thoroughly familiar with the forms.

EDA has conducted a pilot test for each of the evaluation studies which have been completed in the past few years. These pilot test efforts have varied in complexity. In one case, a five-day training session was conducted using video tape scenarios showing various interviewing situations. Interviewer and interviewee roles were played by EDA personnel experienced in field interviewing techniques.

A major problem is the selection of the place or places to conduct the pilot test. Projects selected for a pilot test must be representative of the total group of projects to be evaluated. If the evaluation effort will be performed by several teams of individuals, at least one member of each of the teams should participate in the pilot test.

The pilot test extends beyond the field work. The data collected must be

Questions	Subquestions
1. Has EDA Been Effective in Creating a Viable Institution?	1A. What Is Reputation of the Institution? 1B. Is the Institution Financially Sound? • • • (Example for Vocational Training)
4. Have Projects of This Type Been Successful in Helping Improve Employment Opportunities for Target Groups?	4A. What Is Total Demand for Training in the Community? 4B. What Fraction of This Demand Does Grantee Meet? 4C. How Does Grantee Select Trainees? 4D. How Is Focus on Target Groups Maintained? 4E. What Do Trainees Think About Training They Received? 4G. How Do *Employers* Assess the Training? • • •

Figure 6–4. Translation of Questions into Subquestions (Evaluation of an Economic Development Group)

analyzed and a report prepared, at least in detailed outline form, to insure that all possible problems in the evaluation effort have been identified.

As a result of the test, necessary revisions in forms and interviewing procedures are made. If these are major, a second pilot test is performed as a check on the changes that have been made.

Full-Scale Implementation

Upon completion of the pilot test, the evaluation methodology has been refined to the point where it is ready for implementation. The length of the typical interview and the approximate number of people and organizations to be seen

Subquestions	Data Elements
1B. Is the Institution Financially Sound?	1. Assets and Liabilities 2. Historical Budget Performance 3. Income and Expense Projections 4. Funding Commitments from Other Groups 5. Completeness of Financial Reports
4F. How Do Employers Assess the Vocational Training?	*Actions* 1. Number Previously Unemployed Who Obtained Employment 2. Types of Jobs 3. Earnings 4. Number Who Changed Job Title or Received Increase in Earnings 5. Types of Jobs (Before/After) 6. Amounts of Increase *Opinions* 7. Qualitative Statement of Why Training Made Man Eligible for Job or Promotion

Figure 6-5. Translation of Subquestions into Data Elements (Evaluation of an Economic Development Group)

have been established. To gain optimum use of time and available personnel, detailed schedules are developed for each project to be evaluated. This involves assigning personnel specific days to evaluate each project.

During the implementation phase, the problem of applying uniform standards for the collection of data on each project is encountered. This is crucial for insuring that the data collected are homogeneous and can be used for cross-project comparisons. Numerous procedures for cross-checking the data have been adopted. In evaluating a project, all segments of the community acquainted with the project are interviewed. An attempt is made to interview a balanced sample, representing both favorable and unfavorable views.

Collecting useful information from EDA project grantees is sometimes very difficult. One source of difficulty is the grantee who exaggerates the positive in an attempt to promote a future grant. Another is the grantee who has become frustrated with government "red tape" and has little or no time for what he considers another bureaucratic exercise.

The primary evaluation techniques EDA has employed are on-site interviews, mail-telephone surveys, or a combination of both. An examination of four studies will serve to illustrate many of the problems encountered during evaluations.

The public works evaluation performed in the spring of 1970 involved two studies conducted simultaneously, one by an outside contractor working in the field and the other by an in-house team using mail-telephone techniques. The field interviewers found the most commonly encountered problems to be a lack of local knowledge concerning the EDA project being evaluated, citizen availability for interviews, and the reluctance of firms' management to cooperate, especially in the completion of employee questionnaires.

Lack of citizen awareness was a problem common in large urban sites where the project was relatively small in comparison to the magnitude of the development area. Conversely, in small and isolated rural villages, the dearth of designated local leaders often forced the evaluators to turn to neighboring communities for information. Unfortunately, few of these local leaders were aware of the specific project being evaluated and were therefore not able to adequately assess the impact of the project on the economic development process.

A number of barriers were encountered in the process of attempting to obtain information from firms whose employment levels were affected by EDA projects. The most important was management's unavailability for interviewing and reluctance to reply to sensitive questions. Frequently, the evaluator was referred to higher authorities for a reply. Less frequently encountered was a reluctance to answer questions because of fear of labor union problems.

In the public works evaluation, several problems emerged with respect to the completion of employee forms. The principal problem was encountered with those firms whose work force was not on the premises because of the seasonal nature of the work or deployment in the field. In the case of concerns using assembly lines or automated operations, management viewed stopping for the interviewing process as a costly hindrance. In some cases, the forms had to be left with management to be completed and returned by mail to the evaluator. This reduced the return rate.

The primary difficulties faced by the mail-telephone evaluators were caused largely by the natural limitations of the questionnaires. To encourage return of mail questionnaires, the forms were reasonably short, with the result that some desired descriptions or answers were sacrificed. This sometimes resulted in confusion as to whether questions were interpreted as they were intended.

Another difficulty in the mail-telephone procedure was encountered in the selection of local information sources. Since team members were not intimately familiar with the communities where the projects were located, reliance was placed on lists provided by EDA field personnel. In some cases, the designated information sources were not current or were not completely familiar with the EDA project, so that the reliability of their answers was questionable. In other cases, the source had a vested interest in obtaining more federal funds, and thus was suspected of not providing objective answers.

A problem that arose in conjunction with the business loan evaluation conducted by an outside contractor during spring of 1970 was the mistrust by some interviewees of any individual or group connected with the federal government. While the number of such people is relatively small, this attitude can be detrimental to the effective evaluation of a project.

The contractor conducting the technical assistance evaluation undertaken during the same period faced similar difficulties to those discussed above. Persons connected with the EDA project had sometimes left the area, and were unavailable for interview. In other instances interviewers felt that they were not receiving a complete picture of the impact of EDA technical assistance efforts because of interviewee biases. If the applicant, who frequently supplied names for interviews, had a favorable attitude toward the project, most respondents usually had the same attitude. If the applicant were negative, the other respondents were negative.

Another of the analyses conducted during the spring of 1970 as part of EDA's expanded and accelerated evaluation effort was a study of the effectiveness of agency planning grants. In conducting field work for the planning grant evaluation, the major sources of information were local staff members of economic development districts and officials of redevelopment area county governments. In general, interviewers were received courteously by the district staffs, who were usually very helpful. However, in a number of districts there was a refusal to answer some questions. Refusals to respond were usually on the grounds that the information was either none of EDA's business or unknown to the district staff.

Another problem often encountered was that the district wanted no public credit for particular projects. They adopted this posture for the purpose of maintaining good relationships with the cooperating units of government. Usually, however, district directors were careful to point out that they could not establish how much credit they should receive for particular projects.

A major constraint, common to most of the field evaluations, was a lack of time to conduct all desired interviews. It was particularly difficult to synchronize the interviewers' schedules with those of the interviewees. Another problem was that of selecting objective local information sources. When interviews were scheduled in advance of the field visit, it was sometimes felt that the interviewer was being given a prepared speech. Problems of objectivity were compounded where the interviewer received conflicting viewpoints from seemingly reliable sources.

An issue common to all evaluations is the lack of understanding at the local level of the purpose of evaluations. In some cases, interviewees appeared to believe that they were being investigated in a negative sense, rather than being asked to help improve present policies.

The evaluation of EDA's training-related projects described in chapter 12 offers many examples of the serious problems evaluators encounter because of the poor files and record keeping associated with many projects. Skill centers often have multiple funding sources and may be required to keep different types of records for the different grants. Most often this results in a total breakdown in the record system with no comprehensive listing of all trainees.

In the training evaluation, an attempt was made to randomly sample past participants in the skill center programs to determine the impact of training on earning ability and general socioeconomic status. In order to select a random sample, it is necessary to have a complete record of all trainees. This was available in only one of the fifteen projects that comprised the evaluation. In the remaining fourteen projects, some combination of the school files, teacher class lists, placement records, etc., were necessary to reconstruct complete lists.

Another difficult problem was locating the people finally chosen as the sample. In practice, only about one out of every three people in the sample was actually interviewed. This attrition was caused by several situations: trainees had moved from the area; the interviewers were not able to contact trainees; and evaluators were unable to set up a mutually convenient interview appointment.

Analysis

While analysis is conducted throughout the evaluation process, the bulk of the analytical work occurs after all data collection efforts have been completed. At this point:

1. Findings must be checked for accuracy and consistency;
2. Tentative conclusions must be thoroughly reviewed;
3. Recommendations must be developed for improving the program; and
4. All of this must be summarized in a form which can be used by a wide variety of people.

Many sophisticated analytical techniques, such as linear programming and multiple regression, have limited value for evaluation of economic development programs. These techniques were developed for more scientific problems, where the constraints are more precise and the environment more predictable. Most of the analytical techniques used by EDA have been relatively simple ones, as discussed earlier in this chapter.

To a large extent, EDA's evaluation efforts have consisted of:

1. Determining the types of benefits which are relevant for a given project type;
2. Quantifying those benefits which can be measured (typically jobs and income changes);
3. Assessing the quality and importance of benefits which cannot be measured precisely; and
4. Comparing all benefits with the costs of the activity.

Analysis of economic development programs poses a number of difficult problems. One is determining which benefits to include in the analysis. For example:

1. If EDA projects help some people who already have good jobs, should these benefits be weighted as heavily as jobs for the unemployed?
2. If an unemployed person is hired for a job vacated by someone hired at an EDA-assisted project, should this "musical chairs" effect be considered?
3. If a previously employed person resigns after a year and an unemployed person is hired in his place, should this be included in the analysis?

In practice, EDA has tried to determine the distribution of program benefits to different population groups as well as the level of benefits. Moreover, a study has been done of the "musical chairs" effects of the Business Loan Program. The third question has not yet been addressed, primarily because most EDA evaluations have focused on conditions at one point in time. However, longitudinal evaluations, which would trace program impact over a period of several years, are under consideration.

Many economic development activities produce benefits in addition to increased employment and income. And even increased employment and income may be produced in indirect, hard-to-trace ways. This is commonly the case with public works and technical assistance projects. How can the increased access provided by a road to an industrial park be evaluated? How many jobs should be attributed to the access road, as compared with water and sewer services, low-interest loans for businesses in the park, or training provided at a nearby skills center?

There may be many different sources of funds—including EDA, other federal agencies, local government, and private sources—for all of these activities. Which source should be given primary credit for the benefits? This may be particularly hard to resolve if all the projects were essential to the individual success of each.

Another problem is the consideration of intangible benefits. For example, if a depressed community begins to grow, local residents who would otherwise have had to leave to obtain employment will be able to remain at home. Is this an important benefit? How important is it? Alternatively stated, how much is EDA willing to pay to acquire this benefit? How should these benefits be measured?

Another intangible benefit is increased cooperation among different local groups, who may be working together for the first time. How much consideration should be given to benefits of this type, as compared with employment and income? Some evaluations, such as that of the Public Works Program, have included subjective ratings of improvements in the local economic development process.

Geographic considerations also present problems. Although EDA is trying to stimulate growth in lagging areas, should it ignore the impact projects may have on other areas? What if a redevelopment area places a high priority on a project which would impose costs on a nondesignated area? What if some employees at an EDA-assisted project had previously been unemployed but live in a nondesignated area? How should benefits for them be weighted as compared with those for employees who live in the area but had previously been employed?

Another problem is the assessment of the total impact of all EDA investments in a community. Simple analysis of changes in area statistics can be misleading. For example, if EDA successfully stimulates employment growth in a depressed area, in-migration to the area and frictional unemployment may increase. In this case, the area's unemployment rate might remain unchanged (or even increase), although the long-term structural unemployment problem may have been resolved. In the past EDA has not relied upon changes in an area's economic statistics as an evaluation measure. Instead, measures are more directly tied to EDA's investments.

Finally, there is no way to tell what might have happened in an area if it had not received EDA assistance. Even if the area's economy did not improve significantly, it might have become worse without EDA aid. There is no available control group of non-EDA-assisted areas which are otherwise identical to EDA-assisted areas. If there were, comparisons between the two groups might provide indications of agency effectiveness.

When the analysis has been finished and recommendations developed, considerable attention must be given to the manner of presentation. Operating officials may be understandably defensive about any criticism of programs they have worked long hours trying to implement. Since the evaluators must rely on operating officials to implement their recommendations, considerable attention should be given to resolving communication problems. A consensus of support must be built for the analysis at all stages, if the ultimate recommendations are to have any chance of adoption.

7

Summary of Initial Results and Conclusions

The methodology described in chapter 6 evolved over a two-year period. It has not yet been applied comprehensively to the EDA program.

The first evaluations of EDA program tools emphasized the collection of information relating to job, economic structure, process, private investment, and service impact. Those categories received different emphasis, depending on which project type was being evaluated. Jobs per dollar, for example, could not be considered a major criterion for the evaluation of technical assistance projects. The word "project" should be emphasized, for as previously described, the first evaluations were almost exclusively project-oriented. For the most part, program conclusions were reached by aggregating project data.

The following is a brief summary of the results of the initial evaluations carried out by the agency between December 1969 and July 1970. Subsequent chapters will describe the results of program-oriented studies, which also had project emphasis, but which were designed to answer questions about specific program strategies.

Public Works Evaluation

Background

As of December 1969, when an expanded and accelerated evaluation of EDA programs was initiated, the agency had approved 1,672 public works projects. Of this number, 1,529 had been obligated, involving $802.5 million in EDA funds. For the purposes of evaluation, it is only reasonable to consider public works projects that have been completed for a year or more. Newer projects have not been completed long enough to produce significant impact. In January 1970, when an expanded evaluation was initiated, approximately 330 public works projects had been completed for a year or more. Two hundred and seventy-four, or 83 percent, of these projects were randomly selected and studied during the evaluation. These projects represented EDA investments of approximately $77 million. The remaining 56 projects were not evaluated because of the limited time and funds allotted to the evaluation.

In January 1969, EDA initiated a Request for Proposal to develop a methodology that could be utilized in evaluating the total range of public works projects. These projects include water/sewer systems; industrial/commercial

103

development; street and road building; tourist facility development; and construction of community buildings, educational facilities (primarily vocational schools), and health facilities. Most public works projects fall into two categories: water/sewer and industrial/commercial. Water/sewer projects include waterworks, water lines, sewers, and sewage treatment facilities. These projects are intended primarily to improve the infrastructure of a community and increase its prospects for long-term economic growth. Industrial/commercial projects include industrial parks, harbor facilities, shell buildings in industrial parks, and airports. The main emphasis of these projects is the creation of jobs.

Two firms, including Boise Cascade Center for Community Development, were awarded similar contracts to develop evaluation methodologies. Boise Cascade submitted its report, *A Methodology for Evaluation of the Economic Development Administration's Public Works Program*, in May 1969. It was judged by EDA to be superior to the report submitted by the other firm. As a result, Boise Cascade received a follow-up contract to further refine and field test its methodology with twenty-four projects selected to represent a cross-sample of all public works projects approved under EDA. This effort was completed in November 1969, and documented in a report entitled *A Pilot Evaluation of Twenty-Four EDA Public Works Projects.*

In January 1970, EDA requested Boise Cascade to evaluate an additional 125 projects. This was accomplished by May 1970, and brought the total number of projects reported on by Boise Cascade to 149.[1]

In addition to the projects analyzed by Boise Cascade, a task force of EDA personnel evaluated 125 public works projects utilizing the same criteria for measurement. This undertaking was initiated in January 1970, and completed in May.[2] Because all projects, whether evaluated by Boise Cascade or the EDA task force, were judged according to common criteria, results of the two studies were merged into one set of findings regarding public works projects.

Evaluation Approach

Boise Cascade used an in-depth field interview technique. Essentially one man-week was devoted to the evaluation of each project. Field interviews were conducted with local community leaders, applicants, and relevant employers.

The EDA task force conducted a telephone/mail survey. Members of the in-house evaluation team telephoned over 1,200 EDA project applicants, community leaders, and employers to request their cooperation in surveying the impact of EDA public works projects. Questionnaires were then mailed to each of these individuals to obtain the information necessary for the survey. In many cases, telephone interviews were conducted to supplement the questionnaires. An average of approximately 2.3 man-days was required to evaluate each project.

Major Results

Job Location Impact. For the 274 projects evaluated, a total of 33,486 direct and indirect job equivalents at a $6,500 annual salary resulted. This represents an average of 122 job equivalents per EDA project. The total EDA investment in these 274 projects was $76,684,000, or an average investment of $280,000 per project. Based on this data, it was determined that on the average, the creation of one job equivalent cost the agency $2,290.

Total project costs for the 274 evaluated projects were $125,426,000. These costs included local, state, and federal government funds, of which EDA contributed approximately 61 percent. A breakdown of the number of projects and the associated EDA investment per job equivalent is presented in table 7-1.

The 103 projects without job impact were analyzed in terms of expected economic impact as opposed to actual job impact. Results indicated that only 17 projects reflected a definite failure to accomplish proposed job impact. In 19 other cases, jobs were identified as being connected with the EDA project, but there was difficulty in attributing definite causality to the agency. The remaining 67 projects without job impact were divided almost evenly among three other categories: (1) projects that were intended primarily to build infrastructure or support general economic growth; (2) projects that were only recently completed; and (3) projects that affected firms that were forced to curtail operations because of adverse economic conditions.

Structural Impact. An evaluation of the jobs saved or located as a result of the 274 EDA public works projects revealed that the jobs fulfilled the needs of the community for stable employment, were largely diversified, and provided opportunities for the unemployed and underemployed. Both the firms in which jobs were saved or created and the individuals filling those jobs were analyzed in this effort. Jobs were considered saved when an EDA project allowed a firm to remain in business. For example, numerous projects provided the water supply necessary for firms to stay in operation.

Table 7-1
EDA Investment per Job Equivalent for Public Works Projects

Number of Projects	Percentage of Total	EDA Cost Per Job Equivalent
43	15.6%	Less than $500
34	12.4%	$500 – $1,499
25	9.2%	$1,500 – $2,999
69	25.2%	Greater than $3,000
103	37.6%	No job impact
274	100.0%	Average: $2,290

In a majority of the EDA project areas, it was determined that the EDA-generated employment was in established firms that were economically stable, contributed to employment diversification for the area, and served to materially strengthen the area's economy. The actual jobs generated went principally to area residents who were heads of households. Almost half of the jobs went to workers who were not previously employed, and it was found that those workers who had previously been employed generally increased their average weekly incomes as a result of the EDA project.

Economic Development Process Impact. Analyses were conducted to determine changes in the local economic development process in EDA-assisted areas between the project application date and the evaluation period. Then the relationship between these changes and the EDA project being evaluated was determined.

Based on analyses of ten attitudinal and institutional factors, described in detail in chapter 6, it was found that the economic development process in EDA project locations was in varying stages of change. The majority of the changes were favorable to future economic improvement. In more than 80 percent of the cases, the EDA public works facilities were found to have been a contributing factor to positive economic development process changes.

Service Impact. In interpreting the results of the evaluations of service impact, it should be noted that the EDA legislation does not emphasize or encourage this kind of impact, except in those projects granted under the poverty clause. Thus, for most projects, any benefits that accrue in this area are generally by-products of primary goals.

The purpose of the service impact analysis was to identify the extent to which the project was providing new or extended public service facilities to the community at large, and to isolate particular benefits to specific subgroups of the community, particularly low-income groups.

For the 274 public works projects evaluated, the service impact varied significantly by project type. Taken as an entity, 158 water/sewer projects had moderate impact on service to local residents, particularly the poor. However, 83 industrial/commercial projects had very little service impact.

Analysis by Project Cost. When the evaluated projects were examined according to total cost per project, one significant finding was that those projects with a total cost of more than $1 million had a much higher average EDA investment per job equivalent than those projects costing less than $1 million. There were 25 projects with costs exceeding $1 million, and it was found that 19 of these had generated jobs. However, one of the 19 projects that generated jobs was dropped from the sample in conducting further analysis because the total cost of the project was $9,500,000, an amount covered completely by an EDA public works loan. Including this project in the sample would have distorted the analysis because of the magnitude of the cost and the small number of job equivalents generated.

Examination of the remaining 24 projects that had total costs of more than $1 million showed that these projects had an average EDA investment per job equivalent of $6,707, compared with the average of $2,290 for all 274 projects. If only water/sewer and industrial/commercial projects with costs exceeding $1 million are considered, the average EDA investment per job equivalent is $5,978. Table 7-2 provides the relevant statistics for the 24 projects.

Examination of the twenty-four projects individually showed that 10 were in cities with populations ranging from 44,000 to 636,000, one on an Indian reservation with a population of approximately 115,000, and another in a city of 15,000. The twelve projects in places of 15,000 to 636,000 had an average EDA investment per job equivalent of only $4,431, as compared with $14,699 for the twelve projects in cities with populations under 15,000.

This suggests that when considering large projects, there may be a relationship between the job impact per EDA dollar and the size of the community. However, the limited size of the sample (twenty-four) did not allow the development of a firm relationship.

Analysis of Economic Impact Claims. Applications for public works projects contain anticipated economic impact claims. These usually consist of a firm's indication that it will expand or locate in a designated area as a result of a public works project. While there is no legal contract between the firm and EDA to enforce such expansion or location, approval of a project application is partially determined by claims of potential jobs to be generated by these firms.

To estimate the value of these claims, 50 of the 274 public works projects were drawn at random and analyzed. Thirty-seven of these projects (74 percent) listed economic impact claims on the original EDA application. The total jobs

Table 7–2
EDA Investment per Job Equivalent for Projects with Costs Exceeding $1 Million

Project Type	Number	Total Cost (000)	EDA Cost (000)	Number of Job Equivalents	EDA Investment per Job Equivalent
Water/Sewer	11	$18,754	$11,314	1,894	$ 5,974
Industrial/ Commercial	6	$11,711	$ 8,204	1,371	$ 5,984
Others	7	$13,302	$ 4,325	290	$14,914
TOTAL	24	$43,767	$23,843	3,555	$ 6,707

claimed at the time of application amounted to 10,640. Of these, 4,688 (44 percent) were realized. This percentage might be expected because it usually takes over two years for a project to be completed after the date of application. During this period a firm's business outlook might change, thereby affecting its original job claim.

Of the thirty-seven projects with claims, three exceeded their claims, four met their claims almost exactly, and two additional projects came within 25 percent of their claims. Twenty-five projects had job impact, but failed to come within 25 percent of their claims. Three projects had no job impact at all. Of thirteen projects without claims, eleven realized no job impact and two had some impact.

Analysis of Private Investment Generated. Boise Cascade reported that many of the firms that generated jobs as a result of an EDA project also generated private capital investment as a result of that project. An attempt was made to identify the total capital investment of these firms (e.g., land, buildings, and machinery) at their EDA project-related locations. The contractor also tried to determine the increase in local capital investment as a result of the EDA project. This information was available for 93 of the 149 projects evaluated by Boise Cascade. The remaining 56 projects either did not lead to the location of new firms or the firms that were contacted would not supply the relevant data. It was found that for the EDA projects that led to the location of firms, each dollar invested by EDA generated $8.55 of private capital investment. Table 7-3 presents a breakdown of average private investment by project type.

Analysis of Impact on Target Population. On the basis of the data in table 7-4, it was concluded that the EDA Public Works Program had been successful in generating jobs for residents of designated areas when jobs resulted from public works projects. In addition, it was found that projects generating jobs had provided a substantial number of jobs for the formerly unemployed. The values in table 7-4 are based on a sample of seventy-nine public works projects,

Table 7–3
Effects of Public Works Projects on Private Investment

Project Type	Number	Average EDA Project Cost	Average Private Investment per Dollar of EDA Investment
Water/Sewer	61	$280,000	$9.48
Industrial/ Commercial	32	$380,000	$7.24
All Projects	93	$314,000	$8.55

Note: Data only available on 93 of the 149 projects.

Table 7-4
Distribution of Jobs Created by EDA Public Works Projects

Project Type	Number of Projects	Jobs Generated	Percentage to EDA Area Residents	Percentage to Heads of Household	Percentage to Unemployed
Water/Sewer	41	7,682	91%	60%	42%
Industrial/ Commercial	31	4,184	88%	67%	51%
Other Facilities	7	298	60%	87%	47%
TOTAL	79	12,164	90%	61%	45%

Note: Data only available for 79 projects.

representing a total of 12,164 jobs generated. Data were available for only these projects. The remaining projects either did not lead to the location of jobs or the employers would not supply the data. This is quite reasonable since there is no legal obligation for these firms to provide data on their employees. The sample includes projects evaluated by Boise Cascade and by the EDA task force.

Costs of the Public Works Program

A separate analysis of the costs of EDA's Public Works Program was initiated in December 1970.[3] The study was performed by a member of EDA's evaluation staff and Joseph Noah, an independent consultant. It covered the five fiscal years between August 26, 1965, and June 30, 1970.

The analysts found that on a per dollar obligated basis, EDA grants cost about 1.8 times more than loans. They also found that total opportunity costs for grants and loans ($901.3 million) represented about 95 percent of the total costs of the Public Works Program. The remaining costs were for administration. Other major findings of the analysis were as follows.

1. Future administrative costs related to the five-year period will total $10,616,000. This is 24 percent of the total administrative costs of $44,189,000.
2. Grants represented over 87 percent of the total public works obligations of $960.0 million. More than 55 percent of these obligations for the five years were undisbursed on June 30, 1970.
3. The public works costs of administering the regional offices were slightly more than one half of the total public works administrative costs, including future costs. This indicates a decentralization of personnel.
4. The Atlantic Regional Office was the most expensive to administer, both

absolutely and on a per-grant and a per-loan basis. Costs of the other area offices were significantly lower than that of the Atlantic office, but about equal to each other.

Business Loans Evaluation

Background

EDA makes long-term, low interest loans to stimulate private industry to provide the jobs needed in the nation's economically distressed areas. These loans enable EDA to attract private capital investments to areas experiencing adverse economic situations. Through December 31, 1969, EDA had approved 216 business loan projects, representing $183 million in agency obligations and $97 million in disbursements. On the average, the agency had contributed 45 percent of the total cost of business loan projects.

Past evaluation efforts had consisted of the development of an evaluation methodology and an analysis of forty loans. As part of the accelerated evaluation effort, Booz, Allen, & Hamilton Inc. revised the methodology, evaluated an additional forty-four loans, and performed in-depth analyses of ten loan projects, two of which were included in the group of forty-four.[4] In addition, a separate investigation was initiated to determine the characteristics of persons filling jobs vacated by employees currently working for EDA-assisted firms. Chilton Research Services conducted this analysis, and it is referred to as the "multiple job shifts" study.[5] The following is a summary of the results of this study and of Booz, Allen's evaluation of fifty-two business loans.

Evaluation Approach

Loan Evaluation. Booz, Allen designed questionnaires for data gathering. These forms were completed by employees and employers of forty-four EDA-assisted firms. The data obtained from these forms enabled a thorough analysis of the effects of loans on the employees of the recipient firm. Among the factors examined were previous employment status, previous residence, and increase in income as a result of the new position.

Ten in-depth studies of individual loans were also prepared by Booz, Allen. These analyses identified specific indirect benefits attributed to the loans. An effort was made to describe both tangible and intangible benefits to the community that resulted from EDA loan assistance. Although some demographic data were scrutinized, field interviews with community leaders were the primary data source for the case studies.

Multiple Job Shifts Analysis. Chilton used a three-tiered approach to examine the multiple job shifts resulting from business loans. The first step involved obtaining some of the information elicited by the Booz, Allen questionnaires, such as the past and present incomes, residences, and other demographic data on employees whose jobs were created or saved as a result of an EDA loan. The objective of the analysis was to ascertain if jobs vacated by individuals currently employed by EDA-assisted firms had been filled and, if so, by whom. For example, assume that Firm A received an EDA loan and one of its employees previously worked for Firm B. Contact was made with Firm B to determine if the vacated job had been filled. If the job had been filled, the replacement was asked to provide information on his salary, previous position, and other relevant factors. The analysis continued to Firm C.

Major Results and Conclusions

Jobs and Income Generated. The Booz, Allen study concluded that the EDA business development program had been effective in locating jobs and firms in EDA-designated areas. According to Booz, Allen's figures, the program had stimulated the location of an estimated 16,211 jobs directly and 7,852 jobs indirectly. The number of indirect jobs was estimated by applying a multiplier to the number of direct jobs. A discussion of this technique appears in appendix B. The annual payroll of the direct jobs was estimated at $96,261,000, with an average annual wage per job of $5,938. The annual payroll of the indirect jobs was estimated at $32,138,000, with an average annual wage per job of $4,093. In total, an estimated 24,063 jobs had been located by EDA business loans with an annual payroll of $128,399,000, and an average wage per job of $5,335.

Sixty-four percent of those who shifted jobs as a direct or indirect result of an EDA loan increased their earnings. The average immediate increase in annual income was $350, or a 6 percent increase over previous income.

Job Characteristics. In general, the characteristics of the direct jobs provided by the EDA-assisted firms were consistent with the characteristics of the local labor force and, where this did not occur, the firms tended to provide training. Of the direct jobs, 83.3 percent were for full-time employment and 84.2 percent of all direct jobs were in the "blue-collar" category. Booz, Allen found that 67.8 percent of all persons receiving the EDA jobs were heads of households, while 19.8 percent of those employed as a result of the EDA loans were previously unemployed or part-time workers.

Study results also showed that 84.3 percent of the persons receiving the jobs lived in the county in which the EDA-assisted project was located or in a contiguous EDA-designated county. In addition, 17.7 percent of the persons filling the located jobs were members of minority groups. The analysis did not include estimates of the future jobs that would be created if the recipient firms grew.

Cost of the Business Loan Program. Because loans are repaid, the EDA loan investment is different than EDA cost, which includes such items as administrative costs, estimated losses, and opportunity costs. The ratio of business loan dollars to EDA cost dollars was approximately 4 to 1. EDA costs were projected over the repayment period for loans; that is, future expenditures for servicing loans in the current portfolio were estimated. Payments to the Small Business Administration for loan servicing were also included in the cost analysis and constituted 15.6 percent of program costs. Based on these estimates, the present value of total program costs was found to be $79,065,000. This figure was calculated through the use of a discount rate of 5 percent with present value placed at June 30, 1970. The use of a discount rate suggests that loan dollars would be alternatively invested; in this case, a 5 percent return on investment was assumed.

Cost-Benefit Analysis. The estimated EDA cost per direct job located was $1,911. However, when considering the total of direct and indirect jobs located, the estimated EDA cost per job located was $1,288. In terms of EDA loan funds (or EDA investment), one direct job was located for every $7,534, while the EDA investment for both direct and indirect jobs was $5,075.

Categorization of EDA Investments. Analysis of the ten case studies indicated that EDA business loans can be classified into three economic impact categories:

1. Growth investments, which increase the level of a local economy
2. Recovery investments, which cause a local economy to return to a level achieved in the recent past
3. Stabilization investments, which help a local economy in danger of declining stabilize

The ten case studies showed that the direct economic impact of a business loan differed depending on whether the loan was made to a capital-intensive or a labor-intensive firm. In general, capital-intensive firms generated greater tax revenues for the local area, but required greater EDA loan investment per direct job.

Public improvement impact also varied according to the type of investment. Growth investments were more likely to offer potential for new public improvements, because they increased the level of the local economy and part of the increase was in the public sector. Recovery and stabilization investments offered less potential for immediate improvements in the public sector because these investments generally returned the local economy to a previous high level or prevented it from declining. Therefore, significant increases in municipal revenues did not occur.

However, Booz, Allen found that recovery and stabilization investments could be considered critical in terms of the negative impact to the local municipal budget that would occur if the investments were not made. Increases in local taxes from these investments had the potential of being directed toward improving public services because the public works requirements to support the firms generally were present prior to location. Impact on public improvements also depended on such other factors as the size of the firm (in relation to the local economy) and local decisions.

Additional Impacts of EDA Loans. Ten in-depth business loan case studies were conducted to provide additional information for the evaluation. The significant findings of these case studies were:

1. In five of the ten case studies, it was determined that other firms had been attracted to the EDA-designated area as a result of firms that received EDA assistance. This created further employment opportunities. These additional firms located either because they supplied or used a product of the EDA-assisted firm, or because they were encouraged by the success of the EDA-assisted firm.
2. Few instances of growth in retail and service activity were observed. This was attributed to the fact that excess capacity in these trades generally existed in the area prior to the location or expansion of the EDA-assisted firm.

Multiple Job Shifts Analysis. Chilton Research Services contacted a sample of 1,742 of the employees of thirty-one firms that received EDA business loans. The jobs of these employees were directly attributable to the agency's assistance. The thirty-one firms were chosen at random from the forty-four firms surveyed by Booz, Allen. Since Booz, Allen reported on forty-four loans and Chilton reported on thirty-one, there is a slight variance in results.

As a first step, Chilton determined the previous status of the 1,742 employees (tier 1). The results of this effort are presented in table 7-5.

After determining the previous status of the employees of the EDA-assisted firms, Chilton sought to identify the condition of the jobs vacated by those employees (tier 2). It was found that 45 percent of the jobs were not refilled and disappeared from the market. Of the remaining jobs, 60 percent were filled by workers who had been previously employed, and 40 percent were taken by persons who were formerly farm workers, part-time employees, unemployed, or not members of the labor force.

Chilton traced the vacated jobs through one more level. At this level (tier 3) it

Table 7-5
Previous Status of Employees

Previous Status	Percentage
Employed Full-Time	59%
Employed Part-Time	11%
Farm Workers	7%
Unemployed	10%
Not Members of the Labor Force	13%

was determined that approximately 50 percent of the jobs disappeared, 30 percent were filled by persons previously employed, and 20 percent were taken by individuals in the remaining categories.

These data implied that if 100 jobs were directly located through an EDA business loan: (1) 41 would be filled by persons who were previously unemployed, farm workers, part-time employees, or not members of the labor force; and (2) As a result of multiple job shifts at tiers 2 and 3, another 20 jobs would be taken by workers in the same categories.

Technical Assistance Evaluation

Background

In late 1969, EDA funded two studies to develop methodologies for evaluation of technical assistance projects. The procedure developed by CONSAD Research Corporation was adopted. In a study commencing in January 1970,[6] this procedure, with modifications, was used to evaluate:

1. All projects in Philadelphia, Pennsylvania, and Cleveland, Ohio.
2. All projects in rural Georgia and California.
3. Five university centers, including ten projects in each.
4. Thirty-four randomly selected projects distributed throughout the country.

This sample was structured to include a representative range of projects from the standpoint of geographic location and project type.

Evaluation Approach

The analysis began with a thorough study of the background material in EDA files. Next, data were collected in the field and tabulated by trained survey teams. The evaluation methodology was then applied to the data, and conclusions were drawn as to the effectiveness of projects.

Field work was performed by a group of interviewers employed by TransCentury Corporation under subcontract to CONSAD. The field group was organized into three teams, each consisting of two interviewers. Under the close supervision of CONSAD and EDA personnel, the field group talked with the applicants, contractors employed on the project (if any), and EDA project officers. In each community containing a project, they interviewed representatives of the local development corporation, elected officials, bankers, poor or minority group members, and a representative of the local news media.

The report focused on specific results obtained as a result of the EDA assistance and the impact of the project on the economic development process in the community. In addition, the impact of the project on jobs, employment structure, and community services was identified.

Results and Conclusions

The CONSAD analyses emphasized the broad-based nature of EDA's Technical Assistance Program and the variety of impacts registered by technical assistance projects. CONSAD reported that EDA technical assistance had been responsible for:

1. Creating jobs at relatively low investment levels.
2. Involving the community in activities related to economic development.
3. Aiding in understanding the public sector's role in ghetto development and in developing ghetto training programs.
4. Building institutions as sources of technical and management competence.

The evaluators also found that technical assistance projects aimed at developing tourism and natural resources were less successful on the whole than other types of projects.

Some of the reasons for these characterizations of the effects of technical assistance projects are presented in the following paragraphs.

Although technical assistance is more frequently linked to institution building and product exploitation than to job creation, the evaluators concluded that EDA's Technical Assistance Program had achieved significant success in creating jobs. For all projects analyzed, it was found that EDA activity had resulted in a new or retained job for each $238 of project cost, excluding summer and potential jobs. Projects in large urban areas were judged most likely to yield early impact in terms of identifiable, directly attributable jobs.

Technical assistance was also found to involve the community and affect attitudes of area residents. Approximately 200 community leaders were interviewed. Of this number, 80 percent were aware of the EDA aid and were optimistic about future results. Sixty percent felt that the assistance had already been helpful to their community. A significant number of these leaders had also become more active in planning and participating in activities designed to effect economic development. The analysts reported that several innovative procedures to stimulate and channel the economic development process had been developed and implemented through EDA's Technical Assistance Program.

The evaluators found that the success of technical assistance projects in urban areas had provided EDA, and thus the entire federal government, with valuable insight into the role of the public sector in ghetto development. The development orientation of the technical assistance urban projects was particularly consistent with the interest groups advocating ghetto development and with those who recognize that ghetto development and dispersal are not competing, but complementary strategies.

The evaluators also found that EDA's Technical Assistance Program had been especially effective in aiding the development of unconventional but successful programs for ghetto young people and adults. EDA had been particularly successful in helping or fostering comprehensive job-training matching efforts. At the time of the evaluation, these efforts were relatively new on the urban scene and optimal procedures had not been clearly identified. The most popular types of training were entrepreneurial and managerial programs. Social learning, or self-image training, had played an important role in these programs, as well as basic skills programs, including secretarial, clerical, and service industry training.

The leverage associated with the university center projects was also encouraging. The analysts reported that such centers provided the most comprehensive regional development effort of any type of project. In spite of this great potential, their limitations were severe. One strength of the university centers was supposed to be their access to the technical skills and talent of the university; yet in many projects, sophisticated managerial and technical advice either had not been given or had not been followed by the client. In cases where advice was not followed, there was some evidence that it was not practical from the client's standpoint. The centers had been able to provide adequate, highly-trained staff and consultants to solve all of the complex business problems encountered. In addition, the valuable knowledge of the centers' field staff personnel had not been used in regional planning because no planning staff or funds were available to them.

Nevertheless, CONSAD concluded that the centers offer long-term attention to a wide variety of problems such as industrial management, resource development, and industrial park development. Two reasons such centers were judged valuable were: (1) their consultants were readily available for advice at critical times; and (2) these consultants' background knowledge of their region was unmatched by other types of development groups or consultants.

CONSAD found that results from projects to develop tourism facilities and scenic areas were mixed. A well-organized cooperative effort on the part of state, federal, and local governments is often necessary in implementing such projects. This is difficult to achieve, especially when large amounts of capital must be provided by state or local sources, and when several sites within a state are competing for development funds.

Although EDA-financed mineral surveys in rural areas might be expected to have large impacts in terms of mining activity, the evaluators found no evidence to support this notion. Mining firms had shown interest in some EDA survey reports, but early investment had not occurred. Successful resource development occurred where a processing plant existed, and expansion was feasible, or where the resource was an agricultural or forest product already being exploited. However, even in the case of such traditional products, difficulty was encountered if technological improvements in harvesting and processing were not available. Nevertheless, this type of project was extremely successful in the cases where impacts did occur (about 20 percent).

Planning Grants Evaluation

Background

Among the four primary EDA program tools, planning grants have the smallest budget, accounting for a fiscal year 1970 obligation of only $4.5 million. However, it is the District Program, funded by planning grants, which most clearly distinguishes EDA from its predecessor, the Area Redevelopment Administration (ARA). ARA originally viewed the county as the most useful level through which to plan and fund economic development programs. Experience soon indicated, however, that the county represented too small a geographic entity for effective planning.

In recognition of this fact, Congress legislatively authorized EDA to create economic development districts. These consist of at least two agency-designated redevelopment areas and a town designated as an economic development center. Together, these counties contain the resources necessary to permit useful planning and implementation of projects designed to effect economic development.

The bulk of planning grant funding is expended in such multicounty economic development districts, where it is under the control of local groups for use in staffing economic planning and development organizations. As of December 31, 1969, 84 development districts had been designated with another 50 authorized. These units included 1,089 counties, of which 598 were qualified as redevelopment areas under EDA's designation criteria.

Evaluation Approach

The methodology for evaluating the Planning Grant Program was based on field examination of twenty districts, four Indian reservations, and two redevelopment areas. Approximately one week was devoted to each case, and supplemental information was obtained from interviews in Washington with responsible agency personnel. Additionally, the complete project file of each recipient was read in preparation for the field interview investigation.

Representatives of the contractor, Battelle Memorial Institute, met with the executive director, representatives from the board of directors, the new media, and the target groups in each case. Finally, information from all sources was collated, and a cross-district analysis was prepared, supported by the individual field reports.[7]

Major Results and Conclusions

The following were among the conclusions reached by Battelle as a result of evaluating the Planning Grants Program.

1. The impact of a planning grant on an area's economic development process has generally been very high.
2. The program has provided staff expertise which, for the most part, was nonexistent before the grant.
3. The "key to success" of the program has been the degree of involvement of the local power structure.
4. Planning grants have acted as catalysts to increase communication between the jurisdictions served.
5. Concern with effective economic planning in Overall Economic Development Plans (OEDPs) is sometimes negligible. In many instances, they do not set meaningful priorities.

Four roles are stressed by planning grants recipients. These include the provision of technical assistance to local governments, ranging from advice regarding village, town, and city zoning ordinances to the furnishing of computer programming capabilities. Industrial prospecting, both direct and indirect, is also provided. This can consist of supplying information to Chambers of Commerce, as well as initiating contacts with likely prospects. Considerable staff time is devoted to economic planning functions in many funded areas, while the fourth major role involves seeking out and applying for loans and grants relative to community needs from both state and federal agencies.

Battelle's analysis revealed that the key to success (defined in terms relevant to activities of the staff hired with planning grant funds) was organizational involvement of the local power structure, both political and economic, in area economic development activities. Indeed, the most significant activity of the entire Planning Grant Program was the increased participation and cooperation of such local leaders. This finding, brought out by direct analysis of the planning grants, was amplified through the case studies. This effort found that almost all local organizations had been successful in achieving this involvement.

The Planning Grant Program had also acted as a catalyst to increase communication between local town and county jurisdictions. Given the frequent history of animosity between such competing jurisdictions, which is detrimental to all involved, this achievement is by no means negligible.

Such communication frequently had resulted in concrete payoffs to areas. For example, in the Pennsylvania Turnpike Economic Development District, several towns needed solid waste treatment plants. None could afford one by itself. The district provided a common meeting point, and the staff demonstrated the feasibility of a joint plant to service the entire group. Economies of scale permitted each to afford what was needed. In the Coastal Area District of Georgia, the district staff instituted a joint highway accident reporting system for all police jurisdictions. The evaluators found that every community along U.S. Route 17 (the highway to Florida) had used this system as a data base to approach the State Highway Department with proposals to straighten the roadway.

Common lobbying, brought about by recognition of joint interest through the district, had maximized the impact of numerous small jurisdictions. In Aroostook County, Maine, the two principal towns of Presque Isle and Caribou have a long history of rivalry, stemming from competition for industry. However, planning staff members convinced both towns that any economic activity coming into the county would benefit both, and that they should mutually support any prospective locator.

It was found that the poor and minorities were frequently not effectively represented on the governing boards of redevelopment areas and economic development districts. Battelle suggested that a close relationship between the power structure and the target groups could not be established without communication between the leadership of both groups. Since, at the very least, optimistic attitudes about potential for the improvement of economic conditions are considered an important part of the development process, it was recommended that target group representation be strongly encouraged.

Battelle's evaluation of twenty-six planning grants resulted in several suggestions for making Overall Economic Development Plans (OEDPs) more successful by permitting greater freedom to local staffs and organizations in structuring the documents. All districts do not have the same problems. Thus, the contractor concluded that OEDPs would be more effective planning and strategy documents if areas structured them to their own needs. Battelle suggested that only enough economic and demographic data be provided to demonstrate that areas recognize their needs. Some change had already been implemented through the two-stage OEDP requirement. However, the sample contained too few cases of such OEDPs to draw valid conclusions regarding them.

Difficulties relating to attribution were noted with regard to other EDA program tools such as business loans and public works, despite their proximity to actual jobs. Planning grants are far removed from jobs, and attribution in a quantitative sense is impossible. However, Battelle's qualitative evaluation supported the belief that a high, but indirect, payback in job development results from the Planning Grant Program.

Urban Development Activities Evaluation

Background

EDA has funded a wide variety of projects in urban areas under different circumstances and with varying results. To assess EDA's total impact in five cities, the agency contracted with Roy Littlejohn Associates, Inc., in association with Booz, Allen, & Hamilton Inc., to prepare studies of the EDA investments. The cities were selected on the basis of the following criteria: (1) they were large urban areas; (2) substantial EDA investments had been made in them; and (3) more than one program tool had been used in each city.

The five cities analyzed were New York (Brooklyn Navy Yard), Chicago (stockyards area), Los Angeles (Watts), Pittsburgh and Providence-Pawtucket. At the time of evaluation, EDA had committed itself to an investment of $52.9 million in these cities. However, as of April 1, 1970, only $26.2 million had been disbursed: $1.0 million in New York; $6.3 million in Chicago; $1.6 million in Los Angeles; $4.6 million in Pittsburgh; and $12.7 million in Providence-Pawtucket. In addition to studying EDA efforts in these areas, existing evaluations of EDA activity in a sixth city, Oakland, California, were updated. EDA's approved projects in Oakland amounted to $32.1 million, with $10.4 million disbursed as of April 1, 1970.

Evaluation Approach

The methodology for assessing EDA's urban development activities consisted of two parts. First, a wide range of people were interviewed in each city. Interviewees included the EDA field staff, project applicants, project beneficiaries, city officials, representatives of local development groups, representatives of the business and financial community, labor representatives, and other community leaders and residents. Approximately ten to fifteen man-days in each city were required for the interviewing. Secondly, the information was analyzed and the urban studies were written. A cross-city analysis was then prepared that made general comparisons, conclusions, and recommendations about EDA activities in the cities.

Major Results and Conclusions

Since EDA's development programs in the cities were relatively new at the time of evaluation, it was difficult to estimate the number of jobs that would be generated as the result of the agency's activities. However, at that time, more than 3,600 new jobs had been directly created in the five cities (New York, Chicago, Los Angeles, Pittsburgh, and Providence-Pawtucket). An additional 1,650 jobs had been directly saved as a result of EDA involvement, and approximately 6,200 indirect jobs had been created. The number of indirect jobs was calculated by applying a multiplier to the number of direct jobs as described in chapter 6.

Based on a direct and indirect job count of 11,450 jobs and on EDA disbursements of $26.2 million, the average EDA investment per job in the five cities was approximately $2,300. This implied that in terms of costs and benefits, the agency had been as effective in the cities as in rural areas.

Local Development Corporations. Local development corporations had experienced mixed success, but, on the whole, were judged to be a useful type of EDA investment. For example, the Commerce Labor Industry Corporation of Kings County in New York City, which had assumed responsibility for the operation and administration of the Brooklyn Navy Yard, had attracted fourteen firms to the yard with an associated employment of 1,300 persons. However, the evaluators noted that future progress might depend on the establishment of a viable training program to move the unskilled residents into the available jobs.

One of the most important contributions attributed to these corporations was their assistance in removing impediments to economic development, such as the lack of well-trained businessmen and the inaccessibility of private capital. Perhaps the most successful of the local development groups analyzed in the study was the Business and Job Development Corporation (BJD) in Pittsburgh. BJD's diverse activities included planning an industrial park, owning a plant with 50 employees, running small training programs for businessmen, and packaging loans for minority businessmen.

One recommendation stemming from the urban studies was that more effort be expended on the search for effective ways of assuring that EDA investments benefit the target population. The need for training was particularly emphasized. For example, the Seatrain Shipbuilding Corporation planned to employ 3,000 workers, many of them skilled, at the Brooklyn Navy Yard. The evaluators concluded that unless a more adequate training program was established, the unskilled residents of the communities surrounding the yard would not benefit significantly from Seatrain's EDA-assisted activities.

Another conclusion was that EDA must improve project coordination within individual cities. In the past, EDA had funded organizations that bonded minority contractors, while in the same city, another EDA project funded construction activity. Although coordination would obviously have been beneficial, no attempt was made to link the two activities. Moreover, EDA had funded Opportunities Industrialization Centers (OICs), which provide prevocational training, in a city where other EDA activity was generating employment opportunities, and these activities proceeded with no relation to each other.

The following were additional conclusions of the studies of EDA activities in urban areas.

1. EDA has only been involved in urban economic development for a short time, and there is no likelihood that a universal approach to such development will be devised in the near future. Therefore, the agency should continue to maintain sufficient program flexibility to respond to varying local situations.
2. The agency should continue with its increased efforts to give target group members equal opportunity to perform construction work associated with EDA projects.

Also as a result of these preliminary studies, a decision was made to conduct more detailed analyses of EDA activities in specific urban centers. Appendix A contains a summary of the results of the pilot test of the methodology structured for performing these analyses.

Rural Development Activities Evaluation

Background

Studies of EDA's rural development activities were conducted in twenty-three development districts, redevelopment areas, and Indian reservations. The studies were initiated to determine EDA's impact on an area rather than on a project basis, and to provide a foundation for initiating a detailed evaluation of the agency's impact on development districts and redevelopment areas. This set of detailed evaluations was considered particularly appropriate because at the time of evaluation approximately 80 percent of all EDA obligations had gone to aid rural areas. In conducting the studies, particular attention was directed to four issues: (1) the interaction between projects; (2) the projects' impact on target groups; (3) the successful types of projects; and (4) the reasons for project success.

Two groups were employed to assess EDA's impact in these selected rural areas. Planning Research Corporation examined four development districts and four redevelopment areas. A fifteen-man EDA task force, representing a number of divisions within the agency, studied four development districts, seven redevelopment areas, and four Indian reservations. Both "good" and "bad" areas were included in the sample. These determinations were made by those EDA field staff and Washington personnel who were most familiar with the program.

Evaluation Approach

Both groups conducted a considerable number of field interviews averaging four man-weeks of field work for each district and two for each redevelopment area. EDA's development impact was assessed in two categories: project impacts and program impacts. Project impacts were such measurable direct and indirect consequences of projects as increased employment and investment, and improvements in local facilities and public services. Program impacts were usually less tangible, involving positive changes in the local development process, or in the prospects for inaugurating this process. The evaluators measured changes in: (1) local planning efforts; (2) community attitudes and participation in economic development activites; and (3) attempts to benefit target groups.

For the most part, subjective criteria were used to measure these impacts. Quantitative data on projects funded by each of the agency's program tools were presented earlier in this chapter.

Major Results and Conclusions

The number of jobs realized as a result of EDA projects was generally modest in most of the economic development districts evaluated. However, this was partially attributed to the fact that most districts were relatively new. The evaluators also placed the finding in a different perspective by estimating that job impact would increase considerably over the next two years. In redevelopment areas, on the other hand, the realized job impact per EDA dollar invested was much higher. For example, the agency was credited with saving or creating 608 direct jobs in the redevelopment area of Fayette County, Pennsylvania. It was found that, in both redevelopment areas and districts, the presence of a strong economic development process increased the actual and potential number of jobs generated by EDA assistance.

Although large amounts of capital investment resulted from some public works projects, the average capital investment induced at the time of evaluation in districts and redevelopment areas as a result of EDA projects was modest.

The additional public services generated by EDA projects in districts and redevelopment areas were generally substantial. Many projects provided public water and sewer services to residents previously without them. Target groups, especially minority members, acquired most of the increased services.

Because of the strong emphasis on obtaining grants and organizing the development effort, planning efforts in districts were generally minimal. The study teams suggested that planning is a necessity because it: (1) provides a necessary basis for sound project selection; (2) builds a foundation for effective initial district staff leadership where the local leadership is not yet organized; and (3) provides evidence to the local community and the power structure that the staff knows what it is doing.

For this reason, it was recommended that the EDA should take steps to help district staffs understand the kind of planning they should be doing and its potential contribution to the development process.

In several of the districts, it was found that the staff resources available were totally inadequate to carry out their vital function of stimulating a sustained development process. EDA had not sufficiently funded district staffs, although this program tool is the critical factor in EDA's attempt to maximize the returns from project assistance. For example, the Kiamichi District, Oklahoma, which is one of the poorest areas in the nation and a very large, heterogeneous territory of over 8,000 square miles, had a very low morale with regard to its future and lacked any regional cohesiveness. Kiamichi's staff was funded for less than three professional positions.

The evaluation indicated that district organizations that included the local power structure were more successful in fostering the economic development process. It appeared that when the power structure became more involved with the district staff, the local residents took the development effort more seriously and provided the reinforcing local actions necessary to stimulate the development process.

No special emphasis on helping target groups was noted by the evaluators. However, target groups generally benefited from EDA assistance. There was a tendency for development impact on the target group to rise as the relationship between the leaders of the development organization and the target group improved.

In conclusion, the evaluators stressed the fact that the EDA programs were very new in terms of conception and implementation. While there were successes and failures among the cases studied, those performing the analyses were more impressed with the successes than the failures. In most cases, the failures and unresolved problems appeared correctable, and the wide incidence of successes suggested that EDA programs had a great potential to yield impressive benefits to society. The evaluators reached the conclusion that EDA programs were effective means of stimulating economic development in rural areas, thus providing reasonable alternatives to unemployed and underemployed residents who might otherwise migrate to urban ghettos.

8 Growth Centers: The Wave of the Future

Numerous theoreticians suggest that rural America cannot be revitalized through direct investment in economically distressed small towns.[1] These theorists recommend allocating public investment according to the principle of "development poles,"[2] and thereby accelerating the maturation of already growing places, referred to as growth centers. Their contention is that the modest amounts of public investment available through programs such as EDA's are not sufficient to revive declining small towns. According to these theorists, a better approach to assisting residents of such depressed areas is to accelerate the development of nearby growth centers to which they can migrate or commute to work. This chapter discusses an evaluation of EDA's implementation of this development approach.

The EDA Growth Center Strategy—Rationale and Experience

EDA's Concept of the Strategy

As viewed by EDA, growth centers can be thought of as functioning according to the simplified illustration presented in figure 8-1. They are considered to be part of a wider subregional or economic development district strategy with the center serving as a focal point of development for a multicounty (district) area.[a] The center is expected to provide infrastructure, jobs, and services not otherwise available to residents of the surrounding distressed hinterland. In addition, it is expected to serve as a center for migration in the area.

The evaluation results presented in this chapter show that EDA growth centers are not functioning in this prescribed manner,[3] but they do not disprove the a priori argument that a growth center strategy is a viable approach to regional development. It seems clear, however, that although regions as a whole could profit substantially from the growth center approach to development, the benefits are concentrated in the centers and result in considerably less impact on the distressed hinterland than theorists predicted.

---

[a]Typically a district is comprised of eight counties, at least two of which are designated as severely distressed (redevelopment) areas.

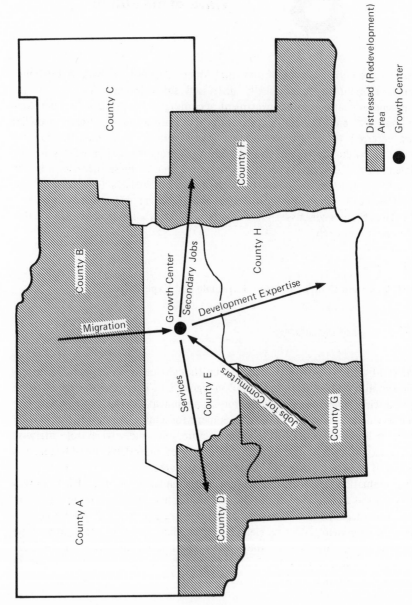

Figure 8-1. The Economic Development District Concept

History of the Growth Center Strategy

Under the Economic Development Administration's predecessor, the Area Redevelopment Administration, only areas with substantial and persistent unemployment or low median family income were eligible for program benefits. Moreover, with the exception of a few experimental cases, the Area Redevelopment Administration (ARA) program was administered on a single-county basis. The agency's enabling legislation contained no provisions to encourage counties to cooperate in an effort to solve common problems.

The single-county approach employed by ARA drew criticism from economists and planners in other agencies. These individuals also questioned the efficiency of assisting residents of distressed areas by spending money in those areas. As an alternative to such an approach, they recommended funding projects in more prosperous places whose growth would benefit residents of depressed areas. Proponents of this "growth center" strategy argued that industry would be more interested in such sites and that it would be less expensive to create jobs in communities with developed infrastructures.

After a 1963 trip to Carbondale, Illinois, on a tour of areas aided by ARA, the agency's Advisory Committee joined the supporters of the growth center strategy. Carbondale had just been taken off the agency's list of designated areas at the time of the committee's visit, and its leaders presented an impressive case to the committee as an argument against its de-designation. Their claim was that ARA should continue to fund projects in Carbondale because it was a growth center serving nine counties, a number of which were designated redevelopment areas.

The apparent validity of this position and the community leaders' persuasiveness in presenting it made a lasting impression on the Advisory Committee. As a result of their experience in Carbondale, members of this group began to advocate revising the ARA legislation to include the growth center concept.

The concept did not stimulate the same degree of enthusiasm within the agency. A number of ARA officials accepted the strategy in principle, but viewed it as politically undesirable and impractical. These individuals argued that employing the strategy would result in competitive fighting among cities and resentment on the part of residents of rural areas whose project applications were rejected in favor of growth center projects.

Despite such skepticism about the feasibility of implementing the growth center concept through a program such as ARA's, agency policy makers could not ignore the growing interest in such a strategy nor its potential value to future development efforts. As a result, studies were funded through ARA's research program to define districts and centers in several states. A study was also funded to identify European experience with the growth center concept and to determine how that concept could best be applied through a program such as ARA's. In addition, in-house studies were conducted to structure a program that combined the growth center strategy with a regional approach to area redevelopment. The results of these efforts proved useful to congressmen, state governors, and EDA officials involved in structuring and implementing the agency's District Program.

By fiscal year 1965, when efforts to draft new legislation for assisting economically distressed areas were initiated, both Congress and the administration favored including some form of the growth center strategy. On March 25, 1965, President Johnson submitted a message to Congress on area and regional economic development. In this message, he stated that the program proposed by the administration to replace ARA was primarily based on the experience of the accelerated public works program, ARA, and the Appalachian Regional Development Commission.

A major portion of the president's message was devoted to explaining the organizational format of the new program. In addition to working through redevelopment areas, the proposed program was to be organized on the basis of economic development districts, regional action planning commissions, and economic development centers.

The president identified economic development centers as "places where resources can be most swiftly and effectively used to create more jobs and higher income for the people of the surrounding area."[4] In discussing these places, he indicated that they need not be distressed themselves to receive designation as a center. The rationale he gave for designating such places was that development succeeds more frequently when activities are located in a single community large enough to offer the advantages that flow from size itself. He also said that clusters of industry tend to attract other industry, and that such clusters offer the prospect of improving the economic conditions of the entire area.

During the congressional hearings that followed submission of the administration's proposal, another rationale was given for implementing the growth center strategy. One of the goals of the new program was to stem migration from the nation's depressed areas. Proponents of the growth center strategy asserted that funding projects in designated centers would help to achieve this goal. Their position was based on the assumption that accelerating and increasing the growth and prosperity of such centers would encourage residents of nearby depressed areas to seek work in the growth center instead of migrating to other areas.

The growth center strategy proposed by the administration for inclusion in the area and regional economic development legislation was accepted by Congress, and became law with the August 1965 signing of the Public Works and Economic Development Act. This act linked the growth center concept to another new approach to economic development, the Economic Development District Program. Reflecting the belief that certain areas could not mount effective attacks on unemployment and low income on their own, this program encourages counties to pool talents and resources to achieve common aims. This is accomplished through the formation of multicounty economic development districts.

The Public Works and Economic Development Act of 1965 stipulates that each economic development district is to contain two or more redevelopment areas and to be of sufficient size or population and have sufficient resources to foster economic development on a multicounty basis. In addition, the legislation states that each district must have one or more growth centers of sufficient size and potential to foster the economic growth activities necessary to alleviate the distress of the redevelopment areas within the district. These places can be located in redevelopment areas or in nondesignated counties.

In empowering the Secretary of Commerce to designate such places as economic development centers, the legislation lists three specific criteria for center selection.

1. The center must be identified and included in an approved district overall economic development program (OEDP) and recommended for such designation by the state or states affected.
2. Each center is to be geographically and economically so related to the district that its economic growth may reasonably be expected to contribute significantly to the alleviation of distress in the redevelopment areas of the district.
3. No center can have a population in excess of 250,000.

Once designated, centers are eligible for EDA assistance if proposed projects meet three basic criteria. The project must further the objectives of the district OEDP, and either enhance the economic growth potential of the district or result in long-term employment opportunities commensurate with the amount of federal financial assistance requested. In addition, the level of federal assistance requested must be reasonably related to the size, population, and economic needs of the district.

The EDA legislation authorizes an annual appropriation of up to $50 million for funding such projects. This amount also covers a 10-percent bonus on grants to redevelopment areas participating in district programs.

Implementation of EDA's Growth Center Strategy

Policy Decisions. The EDA legislation stipulated that these financial provisions be withheld for a period of one year after the agency began operations, during which time planning for implementation of the District Program could be accomplished. However, the need to obligate a year's appropriation in less than nine months obscured other considerations during most of the 1966 fiscal year, and no action was taken on the District Program until February 1966. At that time, Assistant Secretary Foley invited state governors to submit recommendations on economic development district boundaries. In addition, he appointed a task force to develop and recommend an approach for implementing the District Program. This task force spent several months discussing such subjects as regional commission administration of the program and gubernatorial authority, but reached no concrete decisions.

As previously described, the 1967 fiscal year with its funds for growth centers was less than a month away when Foley delegated authority for organizing the program to William J. Nagel. The new program director and his staff were charged with establishing organization guidelines and giving preliminary recognition to districts and economic development centers.

Responses to the Assistant Secretary's request for district boundary proposals had provided more potential districts than could conceivably be funded during the 1967 fiscal year. In determining which districts to assist, EDA officials considered the percentage of district population living in redevelopment areas; per capita income in the district; percentage of families with annual incomes under $3,000; trading area and transportation patterns; and existence of a well-located economic development center.

By September of 1966, sixty-seven districts had been authorized for establishment, and a number of these newly formed entities had been designated as recipients of EDA-funded planning grants. The staffs funded by these grants worked with local residents to prepare OEDPs for submission to District Program officials in Washington. Included in these OEDPs were proposals for the designation of growth centers.

The first growth center was designated in December of 1966 with the acceptance of an OEDP for the Coastal Bend Economic Development District in south Texas. By the end of fiscal year 1967, twenty-two such centers had been designated, and a number had succeeded in obtaining approval for EDA projects.

On January 6, 1967, only a few days after designation of the first growth center, the agency issued an Economic Development Order on the "Qualification and Delineation of Economic Development Centers." This policy statement was primarily a reiteration of the legislative stipulations regarding growth centers. The first of its four major points was that cities or contiguous groupings of incorporated places could be designated as centers if the Secretary of Commerce determined that they met two criteria: (1) that they were the most likely places within economic development districts to have potential for growth that might reasonably be expected to contribute to the alleviation of economic distress in district redevelopment areas; and (2) that their designation was necessary to carry out the economic development program of the district effectively.

Other points covered by the order included the legislative restriction against designating places with populations exceeding 250,000, and a statement that selection and designation of a district's growth center would be based primarily on facts and arguments presented in the district OEDP. In addition, EDA's policy governing the boundaries of economic development centers was discussed. While stating that the recognized boundaries of cities or groupings of incorporated places would ordinarily serve as the boundaries for the growth center, the order announced that such boundaries could be expanded to include an adjoining minor civil division. This would be accomplished in the event that a public works or business development project consistent with the district OEDP and eligible for EDA financing was proposed and approved for location in the adjoining division.

No further policy statements regarding EDA's growth center strategy were issued for more than a year. Then, on March 11, 1968, the agency published a revised version of the earlier Economic Development Order. This statement on the "Economic Development Center Strategy," which specified for the first time centers' obligations to nearby redevelopment areas, is still in effect.

Although a number of issues are discussed in the revised order, it is basically concerned with insuring that EDA expenditures in growth centers benefit redevelopment areas and their residents. These benefits can be in the form of employment, public services, increased economic activity, or reduction in the rate of migration to large urban centers.

In discussing the agency policy on project development the document states that primary emphasis will be placed on those projects within centers that will: (1) directly improve the employment opportunities of unemployed or underemployed residents of redevelopment areas; and/or (2) make public services and facilities more readily available to residents of such areas. In addition, it indicates that priority will be given to projects that materially improve the environmental facilities essential to accelerating the center's growth.

The March 1968 order added administrative criteria to the legal requirements for designating growth centers. Among these is the stipulation that the center be establishing or implementing a comprehensive planning program at the time of designation. This program must include a development strategy involving the assimilation of unemployed and low-income residents of redevelopment areas into the growing economy of the center. In addition, each center should have a sizeable local market, a relatively large well-trained labor force, the prospect of developing a diversified economy, and (normally) a population base of at least 25,000. The order also states that with the exception of location, redevelopment centers should meet the same criteria as economic development centers. (Redevelopment centers are located in district redevelopment areas, while economic development centers are located in nondesignated counties.)

Through the order, a number of guidelines were established for use in approving projects in growth centers. These include giving priority to projects from centers located in districts ranked high in terms of economic distress, and considering no projects from a center until it has outlined a Positive Action Program detailing the steps it will take to insure that unemployed and underemployed residents of redevelopment areas benefit from its growth. The order indicates that the Positive Action Programs will be reviewed at the preapplication conferences that precede the submission of each growth center project.

Among the other topics covered by this policy statement is responsibility for its implementation. District organizations, EDA field offices, and the agency's Washington staff are all assigned roles. For example, district organizations are given responsibility for assessing the plans and programs of growth centers, while primary responsibility for selecting and developing growth center projects is delegated to area (regional) office personnel.

Since issuance of the revised Economic Development Order (MEDO) in March 1968, the agency's policy with regard to projects in growth centers has not changed. Although a guide was published in September of 1968 for communities to follow in preparing Positive Action Programs, no Economic Development Order has been issued on the subject.

Data on Designated Centers and Project Funding. As of March 31, 1971, EDA had designated 139 economic development centers and 67 redevelopment centers in 105 districts from Maine to California. The economic development centers had received obligations of approximately $104 million through EDA's Public Works, Business Development, and Technical Assistance Programs. In addition, the 105 districts had received approximately $17 million in EDA planning grant funds.

Table 8-1 presents a breakdown of EDA growth center expenditures and district planning grants by region.

Evaluation of EDA's Growth Center Strategy—Concept and Approach

Rationale

When EDA initiated a major evaluation effort in January 1970, only three years had elapsed since designation of the first growth center. As a result, few growth center projects had the one-year completion status required by the analysts for inclusion in the evaluation. Because the number of projects that met the completion requirement was so small, the evaluators were primarily limited to making subjective judgments about the success of the strategy.

During the course of the evaluation effort, the White House's Office of Management and Budget (OMB) submitted a set of policy-oriented questions to EDA, requesting that they be addressed as part of the evaluation. One of these asked whether EDA should concentrate assistance in development districts, especially in economic development centers, or in depressed areas. Although the evaluators attempted to address this issue, the limited amount of data on growth

Table 8-1

EDA Assistance to Economic Development Centers: March 31, 1971

Region	EDA Obligations in Economic Development Centers			District Planning Grants[a]
	Public Works	Business Development	Technical Assistance	
Atlantic (Conn., Del., Me., Md., Mass., N.H., N.J., N.Y., Pa., P.R., R.I., Vt.)	$ 6,768,000	$ 4,775,000	$ 301,920	$ 1,563,000
Mideastern (Ky., N.C., Ohio, Va., W.Va.)	$ 7,487,000	$ 2,452,000	$ 38,435	1,737,000
Southeastern (Ala., Fla., Ga., Miss., S.C., Tenn.)	$27,469,000	$10,902,000	$ 335,721	4,584,000
Midwestern (Ill., Ind., Iowa, Mich., Minn., Mo., Neb., N.D., S.D., Wis.)	$ 7,329,000	—	$ 267,854	2,603,000
Southwestern (Ariz., Ark., Colo., Kan., La., N.M., Nev., Okla., Tex., Utah, Wyo.)	$29,181,000	$ 5,701,000	$ 427,891	5,686,000
Western (Alas., Cal., Haw., Idaho, Mont., Ore., Wash.)	$ 1,057,000			780,000
TOTAL	$79,201,000	$23,830,000	$1,371,821	$16,953,000

[a]As of February 28, 1971

Source: Economic Development Administration Budget Division, April 1971

center projects gave them no factual basis for a response. Their answer, which indicated that the agency should and would continue to combine the two approaches, was primarily based on the same theoretical concepts applied in structuring the EDA legislation four years earlier.

These experiences and the impending expiration of the EDA legislation impressed agency policy makers and OMB officials with the need to learn more about the effectiveness of the growth center strategy as implemented by EDA. As a result, an in-house task force was appointed in December 1970 to analyze the agency's implementation of the growth center strategy outlined in the Public Works and Economic Development Act of 1965. This chapter presents the results of that evaluation of EDA's growth center strategy.

Evaluation Goals

Two major goals were identified in connection with this analysis: (1) to evaluate the impact of EDA expenditures in growth centers; and (2) to estimate the potential of counties to serve redevelopment areas as growth centers. The methodology developed to achieve these goals consisted of in-depth case studies of EDA growth centers and an economic assessment of counties in and near economic development districts. The results of the analysis conducted to achieve the second goal are discussed in chapter 9, "A Growth Center Identification System."

Center Selection

Two major criteria were applied to select the economic development centers to be evaluated in the case study portion of the analysis. First, each center was required to have a completed EDA public works or business loan project that had been approved subsequent to the town's designation as an economic development center. Moreover, only those projects approved subsequent to a town's designation as an economic development center were considered valid subjects for the evaluation. Earlier projects were not approved in conjunction with the growth center strategy and could not in fairness be used to measure the strategy's effectiveness or success. This criterion narrowed the list of potential evaluation subjects from 135 centers to 14.

Secondly, within the limits of the project completion criterion, the centers were chosen to represent a wide geographic distribution and a variety of population levels. The dollar amount of EDA expenditures and the length of time elapsed since project completion were also considered in making selections. This narrowed the list to ten. After ten EDC's were selected, two more centers were added to the sample. These centers were included because, together with one of the original ten EDCs they are located in a district involved in a unique effort to obtain government assistance in undertaking a comprehensive district-wide development program.

Evaluation Criteria

In developing the methodology for analyzing selected growth centers, the evaluation team reviewed the legislative provisions for growth centers, agency policy statements relating to the growth center strategy, and techniques employed in past evaluation studies. In an attempt to keep the evaluation focused on one specific agency policy, the team sought to analyze those areas which that policy had clearly been intended to influence.

On the basis of information gained through the review, a decision was made to examine three major areas in evaluating each growth center. Centers were analyzed in terms of EDA project impact, effectiveness of the Positive Action Program, and the role played by the district staff and board in implementing the growth center strategy. In addition, the evaluators measured the status of the local development process in each center, placing particular emphasis on the center's efforts to assist neighboring redevelopment areas. EDA's impact on changes in process status was determined.

EDA Project Impact. One premise of EDA's growth center strategy is that funding projects in growth centers will benefit residents of nearby redevelopment areas. To determine the validity of this assumption, the methodology called for an evaluation of completed projects in each growth center. Emphasis was placed on identifying benefits to redevelopment areas and to unemployed and underemployed residents of the center. However, overall project benefits were also noted in order to evaluate the project's impact on the growth center and to permit comparison of growth center projects with similar projects analyzed in previous evaluation efforts.

For each completed EDA growth center project, data were collected on the total number of jobs which could be attributed to the project, as well as on the amount of income generated. A discussion of the specifics of this analysis was presented in chapter 6.

For the purposes of this study, it was considered necessary to emphasize the benefits accruing to present and former residents of redevelopment areas. For this reason, job location impact was broken down to identify the effects on these individuals. In determining the effectiveness of each project, the number and type of jobs taken by present and former redevelopment area residents were examined, as well as the income generated by these jobs. Present and former RA residents were identified through employee questionnaires which requested information on current and past residence. Another approach used to measure project effectiveness involved calculating the agency investment per direct job created for present and former redevelopment area residents.

Because EDA is committed to assisting the unemployed and underemployed residents of redevelopment areas, the methodology was structured to identify which present and former redevelopment area residents were unemployed or underemployed prior to taking their current jobs. (Underemployed workers are persons who were previously part-time employees seeking full-time jobs and workers who were members of poor households. Former housewives working to supplement family incomes previously more than $1,000 above the poverty level are not counted as previously unemployed or underemployed persons.) Table 6-4 in chapter 6 presents an updated version of the standard used to determine whether households were "poor."[b]

---

[b]The OEO poverty guidelines used for the growth center evaluation were set in December 1970 and were slightly lower than the income figures given in table 6-4. The differences ranged from $100 lower for a household of one to $300 lower for a household of seven.

Other information acquired for present and former RA residents included average income change as a result of EDA-associated jobs, number of families raised above the poverty level, and amount, type, and effect of training received. The methodology employed also allowed evaluators to estimate the number of jobs that would go to these individuals upon realization of employers' present expansion plans. Such estimates were based on information provided by each employer.

Administrators of EDA's Development District Program emphasize a growth center's responsibility to provide assistance to unemployed and underemployed residents of the community. To measure centers' effectiveness in meeting this responsibility, the evaluation methodology called for analysis of jobs to such individuals. Employees of EDA-associated firms who were previously unemployed, involuntary part-time workers, or members of poor households looking for work were identified according to race and status in family. The total number of jobs to such individuals was also reported, as well as total income generated.

As with jobs to present and former redevelopment area residents, the methodology called for computing the average income change and the number of families raised above the poverty level as a result of jobs taken by unemployed and underemployed residents of the growth center. The amount, type, and effect of training received by these individuals in connection with their EDA-associated jobs were also determined. In addition, future jobs for unemployed and underemployed center residents were projected on the basis of employers' plans for expansion.

One of the premises of the growth center strategy is that the creation of jobs in centers will lead directly to the location of other employment opportunities. The theory is that employers who locate in growth centers often attract suppliers and distributors to the area and that these concerns furnish additional employment to local residents. According to EDA's Economic Development Order 1-28 (Revised), "The spillover effect of the Center growth can produce new jobs within nearby Redevelopment Areas. This might include such activities as subassembly plants serving major producers located in the Center." To test this theory, the evaluation methodology included provisions for identifying such employers and determining the number of new jobs they located in the area.

EDA-assisted employers were asked to identify suppliers, and distributors; personal contact was made with these firms. Any employment or income generated by new firms as a result of the EDA beneficiary firm was noted as a secondary impact of the project. The methodology also allowed the identification of new jobs created by the EDA-attributable expansion of suppliers and distributors already located in the area. These jobs were included in the job count for each center.

Another major premise of the growth center strategy is that indirect benefits from projects in growth centers will spill over into the district's redevelopment areas. The evaluation methodology called for testing this theory through two measures. First, data were collected on the expenditures of redevelopment area residents employed by EDA-assisted firms and local suppliers and distributors who established or expanded operations as a result of EDA project impact. This information allowed the evaluators to determine how much money these individuals were spending in their home counties.

The second measure used to test the indirect economic spillover theory involved the dollar value of purchases made in redevelopment areas by EDA-assisted firms and their local suppliers and distributors. Through personal interviews with management personnel, evaluators determined the amount of money spent by these firms in redevelopment areas.

The growth center strategy implemented by EDA assumes that accelerating and increasing the growth and prosperity of economic development centers will encourage residents of nearby depressed areas to commute or migrate to the center for work instead of remaining unemployed or migrating to more distant urban centers. To test the validity of this assumption, the evaluation methodology—through data collected with employee questionnaires—provided for determining:

1. The percent of employees in EDA-assisted and associated firms who migrated to the growth center from a redevelopment area.
2. The percent of employees who would have migrated from a redevelopment area to an urban center of over 500,000 if their present jobs had not been available.
3. The percent of employees who would have migrated from the economic development district if their present jobs had not been available.

In addition, a random survey was made of former residents of the redevelopment areas associated with the various growth centers. Individuals who had migrated from such areas during the past two years were queried as to their reasons for moving. This survey provided another basis for evaluating the theory that providing jobs in a growth center will help to stem out-migration from the redeveloped areas and/or the district. For each center, if a statistically significant number of the participants indicated that they would have remained in the district had employment opportunities been available in the center, it was concluded that the theory was valid for that particular center.

The growth center strategy defined by EDA policy makers includes a provision for funding projects that materially improve the environmental facilities of a center if those facilities are essential to accelerating the center's growth. Among the items considered by EDA before approving such projects is the ability of the district organization and the center leadership to assure that the facilities will be available to low-income or unemployed residents in surrounding redevelopment areas.

To evaluate public facility projects in growth centers, the investigators first considered the overall benefits provided by the project. This portion of the evaluation included a judgment as to whether the facilities were essential to the center's growth. In each case, this judgment was based upon information gathered from public agencies, elected officials, and community leaders concerning the type of service provided and the neighborhoods and establishments served by each EDA project. Emphasis was then placed on determining the types of individuals benefiting from the project. Three categories of beneficiaries were analyzed: redevelopment area residents, low-income growth center residents, and minority group members.

In evaluating benefits to redevelopment area residents, factors considered were the number of households being served, the percent of service to minority households, the percent of the project's benefits going to low-income households, the percent and number of low-income households being served, the change in service resulting from the project, and the change in service to low-income residents. Similar factors were considered in analyzing benefits to low-income growth center residents and minority group members. These data were provided by the agency responsible for managing each public facility project, and were verified whenever possible through other public and private sources.

Data were collected on other funding stimulated by the EDA investment including federal, state, and local monies. Private investment directly associated with or stimulated by the EDA project was also measured as an element of project impact.

Effectiveness of Local Implementation (Positive Action Program). The second major area examined in connection with the in-depth evaluation of selected centers involved determining the effectiveness of program implementation at the local level. Guidelines for this implementation were contained in the EDA policy statement issued in March 1968. This statement stipulates that no growth center will receive project funding until it has outlined the steps it is willing to take to insure that the unemployed and underemployed from redevelopment areas benefit from the center's growth. This outline is referred to as a Positive Action Program (PAP), and is to be prepared in cooperation with the district organization.

The first step taken in evaluating Positive Action Programs entailed determining the PAP's status. Date of preparation and number of updates were considered in judging the present relevance of the document. In addition, emphasis was placed on analyzing the actual preparation of the PAP. Authorship was determined, and factors involved in author selection were identified. Problems encountered in preparing the document were also examined.

The methodology used to evaluate Positive Action Programs required an initial review of such documents. This review focused on the identification of specific programs the town promised to undertake in connection with its responsibility to serve the surrounding area as a growth center.

The evaluation team queried elected officials as well as individuals responsible for PAP programs in each center. The objective was to determine these individuals' understanding of the PAP and growth center concept, and to identify tangible commitments toward accomplishing goals set forth in the document. These sources were used to measure the degree to which each center recognized its responsibilities to nearby redevelopment areas.

The next step in the PAP evaluation methodology consisted of determining the center's progress in implementing the programs described in the Positive Action Program. Evaluators scrutinized each program through interviews with program administrators and their peers in other community groups to determine accomplishments, beneficiaries, and future plans. Emphasis was placed on identifying benefits to redevelopment area residents and the growth center's unemployed and underemployed population.

Another aspect of the PAP evaluation concerned the new effort exerted by the growth center as a result of its Positive Action Program. The evaluators identified those activities directly attributable to the PAP: programs that would not have been undertaken in the absence of the Positive Action Program.

This portion of the analysis included a categorization of such programs. Of greatest importance in terms of the growth center strategy were those programs that provided the most benefits to redevelopment area residents, particularly the unemployed and underemployed. Programs that assisted unemployed and underemployed growth center residents were ranked next in value. Third, and least important from the standpoint of the growth center strategy, were those programs that primarily benefited middle- and high-income growth center residents.

To obtain a more accurate picture of the PAP's value, evaluators, when possible, compared projects funded before PAPs were required with projected funded after centers had prepared such documents. Emphasis was placed on determining what differences, if any, existed with relation to project impact on present and former redevelopment area residents.

Interviews with a wide range of community leaders also provided insights on how the PAP, its preparation, and execution had influenced attitudes, cooperation, and awareness in the community. The evaluation, in effect, attempted to grasp the human and intangible results associated with this requirement.

Role of District Staff and Board. An analysis of the role played by district staff and board members was the third major portion of the in-depth evaluations of selected centers. This effort did not involve an evaluation of the entire range of services provided by these groups. Rather, it focused on those activities directly related to implementation of the growth center strategy for the particular center under consideration.

The methodology developed for evaluating the district organization's role in implementing the growth center strategy called for analyzing the attitudes of the district staff members and board of directors. District staff and board members were evaluated in terms of their concepts of and attitudes toward the strategy. Particular attention was given to the views held by board members from redevelopment areas.

Other criteria used for evaluating the district organization's role in implementing the growth center strategy included the location of the district office and its effect on the strategy. The composition of the board and the relative influence of each of its members were also considered. In addition, the evaluation methodology provided for an analysis of the financial support provided by the district's member counties, and the effect of this support on the growth center strategy.

A number of criteria were applied in evaluating the services of the district staff and board with relation to the growth center strategy. These included the amount and quality of technical assistance provided by the district staff in promoting the growth center strategy. Examples of such assistance are help in preparing Positive Action Programs, and aid to growth center leaders in setting priorities for proposed projects. Other criteria were the amount and quality of assistance provided to board members from nondesignated counties. The degree to which information flowed between board members from the two types of counties also served as a criterion for evaluation.

In cases where the district staff served more than one board, the evaluators judged the staff's performance as an agent for exchanging information. Additionally, and perhaps most importantly, the staff and board were evaluated on their role in developing and implementing projects designed to carry out the growth center strategy.

Status of Economic Development Process. Techniques for measuring the impact of EDA expenditures on a community's economic development process are discussed in chapter 6. That discussion identifies a series of factors considered in the process analysis and presents a rationale for their selection. In addition to the elements described in chapter 6, the factor "concern for redevelopment area residents" was studied as part of the growth center process analysis. This factor was designed to describe the kinds of programs and services made available to redevelopment area residents in the economic development center. Where most of the development programs and services in the center were clearly made available to such persons, the center received a high rating for this factor.

In evaluating the development process in the various growth centers, each of the factors was analyzed in several different ways. The level of these factors was measured at two points in time: before growth center designation; and at the time of the evaluation. This allowed for determining changes in the economic development process. Attributing changes in the process to the growth center strategy was then accomplished by asking community representatives about the relationship between those changes and the PAP, district staff activities, EDA field staff activities, and EDA projects.

Data Collection

The evaluation team collected data through field interviews, telephone conversations, and questionnaires. From three to eight man-weeks were spent in each center evaluated, where team members interviewed at least forty and, in some cases, as many as seventy or more individuals. The large number of interviews held in connection with each center provided reasonable assurance of obtaining an accurate picture of each center and its effect on the district's redevelopment areas.

Typical data sources included district staff and board members, elected officials of the growth center, and elected officials of district redevelopment areas. These individuals provided insights into the relationships between the growth center and nearby redevelopment areas. Other data sources were the initial project applicants, and employers and employees in firms that located as a result of EDA projects. The project applicants, who were often community leaders and elected officials, provided detailed descriptions of projects and their impact on the growth center and district redevelopment areas.

Questionnaires were used to obtain information from the employers and employees. These questionnaires elicited data on the job impact of the EDA project, its contribution to the local economy, and the characteristics of employees. Community leaders in the growth center and in nearby district counties were interviewed to determine the development process in each of the growth centers. In some cases, EDA Economic Development Representatives and Regional Office personnel were interviewed to obtain insights into the commitment of the growth center to assisting the target population, and the effects of the EDA projects.

In addition, the evaluators conducted telephone interviews with individuals who had migrated from centers and nearby district redevelopment areas during the past two years. The recent migrants provided insights into the factors causing out-migration, and the effect creating additional jobs in centers might have on the exodus.

Evaluation Findings

EDA's activities in economic development centers (EDCs) were evaluated through in-depth case studies of twelve communities in which EDA projects had been approved and 90 percent disbursed since preparation of the community's

Positive Action Program (PAP). The centers, which are shown in figure 8-2 and identified in table 8-2 by population, project approvals, and project completions (90 percent disbursed), were selected to insure as much diversity as possible in terms of geographic location, population, and project type.

The field work for this portion of the evaluation was conducted between February and April of 1971. More than 500 on-site interviews were held during this period, and forty-five EDA projects were analyzed. Thirty-two of these were completed or had reached the stage where project impact could be determined.

Impact of EDA Projects in Growth Centers

Overall Job and Economic Structure Impact. The 28 completed EDA public works and business loan projects in the growth centers evaluated had resulted in the creation of 2,825 direct jobs, at an average annual salary of $5,900. Thus, the projects had generated $16.6 million in yearly salary. In addition, they had led to approximately $43 million in private investment. EDA's investment per job for these projects was $7,167. Eliminating the EDA investment and jobs for the two "environmental" projects reduces the number of jobs created to 2,822, and lowers the agency's investment per job to $6,908.

The four completed technical assistance projects had not had an appreciable impact on employment. However, one was partially responsible for the location of eight jobs in an industrial park being studied.

Most of the jobs created through EDA's growth center projects were found to be in stable firms with year-round operations. There was no evidence that these firms had diversified local economies, but this is partially explained by the fact that most of the centers examined differ from redevelopment areas because they already possess diversified economic bases. Thus, EDA projects in such places are less likely to have this type of impact.

Approximately 30 percent of the 2,825 employees at EDA-associated firms in the growth centers were unemployed or underemployed prior to obtaining their present positions. One-fifth of these individuals were members of minority groups. The EDA projects in growth centers had raised 674 households above the poverty level and resulted in increased incomes for 84 households still below the poverty level. Thus, of the households affected by EDA growth center projects, 24 percent were raised above the poverty level as a result of the projects, while 3 percent remained below the poverty level. Seventy-eight percent of the jobs created by EDA were held by heads of households.

The average annual increase in salary for previously unemployed persons as a result of EDA-created positions was $5,200. Previously employed workers increased their yearly wages by $1.7 million, for an average of $1,400 per person.

In addition to obtaining jobs as a result of agency projects, approximately

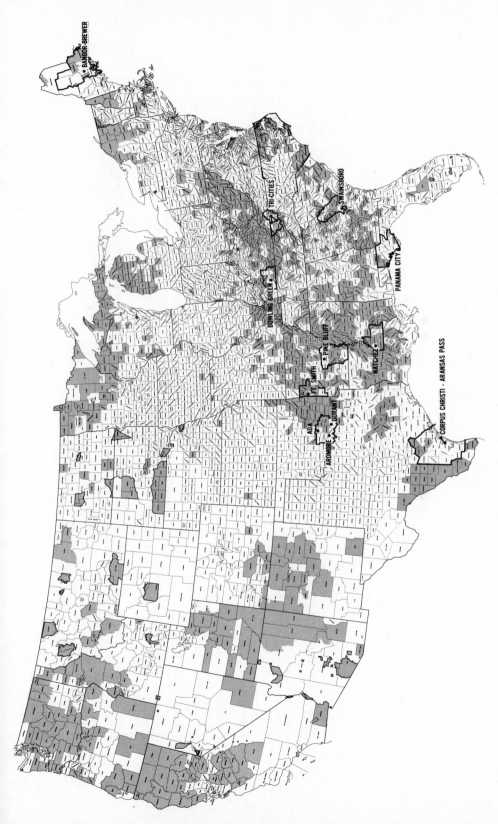

Figure 8-2. Economic Development Centers Evaluated

Table 8-2
Centers Examined Through In-Depth Analysis

Economic Development Centers	Population	Approved Projects (000)	Completed Projects (000)
Ada, Ardmore, Durant, Oklahoma	46,858	$ 3,485 10P's, 1B, 1T	$ 1,214 3P's, 1B
Bangor-Brewer, Maine	42,468	$ 4,172 2P's, 2B's, 2T's	$ 1,859 2B's, 1T
Bowling Green, Kentucky	36,253	$ 1,504 3P's	$ 1,504 3P's
Corpus Christi-Aransas Pass, Texas	210,338	$ 3,188 5P's, 2B's, 1T	$ 1,187 2P's, 2B's, 1T
Ft. Smith, Arkansas	62,802	$ 3,099 6P's	$ 1,050 3P's
Natchez, Mississippi	19,704	$ 597 1B, 2T's	$ 555 1B, 1T
Panama City, Florida	32,096	$ 2,075 1P	$ 2,075 1P
Pine Bluff, Arkansas	57,389	$ 1,481 2P's	$ 1,481 2P's
Swainsboro, Georgia	7,325	$ 1,908 3P's, 1B	$ 1,832 2P's, 1B
Tri-Cities (Bristol, Kingsport, Johnson City), Tennessee-Virginia	100,659	$ 9,767 4P's, 2B's	$ 7,585 3P's, 2B's
TOTAL		$31,276 36P's, 9B's, 6T's	$20,342 10P's, 3B's, 3T's

P = Public Works Grant or Loan
B = Business Loan
T = Technical Assistance

Source: *Program Evaluation: The Economic Development Administration Growth Center Strategy*, Washington, D.C.: U.S. Department of Commerce/Economic Development Administration, February 1972, p. 15

1,900 individuals had received on-the-job training in connection with their new positions. Moreover, 69 percent of those persons had advanced as a result of the training, either by receiving more responsibility or increases in salary. Approximately 800 employees had received other types of training, and 69 percent of these individuals had received promotions or pay increases as a result of such training.

Table 8-3 summarizes the overall findings of the in-depth evaluations.

Job Impact on Present and Former Redevelopment Area Residents. Fourteen percent (392) of the jobs created through the public works and business loan projects in growth centers had been filled by present and former residents of EDA-designated redevelopment areas (RAs). However, this figure is misleading because if the 600 jobs created by three interrelated projects in Bowling Green, Kentucky, are eliminated from the data base, less than 6 percent of the remaining jobs were held by RA residents.

For all projects, EDA's investment per job to a present or former RA resident was $50,000. Excluding the unique case in Bowling Green raises this figure to $116,000.

Of the present and former RA residents employed as a result of EDA projects, just over 26 percent were previously unemployed or underemployed. Approximately 13 percent of these previously unemployed or underemployed

Table 8-3
EDA Employment Impact[a]

Analysis Category	EDA Impact
Jobs Generated	2,822
• Jobs to Present and Former RA Residents	392
• Jobs to Previously Unemployed and Underemployed	875
• Jobs to Members of Minority Groups	271
• Jobs to Heads of Households	2,211
• Number of Families Raised Above Poverty Level	674
EDA Investment per Job	$ 6,908
EDA Investment per RA Job	$50,000
Average Salary	$ 5,900
Training	
• On-the-Job	1,931
• Other	782

[a]Excluding two "environmental" projects

Source: Program Evaluation: The Economic Development Administration Growth Center Strategy, Washington, D.C.: U.S. Department of Commerce/Economic Development Administration, February 1972, p. 17

individuals were members of minority groups. Ninety-six families who live in RAs or formerly resided there were raised above the poverty level as a result of EDA projects in growth centers, while 8 remained below poverty level, despite the income from the job created by EDA.

The average annual salary for present and former RA residents with EDA-associated jobs was $6,400. The average annual salary increase for previously unemployed RA residents was $5,600, while previously employed RA residents averaged an annual salary increase of $1,200.

Approximately 92 percent of the present and former RA residents were heads of households. Two hundred sixty-six, or 68 percent, had received on-the-job training as a result of the job created by EDA, and 77 percent of those who received this training improved their positions as a result. In addition, 237 of the present and former RA residents also received other types of training, and 172, or 72 percent, were promoted or received salary increases in connection with this.

Job Impact on Unemployed and Underemployed Residents of the Growth Center and Nondesignated Counties. Of the 2,825 persons employed as a result of EDA projects in growth centers, 2,430 lived in growth centers or nondesignated counties prior to taking their present positions. Of this number, 771, or 32 percent, were previously unemployed or underemployed residents of growth centers or nondesignated counties.

Approximately 20 percent of these previously unemployed and underemployed persons were members of minority groups, and 71 percent were heads of households. By creating jobs for these persons, EDA raised 418 households above the poverty level, and increased the family income of 33 households that are still below the poverty level.

The average annual increase in salary for previously unemployed persons was $5,200; previously underemployed workers averaged a $2,600 increase in yearly income as a result of EDA projects. Of the previously unemployed or underemployed workers, 58 percent, or 450, had received on-the-job training in connection with their new jobs. In addition, 143 persons had received other types of training. Of those who were trained, 283 received promotions or salary increased attributable to the training.

Secondary Job Impact in Redevelopment Areas. At the time of evaluation, no suppliers or distributors had located in or near growth centers as a result of the twenty-eight EDA public works and business loan projects evaluated. In a number of cases, local suppliers had increased business as a result of the location or expansion of an EDA-associated firm, but, as far as could be determined, the increases had little or no impact on the suppliers' employment. In no case could a supplier state that he had added employees as a direct result of improved business associated with the location or expansion of a firm benefiting from an

EDA project. However, evaluators were able to ascertain that sixteen secondary jobs were saved in Bangor-Brewer, Maine, as result of EDA's loan to Eastern Fine Paper Company.

Indirect Economic Spillover to Redevelopment Areas. At the time of evaluation, there was no evidence that EDA projects in the twelve growth centers had resulted in significant indirect benefits to redevelopment areas. Jobs created through growth center projects represented approximately $16.6 million in annual wages. The 338 present RA residents employed by EDA-associated firms spent an average of $331 per month in their home counties, for a total annual expenditure of $1.4 million. Thus, only 8 percent of the salaries generated by EDA growth center investment were spent in redevelopment areas.

The twenty-eight firms directly assisted by EDA or benefiting from EDA projects in growth centers purchased just over $5 million annually in supplies and services from RAs. However, 90 percent of this amount represented the expenditures of two firms. Moreover, both firms had purchased a similar amount of supplies in RAs before receiving EDA assistance. Thus, approximately $22 million of EDA investment had generated only $1.9 million in new economic spillover benefits to redevelopment areas.

Effect on Out-Migration. As far as could be determined, those EDA projects analyzed in this evaluation had a negligible impact on out-migration from redevelopment areas and economic development districts. Less than 1 percent of the 850 employees contacted at EDA-associated firms in growth centers said they would have migrated from the area if their present jobs had not been available. The percentage of workers who indicated they would have moved to one of the nation's major urban areas in the absence of the EDA-created job was even smaller.

The employee survey showed that only 2 percent of the workers at EDA-associated firms in growth centers had moved from a redevelopment area to the growth center upon taking their present jobs. Moreover, only 11 percent of the employees presently resided in RAs, and this figure drops to 4 percent when the Bowling Green statistics are eliminated.

These findings suggested a need for careful reexamination of EDA's assumption that accelerating and increasing the growth and prosperity of EDCs will encourage residents of nearby depressed areas to commute or migrate to the center for work. However, a straw poll of recent migrants from RA counties near six of the twelve growth centers indicated that the assumption might have some validity. (The six centers were Ada, Okla., Bangor-Brewer, Me.; Bowling Green, Ky.; Corpus Christi, Tex.; Natchez, Miss.; and Swainsboro, Ga.)

Of the sixty-six persons contacted through the poll of recent migrants, thirty-three moved for reasons over which EDA has no control. For example, thirteen of the persons were doctors, teachers, lawyers, or employed as a result of EDA projects. Another nine moved for personal reasons that had nothing to do with employment opportunities.

Of the thirty-three persons who could have been influenced by the creation of jobs in the growth center, nineteen, or 58 percent, indicated they would have remained in the area if "decent-paying" jobs had been available in the growth center. Nine of these stated they would have remained in the RA and commuted to the growth center for work. The other ten said they would have moved their place of residence to the growth center. However, a number of persons expressed doubt that attractive employment opportunities could be created in the growth centers. This was particularly true with respect to Swainsboro.

Improved Public Services. Several of the water systems funded by EDA in the economic development centers provided service to growth center residents. One of these projects had improved service to RA residents, although it was unique in that the facility was physically located in a redevelopment area bordering the growth center county. However, none of the water system projects was submitted or approved primarily for the purpose of providing service. Each was linked to industrial development: the direct creation or saving of jobs.

As indicated previously, the growth center strategy defined by EDA policy makers includes a provision for funding projects that materially improve the environmental facilities of a center if those facilities are essential to accelerating the center's growth. Only two of the twenty-eight completed projects fell into this category: a scientific library built in Ft. Smith, Arkansas, and a marine-oriented research facility in Corpus Christi, Texas. However, the justification given in the project applications for these facilities placed emphasis on the projects' employment generating capabilities as well as their effect on the cities' environmental facilities. A third project was also approved for the purpose of improving a center's environmental facilities; however, this vocational-technical school in Ft. Smith was not completed at the time of the evaluation.

None of these projects was judged by the task force as essential to accelerating the growth of the town in which it was located. The library had no more volumes than the structure it replaced; the research facility employed only nine persons (three attributable to EDA) and had completed few studies; and the vocational-technical school, while a valuable addition to the local infrastructure, represented too small an investment to appreciably accelerate the growth of the entire city.

Moreover, neither of the completed "environmental" projects—the library and research center—benefited RA residents. In fact, the Fort Smith library charged a service fee to residents of other counties. The research facility in Corpus Christi, which was severely damaged in Hurricane Celia, had produced no studies linked to increased job opportunities for RA residents through exploitation of the area's marine and mineral resources. Finally, sources indicated that when the Fort Smith voc-tech facility was completed, the old school's practice of charging RA residents double tuition might well be continued.

The individuals benefiting from the environmental and water facility projects appeared for the most part to be middle-income residents of growth centers. Only the water system in Durant, Oklahoma, and Ft. Smith, Arkansas, which serviced numerous low-income housing units, were having substantial impact on EDA's target population.

Effectiveness of Local Implementation (Positive Action Program)

Every center visited had prepared a Positive Action Program (PAP), and in eight of the twelve centers, the PAP had been updated or was in the process of being revised. Center leaders had assumed full responsibility for preparation of the PAP in only two of the twelve centers. In the remaining EDCs, the PAP was written either through a joint effort on the part of the district staff and local leadership or entirely by the district staff or district director. PAP Committees had functioned at one time in four of the twelve centers, but were active at the time of the evaluation in only three.

In almost every case, the PAP consisted of a description of ongoing federal, state, or local programs aimed at improving conditions in the growth center itself. The community's responsibility to surrounding depressed areas was seldom articulated in the PAPs studied, and in the few cases where some mention was made of the center's relationship to such areas, its service role was not emphasized. The absence of programs designed to benefit RA residents indicated a misunderstanding of the PAP's purpose.

Center leaders and district staff members in several of the EDCs indicated that they view the PAP as a paper requirement of the federal bureaucracy in Washington. In a few centers, the PAP was praised as a useful planning tool, a catalyst that brought together various segments of the community, and a means of acquainting local leaders with growth center programs aimed at assisting the unemployed and underemployed and members of minority groups. However, in no case did center leaders view the PAP as a means of insuring that unemployed and underemployed residents of redevelopment areas benefit from their community's growth. In most centers, only the limited number of persons involved in preparing the PAP remembered the document, and most of them responded with vague answers when questioned about its content.

Several centers listed specific goals, such as establishing a vocational-technical school, in their Positive Action Programs. Goals of this type usually received widespread support within the growth center communities. Goals that concerned improving conditions for the poor and minority group members appeared to be less readily accepted. However, the reaction to them varied considerably among the centers.

Although some of the goals listed in Positive Action Programs received local support, none was recognized as a PAP goal by residents of the growth centers.

If not viewed as local government aims or vague, community-wide goals, they were identified with specific interest groups, such as Chambers of Commerce, Lion's Clubs, and religious organizations.

Some of the PAP goals aimed at improving facilities or initiating projects in growth centers had been achieved. In a few instances, programs to assist poor persons and members of minority groups residing in growth centers had also been implemented. However, none of the programs designed to assist redevelopment area residents had been undertaken.

No evidence was found that benefits had accrued to redevelopment area residents as a direct result of the PAPs associated with these 12 growth centers. The few programs initiated as a result of PAPs primarily served middle- and high-income residents of growth centers.

The few projects in these twelve centers funded before establishment of the PAP requirement (March 1968) had essentially the same impact on present and former redevelopment area residents as those funded since that time. The PAPs had not increased EDA project benefits to these individuals. Moreover, as indicated above, no projects or programs in the centers evaluated had been initiated to benefit RA residents as a result of PAPs.

Effectiveness of District Organization in Implementing the
Growth Center Strategy

Although there were notable exceptions, the majority of the district board and staff members interviewed had only a vague conception of EDA's growth center strategy. The most prevalent view was that EDA funds projects in growth centers because centers are more prosperous than other places in districts. The possibility of growth center projects providing direct benefits to residents of RA's and the responsibility of growth centers to provide services and assistance to RA's were recognized in only a few instances.

District staff members appeared to have a better understanding of the strategy than did members of district boards. However, in only one of the ten districts visited had the staff made any attempt to insure that RA residents benefited significantly from growth center projects. The staffs appeared to believe that projects in growth centers will eventually benefit RAs without any special effort on the part of the growth center or the district staff. Several board members from redevelopment areas felt the district staff had neglected their counties and placed undue emphasis on growth centers.

In at least three cases, the task force felt that the location of the district office had affected implementation of the growth center strategy. In each of these cases, the needs of the center in which the office was located appeared to dominate the staff's attention. Since no effort was made to extend benefits of EDA projects in these centers to RA residents, the district redevelopment areas were not adequately served.

This was particularly true in Texas' Coastal Bend Economic Development District, where the district staff office is located in Corpus Christi, approximately eighty miles from the nearest RA community. Celia, a hurricane that ravaged Corpus Christi, and the personal predilections of the district staff combined to create a situation where most staff time was allocated to the problems of Corpus Christi. Prior to the evaluation team's arrival, no RA had been visited by a staff member for more than seven months.

Growth center residents outnumbered RA residents on only two of the ten district executive boards examined. RA residents, on the other hand, outnumbered growth center residents on four executive boards. For the most part, no single county dominated the activities of the district board; growth center representatives and redevelopment area representatives appeared to have an equal voice in determining board priorities and projects.

The growth center county or counties contributed the largest portion of the district's budget in all of the districts visited. In most cases this was the result of per capita levies. However, as indicated above, growth center representatives were not dominating the boards in most of the districts.

The district staffs had provided considerable assistance to growth centers in their efforts to prepare Positive Action Programs. In several instances, the district staff assumed full responsibility for the PAP's preparation. However, there was little evidence that the staffs provided any assistance with respect to implementing the growth center strategy. The PAPs did not reflect new commitments to helping redevelopment areas; they usually were summations of on-going local, state, and federal programs aimed at improving conditions for residents of the growth center. Moreover, neither district staffs nor boards had intentionally developed or implemented projects designed to carry out the growth center strategy.

Board members from growth centers and nondesignated counties had provided technical assistance to RA representatives on several occasions. However, these appeared to be chance occurrences. The majority of the growth center representatives interviewed did not feel any responsibility to pass on job information or advice to board members from redevelopment areas.

Status of the Economic Development Process

In seven of the twelve EDCs examined, the local government played a leading role in initiating and implementing development activities. In the remaining five centers, local government officials either exhibited a cautious attitude toward development projects or were strongly opposed to disturbing the community's status quo.

EDA projects and district staff activities had stimulated civic leaders in four of the seven centers where the local government supported development activities. In one center, the district staff was exerting considerable effort to persuade local government leaders to sponsor development-oriented projects. However, no results were visible at the time of the evaluation.

Average loan-to-deposit ratios for lending institutions in 9 of the 12 centers were between .55 and .60, representing a generally conservative banking approach. In Ardmore and Corpus Christi loan-to-deposit ratios averaged .45 and .50 respectively, indicating an extremely conservative lending policy. Swainsboro's bankers had the highest ratio, averaging .68. In all cases, EDA appeared to have had little or no impact on the policies of growth center banks.

The dominant economic group or groups in seven communities were generally in favor of development projects. These were the same communities whose elected officials supported such activities. In the other five centers, the dominant economic groups were suspicious of development activities. EDA projects and activities had resulted in a more favorable attitude toward development projects on the part of the economic leaders in four centers.

Community organizations were not heavily involved in economic development projects in any of the twelve centers visited. Most projects sponsored by these groups were aimed at:

1. Benefiting worthy individuals (e.g., scholarship awards).
2. Improving the center's atmosphere (e.g., beautification drives and collecting books for donation to the library).
3. Extending charity to underprivileged residents (e.g., distributing canned goods to poor families at Thanksgiving and Christmas).

EDA involvement in the centers had not affected the activities of such organizations.

Some planning was taking place in each of the twelve centers visited. However, the quality and quantity varied considerably. The smaller centers had planning boards composed of community leaders. These boards had no staffs, met at night, and became involved only in traditional land-use type planning. In Panama City, where zoning requirements had been defeated three times, the district employees were the only professional staff available to the local planning commission.

In the larger centers, such as Corpus Christi, Tri-Cities, and Ft. Smith, full-time planning staffs were employed by the city governments. However, even there, primary emphasis was placed on physical planning, and the staffs were generally not influential in guiding local development. Some of the centers were using grant funds from the Department of Housing and Urban Development's planning program to finance planning activities.

EDA-funded district staffs had assisted local planning boards in five of the twelve centers, and encouraged these entities to do more comprehensive planning. EDA had not had any impact on planning activities in the remaining seven centers.

Three of the twelve centers had active private development corporations working to attract industry. The industrial development foundation in Bowling Green had been particularly successful. In seven other EDCs, city, county, and Chamber of Commerce groups or officials served the same function and appeared to be having some success. No groups were actively engaged in industrial prospecting in the remaining two centers.

PAP Committees were functioning in three of the twelve centers, but in no case was seeking industrial prospects a major activity. EDA projects and district staff assistance had supported local groups' efforts to attract industry, often allowing them to achieve concrete results.

The results of past votes on bond issues and tax increases indicated that residents of six EDCs were willing to finance local improvements through such measures. Residents' attitudes toward supporting local improvements in the other six centers ranged from a willingness to pay for certain types of projects in Swainsboro and Ft. Smith, to a lack of support for all but the most essential service projects in Natchez. There was no evidence that EDA had any impact on these attitudes.

Each of the centers examined through the in-depth case studies was judged to be playing a leading role in the activities of the district organization. In every case, the district board's elected officials included a representative from the EDC being evaluated.

The effectiveness of the center's leadership was more difficult to judge, but a surface inspection indicated that Corpus Christi-Aransas Pass was the only center not providing adequate leadership. Moreover, this failure to provide effective leadership was primarily a result of the board's infrequent and poorly attended meetings, and not because of the poor performance of the board's growth center representatives.

Ten of the twelve centers were taking advantage of programs sponsored by such federal agencies as the Office of Economic Opportunity (OEO), the Department of Housing and Urban Development (HUD), and the Department of Health, Education, and Welfare (HEW). Only Natchez, Panama City, and Kingsport—one of the towns in the Tri-Cities growth center—exhibited a reluctance to obtain certain types of federal assistance. This reluctance appeared to stem primarily from the requirements of these particular federal programs. State assistance programs were being used in all the centers.

District staffs had encouraged centers to make use of such programs whenever possible. In addition, district staffs had assisted in the preparation of applications to EDA and other federal and state programs. Moreover, completed EDA projects had shown center leaders what can be accomplished through local-federal cooperation, and stimulated them to investigate other federal programs.

In no center were the majority of the development programs planned for the benefit of members of poor and minority groups. However, each center was taking advantage of at least one federal program designed to assist underprivileged persons. These included HEW's food stamp program, HUD's low-income housing program, and HEW's Head Start Program. Churches and service clubs in the centers did not appear to be engaged in significant ongoing efforts to alleviate the economic and social hardships suffered by the poor and members of minority groups.

EDA projects and the efforts of districts staffs did not appear to have resulted in more positive attitudes toward helping these individuals.

The one characteristic shared by the twelve centers was their citizens' lack of concern for residents of nearby redevelopment areas. No growth center development programs were planned for the benefit of RA residents, and most center leaders questioned the practicality of attending to the needs of other counties before solving local problems.

In a few isolated instances, EDA projects and district staff efforts had caused EDC residents and employers to recognize the situation facing RA residents and to consider hiring them for jobs in the growth center. However, with the exception of Chrysler's outreach program in Bowling Green, little had been accomplished.

Summaries of Individual Growth Center Evaluations[5]

Ada, Ardmore, and Durant, Oklahoma. The Southern Oklahoma Development Association (SODA) Economic Development District has three designated economic development centers: Ada, Ardmore, and Durant. Ada, which had a 1970 population of 14,859, was designated on February 21, 1967, when the ten-county district was officially recognized by EDA. Ardmore and Durant, with populations of 20,881 and 11,118 respectively, were designated ten months later on December 5, 1967.

As shown in figure 8-3, the centers form a triangle with corners in the north central, southeastern, and southwestern sections of the district, and each is located within fifteen miles of one of the district's three redevelopment areas. However, in each case the distance between the growth center and the largest town in the redevelopment area slightly exceeds thirty miles.

Ada was originally chosen as the sole subject of the in-depth evaluation. However, consideration of two factors led to a decision to include Ardmore and Durant in the analysis: (1) Durant was the site of a completed EDA project; and (2) all three centers were involved in the SODA District's unique effort to obtain government assistance in designing and implementing a comprehensive development program. A three-man EDA evaluation team visited the centers during the period between March 31 and April 9, 1971.

EDA Project Impact. Since their designation, the three centers had obtained approval for EDA projects in excess of $4 million. However, as of December 31,

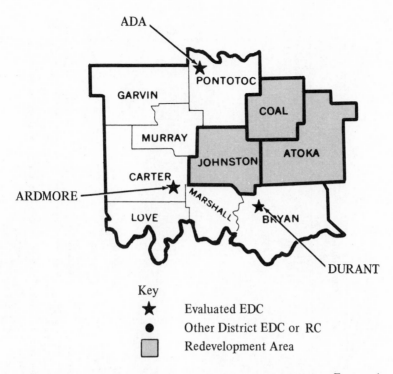

Key
★   Evaluated EDC
●   Other District EDC or RC
▨   Redevelopment Area

Figure 8-3. Southern Oklahoma Development Association Economic Development District

1970, only four projects, representing EDA funds of $1,213,500, were 90 percent disbursed. These consisted of:

1. A $183,500 public works grant to finance a storm sewer and streets for an industrial park in Ada.
2. A $113,500 public works grant to build an access road to the Brockway Glass plant in Ada.
3. A $500,000 business loan channeled through the Pontotoc County Industrial Development Authority to enable Solo Cup Company, a Chicago-based manufacturer of plastic cups, to locate in Ada.
4. A $417,000 public works grant to extend water service facilities in the city of Durant.

Through these projects, EDA had helped locate 225 jobs in Ada and 50 jobs in Durant. In addition, the water system project in Durant serviced 150 units of low-income housing. Table 8-4 presents additional data on each of the projects. Future job impact at a Uniroyal facility in Ardmore will add 1,000 jobs to

Table 8-4
EDA Project Impact in Ada and Durant

Evaluation Category	Durant Water System	Solo Cup Company (Ada)	Ada Industrial Park	Access Road (Ada)	TOTAL
Project Cost	$834,000	$2,000,000	$367,000	$226,000	$3,427,000
EDA Participation	$417,000	$ 500,000	$183,500	$113,500	$1,214,000
Percentage Occupied or Operational	100%	50%	45%	100%	—
EDA-Attributed Jobs	50	165	60	0	275
EDA-Attributed Jobs to RA Residents	0	4[a]	9	0	9
EDA-Attributed Jobs to Unemployed and Underemployed Persons	14	No Data	23	0	37
EDC Residents	14	No Data	15	0	29
RA Residents	0	No Data	3	0	3
EDA Investment Per Job	$ 8,340	$ 3,030	$ 3,058	—	$ 4,415
EDA Investment Per RA Job	—	$ 125,000[a]	$ 20,389	—	$ 79,333
Yearly Salary Generated	$312,000	$ 699,000	$295,000		$1,306,000

[a]Based on employer's estimate and not included in aggregate figures

Source: *Program Evaluation: The Economic Development Administration Growth Center Strategy*, Washington, D.C.: U.S. Department of Commerce/Economic Development Administration, February 1972, p. 31

the total presently attributable to EDA at a public works investment of $1,292,000. In addition, Solo Cup Company in Ada plans to add 135 jobs by the end of 1971. This will increase the total job impact to 1,410 and lower EDA investment per job to $1,777. The Le Tourneau Plant to be constructed in Durant was projecting employment of 400. Since construction was not to be completed within one year of the evaluation, these jobs were not included in the future impact figures.[c]

Effectiveness of Positive Action Program (PAP). Ada's original PAP was prepared by a SODA district staff member in conjunction with Ada community leaders and submitted to EDA in May 1968. This document, whose content was similar to the Economic Development Profile previously required as part of project applications, was updated in January 1969 in connection with a business loan application for Solo Cup Company. The updated PAP contained no provisions for filling the jobs created by Solo Cup with unemployed and underemployed residents of nearby redevelopment areas, and identified no new programs designed to benefit such individuals.

In January 1971, Ada submitted the draft version of a revised PAP and a progress report on local redevelopment efforts. Prepared by the Chamber of Commerce in conjunction with the SODA district staff, the new document was distributed locally and in neighboring RA's for comment. While some of the activities given priority by those who responded to the proposed PAP could have regional impact (e.g., a voc-tech school and general industrial development), the majority were concerned with the development of Ada and only remotely tied to regional growth.

No new or significantly increased commitment to improving the condition of unemployed and underemployed RA residents was identified in the report summarizing the responses. Moreover, almost without exception, the activities affecting the poor were tied to existing projects that would have been implemented in the absence of the PAP or designation as an EDA growth center.

Ardmore's Positive Action Program, which was originally submitted to EDA in June 1968 and updated in January 1969, was prepared by the city manager and his staff. The initial document stressed the city's efforts to promote better race relations, while the update placed emphasis on the creation of job opportunities for the economically disadvantaged, including residents of redevelopment areas.

However, the majority of the programs mentioned were limited to assistance for growth center residents. For example, the State Employment Security Office and the Human Relations and Job Placement Center, both tied to outreach for the unemployed and underemployed, serviced only citizens of Ardmore (Carter County) and nondesignated counties. Moreover, none of the programs described in the document was initiated as a result of the PAP.

[c]The technique used to estimate future jobs was described in chapter 6.

In June 1968, Durant submitted a Positive Action Program to EDA detailing efforts to help the growth center's minority (Indian) and poor population. This document, which was prepared by the Chamber of Commerce on the basis of information provided by community leaders, was updated in November 1970 in connection with an application for an EDA project. Prepared by a SODA staff member under the supervision of the local Chamber of Commerce, this update indicated a clearer recognition of Durant's responsibility to the redevelopment areas. The plans to develop a skills training center and a curriculum for certain health professions in conjunction with an outreach program to recruit RA residents for such training were particularly significant.

At the time of the evaluation, however, these plans had not been implemented, so none of the impacts on adjoining redevelopment areas indicated in the plans had been realized. Furthermore, even if the plans are implemented, their relationship to the PAP is questionable. Community leaders, both economic and political, were not familiar with the PAP and its purposes, suggesting that the PAP had no initiatory impact, but merely recounted ongoing programs and previously conceived plans.

Role of the District Organization. The SODA District organization had focused on providing equal assistance to the individual counties in the district. However, because of a number of factors, including their relative prosperity and size, the growth center counties had acquired a larger proportion of federal and state projects than had the other seven counties. Because the centers made the most demands on its time and because its members did not believe the RAs were economically viable, the district staff had devoted the majority of its time to the growth centers. In addition, representatives of the three centers appeared to dominate the district board and its executive committee.

Despite the emphasis placed on the growth centers, the evaluation team concluded that the district organization had not achieved significant success in implementing the growth center strategy. This was primarily because the staff's efforts to insure that center projects benefited residents of redevelopment areas had been ineffective. Although job vacancies in growth centers were reported to Community Action Program Agencies in RAs, no follow-up activities had been initiated to determine the results of this service. Moreover, no attempt had been made to explain to EDA-associated employers the importance of hiring unemployed and underemployed RA residents. The one tool that EDA provided for extending benefits to redevelopment area residents, the PAP, was viewed by the district staff as a useful educational device, not a vehicle for obtaining new commitments from the growth centers to assist residents of neighboring redevelopment areas.

Another reason for the district organization's apparent failure to successfully implement the growth center strategy involved the characteristics of the towns selected as centers. Excluding the metropolitan areas of Tulsa and Oklahoma

City, the state of Oklahoma exhibited a 4.9 percent population increase during the 1960-70 decade. Not only did the counties in which Ada and Ardmore are located decline in population during this period, but the towns themselves failed to match the state's population growth, registering increases of 3.5 and 3.6 percent, respectively. Moreover, Ada and Durant, with 1970 populations of 14,859 and 11,118 are probably too small to exert a significant economic influence on neighboring redevelopment areas.

Status of the Economic Development Process. The evaluators found that both the power structure and the general public in Ada favored development-oriented activities. For more than a decade private citizens, an active Chamber of Commerce, and, to a certain extent, the city government had worked to diversify the town's economy. At least four local corporations were engaged in efforts to attract industry to the area, and a fifth association, the East Central Oklahoma Building Authority, was involved in the construction of a Regional Health and Social Services Center. When the center is completed, its personnel will work not only in Ada, but also in the redevelopment area counties of Johnston and Atoka. Residents of Coal County (an RA) were unable to contribute their share to the project and thus will have to travel to Ada to take advantage of the Center's services.

Banks in Ada had participated in a positive manner in each of the EDA-associated projects. In addition, community organizations had begun to support the Chamber of Commerce in its effects to promote support for city-wide projects and bond issues. The survey conducted with relation to the proposed PAP had also had an impact in that it made residents aware of the need to set community-wide goals and to improve city and county planning activities, which at the time of evaluation were handled by one part-time consultant.

The attitude of Ada's power structure toward the poor and members of minority groups both in Ada and in the redevelopment areas was influenced by pragmatic considerations. No real understanding of the plight of these groups appeared to exist. However, members of the Ada business community spoke frankly of their desire to see such individuals improve their economic status so that Ada merchants could benefit from their increased purchasing power.

While EDA projects and activities had provided facilities and services the community would not have been able to afford on its own, they had not significantly stimulated the development process in Ada.

The status of Ardmore's development process had fluctuated considerably since the 1940s. Each time a climate favorable to development existed, some setback, such as the closing of a major airbase, occurred. As a result, the evaluators found both the town's leadership and the general citizenry to be cautious about future development efforts. The aging representatives of the oil and cattle industries were particularly conservative, and the younger, more progressive leadership was splintered. With one exception, the banks were highly conservative in their lending policies, and Ardmore's citizens appeared to have little or no sympathy for the residents of redevelopment area or for that segment of their own population that was economically distressed.

Despite these attitudes, external factors favor increased development in Ardmore. The town is located on an Interstate Highway between two major metropolitan areas, serves as a terminal for the recently revised railroad system, and is the site of a new Uniroyal plant that plans to employ up to 1,400 persons. Moreover, certain internal factors indicated that Ardmore's development process was being stimulated. Not only were the various groups of younger leaders making progress with respect to individual development projects, but the location of the Uniroyal facility had stirred some hope among citizens interested in Ardmore's development. However, EDA activities and projects appeared to have had no impact on the development process.

The development process was first stimulated in Durant in 1968 when Corning Ware turned down the city's invitation to locate a plant there. Unlike the situation in Ardmore, Durant's younger, more progressive leaders had managed to unite and gain the support of the older cattle and farming interests, and these groups asked Corning Wares to explain its decision not to locate in Durant. Upon learning that the inadequacy of Durant's health facilities, the lack of housing, the appearance of the town's central business district, and the lack of various amenities were among the factors that led to the firm's decision, Durant's leaders initiated action to remedy such conditions.

Although the evaluators found Durant's leadership to be close-knit, competent, and unusually progressive, local development efforts were handicapped by some of the same roadblocks faced in Ardmore. The banks were still highly conservative in their lending policies, and the general public was much more cautious than the leaders. Moreover, a strong bias existed against poor persons in general. However, past experience indicated that Durant citizens were willing to tax themselves to support development-oriented projects.

The situation was more promising with respect to assisting residents of redevelopment areas. Long dominated by the larger Texas towns of Denison and Sherman, Durant was trying to establish its own sphere of influence. Commercial interests in Durant recognized the need to secure the assistance of redevelopment area residents if they were to succeed. Therefore, they viewed local hiring of such individuals more favorably than was previously the case.

The insights gained from the experience with Corning Ware and the energetic efforts of the town's younger leaders had played the major role in stimulating the economic development process in Durant. EDA projects and activities had supported these efforts, but had little impact on the process itself.

Bangor-Brewer, Maine. Bangor-Brewer, Maine, a city with a population of 42,468, is the one designated economic development center of the six-county Eastern Maine Economic Development District. Technically two distinct municipalities sitting astride the Penobscot River, Bangor-Brewer functions as one unit, economically and socially.

Both the center and district were first designated by EDA on March 13, 1968. Redevelopment areas included in the district are the entire counties of Washington and Knox; four labor areas designated on the basis of sudden rise in unemployment; and Indian Island, a State of Maine Indian reservation. These areas, which are identified in figure 8-4, are, with the possible exceptions of Indian Island and the small labor areas of Lincoln in northern Penobscot County, isolated from Bangor-Brewer by distance and bad roads. EDA field evaluators visited the district in March 1971, to evaluate the impact of EDA projects, PAP effectiveness, the local development process and the district organization.

EDA Project Impact. At the time of the evaluation, three major projects had been completed in the growth center. Two others, the Bangor International Airport Terminal and the Brewer Industrial Park were in the design and construction phases, respectively. Two of the three completed projects were business loans to Eastern Fine Paper Co. and Chapman Precision Products, companies that otherwise would have gone out of business. The third project was a feasibility study for an industrial park at the airport in Bangor.

Job impact, as outlined in table 8-5 had been moderate within Bangor-Brewer. The total number of EDA-attributable jobs was 450. However, not one of these was taken by a present or former resident of a redevelopment area, and only 76 jobs went to previously unemployed or underemployed residents of the center itself. EDA investment per job in Bangor-Brewer was $4,111.

Brewer, where Eastern Fine Paper Co. is located, is a one-industry town, and the shutdown in March of 1968 of Eastern Fine's predecessor company with its 700 employees was a blow to the city's economy. The firm, which reopened with EDA's help six months later, purchased supplies from two RA companies, both of which maintained they could dispose of their products elsewhere. Thus, employment at these firms was not attributable to EDA. Local shipping and warehousing outfits, however, indicated that sixteen jobs were saved as a result of Eastern Fine's reopening.

EDA's $300,000 business loan to Chapman Precision was designed to enable the company to move from its Old Town location to new industrial space at Bangor International Airport, purchase new equipment, diversify its product line, and expand employment to 153 persons. Two years from approval date of loan, Chapman's work force was thirty-seven persons, a slight decrease from the forty-two employed when the loan was made. Approximately 12 percent of the employees were unemployed or underemployed prior to taking jobs at Chapman. Virtually all supplies were purchased from outside the state and 95 percent of all products were sold to a single manufacturer in Connecticut.

EDA's $9,000 grant funding a study of optimum land use at the former Dow

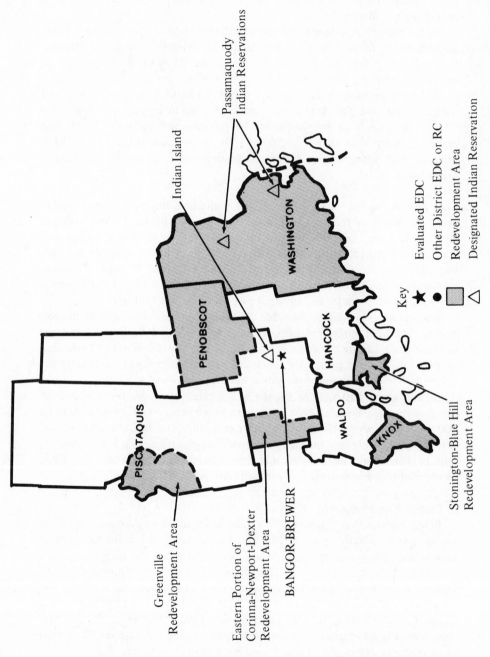

Figure 8-4. Eastern Maine Economic Development District

Key

★ Evaluated EDC
● Other District EDC or RC
▨ Redevelopment Area
◁ Designated Indian Reservation

Passamaquody Indian Reservations

Indian Island

Stonington-Blue Hill Redevelopment Area

Greenville Redevelopment Area

Eastern Portion of Corinna-Newport-Dexter Redevelopment Area

BANGOR-BREWER

PISCATAQUIS

PENOBSCOT

WASHINGTON

HANCOCK

WALDO

KNOX

Table 8-5
EDA Project Impact in Bangor-Brewer

Evaluation Category	Eastern Fine Paper Co.	Chapman Precision Products	TOTAL
Project Cost	$2,650,000	$400,000	$3,050,000
EDA Participation	$1,550,000[a]	$300,000	$1,850,000
Percent Occupied or Operational	100%	100%	
EDA-Attributed Jobs	413 (saved)[b]	37 (saved)	450 (saved)
EDA-Attributed Jobs to RA Residents	0	0	0
EDA-Attributed Jobs to Formerly Unemployed and Underemployed Persons	74	2	76
EDC Residents	74	2	76
RA Residents	0	0	0
EDA Investment Per Job	$ 3,753	$ 8,108	$ 4,111
EDA Investment Per RA Job	—	—	—
Yearly Salary Generated	$3,000,000[c]	$200,000	$3,200,000

[a] A subsequently approved $300 thousand working capital guarantee is not included in this figure.

[b] Includes sixteen secondary jobs in firms serving Eastern Fine

[c] Includes salary generated from secondary jobs in firms serving Eastern Fine. Yearly salary for the secondary jobs was based on estimated rates of $5,200 per year for each of sixteen jobs.

Source: Program Evaluation: The Economic Development Administration Growth Center Strategy, Washington, D.C.: U.S. Department of Commerce/Economic Development Administration, February 1972, p. 37

Air Force Base was partially responsible for the location of a bank in Bangor's air industrial park. This bank was staffed by eight employees, all of whom resided in the growth center; it purchased no supplies from redevelopment areas.

Future impact of EDA's investments in Bangor-Brewer was estimated on the basis of expansion and construction plans of EDA-associated firms. Expansion at Eastern Fine and completion of the new air terminal at Bangor International Airport were expected to generate approximately forty-five jobs. (This figure is based on employer plans and a discounting system discussed in chapter 6, Evaluation Approach.) Since construction on another project, the East-West Industrial Park, had not yet begun at the time of the evaluation, no employment projection could be made. When the figures for future employment are included in the aggregate for Bangor-Brewer, EDA's total investment is $3,502,000 and the agency's investment per job increases to $7,074.

PAP Effectiveness. Because the PAP Committee in Bangor-Brewer had been recently restructured, its members were in the process of defining their functions and goals. The original PAP document was primarily a listing of ongoing community activities that would have been conducted in the absence of the PAP. The new committee viewed itself as a vehicle for improved communication within the growth center and as a group to help identify problems. At the time of evaluation, there had been no visible accomplishments. One new program mentioned in the first PAP proposed bus service to low-income housing areas in the city. This effort was attempted, but proved unworkable primarily because of cost.

The district staff and some members of the committee were aware that, as a growth center, Bangor-Brewer should be serving poorer areas of the district. However, they indicated that the distance between those areas and the EDC, combined with Bangor-Brewer's problems of poverty and unemployment, made it unlikely that the center would provide significant assistance to RA residents.

Role of the District Organization. Since the Eastern Maine Development District's designation, the district staff had been actively involved in development activities in the area. The staff allocated its time according to need and, in fact, maintained a full-time staff member and field office in Washington County, the largest RA. It was managing a Law Enforcement Assistance Grant and working with the state planning agency to rationalize conflicting substate boundaries.

The staff was serving the district effectively in the areas of grantsmanship, planning, and communications. Its members viewed the growth center strategy as useful in theory but largely unworkable because of the district's size and road system. Because the staff had received limited and conflicting guidelines on the PAP and growth center strategy, it had done little to implement the policy.

District board members appeared to have no conception of the growth center strategy. Each was primarily concerned with the needs of his own county.

Status of the Economic Development Process. Perhaps the major cause for the change in attitudes toward development and community problems in Bangor-Brewer was the closing of Dow Air Force Base in 1968. An important source of income and consumers, its abrupt deactivation and the consequent departure of approximately 8,000 servicemen and dependents shocked the community. Residents suddenly realized that the employment and population losses occurring in other New England towns might also occur in Bangor-Brewer, and attitudes toward development activities became more favorable. After Dow's closing, the city was deeded a substantial portion of its land, including an air strip which was being developed as an air industrial park at the time of the evaluation.

The banks remained generally conservative in their lending policies, but the city governments were taking steps to bring in federal programs. Bangor had some low-income housing, an urban renewal project and a manpower training program. Brewer, smaller and a bit more cautious, had recently turned down urban renewal, but was developing an industrial park with EDA funding.

Residents of this area of the country are generally resigned to the existence of poverty. Citizens of Bangor-Brewer are no different. Statutes remained on the books that allow Bangor to return welfare recipients to their county of origin, provided they are given bus fare and spending money. It was generally felt that any willing worker could make a living somehow, even by chopping wood and digging clams. Center residents, especially its merchants, viewed outlying areas as markets for goods and services distributed through Bangor-Brewer. They felt no responsibility to assist economically distressed area; the problems of unemployment and low income within the center itself occupied all available resources.

Bowling Green, Kentucky. Bowling Green is the primary economic development center of the Barren River Area Development District (BRADD). BRADD, which is depicted in figure 8-5, is located in south central Kentucky on the Tennessee border. It consists of ten counties, five of which are designated redevelopment areas. This multicounty area was first designated as a development district by EDA on January 7, 1967. Bowling Green and the secondary EDC of Glasgow in Barren County received growth center designation at that time as well.

Warren County, within which Bowling Green is located, is bordered on three sides by the redevelopment area counties of Butler, Edmonson, and Allen. The U.S. road system appears adequate, and one interstate route passes through the county from south to northeast. Daily commuting to jobs in Bowling Green is common among residents of the redevelopment areas.

EDA Project Impact. Although listed in EDA's project directory as three distinct projects, the agency's assistance in Bowling Green was primarily for the improvement of one industrial site. Water and sewer lines were extended to a location just outside the city at a total cost of $1,812,000, of which $1,504,000,

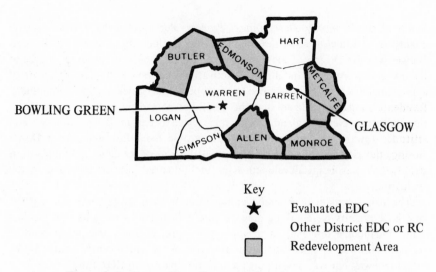

Key

★   Evaluated EDC

●   Other District EDC or RC

▢   Redevelopment Area

Figure 8–5. Barren River Economic Development District

or 83 percent, was funded by EDA. Forty percent of EDA's investment was a public works grant, while the remaining 60 percent was a public works loan. The project was originally designed to attract Chrysler Corporation to Bowling Green. In fact, it was this project which first sparked interest in a development district. The area's EDR, seeing a prospective project, recommended that Bowling Green apply for designation as a growth center. Before this could be done, a district board had to be formed, a staff hired, an OEDP and PAP prepared.

To accelerate the project application process, a group of interested business-men began collecting the information needed even before the new staff was able to develop an OEDP. The vice president of the local bank was assigned the task of preparing a Positive Action Program.

With the promise of new water and sewer facilities, the Chrysler Corporation did decide to locate its Airtemp facility for the manufacture of commercial air conditioning equipment in Bowling Green. In March of 1969, the personnel director for the new plant arrived to begin hiring for production start-up in January 1970. The district's executive director, seeing an opportunity to address some of the employment problems in outlying rural counties, approached the Chrysler personnel man and requested that he recruit in some of these areas. At the director's urging, a series of one-day interviews for prospective employees was conducted in nine small towns outside of Bowling Green. This covered three of the five RAs. Application blanks were left in all places, and an advertising campaign was conducted in county newspapers, on radio, and TV. Although it is Chrysler's policy to hire members of minority groups and the economically disadvantaged, the personnel manager indicated that he would not have made this sort of outreach effort except under the guidance of the development district director.

Approximately 40 percent of the 600 EDA-attributable jobs at Chrysler were held by present or former RA residents. All employees were given an intensive training program of eight to thirteen weeks, depending on the skill level of the prospective job slot. This program combined voc-tech and on-the-job training. Twenty-seven percent of the employees had less than a high school education and 9 percent were black. Annual payroll resulting from this establishment was approximately $4,179,000. The operation had diversified and stabilized employment in Bowling Green: first because its product was unique; and second because it was a job-shop rather than an assembly-line plant. This requires higher skills and wage levels. The labor was unionized and wages were therefore on a standard scale.

Table 8-6 summarizes job impact from the Chrysler project. Although facilities were 100 percent operational at the time of evaluation, expansion was planned which would provide up to 2,200 jobs by 1973. Some increased business for other industries resulted from this project. However, it had not resulted in expansion of employment.

With the exception of a few fire hydrants, Chrysler was the only user of the new water line. However, there had been approximately 50 hookups to the new sewer line. Most were small businesses and commercial establishments that

Table 8-6
EDA Project Impact in Bowling Green

Evaluation Category	Interception Sewer, Water Main, Sewage Collection System (Chrysler)
Project Cost	$1,812,000
EDA Participation	$1,504,000
Percent Occupied or Operational	100%
EDA-Attributed Jobs	600
EDA-Attributed Jobs to RA Residents	237
EDA-Attributed Jobs to Formerly Unemployed and Underemployed Persons	149
EDC Residents	87
RA Residents	37
EDA Investment Per Job	$ 2,507
EDA Investment Per RA Job	$ 6,346
Yearly Salary Generated	$4,179,000

Source: Program Evaluation: The Economic Development Administration Growth Center Strategy, Washington, D.C.: U.S. Department of Commerce/Economic Development Administration, February 1972, p. 43

formerly used septic tanks. According to the Northside Water District—applicant and manager of the facilities—all of these beneficiaries could have continued using septic tanks indefinitely, and had not expanded because the new facilities were made available to them.

The expansion planned by Chrysler would result in 1,600 new jobs. The plant was complete, but hiring for these new jobs had not begun at the time of evaluation. Therefore, the discounting system described in chapter 6 allows 1,200 of these jobs to be counted as future employment. Including these future jobs lowers EDA's investment per job for Bowling Green to $836.

PAP Effectiveness. As indicated above, Bowling Green's PAP, which had never been updated, was written by the vice president of a local bank. It was essentially a Chamber of Commerce-type brochure on the good points of Bowling Green; it contained no new action proposals. The PAP was approved by EDA in the fall of 1968. At the time of the evaluation, the district staff had been working on a PAP for the secondary growth center of Glasgow and had encountered difficulty in getting approval from EDA Washington. This was a somewhat puzzling experience for the executive director since Bowling Green's PAP, which was put together with very little effort, was quickly accepted.

Virtually no one in Bowling Green was familiar with the PAP. There was no committee for its implementation, and the growth center government had neither discussed nor endorsed the concept that Bowling Green should help surrounding counties. It was after the PAP was submitted that the executive director, Chrysler, the CAP Agency, and the Employment Security Office agreed to work together in recruiting employees from RA counties.

A significant number of ongoing programs in Bowling Green addressed the needs of the center's poor and unemployed population. The CAP Agency even had branch offices in some of the outlying counties. This concern, however, was completely incidental to the PAP requirement, which was regarded as a nuisance.

Role of the District Organization. The staff of the Barren River Area Development District is extremely competent, and had succeeded in managing other federal and state grants in addition to EDA's (e.g., LEAA, State Bureau of Outdoor Recreation, and Public Service Careers grants). The staff had provided technical assistance to all the counties of the district, and redevelopment area leaders indicated they could rely on the executive director to travel to their communities whenever he was needed.

The staff had arranged training in budgeting and financial techniques through Western Kentucky University for municipal governments throughout the district. It had also secured the cooperation of Bowling Green's housing authority in helping some of the small communities in the area meet their own public housing problems.

BRADD was the one district visited by the evaluation team where significant employment impact on RAs from a growth center project was achieved or attempted. As discussed above, this resulted from the executive director's work with Chrysler's recruiter in seeking job applicants in the RAs. This effort had nothing to do with the PAP and did not involve a community-wide commitment to helping the RAs. It was the result of a concentrated effort for a limited period of time and for a very specific purpose—jobs to RA county residents.

When queried on the subject of EDA's "growth center strategy," the executive director observed that it was difficult to apply any kind of priority or strategy when funding depended almost exclusively on the decisions of EDA Washington over which the district had little influence.

The OEDP submitted by the Barren River District set priorities, however, and these included the need to make Bowling Green more accessible by improving the district's road system. Coupled with the fact that the district organization had succeeded in mobilizing some of the resources available in Bowling Green to the benefit of the RA counties, this suggested an above-average grasp of the growth center concept.

Status of the Economic Development Process. Development activities in Bowling Green were the result of an interesting mix of circumstances. The local Chamber of Commerce acquired a new manager during the 1960s who is recognized as one of the most effective chamber administrators in the country. Repeatedly, this individual was cited as being a major factor in changing attitudes and in actually locating industry in the city. In the past, members of the Industrial Foundation—the city's industrial development group—had actually been discouraging industrial prospects from considering location in Bowling Green. Some established interests felt that discouraging new industry would hold down wages and insure an adequate labor pool. But new management of the chamber helped change this situation.

Another frequently cited cause for changing attitudes was the shift in city government from a mayor-council to the city manager form of administration. Bowling Green had traditionally been a conservative community which refused to turn tax money over to the city for public improvements. After its first sewer and water facility construction, 30 years elapsed before any substantial extensions or improvements were made. In fiscal year 1971 the city established an engineering department for the first time.

The federal dollar had been another important influence in changing attitudes and conditions in Bowling Green. In 1969 alone, $9.3 million in federal grants and loans flowed into the city. There was an active Model Cities Program which had cooperated with the Bowling Green vocational-technical school to provide skill training for ghetto residents. Two low-income housing projects had been funded, and HUD had provided assistance to the City-County Planning Commission. In addition, an urban renewal project was gradually renovating some of the oldest and worst sections of the downtown area.

Over the last ten years, industrial jobs in Warren County had doubled, largely because of new industry location. The city had encouraged this sort of development by improving industrial land, building shell structures, and leasing space to interested industry. In this way, new industry was freed from property tax burdens. It is interesting to note, however, that the city had supplemented its revenues with an "occupational tax," which is essentially an income tax imposed on all who work in the city, whether or not they live there. Since there is substantial commuting to Bowling Green, this added significantly to municipal income—at the expense of the labor force rather than the employers.

Because Warren County is contiguous to three RA counties and Bowling Green is within a thirty- to forty-five minute drive of these, there is considerable commuting for shopping and services as well as work. Official communication among the district's towns was almost exclusively limited to that involving the district organization. Those interviewed commented that rivalry was more characteristic of relationships among counties and towns than was cooperation. EDA's growth center strategy appeared to have had little impact on the development process in Bowling Green, except in connection with the Chrysler project.

Corpus Christi-Aransas Pass, Texas. Corpus Christi, Texas, was designated as EDA's first economic development center in December 1966. In September 1968, the boundaries of the center were extended to include the city of Aransas Pass, located approximately twenty miles northeast of Corpus Christi. Aransas Pass had a 1970 population of 5,813, which represented a 16.4 percent decrease since 1960, while Corpus Christi's 1970 population was 204,525, an increase of 22 percent during the 1960-70 decade.

The Corpus Christi-Aransas Pass area serves as one of two growth centers for the twenty-county Coastal Bend Economic Development District, which is illustrated in figure 8-6. It is approximately seventy miles from the nearest redevelopment area and eighty miles from the nearest redevelopment area community with a population exceeding 1,000. The growth center area was examined by an EDA evaluation team between March 18 and March 26, 1971.

EDA Project Impact. At the time of the evaluation, four EDA public works and business loan projects in the Corpus Christi-Aransas Pass growth center area were 90 percent disbursed. In addition, a $60,000 EDA technical assistance project to study the district's tourism-recreation potential had been completed, and the Coastal Bend Economic Development District staff had received $136,000 in EDA planning grant funds. The public works and business loan projects, which represent $1,127,000 in EDA funds consist of:

1. A $125,000 public works grant to the Southwest Research Institute for the procurement of scientific equipment for marine laboratories

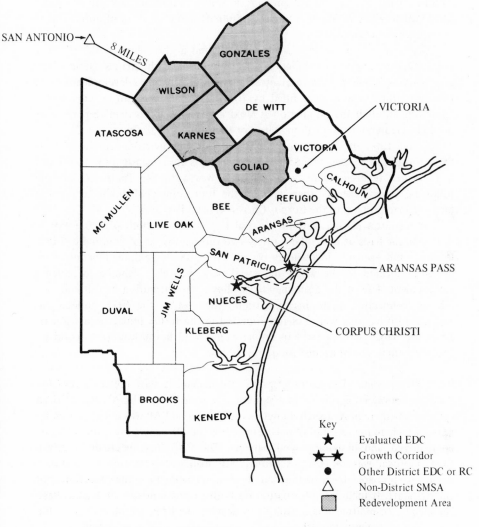

Figure 8-6. Coastal Bend Economic Development District

2. A $234,000 public works grant to the Nueces County Navigation District for the construction of a deep sea oil terminal for loading tankers
3. A $410,000 business development loan to the Sheraton Marina Inn, Inc., for the construction of a hotel-motel facility to accommodate the Corpus Christi tourist trade
4. A $358,000 business development loan to Coastal Freezing, Inc., a shrimp plant located in Aransas Pass, to expand its freezing and processing capacity.

Another partially completed project, a water industrial park, representing $650,000 in EDA funds, had already resulted in the creation of employment opportunities in Corpus Christi.

EDA assistance to these projects had resulted in the creation of 219 direct jobs, which represent approximately $1.6 million in yearly salaries. None of the direct jobs was taken by a resident of an EDA-designated redevelopment area. However, thirteen jobs were filled by former RA residents. In an area where approximately half the population is Mexican-American, less than 15 percent of the EDA-created jobs went to members of that minority group.

At the time of evaluation, EDA's investment per job in the Corpus Christi-Aransas Pass area was $5,367. The agency's investment per job to present and former redevelopment area residents was $86,154. Table 8-7 on the following page presents other data on the four completed public works and business loan projects in the Corpus Christi-Aransas Pass area.

The Sheraton Marina Inn and Coastal Freezing were both planning expansions. On the basis of these plans, thirty-two future jobs can be credited to EDA, lowering the agency's investment per job to $4,858. Benilite, the only firm presently located in the water industrial park, was also planning to increase employment. Use of the discount factor allows the attribution of thirteen new jobs in connection with this expansion. The cost of the EDA project and Benilite's future jobs were not incorporated in the future impact figure above. Since the park itself was still incomplete, it would be misleading to compare Benilite's employment against total project cost.

PAP Effectiveness. The Corpus Christi city manager's staff prepared the first Positive Action Program for that community shortly after EDA's March 1968 announcement requiring such a document. This initial PAP was not approved by EDA, which requested additional information on the city's programs to assist unemployed and underemployed persons. The PAP that eventually received EDA approval was the Corpus Christi city manager's rewritten version of a document prepared by a member of the Coastal Bend Economic Development District staff. It included information on both Corpus Christi and Aransas Pass. No specific committee was organized to develop the PAP, and no official action was taken by the city council.

The Corpus Christi-Aransas Pass PAP identified no significantly increased commitments to the unemployed and underemployed residents of district redevelopment areas. In fact, the only new commitment was directly linked to an EDA project. With the exception of that commitment by one of the firms benefiting from an EDA-financed water system, all of the activities identified in the PAP as having an impact on the poor were: (1) components of ongoing programs; or (2) efforts that would have been undertaken in the absence of the PAP. Moreover, representatives of the organizations responsible for the implementation of such programs were not familiar with the PAP or its objectives.

Table 8-7
EDA Project Impact in Corpus Christi-Aransas Pass

Evaluation Category	Southwest Research	Coastal Freezing	Sheraton Marina Inn	Deep Sea Oil Terminal	Water Industrial Park (Not Completed) Benilite	TOTAL
Project Cost	$250,000	$550,000	$2,935,600	$ 462,000	$1,300,000	$5,497,600
EDA Participation	$125,000	$358,000	$ 410,000	$ 234,000	$ 650,000[b]	$1,777,000
Percent Occupied or Operational	100%	25%	100%	100%	Not Completed	
EDA-Attributed Jobs	3[a]	14	43	150	9[b]	219
EDA-Attributed Jobs to RA Residents	0	0	3	10	0	13
EDA-Attributed Jobs to Formerly Unemployed and Underemployed Persons	0	5	11	25	3	44
EDC Residents	0	5	10	20	3	38
RA Residents	0	0	0	0	0	0
EDA Investment Per Job	$ 41,666	$ 25,571	$ 9,534	$ 1,560	Not Applicable	$ 5,367
EDA Investment Per RA Job			$ 136,667	$ 23,400	Not Applicable	$ 86,154
Yearly Salary Generated	$ 19,000	$ 95,000	$ 164,000	$1,248,000	$ 84,000	$1,610,000

[a]Not included in aggregate figures

[b]Not included in investment per job for this chart

Source: Program Evaluation: The Economic Development Administration Growth Center Strategy, Washington, D.C.: U.S. Department of Commerce/Economic Development Administration, February 1972, p. 49

The one new commitment to helping unemployed and underemployed residents of redevelopment areas had not been realized at the time of evaluation. More closely related to a specific EDA project than to the PAP, this commitment involved advertising and extending preferential recruiting and hiring to the unemployed and underemployed of the redevelopment area counties. The firm that made the commitment had taken no action at the the time of field evaluation. However, as a result of discussions with the evaluators, the firm formally advised its contractors to seek "trainable unemployed and underemployed" from the four redevelopment area counties in the Coastal Bend Economic Development District.

Role of the District Organization. The district organization had played a minimal role in implementing the growth center strategy with respect to projects in the Corpus Christi-Aransas Pass growth center area. Overshadowed by larger, more heavily endowed groups such as the Regional Planning Commission, the four-man district staff had concentrated on acquiring funds for projects in the growth center area as opposed to developing a district-wide development strategy.

Of the approximately $3.5 million in grant and loan money the staff had succeeded in acquiring for district counties, 91 percent had been absorbed in the Corpus Christi-Aransas Pass growth center area. Less than $250,000 went directly to redevelopment areas. One explanation the district staff gave for the distribution was that the redevelopment area counties were unwilling or financially unable to support economic development. In August 1970, Corpus Christi was ravaged by Hurricane Celia and since that time, the district staff had spent close to 100 percent of its time working in the growth center area.

Only token attempts had been made by the staff to influence EDA-associated employers to recruit and hire unemployed and underemployed residents of redevelopment areas. In absolute numbers, the growth center area had more unemployed and underemployed residents than did the four EDA-designated counties, and the district staff questioned the logic and reality of obtaining commitments from the growth center and EDA-associated employers to assist the jobless and underemployed residents of other counties before their own target population had been served.

The district board was an ineffective group that met only once a year. The five-member executive committee met quarterly, but appeared to function only as a rubber stamp for district staff plans and activities. Neither group had any understanding of the growth center strategy articulated by EDA, and their concept of the district strategy was only slightly clearer.

Status of the Economic Development Process. The evaluators reported that certain segments of the business community in both Corpus Christi and Aransas Pass were interested in and working to promote economic development.

Between 1965 and 1970, new development groups devoted to attracting industry were organized in both cities. With the lowering of interest rates, local banks were becoming more involved in development-oriented activities.

A significant portion of the power structure and the general population, however, was more interested in maintaining the *status quo* than in developing economically. This was particularly true in Corpus Christi, where local citizens refused to assist a prospective employer of considerable size. The damage caused by Hurricane Celia in August 1970 resulted in a flurry of activity; however, it was primarily aimed at restoring businesses and infrastructure to prestorm status.

During the five years preceding the evaluation, the number of programs designed to help Corpus Christi's poor and minority group population had increased considerably. However, even with increases in local and federal programs, only a minimum was being accomplished. Data obtained by Community Action Program staff members in 1970 revealed that residents of Corpus Christi's poverty belt fared no better than in 1960. Target neighborhoods were still marked by high unemployment, low income, substandard and crowded housing, limited education, little mobility, and increased ethnic isolation. Corpus Christi's schools still did not meet federal integration requirements, and the community had become polarized over the issue.

Aransas Pass, which has a similar racial composition—55 percent Mexican-American, 45 percent Anglo, and 5 percent black—had a somewhat better record. Among the programs initiated to benefit poor persons were public housing, urban renewal (which Corpus Christi's citizens refused to approve), and low-income housing. Moreover, the town's schools were integrated in the 1950s, and racial problems had been minimal. EDA activities and projects had not resulted in any meaningful impact on the poor and minority group members in either Aransas Pass or Corpus Christi.

No concern was evidenced by residents of the Corpus Christi-Aransas Pass growth center area about the needs of persons living in the four EDA-designated redevelopment areas.

Ft. Smith, Arkansas. Ft. Smith, Arkansas, is the primary economic development center of the Western Arkansas Economic Development District (WAEDD). The district, which was incorporated in August of 1966, is depicted in figure 8-7. The WAEDD consists of six counties grouped along the Oklahoma border in west central Arkansas. Four of these are redevelopment areas, and two are eligible for grant assistance under Title I of the EDA act.

Ft. Smith, which was designated as an EDC in June 1967, is located in Sebastian County and is the largest city in a 100-mile radius, with Little Rock to the east and Tulsa to the west. It is completely surrounded by RA counties. Sequoyah and Le Flore, both in Oklahoma, are to the west; and Crawford, Franklin, Logan, and Scott in Arkansas complete the circle.

Ft. Smith acts as a center for many government services and trade activities.

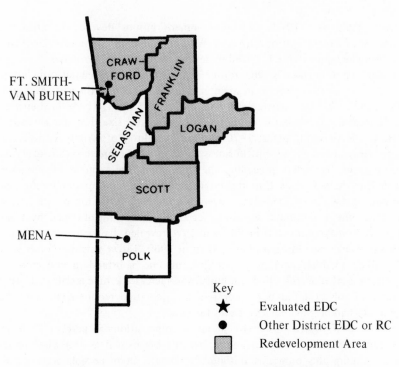

Figure 8–7. Western Arkansas Economic Development District

In 1971, the Employment Security Division estimated that 35 to 50 percent of the town's work force commuted from outside the city limits. The east-west interstate route passing through the growth center facilitates such commuting. Hospital, banking, and educational facilities also serve a wide geographic area, and the Ft. Smith newspaper is the third largest in the state, with subscribers in 14 surrounding counties. EDA evaluators conducted field work in Ft. Smith during March of 1971.

EDA Project Impact. EDA had obligated $3.1 million for six projects in Ft. Smith as compared with approximately $4 million for fifteen projects in the district's RAs. Three of the growth center projects were completed at the time of evaluation. The first Ft. Smith project was approved in June 1967, and involved the construction of a "scientific library" with an EDA cost of $627,000. Justification for this project was twofold. A computer terminal in the library was expected to provide services to technology-based industries already in the area, and the library itself was described as a facility that would improve public services and make Ft. Smith more attractive to new industries.

Although space was set aside for the terminal, it had not been installed at the time of evaluation. EDA could not fund the installation fee and monthly rental charges because of its restriction on rental equipment, and the city had not yet assumed the cost. Even had the computer been installed, however, its utility would have been questionable. Firms without alternative computer facilities are unlikely to have the in-house capability to program their requirements for computer solution. Furthermore, Ft. Smith had a substantial computer service company which local industry already used heavily.

The project's public service impact was also difficult to verify. The district director suggested that one industry located in Ft. Smith because, in addition to the basic requisites for a profitable business, the city possessed the facilities essential to an attractive quality of life. There was no evidence, however, that the library was a significant factor and, in fact, tipped the scales in favor of Ft. Smith.

Service benefits from the library to outlying RAs were minimal. It replaced an older facility but no significant increase in holdings or the volume of circulation had been noted. Residents of other counties had to pay a small charge, and there were no mobile facilities for outreach to RA residents.

A sixteen-inch water pipeline had also been constructed in the growth center with EDA's assistance. This line, which provided service to several industries, was completed at an EDA cost of $43,190 as the first step in an $875,000 water and street improvement project. One of the firms benefiting from the project was Hickory Springs Manufacturing Co. of Arkansas, Inc., a producer of foam rubber. Hickory Springs provided stable employment for over 200 persons and had been expanding in recent years.

With plant demands increasing, local water supply and pressure levels were nearing insurance safety margins. The situation was desperate and Hickory Springs considered leaving the Ft. Smith area. At the recommendation of the local Chamber of Commerce, Hickory Springs decided to relocate in the industrial area serviced by the new water line rather than leave Ft. Smith altogether. Thus, these jobs were attributable to the EDA investment. The firm's management would not allow the EDA evaluators to sample the labor force, however.

Of the other industries serviced by the water line, none located in the area or expanded operations as a result of the project. For this reason, no further jobs could be credited to the EDA investment nor will additional employment result from the future street improvements, because the industrial land serviced is already filled.

The third completed EDA project in Ft. Smith consisted of a $380,000 public works grant to increase the water supply of the city and nearby towns. Funded in April 1968, this project had increased the city water supply by 50 percent to 31 million gallons per day. The expansion resulted in better service to all residential and industrial users in the city and to other towns, which now may purchase surplus water. However, it was not possible to attribute any specific employment impact to the project. The one industrial "bird-in-hand" prospect linked to this project—Owens-Illinois Co.—had not located in Ft. Smith.

EDA funds had also been obligated for three other projects in Ft. Smith. These included two sewage pump stations, a day care center, and an expansion to a vocational-technical facility. The latter was a $1.5 million project financed by the Ozarks Regional Commission, EDA, and local contributors. The facility was not in operation at the time of the evaluation, but college administrators hoped to provide training for RA residents. Unfortunately, prospective students from these places may be deterred by the tuition rates, which at the time of the evaluation were double for persons living outside the growth center county. Table 8-8 presents additional information on the three completed projects in Ft. Smith.

At the time of evaluation, a partially disbursed EDA grant to fund the construction of two sewage pump stations had already resulted in the creation of thirty jobs at Gerber Products Company. However, since the project was not yet

Table 8-8
EDA Project Impact in Ft. Smith

Evaluation Category	Library	Water Line and Street Improvement	Water Treatment Facilities	TOTAL
Project Cost	$1,234,000	$1,336,500	$635,000	$3,205,500
EDA Participation	$ 627,000	$ 43,000[a]	$380,000	$1,050,000[a]
Percent Occupied or		($ 875,000)[b]		($1,882,000)[b]
Operational	100%	100%	100%	
EDA-Attributed Jobs	0	200 (saved)	0	200 (saved)
EDA-Attributed Jobs to RA Residents	0	No Data	0	0
EDA-Attributed Jobs to Formerly Unemployed and Underemployed Persons	0	No Data	0	0
EDC Residents	0	No Data	0	0
RA Residents	0	No Data	0	0
EDA Investment Per Job	—	$ 215[a] ($ 4,375)[b]	—	$ 5,250[a] ($ 9,410)[b]
EDA Investment Per RA Job	—	No Data	—	No Data
Yearly Salary Generated	0	No Data	0	0

[a]Based on Phase I, water line

[b]Based on Phases I and II — Total

Source: Program Evaluation: The Economic Development Administration Growth Center Strategy, Washington, D.C.: U.S. Department of Commerce/Economic Development Administration, February 1972, p. 56

complete, the evaluators felt it would be misleading to include the thirty jobs in the investment per job figure. No additional future jobs could be predicted as a result of the Ft. Smith projects.

PAP Effectiveness. Ft. Smith submitted its first PAP in May of 1968, shortly after EDA issued its policy statement on growth centers. Funds for the library and for expansion of the city water supply had already been obligated before the PAP was written. Only the remaining four projects were approved under the PAP requirement.

Written by the district staff, the PAP listed several desirable programs: expansion of the vocational education school, notifying RA residents of job openings, provision of bus service to RA residents, more low-cost housing, development of a recreation facility, and CAP Agency involvement in Sebastian County. All of these programs except the bus service were being implemented at the time of evaluation. Some, however, had been in operation prior to preparation of the PAP, and it was the consensus of the PAP Committee and other community leaders that even the new efforts would have taken place in the absence of the PAP.

In fact, there was little local interest in Ft. Smith's role in the district, and the PAP was seen simply as an administrative requirement. Most community leaders had never heard of the PAP or what it was supposed to accomplish. This appeared to be a result, in large part, of lack of guidance from EDA when the PAP was being prepared.

Role of the District Organization. The district staff supported the growth center concept, but it was difficult to pinpoint any activities aimed at implementing such a strategy. The staff felt that EDA investments in the EDCs had resulted in greater impact than projects in RAs, but believed that RA projects support the development of the district and should continue to be funded. All eligible counties with the exception of Scott had received EDA projects, and all counties received technical assistance from the staff.

Although the two growth center counties were the largest financial contributors, the RAs were well represented on the board. It appeared that the RA board members were involved in making decisions and were not dominated by the growth center interests.

Status of the Economic Development Process. The evaluators found Ft. Smith citizens to be preoccupied with internal development and spillover to RA counties was incidental. This parochialism was accompanied by a lack of strong leadership. Historically conservative elements had opposed a number of progressive factions which had been unable to join forces.

Mechanization in agriculture accounted for large declines in that sector during and immediately after World War II. Out-migration from the district resulted in a

22 percent drop in population between 1950 and 1960. When the Fort Chaffe Army Base left Ft. Smith in 1962, taking with it the last of a peak troop strength of 100,000, the community realized it had to take action.

For a short period, industrial development activities flourished and out-migration slowed considerably, but at the time of the evaluation, the concern sparked by the fort's closing seemed to have dwindled. The traditional interests of land, lumber, and the furniture industry were resisting change, and the local government had not produced significant new leadership. Issues such as zoning and public bonds had been consistently thwarted.

In January 1969, a city manager form of government was established in Ft. Smith. It may be that this unfamiliar form of government had failed thus far to establish rapport with the public. However, even if there were more popular support and understanding of the new administration, it was not clear that attitudes or efforts toward development and the solution of community problems would significantly improve.

Natchez, Mississippi. The Southwest Mississippi Economic Development District (SMEDD), which is shown in figure 8-8, was incorporated in January 1965, and first funded by EDA in February 1967. The ten counties of the district are grouped into two subdistricts. One group, including two RA counties, is

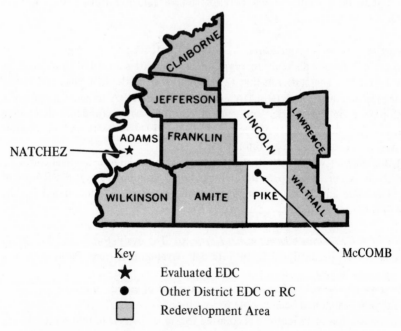

Figure 8–8. Southwest Mississippi Economic Development District

clustered around the secondary EDC of McComb. The second group of five RA counties is oriented toward the district's primary EDC, Natchez, which was visited by an EDA evaluation team in mid-February 1971.

A city of approximately 20,000 persons, Natchez became an EDC at the time of district designation on June 6, 1967. Located on the Mississippi River, the town enjoyed importance as a cotton exchange prior to the Civil War. However, as synthetics gradually cut into the cotton market, agriculture and trading declined, and the areas around Natchez were plagued with unemployment and low income. This situation still existed at the time of the evaluation.

EDA Project Impact. At the time of the field work, only two projects had been completed in the Natchez economic development center. The first was a business loan to Ricks Lumber Company, Inc., for $529,750 out of a total investment of $1.275 million. This company was first established in Natchez in 1959. In 1968, its plant was totally destroyed by fire. Following the loss, management bought an interim yard to maintain service to customers. However, the labor force was reduced from fifty to approximately twenty-two.

With the aid of EDA's loan, Ricks was able to build one of the most modern and highly automated sawmills in the United States. Without the loan funds, Ricks would not have been able to finance construction.

At the time of the evaluation, Ricks had sixty employees working at an average wage of $100 per week. Additional equipment was on order, and with its installment, total employment was expected to increase to sixty-five. In addition, the management indicated that the mill generated fifty temporary jobs for loggers. Approximately $850,000 per year was spent locally for timber, most of which came from redevelopment areas.

Of the jobs that could be credited to EDA (twenty-eight saved and ten new), five went to redevelopment area residents and two were taken by previously unemployed persons. Total annual income generated by these jobs amounted to approximately $197,600. A summary of job impact from this project is given in table 8-9. Since the jobs were an expansion of existing employment, they could not be considered as a diversification of Natchez's economic structure.

The second project, a $25,000 technical assistance feasibility study, involved investigating the possibility of expanding existing port facilities on the Mississippi River. The Natchez port, which was built with city and county funds, was used primarily by International Paper Company for its pulp traffic. Cost to users was based on actual operating expenses and as a public facility, it was tax free. Thus, costs to International Paper were lower than if the company maintained its own facilities.

The feasibility study was initiated because the port had only one loading point, and could not handle any additional traffic. The study recommended the addition of a liquid shipment facility and an extension to the present wharf to permit a second loading point. However, the liquid shipment facility was built

Table 8–9
EDA Project Impact in Natchez

Evaluation Category	Ricks Lumber Company
Project Cost	$1,275,000
EDA Participation	530,000
Percent Occupied or Operational	100%
EDA-Attributed Jobs	38
	(28 saved, 10 new)
EDA-Attributed Jobs to RA Residents	5
EDA-Attributed Jobs to Formerly Unemployed	
and Underemployed Persons	2
EDC Residents	2
RA Residents	0
EDA Investment Per Job	$ 13,948
EDA Investment Per RA Job	$ 106,000
Yearly Salary Generated	$ 197,600

Source: *Program Evaluation: The Economic Development Administration Growth Center Strategy*, Washington, D.C.: U.S. Department of Commerce/Economic Development Administration, February 1972, p. 60

before the report was submitted, and no activities had been undertaken to finance the other expansion. Impact due to the study, therefore, was minimal at the time of evaluation.

A final EDA project in Natchez was a $42,000 study of improvements to the present airport. The improvements involved extending a runway to insure continued commercial air service and preparing land for commercial development. The report had not been completed at the time of the evaluation, and no employment or service benefit was foreseen for some time. Three future jobs were credited to Ricks, lowering the EDA investment per job in Natchez to $12,927.

PAP Effectiveness. The Positive Action Program for Natchez was written by the executive director of the development district in February 1969. The director felt he had been unable to obtain sufficient guidance either from EDA-Washington or the area office in preparing the PAP. Cooperation of the State Employment Service, local school system, minority group members, Chamber of Commerce staff members, and city and county officials was cited in the PAP. However, no committee was instituted for its formulation or implementation.

The operators of programs mentioned in the PAP were not familiar with the document's purpose or content. Community leaders likewise knew little about the PAP. Three of the four district board members from the growth center had not heard of it. The incoming president of the board, also a Natchez resident, was aware of the PAP and had some idea of its general objectives. However, he was unable to identify any of the action programs.

The action programs set forth in the PAP included construction of a new vocational-technical facility in an RA, development of industrial sites in the center, promotion of tourism, provision of employment information to RA residents, and establishment of a licensed practical nurse training program at the city's hospital.

After two years, there had been few accomplishments in the areas cited by the PAP. Vocational-technical training facilities in Natchez did not service any RA residents, and the school mentioned in the PAP had no connection with Natchez, the PAP or EDA's growth center strategy. The one potentially significant program was a job notification system to be operated by the city. A census of available Natchez jobs was to be taken periodically and the results published in redevelopment area newspapers. Interviews with the mayor, leaders of the chamber, and RA residents produced no evidence that these activities were ever undertaken. The State Employment Service, however, had carried out this activity prior to center designation and continued to do so. This, of course, was not a result of the PAP and was not supported by the city or county, but by the state.

Role of the District Organization. The district board was composed of seven representatives from each of the ten counties. Its executive committee consisted of one member from each county, plus all past presidents, and the local share of the district budget was financed by a 20 cent per capita assessment on each county. Thus, the most populous counties, which are those containing the EDCs of Natchez and McComb, were the heaviest contributors. However, this arrangement did not visibly affect policy decisions of the board or activities of the staff. The district offices were located in McComb, but according to the district director, this location had not had a significant impact on the staff's work program.

With regard to the growth center strategy, the district director stated that his objective was to provide equitable distribution of staff time and effort to all district counties. This equality was sought by calling regular board meetings throughout the district. The director, however, believed that the greatest potential for significant economic development lay within the growth centers. Local conditions supported this belief. Any spillover impact to the redevelopment areas was seen by growth center residents as incidental.

There was some feeling, particularly in the RA of Franklin County, that the district staff was overly attentive to the growth center counties. Interviewees in both Wilkinson and Franklin Counties stated that more emphasis should be placed on locating industry in the redevelopment areas. On the other hand, growth center residents opposed emphasizing the goal of providing jobs to RA residents. The fact that RA commuters found employment in Natchez, but provided no tax base because they lived outside the city was particularly aggravating to Natchez residents at a time when revenues were sorely needed. At the time of evaluation, a commuter tax was under consideration.

District staff services consisted primarily of writing the OEDP and PAP, and helping to prepare project applications. The staff assisted the centers and the RAs alike with the latter function, and in fact, more EDA project dollars had been obligated in the RAs than the centers. The district staff did not seem to have assigned any priority to center projects or the center strategy.

Status of the Economic Development Process. Although the development process in Natchez had undergone some changes in recent years, none could be attributed to EDA designation or the growth center strategy. The election of a new city administration in 1968 was seen by some as an indication of more progressive attitudes.

Local leaders suggested that the Adams County government did not promote development as actively as did the city, yet even the county supported such projects as the port improvement. The two largest banks in Natchez were taking part in development activities such as low cost private housing, a new county water system, and the loan to Ricks Lumber Company.

The evaluators reported that the leadership of Natchez was composed primarily of businessmen, bankers, utility managers, and professional men. The remaining aristocracy, whose power was based on fortunes made in cotton, oil, and real estate, was less interested in development than were the younger community leaders. Organizations such as the Chamber of Commerce, the Industrial Development Commission, and civic groups supported and had often taken the lead in promoting development projects. They had solicited the location of industries with some success, particularly in the cases of International Paper and Diamond National.

Panama City, Florida. In April 1971, an EDA field evaluation was conducted in Panama City, Florida, the primary economic development center of the Northwest Florida Economic Development District. The district, which is depicted in figure 8-9, is a ten-county area located in the northwest panhandle of Florida on the Gulf of Mexico. Two of the ten counties—Holmes and Franklin—have had redevelopment area status for some time, and a third, Walton, has recently been qualified as an RA on the basis of a sudden rise in unemployment. The secondary economic development center, Mariana, is located in Jackson County.

Panama City, with a 1970 population of approximately 32,000, was first designated as an EDC in April 1968, at the same time the district was designated. The boundaries of the growth center extend beyond the municipal boundaries of Panama City to include virtually all gulf and bay-front land in Bay County.

The orientation of redevelopment area residents toward Panama City varies according to distance and the presence of nearer facilities. Holmes County is almost an hour's drive from Panama City. Consequently, there is little commuting to Panama City itself, although Holmes County residents do commute to the

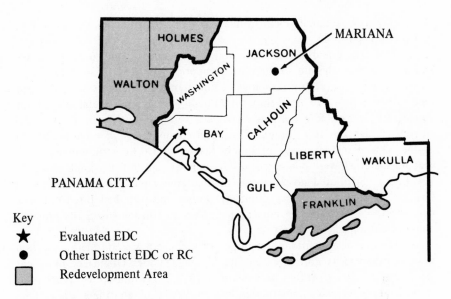

Key
★ Evaluated EDC
● Other District EDC or RC
▨ Redevelopment Area

Figure 8-9. Northwest Florida Economic Development District

beach areas in south Walton and south Bay Counties. Franklin County is almost twice as far from Panama City, and commuting is almost nonexistent.

EDA Project Impact. At the time of evaluation, EDA had funded only one project in Panama City. On October 14, 1968, $2,075,000 in EDA funds were obligated for the expansion of port facilities and improvement of adjacent industrial land in Panama City. A public works grant for $1,035,000 and a public works loan for $1,040,000 accounted for 100 percent of the project cost. Before this expansion was undertaken, the city had two separate docking facilities: one owned and operated by International Paper Company; the other city-owned and operated through the Panama City Port Authority. The latter could accommodate only one vessel at a time.

The additional berth constructed with EDA assistance allowed the port to accommodate two vessels simultaneously, and a new warehouse provided storage space. In addition to increasing the traffic capacity of the port, the project improved adjacent industrial land by removal of concrete foundations formerly used for shipbuilding. It was hoped that these improvements would induce the location of industry that would utilize both the industrial sites and port facilities.

At the time of the evaluation, employment impact from this project was extremely limited, partially because construction was not completed until August 1970. The Port Authority had hired seven full-time employees, and had increased part-time employment, which was estimated to be equivalent to four new full-time positions.

A shipwrecking and salvage operation, Cove Construction Company, which had been located adjacent to the port for approximately ten years, was able to take on thirty new full-time employees. Employment increases were due to the fact that the firm can now ship substantially more scrap metal out of the Panama City port. All of the new employees were previously out of work, and all were residents of Bay County. They received an average of three months of on-the-job training. A survey of supply firms to Cove Construction indicated that no materials were purchased in RA counties, and in fact, suppliers within Bay County attributed no expansion in their employment to Cove's increased business. A steamship agency company serving the port had hired one new employee as a result of the port project. Table 8-10 summarizes the project's employment impact.

At the time of evaluation, a manufacturing concern was considering location near the Panama City Port because of its shipping facilities. Original employment was expected to be 300 with expansion to 1,200 within three years after start-up. However, since construction had not yet begun and there was no firm commitment for a starting date, employment and investment per job figures for Panama City were not adjusted to reflect this possible impact.

PAP Effectiveness. Panama City's original Positive Action Program was written in mid-1968 and accepted by EDA in September of that year. It resulted from a meeting called by the mayor at the instigation of the district's executive

Table 8-10
EDA Project Impact in Panama City

Evaluation Category	Port Project
Project Cost	$2,075,000
EDA Participation	$2,075,000
Percent Occupied or Operational	Port – 100%
EDA-Attributed Jobs	42
EDA-Attributed Jobs to RA's	0
EDA-Attributed Jobs to Formerly Unemployed and Underemployed Persons	42
EDC Residents	42
RA Residents	0
EDA Investment Per Job	$ 49,405
EDA Investment Per RA Job	
Yearly Salary Generated	$ 210,000

Source: Program Evaluation: The Economic Administration Growth Center Strategy, Washington, D.C.: U.S. Department of Commerce/Economic Development Administration, February 1972, p. 65

director. Business and civic leaders were given a general presentation and asked for letters of support to attach to the PAP document. The executive director and staff prepared the actual document which was being updated at the time of the evaluation.

On paper, the PAP appeared to be a straightforward attempt to address problems of low income and unemployment in the district. The action programs dealt with transportation from RAs to Panama City, job placement for RA residents, extra programs for the poor and disadvantaged, etc. The most impressive aspect, however, was the number of supporting letters and their apparent grasp of the PAP's purpose. These letters employed terms almost identical to those in the PAP guidelines EDA distributes to development districts.

Interviews with those signing the supporting letters and persons responsible for various action programs suggested that the PAP was not all that it appeared to be. Almost without exception, these individuals were unfamiliar with the PAP and its purposes. Moreover, none of the proposed programs was initiated as a result of the PAP.

The makeup of the district's board of directors was substantially changed in the fall of 1970, and a new committee was formed to redraw and implement the PAP. Almost all members of the new committee, which included older members of the "establishment," young professionals, one black, and two blue-collar workers, were interviewed during the evaluation. Some were quite dynamic and appeared to be genuinely concerned with making the committee work. However, they had no understanding of the PAP's purpose or their role in relation to it. The consensus seemed to be that the committee would serve as a citizen advisory group for any and all development efforts taking place in Panama City.

Role of the District Organization. The staff and executive director of the Northwest Florida Development Council and Economic Development District were satisfied with the EDA growth center strategy as they perceived it. It had imposed few requirements on them which they would not have undertaken anyway, and they felt that their function was to help the growth center on the same basis that they help any other part of the district, designated or nondesignated.

They had undertaken a reorganization of the PAP Committee as discussed above, but it was not clear that this committee would in fact work to implement a strategy consistent with EDA's goals. Spreading the benefits of Panama City's growth to the redevelopment areas and nondesignated counties of the district played a minor role in the committee's programs. None of the board members contacted had any knowledge of the connection between the center and the redevelopment areas.

Status of the Economic Development Process. The evaluators found that in a state generally associated with lucrative year-round vacation trade, Panama City continued to face many of the problems found elsewhere in the rural south. Surrounding areas had experienced a decline in farm activity, while the city witnessed the boom and bust of wartime ship building, and was for a short time the one-industry town so often associated with large paper mills.

In the past, city administrations exhibited a variety of attitudes toward development. Around 1960, a $7.4 million bond issue for construction of two city marinas, an auditorium, and city hall was approved. Since that time, a more conservative administration had concentrated on balancing the city budget. The present mayor was characterized as being very "middle-of-the-road."

There was some indication, however, that the genuine seat of power in Panama City lay with a few wealthy families, rather than in the visible political structure. These families controlled the banks and a substantial portion of local real estate. They appeared to be the real motivating, or obstructing, force in the city.

In the past, International Paper Company, the largest employer in Panama City (800 jobs), wielded a great deal of power in the county. For a long period, the "company town" of Millville remained independent of Panama City, although at the time of the evaluation, it lay within the municipal boundaries. Another powerful, but somewhat latent economic force in Bay County were the land holders. Up to 50 percent of the county was held by St. Joe Paper Company and an oil company. This not only limited tax revenues, as this type of land carries special tax favors, but hampered development.

A surprising number of those interviewed were quite frank in discussing local attitudes, and most indicated that Panama City, its community organizations, and churches were generally unaware, unconcerned, or at least uninvolved with the problems of the poor. The situation was no different with respect to poverty and distress in the outlying areas of the district.

One factor that seemed to have resulted in cooperation among Panama City leaders was the census finding that the city's population decreased during the 1960-70 decade. This, and the threat that the Naval Research Laboratory might leave the area, had sparked interest in development activities.

EDA appeared to have had no effect on Panama City's development process. However, the district staff was working with local residents on the center's own problems which had to be resolved before it could really begin to serve the more distressed areas of the district.

Pine Bluff, Arkansas. The Southeastern Arkansas Economic Development District (SEAEDD) was organized in April of 1967 and designated in January of 1968. Pine Bluff was designated as the district's primary EDC at the same time. The growth center designation was extended to include Sheridan in adjoining Grant County in March of 1969, forming a growth corridor between the two towns. An additional growth center—Crossett-Hamburg in Ashley County—was designated in August 1970.

The district is a ten-county area, including six redevelopment area counties. It is depicted in figure 8-10. Pine Bluff, which is located in Jefferson County forty-four miles southeast of Little Rock, serves three RA counties to the south.

The 1970 population of Pine Bluff was 57,389, a 30 percent increase over 1960. A telephone survey conducted by the SEAEDD indicated that 20 percent of Pine Bluff's labor force commutes to the city from distances of up to thirty miles. Thirty percent of the district's population of 228,000 is black and 45 percent of these reside in Jefferson County.

Project Impact. EDA had funded two projects in Pine Bluff that were complete at the time of the evaluation. The first was a $275,000 public works grant for an industrial park with a total cost of $601,000. There are 500 commercial acres in the park, and 13 were occupied by three companies at the time of the evaluation. The firms were the Pine Bluff Casket, Pepsi Cola Bottling and Superior Forwarding Companies. Only the employment at the trucking company could be attributed to EDA. Both the casket company and the bottling company were formerly located in Pine Bluff and would have remained within the city even if the industrial land prepared with EDA's assistance had not been available.

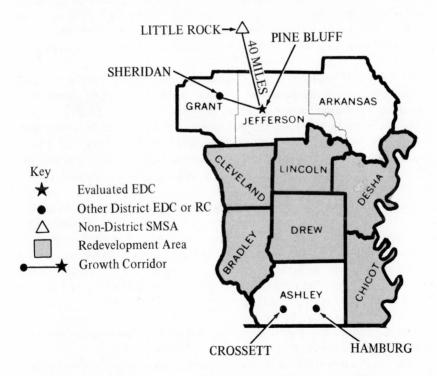

Figure 8-10. Southeastern Arkansas Economic Development District

Superior Forwarding Company employed eleven people with an average annual salary of $9,634 (annual income generation of $105,974). The evaluators reported that the firm was stable and employment was year-round. Therefore, for the industrial park, the EDA cost per direct job was approximately $25,000.

EDA approval in April 1968 of the Jefferson Industrial Park was followed one month later by approval of a port facility and adjacent industrial park project to be owned and operated by the Pine Bluff-Jefferson County Port Authority. A $1.2 million bond issue for a port facility was approved by Pine Bluff voters in 1965. After the town's designation as an EDC, matching EDA funds of $1.2 million were granted, further supplemented by a bank loan of $800,000. The project, completed in March of 1970, includes 372 acres of prepared industrial land, 55 of which were occupied at the time of evaluation. Five public and private facilities were associated with the Pine Bluff Port. However, employment at two of these could not be attributed to EDA.

EDA-attributable jobs were found at two terminal companies and at the Pine Bluff Sand and Gravel Company. Pine Bluff Warehouse Company, the source of eleven attributable jobs, was the successful bidder on a contract to operate the public port facilities for the Port Authority. Because of lack of business, the company would have been forced to lay off seven workers at its major warehouse in Pine Bluff if it had not received the contract. The increased business from the port facility, however, permitted Pine Bluff Warehouse not only to maintain its prior employment, but also to add four persons to its work force.

The Pine Bluff Sand and Gravel Company, under contract with the Corps of Engineers to assist in dredging the Arkansas, added six new employees to its general haulage section because of traffic through the EDA port facility.

Martin Terminals is a bulk chemical shipper, wholly owned by a Pine Bluff resident. The firm had erected storage tanks and portside pumping facilities on land purchased from the Port Authority. At the time of the evaluation, this installation was being enlarged. Employment, including the headquarters staff of the company in Pine Bluff, totaled five persons.

The Strong Company, an indirect beneficiary of the EDA project, began as a contracting firm, but was manufacturing roofing equipment at the time of the evaluation. Vermiculite, part of its roofing compound, is imported from South America. Formerly this was shipped from Louisiana by rail, but the port project enabled the company to bring the material in by barge, at a considerable saving. The owner indicated that between three and five workers would be added to his payroll within the next two years as a result of his better competitive position. The discounting formula discussed in chapter 6 allows three of these jobs to be counted as future employment impact. Including these jobs reduces the EDA investment per job in Pine Bluff to $41,139.

Table 8-11 summarizes the direct job impact attributable to the two EDA projects. All employment was in firms considered to be of intermediate stability

Table 8–11
EDA Project Impact in Pine Bluff

Evaluation Category	Industrial Park	Port Facility and Industrial Park	TOTAL
Project Cost	$601,000	$2,615,000	$3,216,000
EDA Participation	$275,000	$1,206,000	$1,481,000
Percent Occupied or Operational	2.6%	14.8% (Industrial site)	
EDA-Attributed Jobs	11	22	33
EDA-Attributed Jobs to RA Residents	0	1	1
EDA-Attributed Jobs to Formerly Unemployed and Underemployed Persons	7	6	13
EDC Residents	7	6	13
RA Residents	0	0	0
EDA Investment Per Job	$ 25,000	$ 54,800	$ 44,879
EDA Investment Per RA Job	—	$1,206,000	$1,481,000
Yearly Salary Generated	$106,000	$ 136,000	$ 242,000

Source: Program Evaluation: The Economic Development Administration Growth Center Strategy, Washington, D.C.: U.S. Department of Commerce/Economic Development Administration, Feburary 1972, p. 71

(see chapter 6), and there had been no diversification of the economic base. Only one of the thirty-three jobs credited to EDA was taken by an RA resident; however, five of the twelve employees who completed EDA questionnaires were previously unemployed or underemployed residents of Pine Bluff. Neither project had improved public services, and there was no evidence of significant purchases of goods or services from the redevelopment areas by project beneficiaries. Total annual salary generated by EDA-attributed employment was estimated by the three employers to be $242,000.

The evaluators concluded that the port project undoubtedly had long-run potential, but reported that the city had demonstrated a willingness to undertake the project before EDA assistance was available. The value of the industrial park might be questioned because the city already owned an industrial park, which was only partially filled.

A water and sewer project for Sheridan, which is part of the growth center area, was approved in June 1969. Since the facility was not expected to be operational until mid-1971, an extensive evaluation of Sheridan was not undertaken. The project will affect two industrial parks already serving a number of firms, but no specific impact could be projected at the time of evaluation.

PAP Effectiveness. Pine Bluff's Positive Action Program was accepted by EDA in December 1968. It was subsequently updated, with few substantive changes. Although a committee of eleven EDC citizens was formed to prepare the PAP, its members played only a minor role. It was written, in fact, by the deputy director of the district.

All members of the committee were interviewed and none had a clear knowledge of what the PAP was designed to do; some were even unfamiliar with the name of the program. The executive director of the district was quite frank in his assessment of the PAP as being merely a bothersome requirement for the acquisition of federal funds.

Action programs listed in the PAP concerned the provision of vocational education to residents of RAs, formation of a biracial council to address minority problems in Pine Bluff, and provision of health and day care services to residents of outlying areas. Both vocational education institutions within the city predated the PAP and other EDA activities. No expansion of services had resulted from the PAP. The mayor's Human Relations Commission was a functioning group, but the impetus for this group was the violence precipitated by the death of Martin Luther King in the spring of 1968—not the PAP.

The evaluators reported that the Jefferson County Hospital, cited in the PAP as a source of health care for the RAs, offered treatment at a cost that was prohibitive for persons with low incomes. Most of these people traveled to Little Rock, where they obtained free services from the University teaching hospital. Day care centers were available in Pine Bluff, but these were originated by OEO and had no relation to EDA activities. There were frank admissions that the primary concern of Pine Bluff was for its own residents. Outlying areas were considered only as they might coincidentally contribute to the growth of Pine Bluff or Jefferson County.

Role of the District Organization. The district staff was judged to be a group of dedicated professionals. The director was once a state legislator, and had since successfully championed a bill to provide matched-share planning money from the state. He and his staff had been effective in obtaining EDA and other federal grants not only for the growth center, but for the redevelopment areas as well.

The district staff was quite open in its opposition to the PAP requirement. The staff members said they felt it duplicated information already included in the OEDP and that no real commitment could be elicited from Pine Bluff in the absence of substantial federal dollar investments.

The staff's orientation was generally district-wide. The location of the office in Pine Bluff did not visibly affect its strategy. The staff's goal was to to distribute federal assistance throughout the counties in accordance with local ability to provide matching funds. District board members were primarily interested in their own counties and were only secondarily concerned with a "district" outlook. They helped Pine Bluff in its attempts to secure federal funding and expected similar assistance for their own counties in return.

The district board was composed of forty-two members, ten of whom came from the growth center. Unlike the separate PAP Committee, it met regularly and there was good communication among the members. The growth center strategy had a low order of priority in the board's deliberations, though it willingly supported applications filed by the EDC. One of the strongest board leaders came from the redevelopment county of Desha. The heaviest financial contributors were Pine Bluff and Jefferson County, nearly $6,000 each. However, this did not seem to affect the distribution of projects within the district, although Pine Bluff had received the most costly projects. Distribution appeared to be on the basis of need and the ability to provide matching local financial support.

Status of the Economic Development Process. There had been some changes in Pine Bluff's economic development process in recent years. Private developers had taken advantage of HUD rent subsidy programs. About 460 units had been built; two more housing projects were in the planning stage. A city housing authority was finally created in January of 1971, and the mayor, elected in 1965, was enthusiastic about prospects of extensive low-rent housing over the next five to ten years.

The Office of Economic Opportunity had funded day care centers, community centers, and a Head Start program. These served residents of Pine Bluff and Jefferson County. An Urban Renewal Agency for the city had been established, a program begun, and a new city hall had been built in a renewal neighborhood. Local merchants had begun a face-lifting campaign for the shopping district, and the largest bank in Pine Bluff had undertaken a major renovation of its building's exterior.

The two major banks in Pine Bluff are the National Bank of Commerce, and the Simmons First National Bank. Both were actively engaged in development activities, and each had a loan-to-deposit ratio of .60. These activities, however, had no link to the Positive Action Program, EDC designation, or other EDA activities related to the growth center strategy.

Swainsboro, Georgia. Swainsboro, Georgia, was designated by EDA on November 28, 1967, as the first secondary growth center in the country. This action climaxed months of effort on the part of Swainsboro citizens and the staff of the Central Savannah River Economic Development District.

As illustrated in figure 8-11, Swainsboro is situated in the heart of Emanuel County, which is the southernmost county in the Central Savannah River District. In 1970, the town's population was 7,325, which compares with a population of 59,864 for Augusta, the district's primary growth center. Eight of the thirteen counties in the district are EDA-designated redevelopment areas, and three of these are located within a twenty-mile radius of Swainsboro. However, the largest municipality in each of the redevelopment area counties is at least thirty miles from Swainsboro. A three-man EDA evaluation team

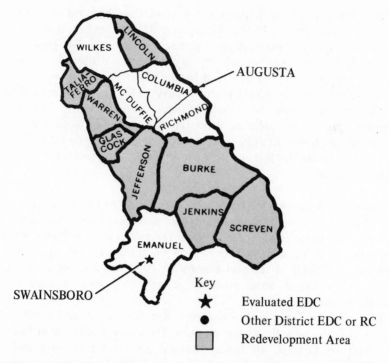

Figure 8-11. Central Savannah River Economic Development District

conducted field work in Swainsboro between February 21 and February 28, 1971.

EDA Project Impact. Two EDA projects had been completed in Swainsboro since its designation and another was approximately 30 percent finished. The completed projects consisted of: (1) a public works grant and loan for the development of a 525-acre industrial park (Magic Mall), four-lane access highway, and related improvements; and (2) a business loan to a manufacturing firm (Keller Stamping & Electric Co.) located in the Magic Mall Industrial Park. The partially completed project was a public works supplementary grant in support of a $1 million water and sewer extension project financed by the Federal Water Quality Administration and the Swainsboro city government.

As a result of EDA assistance to these projects, 387 jobs had been created or saved in Swainsboro. Approximately 8 percent of these jobs were taken by present or former residents of redevelopment areas. This represented an EDA investment of approximately $58,000 per job to an RA resident. Table 8-12 presents data on each of the projects.

Approximately 30 percent of the jobs attributable to EDA were filled by

Table 8-12
EDA Project Impact in Swainsboro

Evaluation Category	Magic Mall Industrial Park	Keller Stamping & Electric Co.	Water and Sewer Extension	TOTAL
Project Cost	$ 816,000	$1,263,910	$1,050,000	$3,131,910
EDA Participation	$ 816,000	$ 821,521	$ 194,000	$1,831,531
Percent Occupied or Operational	5.7%	100%	–	–
EDA-Attributed Jobs	52+ Keller jobs	256	79 (Saved)	387
EDA-Attributed Jobs to RA Residents	10 (28[a])	18	4[b]	32
EDA-Attributed Jobs to Formerly Unemployed and Underemployed Persons	12 (112)[a]	100		112
EDC Residents	12 (97)[a]	85	No Data	97
RA Residents	0 (11)[a]	11	No Data	11
EDA Investment Per Job	$ 15,692 ($ 2,469)[a]	$ 3,209	$ 2,456	$ 4,478
EDA Investment Per RA Job	$ 81,600 ($ 60,649)[a]	$ 68,460	$ 48,500[b]	$ 58,483
Yearly Salary Generated	$ 302,000 ($1,317,000)[a]	$1,015,000	$ 261,000	$1,578,000

[a]Includes Keller jobs
[b]Based on parking lot survey and not included in aggregate figures
Source: Program Evaluation: The Economic Development Administration Growth Center Strategy, Washington, D.C.: U.S. Department of Commerce/Economic Development Administration, February 1972, p. 76

members of poor households, while 27 percent were held by members of minority groups. In addition, 59 percent of the jobs were held by heads of households. Moreover, approximately $20,000 more a year was spent in RA counties by local residents as a result of these jobs.

The secondary effects of the three EDA-assisted projects had been minimal. No suppliers or buyers had located in the area as a result of the projects. However, one firm whose location in the vicinity was partially attributable to the industrial park project reported that it purchased approximately $115,000 worth of timber a month. Approximately 60 percent of this timber came from Emanuel County, but the remaining 40 percent was primarily from the redevelopment area counties of Burke, Jenkins, and Jefferson. The other industries purchased only utilities and clerical supplies locally.

The majority of the employees at EDA-associated plants who were previously employed had increased their incomes. Wages paid by employers located in the

Magic Mall averaged 10 to 15 cents above the minimum hourly wage of $1.60. Training was confined to on-the-job instruction. Attempts to provide more formal training through the Swainsboro Vocational-Technical School had failed because the school's instructors lacked expertise in the relevant technologies.

Two of the firms located in the Magic Mall Industrial Park and another firm which located in Swainsboro as a result of the park were planning expansion at the time of the evaluation. In each case construction was complete but hiring had not begun. According to the discount methodology discussed in chapter 6, the three firms can be credited with a total of fifty-four future jobs. This would reduce the EDA investment per job in Swainsboro to $4,153.

PAP Effectiveness. Swainsboro's Positive Action Program did not reflect any new or expanded commitments on the part of the town toward unemployed and underemployed residents of redevelopment areas. Almost without exception, the programs described in the PAP were related to the development of Swainsboro and Emanual County. Moreover, the majority of these programs were aimed at upper and middle-class residents of Swainsboro.

A number of the programs described in the PAP had been successfully implemented, and progress was being made with relation to others. However, most of these programs were initiated by the local Chamber of Commerce before the town's designation as a growth center. The PAP was credited with providing some impetus for the Chamber to organize and revitalize local committees. However, local leadership changes and the continued development efforts of influential citizens were primarily responsible for such achievements.

Role of the District Organization. Despite the existence of an active, informed board and a well-qualified, competent staff, the Central Savannah River Economic Development District organization had not been particularly effective in implementing the growth center strategy. A number of factors were responsible for this lack of success. Prime among these was the disinterest exhibited by the government and residents of Augusta, the center in the district which displayed the most potential for growth. As a result of the town's attitude, little emphasis had been placed on implementing a growth center strategy through developing projects in Augusta. Rather, the district organization had focused on helping Swainsboro develop as a growth center.

Both the district staff and the Swainsboro representatives on the district board of directors emphasized Swainsboro's ability to serve nearby redevelopment areas. However, board members from other counties, who were willing to help Swainsboro become eligible for more federal funds by supporting its designation as a growth center, privately asserted that it had no more to offer than towns in their home counties. Moreover, the district staff had not encouraged EDA fund recipients in Swainsboro to recruit or give preferential hiring treatment to unemployed and underemployed residents of redevelopment areas. The assumption was that development of Swainsboro would automatically benefit nearby redevelopment areas; that no direct effort to channel project benefits to such places was necessary.

In attempting to implement a growth center strategy through funding projects in Swainsboro, the district staff had been careful to avoid neglecting district redevelopment areas. The staff recognized the parochial attitudes of the various board members and knew that to devote an inordinate amount of time to the development of Swainsboro would result in jealousy and a less effective district program. Thus, efforts were made to insure that federal assistance and staff time were spread evenly among the district counties.

Status of the Economic Development Process. Led by the influence of a local industrial development consultant, the power structure of Swainsboro had become increasingly favorable toward economic development during the past ten to fifteen years. Although a bond election for financing the Magic Mall Industrial Park locally failed in the mid-60s, the 1970 election of an individual closely identified with development efforts suggested that the general public had also become more positive in its attitude toward development. These attitudes were manifested in attempts to attract industry, improve the town's infrastructure, and upgrade service facilities.

The evaluators reported that Swainsboro had actively sought aid from the state and federal government. In addition to EDA assistance, the town had taken advantage of the Federal Housing Administration's (FHA) program providing housing for low-income families, the Office of Economic Opportunity's Head Start program, the Federal Water Quality Administration's sewage treatment program, and several other programs as well.

The local Chamber of Commerce was found to be a particularly effective force for promoting development activities. Through this organization, a number of committees had been established to plan and implement activities aimed at improving the community. These groups met regularly, and had experienced considerable success in implementing projects. Several industrial development groups were also active. Two of the town's major banks had an average loan-to-deposit ratio of .68, and had provided financial support for a number of development projects.

EDA was judged to have played a supporting role with regard to Swainsboro's development process. Development-oriented activities had been initiated and local attitudes were becoming more positive before the town received growth center designation or EDA project funding. However, the psychological lift provided by designation, and the concrete results furnished by EDA project implementation, accelerated local development activities and strengthened the town's commitment to growth.

Tri-Cities, Tennessee-Virginia. The Tri-Cities area (composed of Bristol, Johnson City, and Kingsport, Tennessee, and Bristol, Virginia) was designated by EDA on

June 6, 1967, as the primary economic development center of the First Tennessee-Virginia Economic Development District. The boundary of the Tri-Cities growth center was extended in December of 1968 to include Elizabethton, a community ten miles east of Johnson City in Carter County. The district, which is depicted in figure 8-12, is composed of nine counties, eight of which are located in eastern Tennessee. Three of these, Greene, Hancock, and Johnson Counties, are redevelopment areas.

The growth center cities are approximately 25 miles apart, forming a small triangle in the center of the district. Their combined population has increased from 103,123 in 1960 to 112,898 in 1970. In 1970, the individual populations of the cities were:

1. Bristol, Tennessee-Virginia–34,921
2. Kingsport, Tennessee–31,938
3. Johnson City, Tennessee–33,770
4. Elizabethton, Tennessee–12,269.

Although the mileage between the redevelopment areas and the growth center communities is not excessive, mountainous terrain and poor roads make commuting and routine travel extremely difficult. Field work in the Tri-Cities growth center was conducted by an EDA evaluation team during March 1971.

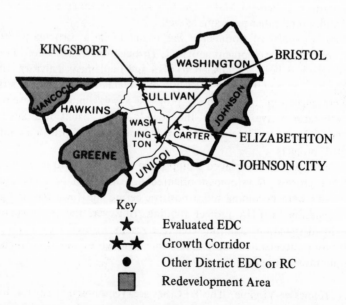

Figure 8-12. First Tennessee-Virginia Economic Development District

EDA Project Impact. EDA had invested heavily in the Tri-Cities growth center. Projects completed at the time of evaluation represented an agency obligation of $7,585,000. An additional $2,325,000 had been obligated for projects not physically completed, or still in the planning stage.

The two major job-creating firms associated with EDA Tri-Cities investments were Jarl Aluminum Extrusion Corporation and Camac Corporation, a producer of synthetic carpet thread. Both firms had received substantial EDA business loans—$4,550,000 and $1,730,000 respectively—and both were also beneficiaries of EDA public works industrial park investments. At the time of evaluation, the two firms employed 107 workers, and had verifiable plans to hire 363 more by the end of 1971.

Camac was located in the Washington County Industrial Park (Virginia), which was funded through two separate EDA projects. These were a $1,008,000 public works grant and loan and a $143,000 public works grant for water and sewage facilities, access roads, storm drainage facilities, and general site preparation. Jarl was able to locate in an industrial park in Elizabethton because of a $154,000 EDA public works grant that provided sewage service.

In addition to the jobs created through Jarl and Camac, EDA-attributed jobs were generated in Bristol Steel Company and Iodent Chemical Company. Bristol Steel had located a steel fabrication plant in the Washington County Industrial Park, and employed eighty-five workers there. Iodent Chemical was located in an industrial park in Carter County, which was served by the same EDA-funded sewage line that served the park in which Jarl was located. Iodent employed thirty-five workers and was credited with fifty-two future jobs.

The major remaining EDA investment in the Tri-Cities area was the Piney Flats Tri-Counties Industrial Park, not physically completed at the time of evaluation. The 800-acre park represented an agency expenditure of $1,885,000 for site preparation. Directly related to the park was an EDA grant of $440,000 for water and sewer lines to service Bristol as well as the park. At the time of the field evaluation, there was no employment in the park. However, Amerace Esna had begun plant construction and expected to employ 225 persons by the end of 1971. Using the discount rate for future jobs reduces this figure to 113. When future jobs and the park investment are included, EDA's investment per job in Tri-Cities increases to $13,126. Table 8-13 presents additional data on the EDA projects in Tri-Cities.

PAP Effectiveness. The Tri-Cities PAP was written by the district organization in March 1968, before the MEDO or guidelines were received from EDA Washington. The PAP was subsequently updated (August 1969) with no significant changes.

The bulk of the PAP was devoted to the development of the Tri-Cities growth center. It emphasized that the cost-benefit ratio for public investment and the potential for growth in general was greater within Tri-Cities because of location and existing social amenities.

Table 8-13
EDA Project Impact in Tri-Cities

Evaluation Category	Jarl[a]	Camac	Wash. County Industrial Park	Carter County Industrial Park	TOTAL
Project Cost	$7,154,000	3,460,000	$1,151,000	$308,000	$12,073,000
EDA Participation	$4,550,000	$1,730,000	$1,151,000	$154,000	$ 7,585,000
Percent Occupied or Operational	15%	45%	60%	50%	
EDA-Attributed Jobs	300	170	85+ Camac jobs (255)[b]	35	590
EDA-Attributed Jobs to RA Residents	31	4	0 (4)[b]	0	35
EDA-Attributed Jobs to Formerly Unemployed and Underemployed Persons	133	96	33[a] (129)[b]	No Data	262
EDC Residents	79	42	33[a] (75)[b]	No Data	154
RA Residents	31	4	0 (4)[b]	No Data	35
EDA Investment Per Job	$ 15,167	$ 10,176	($4,513)[b]	$ 4,400	$ 12,856
EDA Investment Per Job to RA Residents	$ 146,774	$ 432,500	($287,500)[c]	–	$ 216,714
Yearly Salary Generated	$1,779,000	$1,300,000	$ 600,000	$206,500	$ 3,885,500

[a]Employee data for Jarl and the 85 Bristol jobs in Washington County Industrial Park are based on a sample of less than 10 percent of the firms employees
[b]Includes Camac jobs
[c]Based on public works investment in park only

Source: *Program Evaluation: The Economic Development Administration Growth Center Strategy*, Washington, D.C.: U.S. Department of Commerce/Economic Development Administration, February 1972, p. 81

Local leaders were unaware of the existence of the Positive Action Program and showed only limited interest in the concept when it was explained to them. They felt that the needs of each community within the growth center so occupied the available resources that assistance to outlying areas, i.e., RAs, was unlikely. Since the PAP was regional in scope, these individuals felt that the proper place for its design and implementation lay with the district staff rather than with themselves as leaders in the growth center.

Specific steps affecting growth center spillover to RAs were mentioned briefly at the end of the document. They included: (1) professional recruiting and hiring of RA residents; (2) job notification in RAs; (3) expanded vocational technical training for RA residents; and (4) efforts to increase low- and moderate-income housing and public transportation both within the growth center and the RAs. However, job recruitment and hiring is difficult in most of the district's RAs because mountainous terrain and poor roads make commuting impractical. Moreover, the evaluators found that nearly all new industry of any size hired local labor first. For example, the new Westinghouse plant found the local labor pool quite adequate and was not hiring outside a thirty-mile radius of the plant. This excludes the RA counties with the exception of the northwest section of Johnson County.

Attempts to service the RAs were in no way related to the PAP, and the evaluators concluded that the isolation of the RAs made it highly unlikely that the growth center would have substantial impact on those counties. Generally, the RAs had closer economic ties with Morristown and Knoxville. Although there had been expansion of vocational education in the growth center, this had been of little benefit to the RAs. In some cases, voc-tech facilities were limited to county residents. In other cases, where out-of-county students were accepted, no transportation was provided. The result was limited attendance on the part of RA residents.

In the judgment of the evaluators, the PAP in Tri-Cities had not been effective for three primary reasons. First, the document was unknown to the local leadership; second, EDA had not effectively transmitted its concern about the PAP to the district level; and third, geography and road systems severely limited the influence the center might have upon the redevelopment areas. The district staff regarded the PAP as a simple administrative necessity.

Role of the District Organization. The First Tennessee-Virginia Development District was first funded by EDA in November of 1966, and supported a professional staff of almost thirty at the time of evaluation. Based on interviews with the staff and analysis of staff-prepared material, the evaluators judged the director and his employees to be extremely competent. Their assistance went beyond simple "grantsmanship" to the provision of technical assistance and information to member governments, and specialized forms of development planning.

The district organization had succeeded in securing federal assistance from such agencies as the Law Enforcement Assistance Administration, FHA, and HUD. It had also received assistance from the Appalachian Regional Commission and had been designated as an A-95 clearinghouse by OMB.[d]

As previously noted, the Tri-Cities PAP was prepared by the district staff, which found the exercise itself useful, but the document superfluous. The staff spent considerable time in redevelopment areas of the district although its offices were located in the growth center. Their time appeared to be divided equally among the growth center, RA counties, and nondesignated counties.

District staff members had mixed reactions to EDA's growth center concept. They told the evaluators that significant regional development could only take place within Tri-Cities. However, geographic barriers precluded the redevelopment areas from significantly benefiting from such growth. Consequently, the staff had sought to provide the redevelopment areas with whatever projects they could in an attempt to help the local residents.

Status of the Economic Development Process. The city of Bristol lies astride the Virginia-Tennessee state line, which divides its principal business street and commercial center. The Tennessee and Virginia sections of the city have separate forms of municipal government and separate city services, but most residents interviewed felt that cooperation between the two was extremely good. A generally recognized turning point for development activities in Bristol was the founding in 1965 of the joint Bristol, Tennessee-Virginia Industrial Commission. The commission introduced updated planning and zoning requirements and applied for federal assistance.

Between 1967 and 1971, seven new industries located in Bristol. However, some problems of suburban exodus plagued the community. The middle class was leaving the city proper, and municipal revenue and downtown businesses had decreased accordingly. Efforts to revitalize the center of town had not met with much success at the time of evaluation.

Johnson City had experienced substantial commercial growth in recent years. The city had a higher proportion of service and commercial industry than the other towns in the Tri-Cities growth center, but had not experienced as much industrial and manufacturing growth. The evaluators reported that the concentration of hospitals and related facilities, as well as a university and two colleges established Johnson City as an educational and health facility center for the area.

Johnson City had undertaken considerable development in the past five years, primarily due to the willingness of the public to pay for projects of this nature. Water and sewer facilities, industrial sites, and a new school and municipal

---

[d]The function of an A-95 clearinghouse is to review all federal grant applications from a multi-county region and to make recommendations concerning those applications.

building program were some of the development projects that were made possible through public financing. Although it was difficult to pinpoint a group of economic leaders as the real moving force within the community, developments in recent years suggested that diverse groups had been able to work together for the good of the community.

Community leaders expressed a concern for the poverty and unemployment that existed in the outlying redevelopment areas. They recognized, however, the limitations of the road system connecting the city with Hancock County, and believed that the only way Hancock residents could be helped was by migrating to the center or through the location of factories in the RA county itself.

Although only half as old as Johnson City and Bristol, Kingsport had in approximately fifty years matched them in retail trade and services. A large part of this growth was due to the location of Tennessee-Eastman, chemical manufacturer and subsidiary of Eastman Kodak. This plant employed 15,000 workers with a median salary of $12,000 and an unusually high level of education. The plant had made considerable contributions to community affairs, including $225,000 for an environmental education center. Other large employers included Mead Paper, an Army munitions factory, and one of the country's largest printing plants.

The evaluators found that Kingsport, in combination with Bristol, was the major retail trade center for northeastern Tennessee and nearby West Virginia. It was also becoming an educational center with the opening of the new $2.5 million Kingsport University Center. An extensive capital improvements program and a recreational program were among the other activities that the community had begun in the area of development. The community was visibly reluctant to become involved in most federal programs, although the evaluators saw evidence that this situation might be changing.

Elizabethton, which was added to the growth center area in 1968, was beginning to develop a diversified economy at the time of evaluation. A number of new industries had located there, and the town was building its own service sector. Two new shopping centers and the city's first motel were being built.

Traditionally isolated by poor roads, new highway construction promised to make Elizabethton more accessible from the Tri-Cities airport and industrial park to the north. Because of this isolation, Elizabethton's influence on outlying RAs had been minimal. Local leaders believed the city would have greater potential to attract commuters when the road improvements were completed.

City leaders felt that attitudes toward development were becoming more positive. Elizabethton had participated in the construction of a regional industrial park by contributing 13 percent of the project cost. The city had also become involved in some federal programs including urban renewal, a HUD-financed water and sewer system, an OEO Operation Mainstream Program, and public housing leased by the City Housing Authority.

Conclusions

On the basis of the twelve in-depth case studies conducted during the growth center evaluation, it is not yet clear that the growth center strategy outlined in the agency's legislation and expanded in EDA policy statements is workable. Residents of surrounding depressed counties designated as redevelopment areas received almost no employment or public service benefits from the EDA growth center projects surveyed by the evaluation team. Moreover, at the time of evaluation these projects had not resulted in more total job impact than similar projects placed in distressed areas, as had been suggested in the past.

Impact of EDA Projects in Growth Centers

Distressed area projects of the same type, age, and from the same geographic areas were compared with the growth center projects analyzed through the evaluation.[e] The results, which are presented in table 8-14, suggested that RA projects, although substantially less costly, were not necessarily inferior to growth center projects. Although growth center projects resulted in more jobs, there was no significant difference between the EDA investment per job and the percentage of jobs to unemployed and underemployed persons for the two groups of projects.

The EDA growth center projects were similar to the RA projects in that they had created jobs in stable firms with year-round operations. However, the growth center projects differed from similar projects in distressed areas in that they had not diversified local economies. The twenty-six completed growth center projects designed primarily to generate jobs had raised 674 households above poverty level, resulted in wage increases for most workers, and led to training for more than 65 percent of the employees at EDA-associated firms. The relative effectiveness of the projects in these areas could not be determined, however, because such data were not available for RA projects.

With respect to job impact on present and former residents of redevelopment areas, the previously evaluated RA projects were considerably more effective than were projects in the growth centers evaluated. The percentage of jobs taken by present and former RA residents in connection with the control group of RA projects was more than five times that for the growth center projects. Since these RA projects also had as much total job impact per dollar invested as growth center projects, the rationale for placing projects in growth centers when they could be supported in redevelopment areas should be reexamined. It may be that agency investment in RAs is the way to maximize benefits to EDA's

[e]It should be noted that the analysis period for the RA projects was approximately 12 months earlier than that for the growth center projects. This time difference during a period of national economic readjustment raises the possibility that macro-conditions might have adversely affected the impacts of the growth center projects.

Table 8-14

Comparison of Public Works and Business Loan Projects in Redevelopment Areas and Growth Centers

Categories of Analysis	Growth Center Projects (26 Projects)[a]	RA Projects (30 Projects)
Average Project Cost	$1,360,000	$768,000
Average EDA Participation	$ 722,000	$495,000
Average EDA-Attributed Jobs per Project	109	79
Average EDA Investment per Job	$ 6,908	$ 6,275
Percent EDA-Attributed Jobs to RA Residents	14% (6%)[b]	87%
Average EDA Investment per RA Job	$ 50,000 ($ 116,000)[b]	$ 8,164
Percent EDA-Attributed Jobs to Unemployed and Underemployed Persons	31%	28%
Average Annual Salary Generated	$ 5,900	$ 5,300

[a]Does not include two "environmental" projects

[b]Excluding Bowling Green projects from the sample

Source: Program Evaluation: The Economic Development Administration Growth Center Strategy, Washington, D.C.: U.S. Department of Commerce/Economic Development Administration, February 1972, p. 176

target population—the unemployed and underemployed residents of economically distressed areas.

The evaluation team was able to identify secondary job impact in RAs from the EDA growth center projects in only one of the centers examined. In this case, sixteen secondary jobs were saved as a result of an EDA loan. No suppliers or distributors had located in or near growth centers as a result of such projects, and no firms had increased employment as a result of improved business associated with the location or expansion of a firm benefiting from an EDA growth center project. It should be noted, of course, that these projects were relatively new, and there may be impact of this nature in the future.

EDA projects in the growth centers evaluated had resulted in minimal indirect benefits to nearby depressed areas. Approximately $22 million of EDA investment in growth centers had resulted in jobs with over $16 million in annual wages, less than 10 percent of which was spent in redevelopment areas. New purchases in RAs by firms benefiting from these growth center projects totaled less than $1 million per year.

At the time of evaluation, the twenty-eight completed EDA projects in the growth centers analyzed showed no evidence of stemming out-migration from redevelopment areas or economic development districts. Less than 1 percent of the 850 employees surveyed at EDA-associated firms stated that they would have migrated from the area if their present jobs had not been available. The percentage of workers who indicated they would have moved to one of the nation's major metropolitan areas in the absence of the EDA-created job was even smaller.

Moreover, the study of population and migration characteristics of EDA districts described in chapter 10 revealed that the counties in which most EDA centers are located were not serving as migration points. Between 1960 and 1970, 77 percent of economic development centers and 97 percent of redevelopment centers underwent net out-migration. The study also found that absolute population change for all districts was far below that of the nation as a whole, despite a higher birth rate.

The public facilities EDA had funded in these 12 growth centers provided little service to residents of redevelopment areas. Moreover, they did not appear to be stimulating or accelerating economic growth in these centers. The water system projects located in growth centers had improved public services to residents of the centers, but the other two public facility projects—a scientific library and a marine-oriented research laboratory—had resulted in negligible impact on local citizens.

Effectiveness of Local Implementation
(Positive Action Program)

On the basis of case studies of twelve EDA growth centers, the evaluation team concluded that Positive Action Programs were not an effective means of insuring that residents of nearby redevelopment areas benefit from the employment opportunities and public services in growth centers. No observable benefits had accrued to residents of such areas as a result of EDA's requirement that economic development centers prepare these documents. Moreover, few programs had been initiated to benefit residents of growth centers as a result of PAPs.

Discussions with community leaders, district staff members, and EDA Washington office personnel, as well as analysis of PAP impact, led to the conclusion that the concept underlying the PAP was too broad, given EDA's limited resources. The evaluators concluded it was unrealistic to expect that a community would address not only its own problems but also those of other counties and communities solely for the purpose of obtaining EDA funds for one, two, or even three projects.

*Effectiveness of District Organization in Implementing
the Growth Center Strategy*

District organizations analyzed through this study had not effectively implemented EDA's growth center strategy. This was primarily due to a lack of understanding on the part of district staff and board members. Neither the strategy itself nor the purposes of the PAP requirement had been adequately explained to these individuals.

Moreover, the treatment given to PAPs by EDA Washington had led most district staff and board members to the conclusion that the agency was not serious about the PAP requirement. As a result, they did not recognize the importance of channeling benefits from EDC projects to unemployed and underemployed residents of redevelopment areas.

For the most part, district staffs were serving effectively as grantsmen, planners, and agents of change. It is primarily through these individuals that EDA stimulates the economic development process in redevelopment area communities, growth centers, and towns in nondesignated district counties.

Status of the Economic Development Process

In a few of the centers evaluated, agency projects had resulted in more positive attitudes toward development activities. However, such projects appeared to have had little impact on the lending policies of local banks, the cooperation of community organizations, and the willingness of center residents to finance local improvements. Moreover, the projects had not resulted in more positive attitudes toward helping unemployed and underemployed residents of redevelopment areas or the centers themselves.

Possible Program Modifications

The growth center evaluation described above must be regarded as somewhat preliminary. The centers examined represented only 10 percent of all EDA-designated growth centers and may not be completely representative of the universe. Therefore, final conclusions on the effectiveness of the growth center strategy cannot be drawn until a larger sample is evaluated. Moreover, as the study progressed, it became clear that several other analyses would have to be performed to provide more complete insight into the effectiveness and potential of the strategy.

One of these studies—an analysis of the musical chairs effects of growth center projects—was initiated during the fall of 1971 and scheduled for completion by June 1972. This analysis will reveal who took the jobs vacated by employees at firms benefiting from EDA growth center projects. Other proposed studies include an analysis of Social Security data to determine if EDA growth centers are serving as way stations for RA residents on their way to larger urban areas. If RA residents are temporarily residing in growth centers before migrating to larger cities, the potential exists for EDA's growth center strategy to stem their migration from the centers. Analysis of 1970 census data would provide additional information on migration patterns.

Despite the need for further study, a number of program modifications can be tentatively suggested on the basis of the findings of the evaluation team. These modifications are based on the agency's stated policy with regard to centers and center projects. This policy, which is supported by EDA's legislation, clearly states that the primary purpose of EDA growth center investments is to benefit unemployed and underemployed residents of redevelopment areas.

Funding Priorities

In the course of development, many projects are eliminated for a variety of reasons—lack of local matching share, disinterest, loss of prospective industries, or private locational decisions. Even though a number of projects are eliminated for these reasons, the agency still receives more applications than it can fund. Therefore, EDA officials must choose among those which appear to have similar chances of success in terms of job creation, income generation, and provision of services.

To increase the agency's effectiveness in choosing among the various projects, priority should be given to these investments that can be placed directly in distressed (redevelopment) areas. By funding projects directly in distressed areas, the agency will have the most direct, timely, and significant impact on the unemployed and underemployed residents of redevelopment areas. Field experience during the growth center analysis and other evaluations has indicated that spillover from EDA's growth center projects to redevelopment areas is minimal, and heavily dependent on the proximity of the redevelopment areas to the EDC. Even in the case where considerable effort was expended to secure jobs for redevelopment area residents, less than half of the jobs went to RA residents. And, in that case, three RAs were contiguous to the growth center county and were within commuting distance.

Jobs generated by projects located in redevelopment areas, on the other hand, have been taken primarily by RA residents. Approximately 85 percent of the employees associated with redevelopment area projects of the same age and from the same geographic area as the growth center projects were RA residents. Thus, top priority should be given to redevelopment area projects that have a reasonable chance to generate jobs, can be partially supported by local funds, and have the potential for long-term impact on unemployed and underemployed RA residents.

Projects in Growth Centers

If EDA is to alleviate the conditions of unemployment and underemployment in redevelopment areas, it must create jobs and see that they reach the target population (unemployed and underemployed residents of RAs). Since the agency's inception, investments in economic development centers have become more varied and have included such projects as libraries, educational television stations, convention centers, and parking lots. Such projects have been justified on the basis that they accelerate the growth of the center, which in turn benefits redevelopment areas.

In the growth centers evaluated, this had not yet happened. Projects designed to accelerate growth had almost no impact on redevelopment areas or their residents. A library in Fort Smith, for instance, had not provided services to RA residents, had not attracted any industry to the city, and had not visibly affected growth in any way. Moreover, research on the subject of growth centers indicates that the modest public investment which EDA's budget allows has very little effect on either accelerating or retarding the growth of a center and will almost certainly not initiate growth where it is not already taking place.

In addition to funding environmental facilities projects intended to accelerate a center's growth, the agency has funded projects for the purpose of creating jobs in growth centers. As previously discussed, these projects were comparable in terms of employment and income to redevelopment area projects of similar age and location; they were not clearly superior as had been suggested in the past.

For these reasons, EDA should fund only those projects in EDCs that cannot be located in redevelopment areas (e.g., a business loan to a firm that requires services not available in an RA). If other investments are to be made in EDCs, consideration should be given to:

1. Insuring that projects funded in EDCs for service or employment impact have the potential for directly spilling over that impact to unemployed and underemployed redevelopment area residents.
2. The policy of funding EDC projects primarily for the purpose of accelerating growth. Such a policy should be studied more carefully to determine if the types of environmental projects EDA funds have the potential to influence center growth, and if the growth of EDCs automatically results in benefits to redevelopment areas, or if mechanisms should be developed to insure that benefits spill over to economically distressed areas.

More EDA environmental projects in economic development centers should be evaluated before final conclusions are drawn regarding their effectiveness.

Outreach to RAs

Ineffectiveness of PAP. Under EDA's present growth center strategy, the Positive Action Program is the tool by which the agency attempts to insure that the unemployed and underemployed from redevelopment areas benefit from the growth of economic development centers. As indicated, the PAP had not accomplished this in the twelve centers evaluated. No benefits had accrued to RA residents as a result of the program; very few people—even district board members—were familiar with it; and virtually no one recognized that the requirement was intended to benefit redevelopment areas.

In addition, the evaluation team's conversations with Washington personnel revealed that few persons knew what constituted a good PAP. The district directors correctly observed that they had received only fragmentary guidance on how to formulate a PAP and even less on how to implement it.

The reasons for this situation are twofold. The first is administrative. Guidelines were provided to district organizations in September 1968, approximately six months after issuance of the first detailed policy statement on growth centers. This left considerable time during which many districts were forced to guess at what EDA Washington wanted. Even when guidelines were issued, they were not precise.

Under the pressures of time and project processing, PAPs were hurriedly prepared, and even when deficiencies were noted by regional offices or EDA Washington, project approval usually was given. This tended to decrease the credibility of the PAP requirement. In many cases little effort was put into formulating the PAP, because it was viewed as just one more piece of paper to be submitted in connection with projects.

The second reason for the PAP's failure is closely tied to the difficulties encountered in administering it within EDA: the PAP attempts to achieve too much and provides too little guidance or incentive for accomplishing it. The guidelines suggest expanding municipal services, upgrading vocational-educational facilities, providing mass transportation to urban and rural areas, and extending community aid programs to citizens from outside the city or county. They ask that the community make a "commitment of intention" toward the underemployed and unemployed from the RAs, and detail methods to implement that commitment.

Strict enforcement of a requirement such as this, implying sweeping goals and programs, is difficult, if not impossible. In a sense, the PAP requires not only that a community respond to its own problems, but also that it address those of surrounding communities. This is undoubtedly a desirable goal, but scarcely a realistic requirement to impose upon an EDC in connection with EDA project funding. Political realities make it difficult for any mayor or city manager to justify the expenditure of city tax dollars for services to residents of other cities and counties. Moreover, EDA's financial incentives are not substantial enough to outweigh the political disadvantages.

The PAP's deficiencies lead to the conclusion that EDA should discontinue the PAP requirement. This does not mean, however, that EDA should abandon attempts to stimulate the economic development process in districts. To the contrary, this is a primary goal of the district organizations the agency supports through its planning and administrative grants. It is the district staffs who are in a position, through daily community involvement, to change attitudes and influence community decisions in areas that extend beyond EDA's legislative mandate and funding capabilities.

Alternative Approach. The Positive Action Program could be replaced with a more realistic requirement, in terms of both goals and enforcement. It is believed that the job outreach procedures discussed below, or a similar approach, have attainable goals and can be more easily implemented than the PAP. These procedures, which involve requiring a job outreach plan in connection with EDC projects, focus the efforts of EDA, EDC residents, and the district organizations on one specific goal: recruiting RA residents for jobs in growth centers.

The one evaluated EDC project that had a significant impact on RA residents owed its success to the efforts of the district's executive director; its impact had no relationship to the PAP. In that case, a division of Chrysler Corporation located a facility for the manufacture of commercial air conditioning and refrigeration equipment in Bowling Green in connection with several EDA public works projects. At the urging of the development district's executive director, the Chrysler recruiter actually visited surrounding rural counties and conducted interviews.

Before recruiting began, the director arranged for publicity in local papers and on radio and television. Recruiting stations were set up in local CAP Agency headquarters, city halls, and other central locations in nearby counties. As a result of this effort, approximately 40 percent of the 600 jobs created in the new plant were taken by present or former residents of redevelopment areas.

The conclusion then is that all applications for EDC projects having employment impact should include assurances that this type of recruiting will take place. In addition, each district organization should commit a member of its staff to administer the recruitment program, work with employers, and assist in the execution of their commitments to recruit unemployed and underemployed residents of redevelopment areas.

In the case of a business loan, the commitment would be made directly by the loan recipient, while in the case of a public works project, all direct and substantial beneficiaries of an EDA project would participate in an outreach hiring plan. With respect to vocational-technical training facilities, the analogue of an outreach hiring program—a student recruiting effort—should be required. This would entail the recruitment, training, and placement of students from redevelopment areas as well as commitments from school administrators that all services of the facility will be made available to redevelopment area residents.

Responsibility for administering the program should be lodged with the district organization. In this way, the importance of extending benefits to unemployed and underemployed residents of redevelopment areas can be stressed from the beginning of project development. Preapplication activities involving district staffs, EDRs, and regional office personnel should emphasize the outreach aspect as an integral part of a growth center project.

An ongoing evaluation could be undertaken within EDA to determine whether hiring and recruiting commitments are being fulfilled. This evaluation would involve examining a number of projects each year, and result in periodic recommendations on EDA's growth center investments.

9 A Growth Center Identification System (GCIS)

To implement a viable growth center strategy, the cities that are designated as centers must have potential for future growth. This chapter describes a system developed to identify counties with high potential for population growth, a useful proxy for economic growth. The results of the system's implementation are presented for 1,440 counties in and proximate to economic development districts.

This system is by no means the only possible approach to identifying growth centers.[1] In fact, it represents a rather elementary model, but it is easy to implement and probably as accurate as is necessary for differentiating between two types of centers: those with significant population growth potential; and those with little or no potential for population growth. The system is applicable for regions with homogeneous socioeconomic characteristics. However, because the determinants of growth are not well defined, policy makers should not rely solely on this system or any other statistical model for prediction. The system was developed to serve EDA administrators as one of several decision-making aids.

For regions with homogeneous socioeconomic characteristics, the Growth Center Identification System (GCIS) identifies counties with the potential to serve surrounding distressed (redevelopment) areas by providing economic spillover to them.[a] The following paragraphs summarize the various steps in this system as an introduction to a detailed description of each component.

The first step in implementing the GCIS consisted of modifying EDA-designated and authorized districts to include counties that were linked to the districts by trade and commuting patterns. The boundaries of OBE Economic Areas and Rand-McNally Trade Areas formed the basis for this effort. When the modification procedure had been applied to all designated and authorized districts, the modified districts were grouped into thirteen relatively homogeneous regions. The regions were delineated on the basis of Bogue and Beale's "economic regions,"[2] major topographical characteristics, and regional commission boundaries.

---

[a]As discussed in the preceding chapter, the evaluation team concluded that residents of surrounding redevelopment areas will not necessarily receive immediate benefits from EDA projects in growth centers even if such centers have a high potential to provide economic spillover to such areas. On the basis of their field experience, the evaluators judged that some mechanism was necessary to insure that residents of such areas benefit from center projects.

213

Following the delineation of regions, a modified shift-share analysis was employed to isolate those counties in each region with dissimilar employment structures or dissimilar changes in those structures. The types of counties identified through this analysis were: counties that were more depressed than others within their regions; counties with extremely specialized economies, such as recreation, mining, retirement; and counties that appeared to reflect potential for significant further growth and employment growth impact on surrounding areas.

Five criteria were applied to differentiate between counties in the last group:

1. Employment growth in key sectors between 1950 and 1960
2. Ratio of nonbasic employment to total employment in 1960 and ratio of manufacturing employment to total employment in the same year
3. Population growth between 1960 and 1970
4. Location with respect to Standard Metropolitan Statistical Areas
5. Proximity to EDA-designated redevelopment areas

On the basis of these criteria, counties were categorized as Type I, Type II, or Type III centers.

Places identified as Type I centers exhibited high growth potential and their growth could be expected to improve conditions in nearby redevelopment areas. To be identified as a Type I center: (1) a county's manufacturing and nonbasic employment ratios had to equal the same ratios for the region; (2) a county's percent change in population had to exceed that for the entire region; and (3) a county had to be contiguous to a redevelopment area that did not border on an SMSA and be within thirty minutes commuting time from the largest community in that RA.

Type II centers were less likely to grow and affect surrounding distressed areas than were Type I centers, but the possibility that they would do so could not be rejected on the basis of the data examined. Counties classified as Type II centers were contiguous to a redevelopment area that did not border on an SMSA and were within thirty minutes commuting time from the largest community in that RA. In addition, a Type II center had to satisfy one of two conditions: (1) its percent change in population had to exceed that for the region; or (2) its employment growth rate had to exceed that for the region, and its manufacturing and nonbasic employment ratios had to at least equal the corresponding regional values.

Counties that did not meet the above criteria were judged to offer little potential for growth, or impact on redevelopment areas. These were classified as Type III centers.

Two independent analyses were conducted to support the results of the GCIS implementation. These analyses, which are presented in chapter 10, consist of: an investigation of the population and migration characteristics of EDA-designated districts; and a study of employment changes in counties contiguous to EDA-designated or GCIS-identified growth centers.

Description of Data Base Employed

Use of County Data

Growth centers are designated and funded by EDA under the assumption that government investment in these centers will stimulate their economic growth and thus have a positive impact on neighboring redevelopment areas. The "best" centers are those urban areas that have a strong natural potential for growth. It is assumed that by funding projects in these places, EDA achieves greater returns for its investments.

Growing urban centers draw from and contribute to the surrounding area. In terms of population, economic activity, and industrial structure, a viable growth center dominates most of the county in which it is located. Thus, although the growth centers are politically bounded, their economies encompass the entire county. This is the area that will be most strongly affected by the economic activity of the center. If the influence of the growth center is not felt in its own county, it is unlikely that the center will affect other counties. Therefore, county data were used to assess the influence of the growth center.

Other geographic units were considered and rejected. Possibilities were city or SMSA data, and data on the Office of Business Economics (OBE) Economic Areas. City data were rejected because city political boundaries do not reflect the range of a center's economic activity. Moreover, between 1950 and 1970, many cities annexed adjacent territory, making consistent comparisons extremely difficult. In addition, EDA's designation criteria make use of city data inappropriate. These criteria allow the designation of growth corridors between cities, and city statistics do not include such areas. (In cases where EDA had designated a corridor which encompassed more than one county, aggregated data for the combined counties were used in the analysis.)

Data on OBE Economic Areas were not considered appropriate because these areas are too large to reflect the influence of individual growth centers.

Although data on counties were used to identify potential growth centers, only the major city or town within each selected county is recommended for designation. Usually, this place dominates the economic activity of the county, and contains the major portion of the existing infrastructure. Thus, EDA will achieve the greatest economies by investing here, because projects can be designed to take advantage of the existing infrastructure.

Districts and Regions

Economic Development Districts. Economic Development Districts (EDDs) were selected as the basic unit of analysis because they are relatively homogeneous and because a major objective was to identify growth centers within existing district boundaries.

Most districts are multicounty distressed areas where family incomes have remained below the national median, and unemployment has exceeded the national average. Of the 1,094 counties that comprised the 140 districts recognized by EDA as of December 31, 1970, 96 percent had family incomes below the national median and 64 percent had unemployment rates that exceeded the national average.[b]

In addition to having similar income and employment statistics, districts are relatively homogeneous with respect to the socioeconomic variables used by the Bureau of the Census in delineating multicounty State Economic Areas (SEAs), which are defined as "groups of counties within a state which have similar economic and social characteristics."[3]

In most cases, an economic development district is comprised of several SEAs. Most districts include less than 10 counties and, therefore, cover a relatively small geographic area. As a result, socioeconomic characteristics tend to be uniform throughout a district, even if district boundaries do not coincide exactly with those of an SEA. However, approximately two-thirds of the 140 EDDs have boundaries which conform to those of the SEAs.

Modified Economic Development Districts. Modified districts were developed by enlarging existing district boundaries to include those peripheral counties with commuting and trade patterns related to those of the district. In cases where such counties were members of other EDDs, no modifications were made.

The Economic Areas defined by the Office of Business Economics were used as a first approximation for delineating the modified district boundaries. The 173 Economic Areas are structured to minimize commuting across boundaries.[4]

To develop modified district boundaries, EDD boundaries were extended to include all counties associated with their respective OBE economic areas. Then, the enlarged districts were further modified to exclude counties at the periphery of the OBE Economic Areas that did not show significant trade relationships with the district. Rand-McNally Trade Areas were used for this step in refining modified district boundaries.[c] The final results were modified in districts that corresponded closely to the "closed trade areas" of central place theory.[d]

---

[b]Tables 9-1 and 9-2 contain regional income and employment data.

[c]The 50 Major Trading Areas and their components, Basic Trading Areas, which were used for further modifying district boundaries, were delineated by the staff of Rand McNally. The boundaries of these areas were established on the basis of criteria covering physiographic characteristics, population, economic activity, newspaper circulation, highway facilities, railroad service, suburban transport, and field sales reports. Additional information is in *1970 Commercial Atlas and Marketing Guide*, 101st Ed., Ossining, New York: Rand McNally and Company, 1970.

[d]Basically, a closed trade area is an area surrounding a city or urban place where goods and services are purchased locally. The boundaries of the trade area are "closed" when retail sales and service patterns can no longer be associated with a specific city.

The established commuting and trade patterns that exist within the modified districts as developed above make them cohesive planning units. Furthermore, if a growth center is identified in a modified district, it will have strong economic ties throughout the district.

Regions. All districts and modified districts were grouped into thirteen regions for analysis. Each region was constructed to contain districts that were reasonably homogeneous with respect to geographic characteristics and economic activities. Two steps were taken to delineate regions.

First, modified districts were grouped into larger areas approximating the "economic regions" defined by Bogue and Beale. Each of the economic regions is a combination of smaller geographical units that are comparatively homogeneous in terms of topography, climate and economic interrelationships. Second, each of the modified district groupings was altered to conform to the major topographical characteristics (e.g., mountain ranges, plateaus, valleys, and plains) of the area. When feasible, boundary problems between contiguous regions were settled by using the boundaries established by EDA's Title V regional commissions or the Appalachian Regional Commission.

These procedures resulted in the delineation of thirteen relatively homogeneous regions. These regions are depicted in figure 9-1.

The Southwest, Great Lakes, and New England Regions are not composed of entirely contiguous districts or modified districts. The Southwest Region is divided into two parts, both of which lie within the Rocky Mountain and Intermountain Economic Region as defined by Bogue and Beale. For this study, both sections were treated as a single contiguous geographic unit.

The Great Lakes Region also has two geographically separate parts that were combined and treated as a single unit. One of the sections falls within Bogue and Beale's Northern Woods Economic Subregion, while the other is included in the area they identify as the Upper Great Lakes Economic Region. The New England Region is composed of three parts. The two larger sections are located in Bogue and Beale's Eastern Great Lakes and Northeastern Upland Economic Region, and in the northern extension of the Appalachian Plateau. The remaining section consists of one modified district, which lies within New England but does not have the same physical characteristics as the other two parts.

The Terre Haute and Delmarva Regions each consist of one district. The Terre Haute Region is a modified district composed of an SMSA and a few neighboring counties. The Delmarva Region encompasses the entire Delaware-Maryland-Virginia Peninsula. The economic and physical characteristics of these areas precluded them from being combined with the modified districts of other regions. The Rio Grande Region covers four districts and lies wholly within the Gulf Coast and Atlantic Flatwoods Economic Region and the Rio Grande Plain.

The Cascade Mountains and Columbia Plateau were used to delineate the

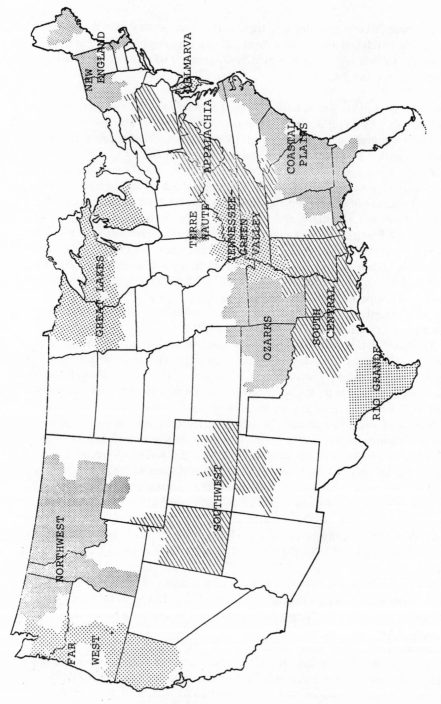

Figure 9-1. Region of Analysis

boundary between the Northwest and Far West Regions. The Northwest Region extends from the Scablands to the Snake River Valley, while the Far West Region covers the area between the Puget Trough of Washington and Napa Valley of California.

The Appalachian Regional Commission boundary and the physical characteristics of the Appalachian and Piedmont Plateaus were used to demarcate the Coastal Plains and Appalachian regional boundaries. The area between the Appalachian and Ozark Plateaus was identified as the Tennessee-Green Valley Region. This area includes the western end of the Ohio Valley, the Kentucky Blue Grass area, and the Wabash Valley. Overall, the economic and geographic characteristics of the area differ considerably from those of the Ozarks and Appalachian Regions on which it borders.

The Ozarks Regional Commission boundaries were used in delineating the Ozarks Region, which includes most of the Ozarks Plateau and the northernmost part of the Mississippi Basin. Only the western portion of Bogue and Beale's Central and Eastern Upland Region was included in the Ozarks Region.

The final region identified was the South Central Region, which borders the Ozarks, Tennessee-Green Valley, and Coastal Plains Regions. This area covers most of the Mississippi Basin, portions of the Gulf Coast and the westernmost part of the Coastal Plain. Most of the region lies in the area identified by Bogue and Beale as the South Center and Southwest Plains Region.

Income and Economic Characteristics of Regions. Table 9-1 shows the family income characteristics for each of the regions. All district counties in the Coastal Plains, Tennessee-Green Valley, Rio Grande, and Terre Haute Regions had median family incomes below the national value in 1960. In that year, more than 99 percent of the district counties in the Ozarks, Appalachian, and South Central Regions had median family incomes below the national median. Only the Far West Region, where 30 percent of all district counties had median family incomes below the national median, appeared to differ considerably from the others.

Table 9-2 shows the unemployment rate characteristics of each of the regions. Again, the regions appear to be uniformly distressed. Only the Coastal Plains Region had more counties below the national unemployment rate than above. In all the other regions, at least 56 percent of the district counties had unemployment rates exceeding the national rate.

System Description

The first step in implementing the Growth Center Identification System involved using a modified shift-share analysis to isolate those counties in the thirteen identified regions with dissimilar employment structures or dissimilar changes in

Table 9–1
Characteristics of Median Family Income in District Counties: 1959

Region	Number of District Counties in Region	Number of District Counties with Median Income Below National Median	Percent of District Counties with Median Income Below National Median
Coastal Plains	191	191	100%
Rio Grande	36	36	100%
Tennessee-Green Valley	106	106	100%
Terre Haute	5	5	100%
Appalachia	199	197	99%
Ozarks	129	128	99%
South Central	181	180	99%
New England	32	30	94%
Delmarva	14	13	93%
Great Lakes	87	79	91%
Southwest	43	39	88%
Northwest	41	34	83%
Far West	30	9	30%
TOTAL	1,094	1,047	96%

Source: U.S. Bureau of the Census, *County and City Data Book, 1962* (A Statistical Abstract Supplement), Washington, D.C.: U.S. Government Printing Office, 1962.

Table 9-2
Characteristics of Unemployment Rate in District Counties: 1960

Region	Number of District Counties in Region	Number of District Counties with Unemployment Rate Above National Average	Percentage of District Counties with Unemployment Rate Above National Average
Far West	30	29	97%
Great Lakes	87	76	87%
Appalachia	199	161	81%
Northwest	41	33	81%
New England	32	25	78%
Delmarva	14	10	71%
Southwest	43	26	61%
Terre Haute	5	3	60%
Ozarks	129	75	58%
Tennessee-Green Valley	106	59	56%
Rio Grande	36	20	56%
South Central	181	102	56%
Coastal Plains	191	84	44%
TOTAL	1,094	703	64%

Source: U.S. Bureau of the Census, *County and City Data Book, 1962* (A Statistical Abstract Supplement), Washington, D.C.: U.S. Government Printing Office, 1962.

those structures. Counties selected by this procedure were then analyzed with respect to: (1) employment growth in seven major sectors; (2) employment structure; (3) population change; (4) location with respect to Standard Metropolitan Statistical Areas; and (5) commuting distance from EDA-designated redevelopment areas. The largest place in each county passing this final group of tests was identified as a potential growth center.

Modified Shift-Share Analysis

Scope of Analysis. A modified shift-share analysis was used to isolate counties for further study.[e] The underlying assumption was that *most* counties in a distressed region have similar employment characteristics and thus offer limited potential for further growth. Counties with dissimilar characteristics are more likely to contain a potential growth center.

The modified shift-share analysis consisted of: (1) a shift-share analysis to determine changes in each county's employment structure; and (2) a correlation analysis to identify the counties with the most dissimilar changes.

Shift-Share Analysis. Use of shift-share analysis to analyze an area's economic potential is based on the assumption that two facts need to be known about its growth. These facts are (1) whether the area has many rapid-growth industries, i.e., a favorable industrial mix, and (2) whether it has an increasing share of particular industry sectors.

While increases in employment are not the same as economic growth, employment data provides a clear and uniform measure of economic activity. In addition, EDA's growth concept is based on the creation of jobs. As previously indicated, the county was selected as the geographic area best suited for an analysis of growth centers. Therefore, the basic data used in this study were figures on county employment in the thirty-two industry sectors for 1940, 1950, and 1960. These sectors are identified in table 9-3.

This analysis separated county employment in each industry into three components.

First, the share *(S)* is that part of an industry's employment growth in a county that can be attributed to total regional employment trends. It represents the increase that would have occurred in a county's employment in a particular industry had it grown at the same rate as the regional average of all industries combined. It is computed by multiplying the county's base year employment in

---

[e]This technique was developed by John A. Kuehn and Lloyd D. Bender in "An Empirical Identification of Growth Centers," *Land Economics*, November 1970, pp. 435-43. Their method is based upon analysis of employment structure and changes in the pattern of employment structure and has the "objective of isolating growth poles within distressed areas."

Table 9–3
Industry Sectors (Employment by Place of Residence)

No.	Industry Sectors
1	Agriculture
2	Forestry and Fisheries
3	Mining
4	Contract Construction
5	Manufacturing: Food and Kindred Products
6	Manufacturing: Textile Mill Products
7	Manufacturing: Apparel and other Textiles
8	Manufacturing: Printing and Publishers
9	Manufacturing: Chemicals and Allied Products
10	Manufacturing: Lumber and Furniture
11	Manufacturing: Machinery, excluding Electrical
12	Manufacturing: Electrical Equipment and Supplies
13	Manufacturing: Transportation Equipment
14	Manufacturing: Paper and Allied Products
15	Manufacturing: Petroleum Refining
16	Manufacturing: Primary Metals Industry
17	Manufacturing: Fabricated Metals and Ordinance
18	Manufacturing: Miscellaneous Manufacturing
19	Transportation
20	Communications
21	Utilities
22	Wholesale Trade
23	Eating and Drinking Places
24	Other Retail Trades
25	Finance, Insurance and Real Estate
26	Lodging Places and Personal Services
27	Business and Repair Services
28	Amusement and Recreation Services
29	Private Households
30	Educational, Medical, and Professional Services
31	Public Administration
32	Armed Forces

that industry by the regional growth rate for all industries, and is the base from which the two shift components are measured.

Second, the composition shift *(M)* is that part of a specific industry's employment growth in a county that can be attributed to that industry's regional growth rate. It represents the number of additional jobs that would have been available in the county had that industry grown regionally at the same rate as the all-industry average. It is computed by subtracting the average regional growth rate of all industries from the regional growth rate of the particular industry under consideration and multiplying this difference by the county's base year employment in the same industry.

Third, the competitive shift *(C)* is that part of an industry's employment growth in a county that can be attributed to the industry growing at a different rate in the county than throughout the region. It represents the number of additional jobs that would have been available had the industry in the county grown at the same rate as it did in the region. It is computed by subtracting the regional growth rate of the industry from the industry's growth rate in the county and multiplying the difference by the county's base year employment in that industry.

Total employment growth of an industry in a county is the sum of the three components.

The two shift components, M and C, are concerned with that portion of an industry's growth in a county that is above or below the regional average growth rate of all industries. That is, the sum of the shift components is equal to the difference between the actual employment change in the industry in the county and the change that would have occurred had the industry's county employment grown at the regional rate of all industries.

The composition shift, M, measures the effect of some industries growing faster on a regional basis than others. The competitive shift, C, measures the difference between the growth rate of a given industry in a county and the growth rate of that industry regionally. Areas that have locational advantages for particular industries should have net upward competitive shifts. Such internal competitive shifts in industrial composition, which often reflect transition from an agricultural to an industrial economy, indicate growth potential.

The three components of the shift-share analysis can be defined mathematically as follows:

Share *(S)*

$$S_{ij} = E_{ij}^O \left[\frac{E_n^t}{E_n^O} - 1 \right]$$

Composition Shift *(M)*

$$M_{ij} = E_{ij}^O \left[\frac{E_{in}^t}{E_{in}^O} - \frac{E_n^t}{E_n^O} \right]$$

Competitive Shift *(C)*

$$C_{ij} = E_{ij}^O \left[\frac{E_{ij}^t}{E_{ij}^O} - \frac{E_{in}^t}{E_{in}^O} \right]$$

Total Employment Change

$$E^t_{ij} - E^0_{ij} = S_{ij} + M_{ij} + C_{ij}$$

where:

S	= Share
M	= Composition shift
C	= Differential or competitive shift
E_{ij}	= Employment in industry i in county j
E_{in}	= Employment in industry i in the region
E_n	= Employment in all industries in the region

Subscript j = 1,2, . . . , n where n is number of counties
Subscript i = 1,2, . . . , 32 industry sectors
Subscript t = Final time period
Subscript 0 = Initial time period

Each of the shift components was summed across the thirty-two industry sectors to give the total composition shift and the total competitive shift of a county:

Total Composition Shift *(TCS)*

$$TCS = \sum_{i=1}^{32} M_{ij}$$

Total Competitive Shift *(TCS*)*

$$TCS^* = \sum_{i=1}^{32} C_{ij}$$

The 32 C_{ij}'s indicated whether county j's share of industry i was growing faster or slower than the same industry regionally. Each of the 32 M_{ij}'s indicated whether county j had some share of industry i that was growing faster or slower than the average of all industries regionally. Summation of the two components provided two more observations for each county, making a total of 66 observations per county.

Correlation Analysis. The 66 observations for a particular county were correlated with the same 66 observations for each of the other $n-1$ counties in the region.

The $(n-1)$ correlation coefficients for a particular county were then summed to give an index of the similarity of the county with the rest of the region. The smaller the sum of the correlation coefficients, the more dissimilar the county. The counties in each region were then ranked according to the sum of their coefficients. The sum of the coefficients is referred to as an index of similarity.

Histograms of the Indices of Similarity. Histograms of the Indices of Similarity were constructed for each of the thirteen regions. This was done to determine an appropriate cutoff point for separating dissimilar places from all others within their respective regions. The histograms show that the distribution of the index values are highly skewed to the right, as would be expected since similar places have larger index values and are more numerous than dissimilar places. Histograms for the ten regions are provided in figures 9-2 through 9-11.[f]

Final cutoff points were established for each region in the following manner. An initial cutoff was selected on the histogram at approximately the point of inflection on the curve. This initial choice was then tested as follows.

The ten counties immediately to the right of the cutoff point and counties selected through a random sample of all counties to the right of the cutoff point were tested under the county selection criteria explained later in this chapter. If any of these counties qualified as a Type I or Type II center, the cutoff point was adjusted to include that county. Then, the procedure was repeated to determine if any of the ten counties immediately to the right of the new cutoff point or any of the counties picked through a random sample of all counties to the right of the new cutoff point met the criteria for Type I or Type II centers. This procedure was repeated until none of the counties—either those ten immediately to the right of the cutoff point or those included in the sample of all counties to the right of the cutoff point—satisfied the selection criteria. When that occurred, it was judged that a satisfactory final cutoff point had been reached.

For the most part, the results of these tests showed that the places to the right of the original cutoff point could not meet the county selection criteria. The exceptions, observed in three regions, are discussed below.

It should be emphasized that the shift-share analysis was used only to reduce the number of counties to be examined under the criteria for county selection. The purpose of the analysis was to eliminate those counties that were similar with respect to distressed economic conditions and would not be potential growth centers. The shift-share analysis was not part of the selection procedure.

---

[f]Histograms for three regions have been omitted. An explanation is provided in the following section on statistical limitations.

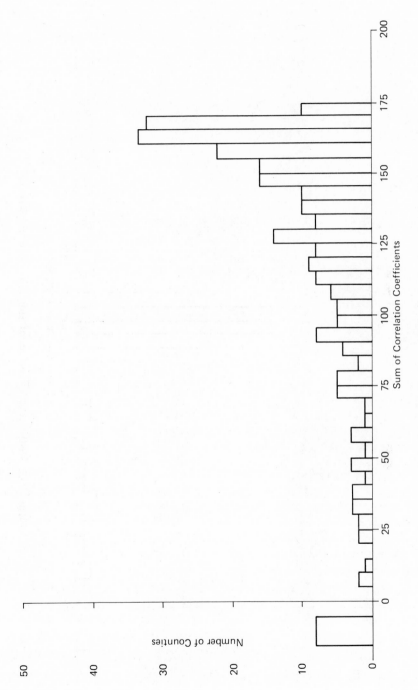

Figure 9–2. Distribution of Indices of Similarity — Appalachian Region

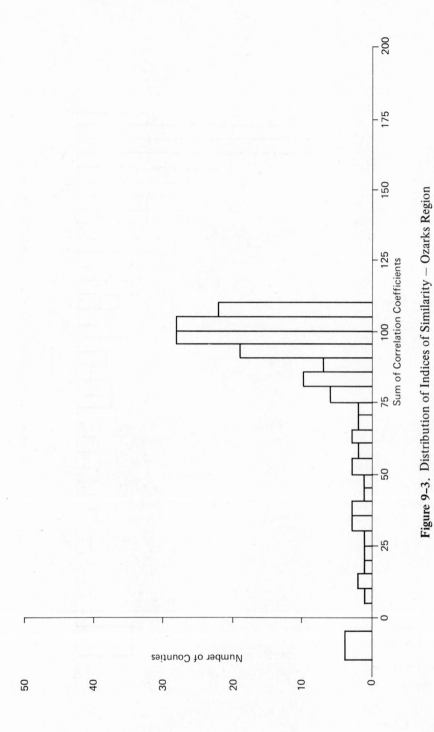

Figure 9–3. Distribution of Indices of Similarity — Ozarks Region

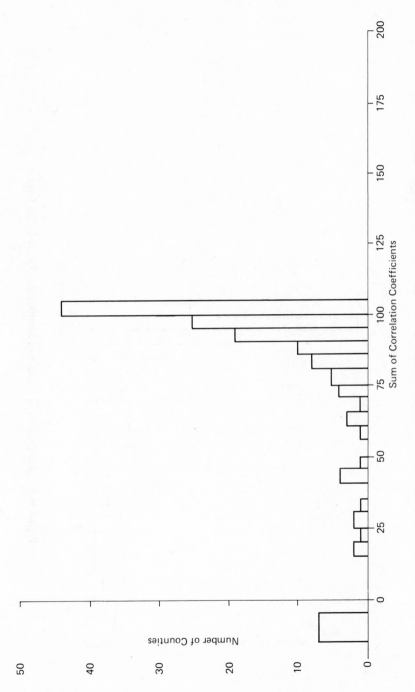

Figure 9-4. Distribution of Indices of Similarity — Tennessee-Green Valley Region

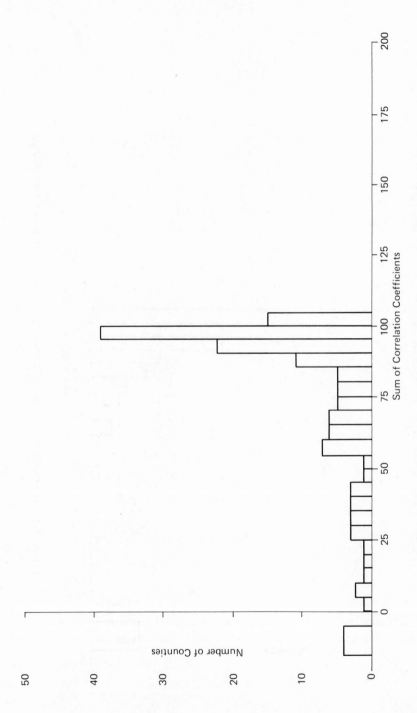

Figure 9-5. Distribution of Indices of Similarity — Great Lakes Region

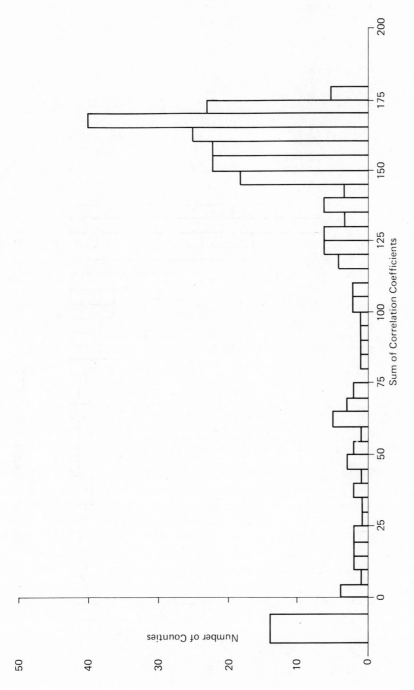

Figure 9-6. Distribution of Indices of Similarity — Coastal Plains Region

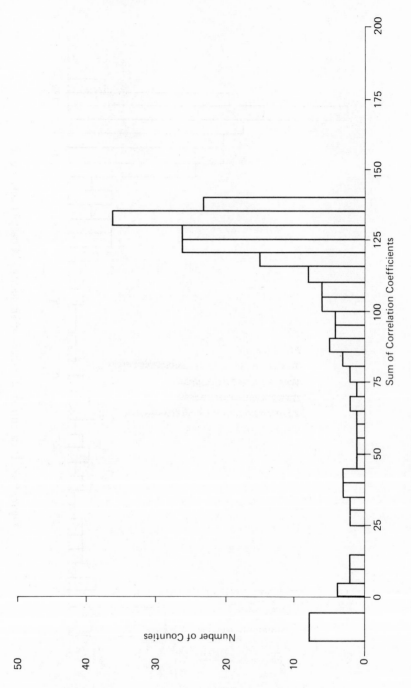

Figure 9-7. Distribution of Indices of Similarity — South Central Region

233

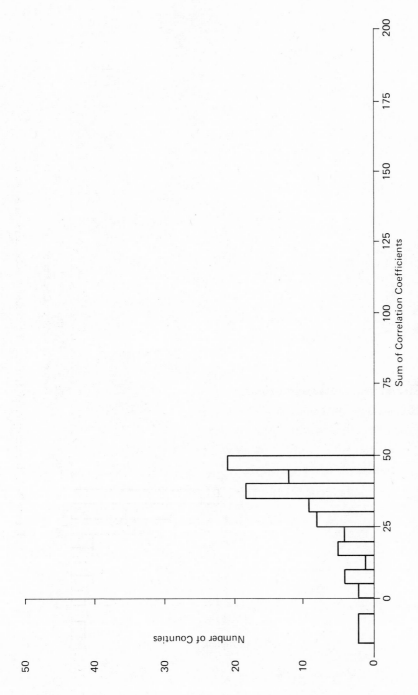

Figure 9–8. Distribution of Indices of Similarity — Northwest Region

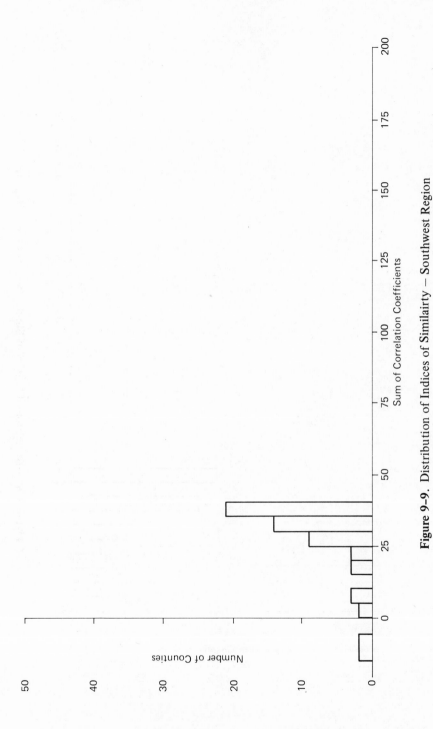

Figure 9-9. Distribution of Indices of Similairty — Southwest Region

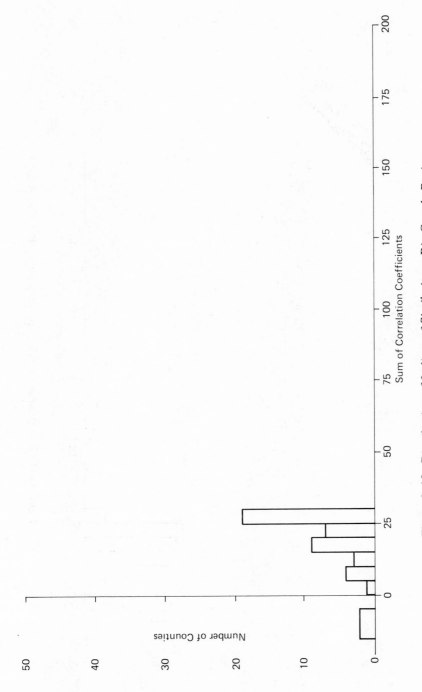

Figure 9–10. Distribution of Indices of Similarity — Rio Grande Region

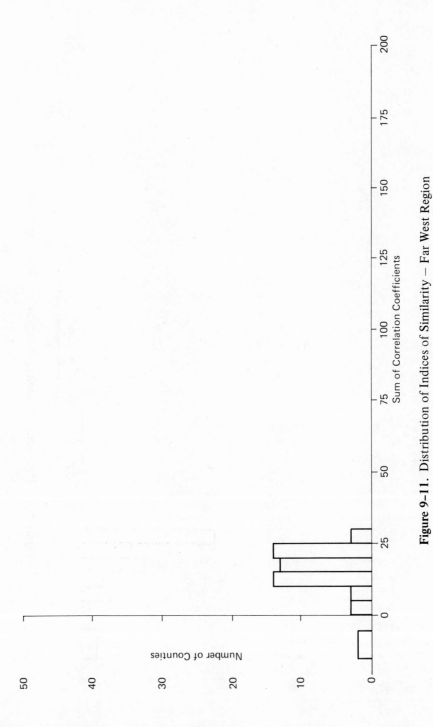

Figure 9–11. Distribution of Indices of Similarity — Far West Region

Limitations of the Statistical Technique. It was found that the statistical technique failed to identify dissimilar places when the number of observations (counties) within a region was extremely small. Three regions were affected: Delmarva, New England, and Terre Haute. The criteria for county selection, discussed below, were applied to all counties within the three smallest regions. All other regions had a sufficient number of counties so that the statistical technique did differentiate between the similar and dissimilar counties. The modified shift-share analysis can only be used on economically homogeneous regions of the country. In nonhomogeneous regions, each county should be examined using the criteria for county selection.

Basis of Criteria for County Selection

Counties selected by the modified shift-share analysis were analyzed in detail with respect to employment and population. Four criteria were employed: (1) percentage change in employment in seven major sectors; (2) ratio of manufacturing employment to total employment; (3) ratio of nonbasic employment to total employment; and (4) percentage change in population between 1960 and 1970. The criteria are discussed later in this chapter. The background for their selection is presented here.

Counties identified by the modified shift-share analysis were: (1) counties that were more depressed than others within their regions; (2) counties with extremely specialized economies, such as recreation, mining, and retirement; and (3) counties that reflected potential for further growth concurrent with employment growth impact in surrounding areas. A minimum requirements approach was used to identify counties of the last type.

The minimum requirements approach determines the minimum percentage of a labor force required in various sectors of an area's economy to maintain the viability of the area.[5] Three modifications were introduced. First, the distinction between basic production (for export) and nonbasic production (for local consumption) for each industrial sector was dropped in preference to aggregating manufacturing employment as the area's basic export sector. Second, employment in the various trade and service industries was aggregated to represent the area's nonbasic employment structure. Last, rather than comparing the employment characteristics of areas with each other, the benchmark for comparison was the average regional distribution of employment by major industrial sectors.[g]

[g]Fundamentals of export base theory are brought into the analysis by the first and second modifications. The distinction between export industries and tertiary or service industries and activities is straightforward. In theory, economic activities directly related to the export of goods and services are said to create a flow of funds into the exporting area which induces further growth and sets the overall level of activity in the local service and trade sectors. See Douglass C. North, "Location Theory and Regional Economic Growth," *Journal of Political Economy*, vol. 63, June 1955, pp. 243-58, and Harvey H. Perloff, et al., *Regions, Resources and Economic Growth* University of Nebraska Press: Lincoln, 1960, particularly chapter 4, "Theories of Regional Economic Growth," pp. 55-62.

Two employment base measures were developed. The first was the ratio of manufacturing employment to total employment. The relative size of an area's manufacturing base is related to national and regional market forces. The greater the demand for an area's manufacturing goods, the larger the relative size of the area's manufacturing base. It was determined that the relative size of an area's manufacturing base was of strategic importance for an area's overall future employment growth. According to Perloff,

manufacturing is one of the largest and most dynamic sectors of total employment. In explaining shifts in total employment, its role is especially important because it is the basic link between resource sectors and consumming sectors of the economy. Because internal and external economies of scale are so often important, a significant segment of manufacturing activity is characterized by a large intra-industry absorption of inputs and outputs and a locational orientation towards "intermediate" inputs and outputs.[6]

The second employment base measure was a ratio of the sum of all employment in the trade and service industries to total employment. This is considered the nonbasic component of an area's industrial structure. It must be large enough to service the area's local market and surrounding counties. Although most economic base studies assume that the nonbasic sector is primarily "adaptive" to changes in the export sector, it was assumed that the relative size of both sectors—basic and nonbasic—is significant in the development process of distressed areas.[7] Thus, the employment structure of an area is considered to offer greater potential for future growth and impact on the surrounding area when the percent employed in the basic and nonbasic sectors is greater than or equal to that of its region.[8] A listing of the industries in both the basic and nonbasic sectors appears below.

The third part of the methodology follows logically from the base analysis described above. If an area's economic base is at least as viable as that of the representative base for the region, overall employment and population growth should be increasing. Two variables were developed to measure the aggregate growth process.[9] The first measures the percent change in employment during the decade preceding the computation of the basic and nonbasic components of an area's employment structure.[h]

Since comparable employment data was not available for the 1960-70 decade, the second variable—the percent change in an area's population—was used as a proxy for estimating continued employment growth.[i] Together, both

---

[h]The employment variable discussed above excludes employment in the military sector as well as employment in major industrial sectors which are declining nationally.

[i]The use of population growth as a proxy for employment growth received support from an experiment performed concurrently with this study. Basically, the percent change in employment for 1,435 counties for the same period. The resulting correlation coefficient was 0.98. When the counties were divided into two groups—growing counties and nongrowing counties as measured by overall population changes—the correlation coefficient for the growing counties (population and employment both increasing) was 0.98. For nongrowing counties, the correlation coefficient was 0.93. These results were sufficiently significant to warrant using population change as a proxy variable for employment growth.

variables described a twenty-year growth path for each of the areas in-cluded in this study.

GCIS Application

Three classification categories—Type I, Type II, and Type III counties—were developed by this analysis. The four variables discussed in the previous section were used to determine a county's classification. Table 9-4 indicates the regional norms that counties were compared to in connection with each of the decision criteria. To satisfy each criterion, a county had to equal or surpass the regional average.

The first variable used in the analysis was the percent change in employment in the following seven major employment sectors: (1) contract construction; (2) manufacturing; (3) trade; (4) finance, insurance and real estate; (5) commu-nications and utilities; (6) services; and (7) public administration. Nationwide, these seven employment sectors experienced growth during the past two decades. Employment in the primary, mining, and railway transportation services sectors declined during the same period. Employment growth could not occur unless the other sectors were able to absorb the employment decreases in the latter three declining sectors.

Military employment was also omitted from this decision variable, although it was not a declining sector. The presence of a military base often stimulates the local service sector, particularly entertainment. If a county has been able to grow by supporting the military, this fact will be reflected in the service sector. As stated in the previous section, the county's employment growth, as defined

Table 9-4
Regional Norms for Decision Criteria

Region	Employment Change 1950–60	Ratio of Nonbasic Empl. to Total Empl. 1960	Ratio of Mfg. Empl. to Total Empl. 1960	Change in County Population 1960–70
New England	12.8%	.53	.32	9.7%
Delmarva	22.3%	.43	.30	7.7%
Terre Haute	11.9%	.50	.25	0.9%
Appalachia	18.8%	.45	.30	3.7%
Ozarks	21.7%	.55	.17	8.9%
Tennessee-Green Valley	22.4%	.49	.18	6.1%
Great Lakes	22.1%	.50	.26	12.2%
Coastal Plains	30.9%	.46	.20	12.0%
South Central	30.4%	.53	.19	11.7%
Northwest	24.0%	.55	.13	4.3%
Southwest	47.0%	.59	.13	25.3%
Rio Grande	31.0%	.57	.09	9.4%
Far West	32.7%	.56	.23	17.9%

above, had to exceed the corresponding regional employment growth rate.

The second decision criterion used two variables. The first was the ratio of manufacturing employment to total employment. The second was the ratio of nonbasic employment to total employment. Nonbasic employment is defined as the sum of employment in: (1) contract construction; (2) trade; (3) finance, insurance and real estate; (4) communications and utilities; (5) services; and (6) public administration. The logic behind the use of these ratios was discussed earlier.

In each case, the ratio for the growth center county had to be equal to or greater than that of the corresponding region. Counties could meet this decision criterion only by having both manufacturing and nonbasic employment ratios greater than or equal to the regional average. This insured that counties selected as Type I growth centers had a sufficient manufacturing and service base to support continued economic expansion.

The third decision variable was the percent change in population between 1960 and 1970. To be selected as a Type I or Type II growth center, the county's population increase had to exceed that for the entire region.

The relationship between the decision criteria and the Type I, Type II, and Type III ratings is summarized in table 9-5. In the chart, a "+" indicates that the criterion must be met; "−" indicates it need not be met.

To contain a Type I growth center, it was necessary for the county to meet both the 1960 base requirements and the requirement for population increase for 1960-70. A county could still be characterized as a Type I growth center if the 1950-60 employment growth rate was below the regional average. The 1950-60 period was viewed as a readjustment or transition period during which a viable economic base might be established to support growth during the following decade.

To contain a Type II growth center, a county had to meet one of three conditions:

Table 9-5
Growth Center Decision Chart

Designation of County	Percentage Change in Employment—1950-60	Manufacturing and Nonbasic Employment Ratio—1960	Percentage Change in Population 1960-70
Type I	+	+	+
Type I	−	+	+
Type II	+	−	+
Type II	+	+	−
Type II	−	−	+
Type III	−	+	−
Type III	+	−	−
Type III	−	−	−

1. *Satisfy both the percentage change in employment criterion and the percent change in population criterion.* If the county had also passed the manufacturing and nonbasic employment test, it would have been a Type I candidate. If it did not pass the manufacturing and nonbasic employment test, it was felt that a population change exceeding the regional rate indicated potential for growth. Thus, the county was designated as a Type II candidate

2. *Satisfy both the percent change in employment criterion and the manufacturing and nonbasic employment criterion.* In this case, growth for the period 1960 to 1970 was not demonstrated, although the county's employment structure appeared to have potential. Therefore, the designation is Type II

3. *Satisfy the percent change in population criterion only.* In this case, the county demonstrated population growth in the period 1960 to 1970, in spite of the fact that employment growth did not previously occur.

Areas that did not meet the conditions outlined for selection as Type I or Type II growth centers were classified as Type III.

The location of the counties selected by the above procedure with respect to Standard Metropolitan Statistical Areas (SMSAs) was considered. When selected counties were contiguous to SMSAs, the central city[j] of the SMSA was designated as the growth center, unless the RA county or counties were contiguous to the selected county and not contiguous to the SMSA. This was done because of the dominance of the SMSA in the area's labor market.

In most cases, counties contiguous to SMSAs are primarily bedroom communities and therefore provide less returns for EDA investment than the SMSA. However, when the RA county or counties were contiguous only to the selected county and not to the SMSA, the selected county was chosen as possibly containing a growth center. In this case, nearness to the RA county or counties was considered more important than the dominance of the SMSA.

EDA's legislation (Public Works and Economic Development Act of 1965) states that a growth center must be "geographically and economically so related to the district that its economic growth may reasonably be expected to contribute significantly to the alleviation of distress in the redevelopment areas of the district." On the basis of this requirement, a county was classified as Type III unless: (1) it bordered on at least one redevelopment area; and (2) the county line of one or more of the contiguous redevelopment areas was no more than 30 minutes commuting time from the largest place within the selected county, which was designated as the growth center.

EDA employee surveys have shown that 95 percent of all workers commute less than one hour to their place of work from their place of residence. The 30-minute time restriction to the county line insured that the majority of persons in the contiguous RA county or counties lay within one-hour commuting distance of the center.

---

[j]If under 250,000 population.

242

Implementation of the GCIS

This section presents the results of applying the GCIS to 1,440 counties (45 percent of the nation's counties). The 1,440 counties include all counties located within authorized and designated economic development districts[k] plus non-district counties linked to the districts by commuting and trade patterns.

The counties and districts were grouped into thirteen regions as described previously. Each of the regions is relatively homogeneous, both geographically and economically. Each can be considered distressed on the basis of income and unemployment.

The objective of the analysis was to identify growth centers within and near economic development districts (EDDs). Most of the growth centers identified were located within economic development districts, but in a few cases, the analysis identified a growth center in a nondistrict county contiguous to a district.

The analysis identified thirty Type I EDCs and fifty-three Type II EDCs and RCs in the thirteen regions. A summary of the findings with respect to EDCs and RCs is presented in table 9-6.

In addition, forty-one other places were identified as Type I or Type II growth centers within the thirteen regions. Five were within designated economic development districts, and thirteen were located outside designated districts, but within the commuting and trade patterns of the district. The remaining twenty-three were located in districts that were authorized or funded (but not designated) at the time of system implementation.

All counties in EDDs designated or authorized at the time of the evaluation were analyzed. As previously noted, modified districts were formed through the addition of counties linked to the district in commuting and trade patterns. No attempt was made to alter specified district boundaries, but only to identify nearby economically related counties that contained growth centers. Five districts were found to possess such a county outside the district boundaries.

Forty-two districts did not include a place considered acceptable as a growth

Table 9-6
Analysis of Presently Designated Centers

Category of Center	Type I	Type II	Type III
Economic Development Centers	30	40	65
Redevelopment Centers	0	13	53

[k]Districts authorized or designated as of December 30, 1970.

center. However, as noted, boundaries could be modified in five of these districts to include a growth center. In one district, none of the designated centers were acceptable, but a nondesignated town did meet the growth center criteria. The remaining thirty-seven lacked a place that could function as a growth center under the assumptions of the GCIS methodology.

Summary findings for each of the thirteen regions are presented below. Statistical descriptions of each of the centers are given in appendix C.

New England Region

The system identified six Type II growth centers in the New England Region, which is shown in figure 9-12. No Type I centers were selected. The Type II centers consisted of three economic development centers, two redevelopment centers, and one additional growth center. Boston, Massachusetts, would have been identified as a Type II growth center if its population had not exceeded 250,000.

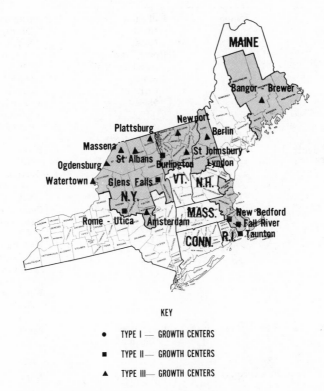

KEY

•   TYPE I — GROWTH CENTERS

■   TYPE II — GROWTH CENTERS

▲   TYPE III — GROWTH CENTERS

Figure 9–12. New England Region

Ten of EDA's EDCs and RCs were classified as Type III growth centers. All ten of these places were so described because of insufficient population increase and inadequate employment base. Five of these places also lacked employment growth.

The New England Region contains six economic development districts with seven economic development centers and eight redevelopment centers. None of these places was classified as a Type I center, and only five of these fifteen EDA centers were identified as Type II centers. These are located in three economic development districts: Southeastern, Eastern Adirondack, and Mohawk Valley. The other districts contained only Type III centers. However, when the district boundary of the New Hampshire-Vermont District was modified, Burlington, Vermont, was identified as a Type II growth center.

A list of the Type II centers and the Type III EDA growth centers is presented in table 9-7.

Table 9-7
Analysis Results for the New England Region

Category of Center	Type I	Type II	Type III
Economic Development Centers	None	Fall River (Bristol), Mass. Rome-Utica (Oneida), N.Y. Taunton (Bristol), Mass.	Amsterdam (Montgomery), N.Y. Bangor-Brewer (Penobscot), Me. Newport (Orleans), Vt. St. Johnsbury-Lyndon (Caledonia), Vt.
Redevelopment Centers	None	Glen Falls (Warren), N.Y. New Bedford (Bristol), Mass.	Berlin (Coos), N.H. Masenna (St. Lawrence), N.Y. Ogdensburg (St. Lawrence), N.Y. Plattsburg (Clinton), N.Y. St. Albans (Franklin), Vt. Watertown (Jefferson), N.Y.
Additional Growth Centers	None	Burlington (Chittendon), Vt.	None
Growth Centers Over 250,000	None	Boston, Mass.	None

Delmarva Region

The GCIS identified two Type II growth centers in the Delmarva Region: Dover, Delaware; and Salisbury, Maryland. Both are EDCs in the Delmarva Economic Development District, and both lacked the manufacturing employment base necessary to be identified as Type I growth centers. No other centers were identified in the region, which is depicted in figure 9-13.

Terre Haute Region

The GCIS identified the only EDC in the region—Terre Haute—as a Type I growth center. The West Central District in Indiana is the only district within the region, which is shown in figure 9-14.

Appalachian Region

The system identified nine Type I growth centers and six Type II centers in the Appalachian Region, which appears in figure 9-15. The Type I centers consisted of eight EDCs, and one center in an authorized district.

Of the six Type II growth centers, five are EDCs and one is an RC. All five EDCs lacked a sufficient manufacturing base to be Type I centers. The RC was not identified as Type I because of inadequate population growth between 1960 and 1970.

Twenty-one present EDCs and RCs were classified as Type III by the system. All twenty-one failed to satisfy the change in population criterion. Fifteen also failed to increase in employment, while five lacked a sufficient employment base.

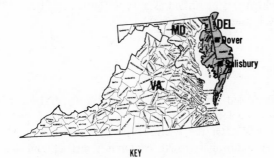

KEY

●   TYPE I — GROWTH CENTERS

■   TYPE II— GROWTH CENTERS

▲   TYPE III— GROWTH CENTERS

Figure 9-13. Delmarva Region

KEY

●　TYPE I — GROWTH CENTERS

■　TYPE II — GROWTH CENTERS

▲　TYPE III — GROWTH CENTERS

Figure 9-14. Terre Haute Region

Cincinnati, Ohio, would have been selected as a Type I growth center if its population had not been over 250,000.

According to the GCIS, six of the fifteen designated EDDs in the Appalachian Region, contain at least one Type I growth center. The Georgia Mountains and East Tennessee Districts each have two Type I growth centers. Two of the remaining designated EDDs contain a Type II growth center, while seven have only Type III growth centers.

In addition, the region has two funded districts and eight authorized districts. One of the authorized districts, Southeast Tennessee, includes Chattanooga, Tennessee, which was identified as a Type I growth center. A list of the center classifications is presented in table 9-8.

Ozarks Region

The GCIS identified seven Type I and twelve Type II growth centers in the Ozarks Region depicted in figure 9-16. The seven Type I centers are all designated as EDCs. Of the twelve Type II centers, seven are EDCs, three are RCs, one is an additional growth center in a district, and one is an additional growth center in a county contiguous to a district.

Ten of the Type II centers exhibited an insufficient employment base, while the other two declined in population between 1960 and 1970. Two Standard

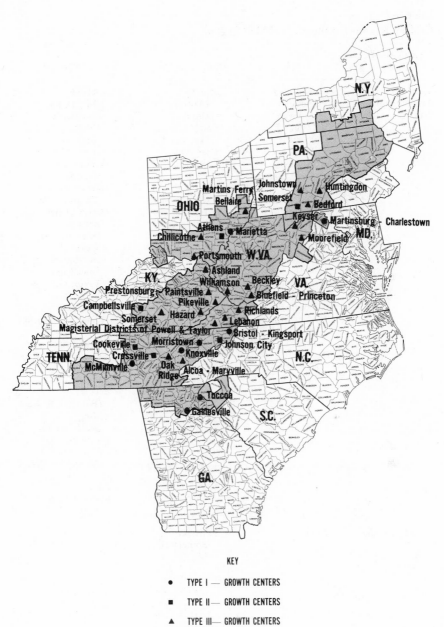

KEY

●   TYPE I — GROWTH CENTERS

■   TYPE II — GROWTH CENTERS

▲   TYPE III— GROWTH CENTERS

Figure 9-15. Appalachian Region

Table 9-8
Analysis Results for the Appalachian Region

Category of Center	Type I	Type II	Type III
Economic Development Centers	Bristol-Kingsport (Sullivan), Tenn.	Athens (Athens), Ohio	Ashland (Boyd), Ky.
	Gainesville (Hall), Ga.	Campbellsville (Taylor), Ky.	Alcoa-Maryville (Blount), Tenn.
	Knoxville (Knox), Tenn.	Cookeville (Putnam), Tenn.	Chillicothe (Ross), Ohio
	Marietta (Washington), Ohio	Crossville (Cumberland), Tenn.	Huntingdon (Huntingdon), Pa.
	Martinsburg-Charlestown (Berkley-Jefferson), W. Va.	Johnson City (Washington), Tenn.	Johnstown (Cambria), Pa.
	McMinnville (Warren), Tenn.		Martin's Ferry-Bellaire (Belmont), Ohio
	Morristown (Hamblen), Tenn.		Magisterial Districts of Powell and Taylor (Scott), Va.
	Toccoa (Stephens), Ga.		Oak Ridge (Anderson, Roane), Tenn.
			Portsmouth (Scioto), Ohio
			Somerset (Pulaski), Ky.
			Beckley (Raleigh), W. Va.
			Bedford (Bedford), Pa.
			Bluefield-Princeton (Mercer), W. Va.
			Hazard (Perry), Ky.
			Keyser (Mineral), W. Va.
Redevelopment Centers	None	Somerset (Somerset), Pa.	

Table 9-8 (Cont.)

Category of Center	Type I	Type II	Type III
			Lebanon (Russell), Va.
			Moorefield (Hardy), W. Va.
			Pikeville (Pike), Ky.
			Prestonburg-Paintsville (Floyo-Johnson), Ky.
			Richlands (Tazewell), Va.
			Williamson (Mingo), W. Va.
Additional Growth Centers	Chattanooga (Hamilton), Tenn.	None	None
Growth Centers Over 250,000	Cincinnati, Ohio	None	None

Metropolitan Statistical Areas, Oklahoma City and Tulsa, would have been identified as Type I growth centers, but exceeded EDA's legislative population limit of 250,000.

Eleven EDCs and four RCs were classified as Type III growth centers by the system. Of the fifteen Type III places, fourteen lacked an adequate employment base, thirteen exhibited insufficient employment growth, and all had declines or small increases in population.

A list of the growth centers and the Type III EDA centers is presented in table 9-9.

The Ozarks Region is comprised of sixteen districts: one in Kansas; three in Missouri; six in Oklahoma; and six in Arkansas. All the districts are designated except the one in Kansas, which is funded. Twenty-five EDCs and seven RCs have been designated in these districts.

The seven Type I growth centers are distributed among five of the fifteen designated districts. Five other districts contain at least one of the ten Type II growth centers. Five of the designated districts contain only Type III growth centers. In addition, the system identified no growth center for the funded district in Kansas.

The Lakes County District in Missouri could be modified to include Joplin in

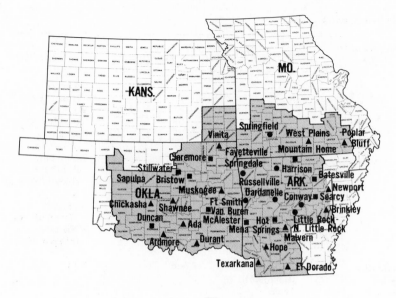

KEY

●   TYPE I — GROWTH CENTERS

■   TYPE II— GROWTH CENTERS

▲   TYPE III— GROWTH CENTERS

Figure 9–16. Ozarks Region

Jasper County, which was identified as a Type II growth center. The South Central District in Oklahoma contains a Type II growth center that is not presently designated. This is the town of Lawton. These two places were the only additional growth centers identified.

Tennessee-Green Valley Region

The GCIS identified nine Type I and four Type II centers in the Tennessee-Green Valley Region (figure 9-17). Two of the Type I centers are EDCs; the other seven are additional growth centers.

    Two of the Type II centers are EDCs, and two are additional centers. Both Type II EDCs lacked the manufacturing employment base necessary to be identified as Type I centers. Three SMSAs would have been identified as Type I growth centers, but all had populations exceeding 250,000.

    Five EDCs and five RCs were classified as Type III growth centers by the system. Eight of the ten declined in population, while the other two exhibited

Table 9-9

Analysis Results for the Ozarks Region

Category of Center	Type I	Type II	Type III
Economic Development Centers	Conway (Faulkner), Ark. Fayetteville-Springdale (Washington), Ark. Ft. Smith-Van Buren (Sebastian), Ark. Harrison (Boone), Ark. Little Rock-N. Little Rock (Pulaski), Ark. Russellville-Dardanelle (Pope, Yell), Ark. Springfield (Green), Mo.	Claremore (Rogers), Okla. Duncan (Stephens), Okla. Hot Springs (Garland), Ark. Mena (Polk), Ark. Mountain Home (Baxter), Ark. Sapula-Bristow (Creek), Okla. Stillwater (Payne), Okla.	Ada (Pontotoc), Okla. Ardmore (Carter), Okla. Chickasha (Grady), Okla. Durant (Bryan), Okla. El Dorado (Union), Ark. Newport (Jackson), Ark. Poplar Bluff (Butler), Mo. Shawnee (Pottawatomie), Okla. Texarkana (Miller), Ark. Vinita (Craig), Okla. West Plains (Howell), Mo.
Redevelopment Centers	None	Batesville (Independence), Ark. McAlester (Pittsburg), Okla. Searcy (White), Ark.	Brinkley (Monroe), Ark. Hope (Hampstead), Ark. Malvern (Hot Spring), Ark. Muskogee (Muskogee), Okla.
Additional Growth Centers	None	Joplin (Jasper, Newton), Mo.	None

Table 9-9 (Cont.)

Category of Center	Type I	Type II	Type III
		Lawton (Comanche), Okla.	
Growth Centers Over 250,000	Tulsa (Tulsa), Okla.	Oklahoma City (Oklahoma), Okla.	

population increases of less than 2 percent. Nine were so classified on the basis of insufficient manufacturing employment base.

The Tennessee-Green Valley Region is comprised of thirteen districts: eight designated districts; three funded districts; and two authorized districts. Nine EDCs and five RCs have been designated within the eight designated districts.

Four of the designated districts have a Type I or Type II growth center. Two other districts could be modified to include a Type I growth center. In three designated districts, the GCIS identified only Type III growth centers.

Two designated districts could be modified to include a Type I growth center. One authorized district and two funded districts each contain at least one Type I growth center.

The rankings of centers are identified in table 9-10.

Great Lakes Region

Three Type I growth centers, and six Type II centers were identified in the Great Lakes Region. The three Type I centers included one economic development center and two additional growth centers. The region is depicted in figure 9-18.

One Type II growth center is an EDC. In addition, three RCs and two additional growth centers were identified as Type II centers. One of the additional places is in a designated district.

Two EDA-designated economic development centers and eight redevelopment centers were classified as Type II by the identification system. All but one declined in population, and all but two exhibited an insufficient employment base.

Minneapolis-St. Paul would have been identified as a Type I center if its population had not exceeded 250,000. A list of the growth centers and the Type III EDA centers is presented in table 9-11.

The Great Lakes Region is comprised of seven designated districts and four authorized districts. Four EDCs and eleven RCs have been designated by EDA within the seven designated districts.

KEY

●   TYPE I — GROWTH CENTERS

■   TYPE II — GROWTH CENTERS

▲   TYPE III— GROWTH CENTERS

Figure 9–17. Tennessee-Green Valley Region

The East Central District in Michigan contains five counties identified as Type I and Type II growth centers by the GCIS. Three of these are designated as the Bay City-Midland-Saginaw Economic Development Center. The other two are Mt. Pleasant in Isabella County and Tawas City-East Tawas in Iosco, both identified as Type II centers.

Three other designated districts contain at least one Type II growth center and three contain only Type III centers.

One of the authorized districts contains a Type I growth center, and one district could be modified to include a Type II growth center.

Table 9-10
Analysis Results for the Tennessee-Green Valley Region

Category of Center	Type I	Type II	Type III
Economic Development Centers	Bowling Green (Warren), Ky. Jonesboro (Craighead), Ark.	Carbondale (Jackson), Ill. Elizabethtown-Radcliff-Vinegrove (Hardin), Ky.	Dexter-Bloomfield (Stoddard), Mo. Glasgow (Barren), Ky. Hopkinsville (Christian), Ky. Madisonville (Hopkins), Ky. Sikeston (Scott), Mo.
Redevelopment Centers	None	None	Batesville (Panola), Miss. Clarksdale, (Coahoma), Miss. Forrest City (St. Francis), Ark. Harrisburg (Saline), Ill. New Madrid (New Madrid), Mo.
Additional Growth Centers	Cape Girardeau (Cape Girardeau), Mo. Corinth (Alcorn), Miss. Jackson (Madison), Tenn. Lexington (Fayette), Ky. Murray (Calloway), Ky. Owensboro (Daviess), Ky. Union City (Obion), Tenn.	Clarksville (Montgomery), Tenn. Paducah (McCracken), Ky.	None

Table 9-10 (Cont.)

Category of Center	Type I	Type II	Type III
Growth Centers Over 250,000	Louisville, Ky. Memphis, Tenn. Nashville, Tenn.	None	None

Coastal Plains Region

The system identified eight Type I and seventeen Type II growth centers in the Coastal Plains Region illustrated in figure 9-19. Seven of the eight Type I centers are EDCs and the remaining Type I center is contiguous to two authorized districts. Of the seventeen Type II centers, twelve are EDCs, one is in a district, and four are contiguous to districts.

KEY

●   TYPE I — GROWTH CENTERS

■   TYPE II— GROWTH CENTERS

▲   TYPE III— GROWTH CENTERS

Figure 9-18. Great Lakes Region

Table 9-11

Analysis Results for the Great Lakes Region

Category of Center	Type I	Type II	Type III
Economic Development Centers	Bay City- Midland- Saginaw (Bay, Midland, Saginaw), Mich.	Tawas City- East Tawas (Iosco), Mich.	Duluth (St. Louis), Minn. Ontanagon- White Pine (Ontanagon), Mich.
Redevelopment Centers	None	Alpena (Alpena), Mich. Marquette- Negaunee- Ishpeming (Marquette), Mich. Traverse City (Grand Traverse), Mich.	Escanaba- Gladstone (Delta), Mich. Houghton (Houghton), Mich. Iron Mountain- Kingsford- Norway (Dickinson), Mich. Iron River (Iron), Mich. Ironwood- Bessemer- Wakefield (Gogebic), Mich. Newberry (Luce), Mich. St. Ignace (Mackinac), Mich. Saulte- St. Marie (Chippewa), Mich.
Additional Growth Centers	Grand Rapids (Kent), Mich. Grayling (Crawford), Mich.	Mt. Pleasant (Isabella), Mich. St. Cloud (Stearns), Minn.	None
Growth Centers Over 250,000	Minneapolis- St. Paul, Minn.	None	None

KEY

●　TYPE I — GROWTH CENTERS

■　TYPE II— GROWTH CENTERS

▲　TYPE III— GROWTH CENTERS

Figure 9–19. Coastal Plains Region

Eight of the Type II centers were identified as such on the basis of an insufficient total employment base, three lacked the necessary change in employment and also exhibited an insufficient employment base, and eight did not meet the requisite population change between 1960 and 1970. One Standard Metropolitan Statistical Area—Atlanta, Georgia—would have been identified as a growth center except that it exceeded EDA's legislative population limit of 250,000.

Eleven EDCs and four RCs were classified as Type III growth centers. Of these fifteen places, ten lacked sufficient employment bases, twelve exhibited inadequate employment growth, and eleven declined or showed only a small increase in population.

The Coastal Plains Region contains twenty designated economic development districts and four authorized districts. The GCIS identified Type I growth centers in seven of the designated EDDs. In addition, when the districts are modified by adding contiguous counties related by trade and commuting patterns, the Waccamaw District of South Carolina includes Charleston, a Type I growth center. Nine of the remaining designated districts include at least one Type II center; two of the four authorized districts have a Type II growth center in a county contiguous to the district.

A list of the centers and their classification is presented in table 9-12.

South Central Region

The system identified four Type I and nine Type II growth centers in the South Central Region (figure 9-20). Two of the four Type I centers are EDCs, and two are located in separate authorized districts. Of the nine Type II growth centers, seven are EDCs, one is in an authorized district, and another is contiguous to a designated district. Six of the Type II growth centers exhibited an insufficient employment base to be selected as Type I, while the other three declined in population between 1960 and 1970. One Standard Metropolitan Statistical Area—Dallas, Texas—was identified as a growth center, but exceeded the legislative population limit of 250,000.

Fourteen EDCs and seven RCs were classified as Type III growth centers through the analysis. Of the twenty-one such places, thirteen lacked a sufficient employment base, twelve exhibited inadequate employment growth, and all declined or showed only a small increase in population.

There are nineteen designated or authorized economic development districts in the South Central Region. The four Type I growth centers are located in four separate districts—two authorized and two designated. The GCIS identified one Type II growth center in six of the districts. One district, if modified, would have one Type II growth center. Seven districts have neither a Type I nor a Type II growth center.

A list of the centers is presented in table 9-13.

Table 9–12
Analysis Results for the Coastal Plains Region

Category of Center	Type I	Type II	Type III

Economic Development Centers	Aiken-
	  N. Augusta
	  (Aiken), S.C.
	Athens
	  (Clarke), Ga.
	Brunswick
	  (Glynn), Ga.
	Carrollton
	  (Carroll),
	  Ga.
	Dothan
	  (Dale-
	  Houston),
	  Ala.
	Greenwood
	  (Greenwood),
	  S.C.
	Wilmington
	  (New Hanover
	  Burnswick),
	  N.C.
		Albany
		  (Dougherty),
		  Ga.
		Augusta
		  (Richmond),
		  Ga.
		Dublin-East
		  Dublin
		  (Laurens),
		  Ga.
		Fayetteville
		  (Cumberland),
		  N.C.
		Florence-
		  Darlington
		  (Florence-
		  Darlington),
		  S.C.
		Hinesville
		  (Liberty),
		  Ga.
		Kinston
		  (Lenoir),
		  N.C.
		Milledgeville
		  (Baldwin),
		  Ga.
		Panama City
		  (Bay), Fla.
		Tifton
		  (Tift), Ga.
		Valdosta
		  (Lowndes),
		  Ga.
		Waycross
		  (Ware), Ga.
			Americus
			  (Sumter), Ga.
			Bainbridge
			  (Decatur), Ga.
			Columbus
			  (Muscogee), Ga.
			Goldsboro
			  (Wayne), N.C.
			LaGrange
			  (Troup), Ga.
			Marianna
			  (Jackson), Fla.
			Montgomery
			  (Jackson), Fla.
			New Bern
			  (Craven), N.C.
			Swainsboro
			  (Emanuel), Ga.
			Washington
			  (Beaufort), N.C.
			Williamston
			  (Martin), N.C.

Redevelopment Centers	None	None	Greenville
			  (Butler), Ala.
			Greenville
			  (Pitt), N.C.
			Orangeburg
			  (Orangeburg),
			  S.C.
			Troy
			  (Pike), Ala.

Table 9–12 (Cont.)

Category of Center	Type I	Type II	Type III
Additional Growth Centers	Charleston (Charleston-Berkley), S.C.	Columbia (Richland), S.C. Gainesville (Alachua), Fla. Jacksonville (Onslow), N.C. Pensacola (Escambia), Fla. Tallahassee (Leon), Fla.	None
Growth Centers Over 250,000	Atlanta, Ga.	None	None

Northwest Region

The GCIS identified four Type I growth centers and two Type II centers in the Northwest Region shown in figure 9-21. The four Type I centers included only one designated EDC: Lewiston, Idaho. The other three Type I centers were additional growth centers. Two other places were identified as Type II growth centers. Both lacked a sufficient manufacturing employment base to be identified as Type I centers.

Two EDCs and two RCs were classified as Type III on the basis of an inadequate employment base and a decline in population.

Eight economic development districts make up the Northwest Region. Five are designated districts and three are authorized districts.

Three economic development centers and two redevelopment centers are located within the five designated districts. Only Lewiston, an EDC in Clearwater District in Idaho, was identified as a Type I center. In the Big Horn District, Hardin was classified as Type III, but Billings, a Type I center, could be incorporated into the district by adding Yellowstone County.

In the Trico District in Washington, the redevelopment center of Colville was also classified as Type III and no center was identified to take its place. In the Inter-County District in Montana, the existing redevelopment center of Butte-Anaconda was classified as Type III through the analysis, but two other towns

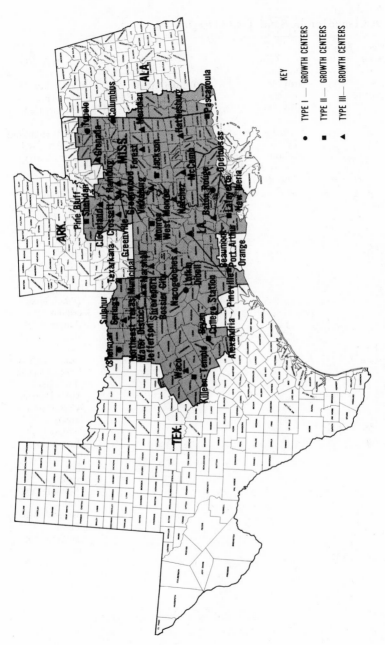

Figure 9–20. South Central Region

Table 9-13

Analysis Results for the South Central Region

Category of Center	Type I	Type II	Type III
Economic Development Center	Baton Rouge (E. Baton Rouge), La. Nacogdoches-Lufkin-Diboll (Nacogdoches-Angelena), Tex.	Bryan College Station (Brazos), Tex. Jackson (Hinds), Miss. Killeen-Temple (Bell), Tex. Lafayette-New Iberia (Lafayette), La. Monroe-West Monroe (Ouachita), La. Pascagoula (Jackson), Miss. Pine Bluff-Sheridan (Jefferson), Ark.	Bossier City-Shreveport (Bossier,Caddo), La. Crossett-Hamburg (Ashley), Ark. Forest (Scott), Miss. Grenada (Grenada), Miss. Hattiesburg (Forrest), Miss. Marshall (Harrison), Tex. McComb (Pike), Miss. Meridian (Lauderdale), Miss. Natchez (Adams), Miss. Northeast Texas Municipal Water District (Cass, Camp, Morris, Upshaw), Tex. Sulfur Springs (Hopkins), Tex. Texarkana (Bowie), Tex. Vicksburg (Warren), Miss. Waco (McLennan), Tex.

Table 9–13 (Cont.)

Category of Center	Type I	Type II	Type III
Redevelopment Centers	None	None	Alexandria-Pineville (Rapides), La. Cleveland (Bolivia), Miss. Greenville (Washington), Miss. Greenwood (LeFlore), Miss. Jefferson (Marion), Tex. Natchitoches (Natchitoches), La. Opelousas (St. Landry), La.
Additional Growth Centers	Sherman (Grayson), Tex. Tupelo (Lee), Miss.	Beaumont-Port Arthur-Orange (Orange), Tex. Columbus (Lowndes), Miss.	None
Growth Centers Over 250,000	Dallas, Tex.	None	None

were identified as centers: Bozeman as a Type II center and Missoula as a Type I center, the latter outside present district boundaries.

Growth centers were identified for both of Idaho's authorized districts. Coeur D'Alene was identified as a Type I center in the Northern District and Boise was identified as an additional Type II center for the Southwestern District.

Table 9-14 depicts the findings for this region.

Far West Region

The system identified only one Type I growth center, and four Type II centers in the Far West Region (figure 9-22). Three of the centers—one Type I and two Type II—were additional growth centers in authorized districts. Portland, Oregon; Seattle, Washington; and Sacramento, California, would have been

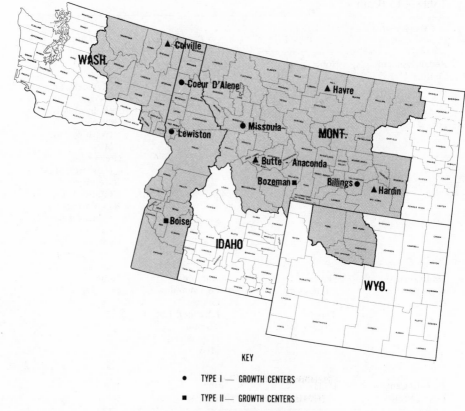

KEY

- •   TYPE I — GROWTH CENTERS
- ■   TYPE II — GROWTH CENTERS
- ▲   TYPE III — GROWTH CENTERS

Figure 9–21. Northwest Region

identified as Type I growth centers if their populations had not exceeded the 250,000 legislative limit. Two RCs were identified as Type II growth centers because they had inadequate manufacturing employment bases.

The Far West Region contains seven districts: one designated; one funded; and five authorized. The region contains no economic development centers and only two RCs, both Type II centers in the Sierra District of California. Three additional growth centers were identified in three authorized districts.

A list of the growth centers is presented in table 9-15.

Southwest Region

Two Type I growth centers and three Type II centers were identified in the Southwest Region depicted in figure 9-23. Both Type I growth centers are

Table 9-14
Analysis Results for the Northwest Region

Category of Center	Type I	Type II	Type III
Economic Development Centers	Lewiston (Nez Perce), Idaho	None	Hardin (Big Horn), Mont. Havre (Hill), Mont.
Redevelopment Centers	None	None	Butte-Anaconda (Silver Bow, Deer Lodge), Mont. Colville (Stevens), Wash.
Additional Growth Centers	Billings (Yellowstone), Mont. Coeur D'Alene (Kootenai), Idaho Missoula (Missoula), Mont.	Boise (Ada), Idaho Bozeman (Gallatin), Mont.	None

additional growth centers (Provo-Orem and Salt Lake City, Utah) that could be added to neighboring economic development districts.

One of the Type II growth centers is an EDC. The other two are additional growth centers in counties contiguous to designated districts. All three Type II centers lacked the manufacturing employment base necessary to be identified as a Type I growth center. Four EDCs and four RCs were classified as Type III on the basis of an insufficient employment base and a decline in population.

The Southwest Region includes four designated economic development districts and one authorized district. In the North Central New Mexico District, the GCIS identified Santa Fe as a Type II growth center, while Las Vegas, a redevelopment center, was classified as Type III. In addition, Albuquerque could be added to the district as an additional Type II growth center.

In the Southern Colorado District, all three EDA growth centers were classified as Type III. The four growth centers designated in the Southeastern and Six-County Utah Districts were also classified as Type III. However, a redevelopment area in the Six-County District could be served by Provo-Orem and Salt Lake City, which are in counties contiguous to the district.

A list of center classifications is presented in table 9-16.

KEY

●   TYPE I — GROWTH CENTERS

■   TYPE II — GROWTH CENTERS

▲   TYPE III— GROWTH CENTERS

Figure 9–22. Far West Region

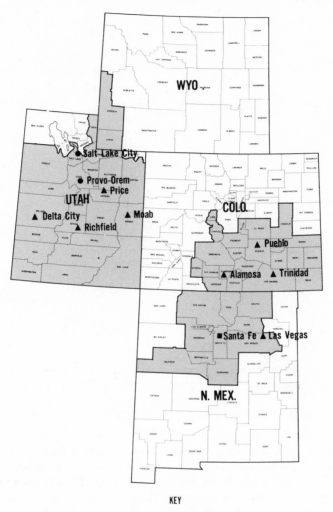

KEY

- TYPE I — GROWTH CENTERS
- TYPE II— GROWTH CENTERS
- ▲ TYPE III— GROWTH CENTERS

Figure 9-23. Southwest Region

Table 9-15
Analysis Results for the Far West Region

Category of Center	Type I	Type II	Type III
Economic Development Centers	None	None	None
Redevelopment Centers	None	Grass Valley-Auburn (Nevada, Placer), Calif. South Lake Tahoe (El Dorado), Calif.	None
Additional Growth Centers	Medford (Jackson), Ore.	Redding (Shasta), Calif. Takoma (Pierce), Wash.	None
Growth Centers Over 250,000	Portland, Ore. Sacramento, Calif. Seattle, Wash.	None	None

Rio Grande Region

The GCIS identified one Type I growth center and three Type II centers in the Rio Grande Region. The Type I center is the economic development center of Victoria. The Type II centers are two RCs, (Del Rio and Laredo) and Eagle Pass, which is an additional growth center. Three redevelopment centers and two EDCs were classified as Type III. The Rio Grande Region is illustrated in figure 9-24.

Although Corpus Christi met the economic criteria for a Type II center, it was classified as Type III because the nearest RA county is more than seventy miles away. San Antonio would have been selected as a growth center if its population had not exceeded the 250,000 legislative limit.

The Rio Grande Region is comprised of four designated districts. The Coastal Bend District has a Type I growth center, while the Middle Rio Grande has two Type II centers, one of which is presently designated as an RC. The South Texas District has one Type II redevelopment center, while the Lower Rio Grande Valley District has only Type III centers.

A list of the centers is given in table 9-17.

Table 9-16
Analysis Results for the Southwest Region

Category of Center	Type I	Type II	Type III
Economic Development Centers	None	Santa Fe (Santa Fe), N. Mex.	Alamosa (Alamosa), Colo. Delta City (Millard), Utah Pueblo (Pueblo), Colo. Trinidad (Las Animas), Colo.
Redevelopment Centers	None	None	Las Vegas (San Miguel), N. Mex. Moab (Grand), Utah Price (Carbon), Utah Richfield (Sevier), Utah
Additional Growth Centers	Provo-Orem (Utah), Utah Salt Lake City (Salt Lake), Utah	Albuquerque (Bernalillo), N. Mex. Colorado Springs (El Paso), Colo.	None

Conclusions

Two major conclusions were reached as a result of the implementation of the Growth Center Identification System: (1) that economic and demographic indicators suggest that the majority of places designated as EDA growth centers offer limited potential for future population or employment growth; and (2) that a significant number of economic development districts do not contain cities with the potential to serve district redevelopment areas as growth centers. However, system implementation also revealed that with only one exception EDA had designated the best possible places within economic development districts. The reason for the agency's apparent failure to designate places with significant potential for future growth stems from the generally depressed nature

KEY

●   TYPE I — GROWTH CENTERS

■   TYPE II — GROWTH CENTERS

▲   TYPE III— GROWTH CENTERS

Figure 9-24. Rio Grande Region

of the districts in which it is legislatively required to work. A substantial number of these multicounty units simply do not include a community with the capacity to serve surrounding areas as a growth center.

Approximately 60 percent of EDA's growth centers did not meet the GCIS criteria for Type I or Type II centers, and thus were judged to have little or no potential for future population or employment growth. The evaluators concluded that the 119 centers that fell into this category were not likely to have an impact on redevelopment areas; in fact, most were experiencing out-migration themselves.

Centers ranked as Type I through the GCIS exhibited a high growth potential,

Table 9–17
Analysis Results for the Rio Grande Region

Category of Center	Type I	Type II	Type III
Economic Development Centers	Victoria (Victoria), Tex.	None	Corpus Christi-Aransas Pass (Neuces, Aransas), Tex. McAllen (Hidalgo), Tex.
Redevelopment Centers	None	Del Rio (Valverde), Tex. Laredo (Webb), Tex.	Brownsville-Harlingen (Cameron), Tex. Uvalde (Uvalde), Tex.
Additional Growth Centers	None	Eagle Pass (Maverick), Tex.	None
Growth Centers Over 250,000	San Antonio, Tex.	None	None

and their growth could be expected to improve conditions in nearby redevelopment areas. Those places classified as Type III centers either offered little or no growth potential or were not located within commuting distance of redeveloping areas. Places identified as Type II centers were less likely to growth and affect surrounding distressed areas than were Type I centers, but could not be classified as Type III centers on the basis of the data examined. Table 9-18 summarizes results of the GCIS implementation for EDA-designated centers.

Of the 103 economic development districts designated or authorized by EDA at the time of system implementation (December 31, 1970), 43 (42 percent) did not contain a place identified as a Type I or Type II growth center. Thus, according to the GCIS, none of these districts contains a city with the potential to serve district redevelopment areas as a growth center. Table 9-19 summarizes the classifications of centers in designated districts.

Two of the thirty-three districts that contain only Type II centers could be modified to include a county with a Type I center. Six of the districts with no Type I or Type II center could be modified to include at least one such place. Four of the six would contain a Type I center, while the other two would have only a Type II center.

Table 9-18
Categorization of Designated Centers

GCIS Ranking	Economic Development Centers		Redevelopment Centers		TOTAL	
	Number	Percentage	Number	Percentage	Number	Percentage
Type I	30	22%	–	–	30	15%
Type II	40	30%	13	19%	52	26%
Type III	65	48%	54	81%	119	59%
TOTAL	135	100%	67	100%	201	100%

Source: Program Evaluation: The Economic Development Administration Growth Center Strategy, Washington, D.C.: U.S. Department of Commerce/Economic Development Administration, February 1972, p. 179.

Table 9–19
GCIS Classifications of Centers in Designated Districts

District Category	Number of Districts
At least one Type I center	27
No Type I center, but at least one Type II center	33
No Type I or Type II center	43
TOTAL	103

Source: Program Evaluation: The Economic Development Administration Growth Center Strategy, Washington, D.C.: U.S. Department of Commerce/Economic Development Administration, February 1972, p. 180

10 Supporting Analysis for the GCIS

Population and Migration Study

Introduction

To support the findings of the Growth Center Identification System (GCIS) and the case studies, a study was conducted to investigate population and migration characteristics of areas in which EDA has implemented its growth center strategy.[1] There were three parts to the study. Part I involved determining whether EDA-designated economic development centers (EDCs) and redevelopment centers (RCs) are migration centers; that is, places that have experienced substantial net in-migration. This segment of the study also investigated absolute population change in EDCs and RCs.

In part II, the migration and population characteristics of EDA-associated districts were examined to determine whether these districts are experiencing out-migration and loss of population. These data were compiled in aggregate form for districts in the twelve[a] regions structured for the GCIS implementation and depicted in figure 9-1. The assumption that growth centers serve districts as migration centers and counter the movement of migrants to large overburdened cities was also examined in this portion of the study. Part III involved an investigation of the population and migration trends in all districts and a comparison with national trends.

Findings and Conclusions

Part I

1. The hypothesis that people are migrating to EDA growth centers was tested and found to be false. 75 percent of all EDA growth center counties underwent net out-migration during the 1950-60 decade: 70 percent of economic development centers and 84 percent of redevelopment centers. This trend increased during the following decade, when 84 percent underwent net out-migration: 77 percent of economic development centers and 97 percent of redevelopment centers.

2. In addition, 42 percent of the counties in which EDA growth centers are located declined in absolute population during both decades.

---

[a]The thirteenth region, Terre Haute, was excluded because it consists of only four counties and one EDC, which is an SMSA.

3. Moreover, 37 percent of all EDA growth centers had net out-migration rates exceeding those of their districts during the decade 1960-70: 30 percent of economic development centers and 48 percent of redevelopment centers.

4. Redevelopment centers appeared to be declining more rapidly than economic development centers. 97 percent of the RCs experienced net out-migration during the last decade. Fifty-nine percent of the RCs declined in absolute population between 1950 and 1960, as opposed to 64 percent during the 1960-70 period.

5. EDCs and RCs in the Great Lakes Region, Northwest, Southwest, New England, and Tennessee-Green Valley Regions appeared to be losing population more rapidly than non-EDC and non-RC counties in those regions. This was also the case, but to a lesser extent, in the Rio Grande Region, Ozarks, Coastal Plains, South Central, and Appalachian Regions.

Part II

1. Loss of population in rural districts seemed to be ending. For the most part, the districts showed no absolute decline in population, a circumstance due largely to a decrease in out-migration rates. This trend occurred despite the fact that a large number of EDCs and RCs declined in overall population.

2. Only four regions (Appalachia, Tennessee-Green Valley, Ozarks, and Southwest) declined in overall population during the 1950-60 period and all regions increased in population during the 1960-70 period.

3. Despite increases in absolute population, most districts were experiencing net out-migration. However, out-migration from districts over the decade between 1960 and 1970 had not been large enough to contribute significantly to the burdens of the nation's cities.

4. Of the twelve regions, nine underwent out-migration during the 1950-60 decade, and ten had net out-migration during the following decade.

5. Districts in Appalachia accounted for 50.6 percent of out-migration for all districts during the first decade and 35.3 percent during the following decade.

6. Only one region, the Northwest, had more out-migrants during the second decade than in the previous ten years. The Rio Grande Region had in-migration during the latter period; the Ozarks had net out-migration during the first period and net in-migration during the second period.

Part III

1. The percentage of the total U.S. population residing in economic development districts (EDDs) recognized by EDA had declined steadily over the last two decades. Absolute population increase within all districts was far below that of the nation as a whole.

2. During the twenty-year span between 1950 to 1970, population in all EDDs increased only 7 percent while the national population increased by 34.8 percent.

Detailed Findings

Part I: Demographic Characteristics of EDCs and RCs. This study contradicted the assumption that EDCs and RCs are migration centers for their respective districts.[b] Seventy percent of the EDCs had net out-migration during the 1950-60 decade; 84 percent of the RCs experienced net out-migration during the same period. In the 1960-70 decade, the percent of EDCs having net out-migration increased to 77 percent, while 97 percent of the RCs had net out-migration.

Net out-migration need not imply an absolute decrease in population. Yet, 34 percent of the EDCs declined in overall population during the first decade and 32 percent during the 1960 to 1970 period. The absolute population decline in redevelopment centers was even higher, with 59 percent of the RCs declining in overall population during the first time period and 64 percent during the latter decade.

Migration and population characteristics of EDCs and RCs located in different regions varied significantly. All EDCs and RCs in the New England, Northwest, Rio Grande, and Southwest Regions underwent net out-migration during the 1960 and 1970 period. More than 80 percent of the EDCs and RCs in Appalachia, the Coastal Plains, Tennessee-Green Valley, the Great Lakes, and the South Central Regions underwent net out-migration during the same period. In all of these regions the number of EDCs and RCs having net out-migration increased over that of the 1950-60 decade.

In the Ozarks Region, the situation improved. Of the thirty-two growth centers[c] in this region, twenty-nine experienced net out-migration during the first decade, and this figure decreased to twenty-one centers between 1960 and 1970. In only two regions—Delmarva (two EDCs) and the West (two RCs)—did the centers show no net out-migration in either time period. Overall, 75 percent of the EDCs and RCs had net out-migration during the 1950-60 decade and this figure increased to 84 percent in the following decade. Summary migration statistics for EDCs and RCs are presented in table 10-1.

In 84 of the 197 growth center counties, out-migration exceeded natural population growth during the last decade. This is interesting for several reasons.

[b]The number of EDCs and RCs included in this study differed from the number analyzed through the GCIS for two reasons: (1) counties which included more than one growth center were treated as individual units of analysis (an example is Bristol County, Mass., which included three EDCs: Fall River, Taunton and New Bedford, and was treated as one EDC); and (2) the Terre Haute Region, which includes one district and one EDC, was excluded from analysis.

[c]"Growth centers" hereafter refers to both EDCs and RCs.

Table 10-1
EDC and RC Migration Data, by Region:[a] 1950-60 and 1960-70

	Economic Development Centers		Redevelopment Centers	
Region	Number with Net Out-migration 1950-60	Number with Net Out-migration 1960-70	Number with Net Out-migration 1950-60	Number with Net Out-migration 1960-70
New England	5 (83%)[b]	6 (100%)	4 (66%)	6 (100%)
Delmarva	0 (--)	0 (--)	No RC's	No RC's
Appalachia	18 (78%)	19 (83%)	12 (100%)	12 (100%)
Ozarks	22 (88%)	14 (56%)	7 (100%)	7 (100%)
Tennessee-Green Valley	6 (67%)	7 (78%)	5 (100%)	5 (100%)
Great Lakes	2 (50%)	3 (75%)	8 (73%)	11 (100%)
Coastal Plains	18 (60%)	25 (83%)	4 (100%)	4 (100%)
South Central	16 (70%)	18 (78%)	6 (86%)	7 (100%)
Northwest	1 (33%)	3 (100%)	2 (100%)	2 (100%)
Southwest	4 (80%)	5 (100%)	3 (75%)	4 (100%)
Far West	No EDC's	No EDC's	0 (--)	0 (--)
Rio Grande	1 (33%)	3 (100%)	3 (75%)	4 (100%)
TOTAL (All Regions)	93 (70%)	103 (77%)	54 (84%)	62 (97%)

[a]The Terre Haute Region was excluded for the reasons cited earlier.
[b]Bracketed figures indicate percent of total EDC's or RC's in the region with net out-migration.

Source: "Current Population Reports, Population Estimates and Projections," series P-25, no. 461, June 1971, and *County and City Data Book,* 1967, U.S. Department of Commerce/Bureau of the Census

First, these counties obviously do not serve as migration nodes. Second, most of these counties were located in regions that were increasing in overall population. Several examples of this can be cited.

1. In New England, eleven of the twelve centers had net out-migration rates that exceeded the region's, and only two growth center counties had population increases even slightly above the regional rate. EDC and RC counties had 64,512 net out-migrants; the remaining counties in the region had 42,534 net in-migrants.
2. In the Northwest Region, three of the five growth center counties declined in overall population; four had net out-migration rates that exceeded the region's, and only one center had an increase in population that exceeded the regional rate. EDC and RC counties had 18,383 net out-migrants or approximately 57 percent of the net out-migrants for the entire region.
3. In the Southwest Region, six of the nine growth center counties declined in overall population, seven had net out-migration rates that exceeded the region's; and only three of the centers grew in overall population. Overall net out-migration from EDC and RC counties exceeded that of non-EDC and non-RC counties.
4. In the Great Lakes Region, nine of the fifteen growth center counties declined in overall population; two increased less than the regional population rate; and four centers were above the regional rate. The region increased in population by 9.2 percent and had a net out-migration rate that was lower than all but one of its EDC or RC counties. Overall, EDC and RC counties had 49,610 net out-migrants; the non-EDC and non-RC counties had 554 net in-migrants.
5. In the Tennessee-Green Valley Region, ten of the fourteen growth center counties had out-migration rates exceeding the region's; eight declined in overall population; and only four increased in population above the regional rate.

This situation prevailed to a lesser extent in the Rio Grande, Ozarks, Coastal Plains, South Central, and Appalachian Regions. The Far West and Delmarva Regions did not appear to follow this trend.[d] Table 10-2 summarizes each region's EDC and RC population change characteristics. The data sources for this and following charts are the same as those cited for table 10-1.

An overview of aggregate 1960-70 EDC and RC county migration characteristics by region and district is provided in table 10-3. The most populous region, the South Central Region, is made up of nineteen districts. Three of these districts do not have designated EDC counties. Of the remaining districts, six had

---

[d]It should be noted that six of the seven districts in the Far West Region do not have designated centers; the remaining district has two redevelopment center counties. The Delmarva Region has only one district which includes two EDC counties.

Table 10-2
EDC and RC Population Data, by Region:[a] 1950-60 and 1960-70

	Economic Development Centers		Redevelopment Centers	
Region	Number with Absolute Population Losses 1950-60	Number with Absolute Population Losses 1960-70	Number with Absolute Population Losses 1950-60	Number with Absolute Population Losses 1960-70
New England	3 (50%)[b]	4 (66%)	1 (17%)	1 (17%)
Delmarva	0 (--)	0 (--)	No RC's	No RC's
Appalachia	5 (22%)	7 (30%)	10 (83%)	12 (100%)
Ozarks	16 (64%)	8 (32%)	7 (100%)	3 (43%)
Tennessee-Green Valley	5 (56%)	3 (33%)	5 (100%)	5 (100%)
Great Lakes	0 (--)	2 (50%)	5 (46%)	7 (64%)
Coastal Plains	5 (17%)	7 (23%)	2 (50%)	2 (50%)
South Central	8 (35%)	7 (31%)	4 (57%)	5 (71%)
Northwest	0 (--)	1 (33%)	1 (50%)	2 (100%)
Southwest	3 (60%)	3 (60%)	3 (75%)	3 (75%)
Far West	No EDC's	No EDC's	0 (--)	0 (--)
Rio Grande	0 (--)	1 (33%)	0 (--)	1 (25%)
TOTAL (All Regions)	45 (34%)	43 (32%)	38 (59%)	41 (64%)

[a]The Terre Haute Region was excluded for the reasons cited earlier.

[b]Bracketed figures indicate percent of total EDC's or RC's in the region with absolute losses in population.

Source: "Current Population Reports, Population Estimates and Projections," series P-25, no. 461, June 1971, and *County and City Data Book,* 1967, U.S. Department of Commerce/Bureau of the Census

Table 10-3

Aggregate EDC and RC County Migration Characteristics by Region[a] and District: 1960-70

Regions	Districts								
	No EDC No RC	-EDC[b] No RC	-RC No EDC	-EDC -RC	-EDC +RC[c]	+RC No EDC	+EDC No RC	+EDC -RC	Total Districts
New England	1	2	2	1	0	0	0	0	6
Delmarva	0	0	0	0	0	0	1	0	1
Appalachia	10	7	4	1	0	0	2	1	25
Ozarks	1	3	1	1	1	1	6	2	16
Tennessee-Green Valley	5	2	1	2	0	1	2	0	13
Great Lakes	4	2	2	1	0	1	0	1	11
Coastal Plains	4	13	0	3	0	0	4	0	24
South Central	3	6	2	4	0	0	4	0	19
Northwest	3	2	2	0	0	0	1	0	8
Southwest	1	1	1	2	0	0	0	0	5
Far West	6	0	0	0	0	1	0	0	7
Rio Grande	0	1	2	1	0	0	0	0	4
TOTALS	38	39	17	16	1	4	20	4	139

[a]The Terre Haute Region was excluded for the reasons cited earlier.

[b]"-" signifies a county with net out-migration.

[c]"+" signifies a county with net in-migration.

Source: "Current Population Reports, Population Estimates and Projections," series P-25, no. 461, June 1971, and County and City Data Book, 1967, U.S. Department of Commerce/Bureau of the Census

EDC counties with net out-migration, two districts had RC counties with net out-migration, and four districts had both EDC and RC counties with net out-migration. A similar situation existed in the second most populous region, Appalachia, which has twenty-five districts: ten without designated EDC or RC counties, seven with EDC counties having net out-migration, four with RC counties having net out-migration, and one with both EDC and RC counties having net out-migration. One hundred thirty nine authorized districts compose the national total; of these, thirty eight do not have designated centers, thirty nine had EDC counties with net out-migration between 1960 and 1970, seventeen districts had RC counties with net out-migration, and sixteen districts had both EDC and RC counties with net out-migration.

Part II: Demographic Characteristics of Economic Development Districts. The regions in which the districts are located all increased in total population during the last decade, ranging from an 0.7 percent increase for the Southwest to 23.5 percent increase in the Far West. During the previous decade (1950-60), four regions—Appalachia, Tennessee-Green Valley, Ozarks, and Southwest—declined. The reversal between the two decades seems to be connected to a decrease in the out-migration rate for the latter four regions. This is summarized in table 10-4.

During the first decade, nine of the twelve regions had overall net out-migration, ranging from 3.0 percent for Delmarva to 42.3 percent for the Southwest. The number of net migrants leaving the twelve regions during this period was 5,486,881, with Appalachia accounting for 50.6 percent of the total. Between 1960 and 1970, ten of the twelve regions had net out-migration but the absolute

Table 10-4
Migration and Population Change, by Region[a]: 1950-60 and 1960-70

Region	Regional Migration Rates		Regional Population Changes	
	1950-60	1960-70	1950-60	1960-70
New England	- 8.9%	- 1.1%	9.5%	9.4%
Delmarva	- 3.0%	- 1.7%	16.4%	7.6%
Appalachia	-34.6%	- 8.6%	-18.5%	2.3%
Ozarks	-20.3%	0.9%	- 6.1%	7.0%
Tennessee-Green Valley	-15.4%	- 6.5%	- 0.5%	4.9%
Great Lakes	-10.3%	- 1.7%	8.7%	9.2%
Coastal Plains	-15.2%	- 8.9%	5.4%	8.0%
South Central	- 9.9%	- 5.2%	10.6%	9.0%
Northwest	0	- 7.3%	18.2%	1.3%
Southwest	-42.3%	-13.4%	-16.1%	0.7%
Far West	10.8%	12.7%	25.9%	23.5%
Rio Grande	43.9%	-20.4%	66.7%	1.7%

[a]The Terre Haute Region was excluded for the reasons cited earlier.

Source: "Current Population Reports, Population Estimates and Projections," series P-25, no. 461, June 1971, and *County and City Data Book,* 1967, U.S. Department of Commerce/Bureau of the Census

magnitude declined 29 percent. Appalachia again contributed the largest share with 35.3 percent of the total. The numbers of net migrants by region, district, EDC, and RC for the decade 1960 to 1970 are presented in Appendix G.

Significant declines in out-migration occurred within specific regions. Net out-migration from New England was 86.8 percent lower during the last decade than during the 1950 to 1960 period. In the Great Lakes, net out-migration declined 82.3 percent; in Appalachia it declined 79.8 percent; in the Southwest by 73.4 percent; and in the Tennessee-Green Valley Region, it declined by 58 percent. Net out-migration also declined, but to a lesser extent, in Delmarva, the Coastal Plains, and South Central Region and actually reversed direction for the Ozarks. The analysts concluded that if these trends continued, the "rural exodus" would be a thing of the past for EDA's rural counties.

In order to give the overall picture some perspective, the analysts decided that consideration should be given to what was happening within these regions as the rate of out-migration declined. Each of the regions cited above was gaining in overall population; each had EDCs and RCs with out-migration rates which exceeded that of the region; and, more significantly, each had EDCs and RCs which were declining in overall population. This latter point was considered particularly important. If the rate of out-migration continued to decline and non-EDC, non-RC residents elected to remain outside the designated growth centers, then growth centers might become "ghost" centers in less than twenty years.

The view that EDCs and RCs could become migration centers for district residents in order to take the pressure off already overburdened cities was termed "misleading." The analysts stated that this argument assumed that out-migration from the districts was large enough to contribute significantly to the problems of the cities. They said that if the fact that out-migrants could move anywhere were disregarded and the unrealistic assumption that all went to existing SMSA's were made, then each of the 224 SMSA's would have had to absorb 7,120 new residents over a 10-year period, or approximately 712 residents per year.

The analysts concluded by saying that if this strict assumption were replaced with the assumption that district migrants moved to the 678 cities with populations exceeding 25,000, then each city would have had to absorb 235 new residents per year. This would hardly seem to be a problem requiring a national commitment to employ a significant portion of the public sector's resources.

Part III: National Comparisons. Very little reported here is analytical; most of the findings are descriptive. The analysts found that comparing district data to national data clearly indicated that economic development districts were not losing absolute population despite their large out-migration rates. For all EDA-designated districts, population growth was slightly above 9.1 percent between 1950 and 1970, while national growth for the same period was 34.8 percent. In general, the districts, whether studied individually or grouped into regions, gained in population during the last decade.

Those conducting the study noted that several trends were worth mentioning, but did not clearly imply what the future holds for individual districts. First, despite an increase in the rate of population growth for the districts (from 1.5 percent for 1950-60 to 7.5 percent for 1960-70) and a decrease in the national rate (from 18.5 to 13.3 percent), the percentage of the total U.S. population residing in EDA-associated districts declined steadily over the last two decades. In 1950, 21.5 percent of the total U.S. population resided in areas that are now districts; this had declined to 17.4 percent by 1970.

A second trend noted was the decline of the high natural population growth rate within districts. For the first decade, the natural rate was 18.4 percent; for the second decade, the natural rate dropped to 12.3 percent. The national natural population growth rate for the same two periods was 16.7 percent and 12.8 percent. Thus, the decline in the district's natural rate exceeded the decline in the national rate by approximately 35 percent. This, coupled with the findings of the preceding paragraph, implies that the percent of the total U.S. population residing in EDA-associated districts will continue to decline sharply. National and regional data are summarized in table 10-5.

Table 10-5
District and National Comparisons

Categories of Analysis	District	National
Population		
• 1950	32,478,177 (21.5%)	150,697,361
• 1960	32,958,769 (18.4%)	179,323,175
• 1970	35,433,661 (17.4%)	203,184,772
Percent Change in Population		
• 1950–60	1.5%	18.5%
• 1960–70	7.5%	13.3%
Natural Rate of Increase		
• 1950–60	18.4%	16.7%
• 1960–70	12.3%	12.8%
Migration Characteristics		
• 1950–60	−16.9% (Net Migration from All Districts)[a]	−7.2% (Median Migration Rate for Nondistrict Counties)
• 1960–70	−4.8% (Net Migration from All Districts)	

[a]Bracketed figures indicate percentage of national population.

Source: "Current Population Reports, Population Estimates and Projections," series P-25, no. 461, June 1971, and *County and City Data Book,* 1967, U.S. Department of Commerce/Bureau of the Census

Contiguous County Employment Profile

Scope of Study

This section summarizes a study of employment changes in counties contiguous to Type I growth centers, Type II growth centers, and Type III growth centers. The results showed that between 1950 and 1960 counties contiguous to both Type I and Type II growth centers usually had more favorable changes in their employment structures than did counties contiguous to Type III growth centers.

The average percentage change in total employment and the average percentage change in nonprimary, nonmilitary employment were computed for the contiguous counties of each Type I, Type II and Type III growth center. Contiguous counties within SMSAs or containing Type I growth centers were not included in the computations. In addition, these two percentage changes were computed separately for the contiguous redevelopment area counties. This provided two sets of measures for each growth center. These determined: (1) whether the growth center was favorably affecting its surrounding area; and (2) whether this impact, if there was any, was also being felt in nearby redevelopment areas.

Results For All Regions Combined

Tables 10-6 and 10-7 present data on median percentage change in total employment and in nonprimary, nonmilitary employment for counties contiguous to all EDA growth centers, by region and for all regions combined.

Table 10-6 shows that the percentage change in total employment was very small for all counties contiguous to Type I centers and, with few exceptions, was negative for contiguous RAs. Since SMSA counties and counties containing Type I growth centers were excluded from the computations, the contiguous counties were primarily rural and had large agricultural sectors. Therefore, the decline in agriculture was the cause of the small increase or the decline in total employment for these centers.

The percentage change in total employment for the contiguous RAs was significantly lower for all three types of growth centers than the change for all contiguous counties. RA counties are characterized by very low per capita incomes and/or very high unemployment rates. These low per capita incomes are indicative of agricultural sectors larger than those of contiguous non-RA counties. This, and the high unemployment rates would account for the larger decline in total employment in the contiguous RA counties.

Table 10-7 shows that the percentage change in nonprimary, nonmilitary employment was about 30 percent for both all counties and for RA counties contiguous to Type I growth centers. Both were about 23 percent for Type II

Table 10-6

Median Percentage Change in Nonprimary, Nonmilitary Employment

Region	All Contiguous Counties			Contiguous RA Counties		
	Type I	Type II	Type III	Type I	Type II	Type III
All Regions	31.9	23.5	13.5	29.0	22.3	12.5
New England	–[a]	9.4	12.9	–	5.4	4.6
Delmarva	–	20.4	–	–	21.3	–
Terre Haute	14.4	–	–	17.1	–	–
Appalachia	38.5	23.5	16.0	41.1	25.9	13.5
Ozarks	24.9	13.9	12.1	24.9	11.1	9.7
Tennessee-Green Valley	29.4	21.9	10.6	32.3	19.8	11.0
Great Lakes	33.6	43.1	–1.6	28.0	40.4	–0.5
Coastal Plains	41.3	37.6	26.9	29.1	30.2	25.1
South Central	28.6	23.8	20.7	24.7	22.5	18.7
Northwest	18.1	21.2	7.4	16.7	12.9	4.7
Southwest	30.0	23.2	4.2	26.4	18.8	2.2
Far West	13.1	34.8	–	13.1	37.1	–
Rio Grande	21.4	17.7	10.7	17.2	10.6	8.7

[a](–) indicates that no growth center existed in the category.

Source: "Current Population Reports, Population Estimates and Projections," series P-25, no. 461, June 1971, and *County and City Data Book,* 1967, U.S. Dept. of Commerce/ Bureau of the Census

Table 10-7

Median Percentage Change in Total Employment

Region	All Contiguous Counties			Contiguous RA Counties		
	Type I	Type II	Type III	Type I	Type II	Type III
All Regions	1.5	–3.6	–9.9	–6.5	–9.5	–15.0
New England	–[a]	1.9	–2.7	–	–0.7	–4.1
Delmarva	–	6.4	–	–	8.4	–
Terre Haute	–5.6	–	–	–3.3	–	–
Appalachia	9.4	–3.9	–8.7	8.6	–7.8	–8.8
Ozarks	–8.2	–14.5	–16.3	–15.5	–19.0	–22.0
Tennessee-Green Valley	–6.8	–9.1	–15.7	–8.5	–9.8	–17.7
Great Lakes	13.4	6.2	–3.1	10.3	2.5	–3.1
Coastal Plains	2.8	–4.0	–5.4	–8.2	–13.4	–17.0
South Central	–0.1	–2.8	–16.4	–5.6	–20.7	–23.0
Northwest	1.9	2.6	–8.3	–4.1	–12.1	–12.5
Southwest	6.8	–0.2	–12.1	2.6	–0.4	–19.5
Far West	8.3	23.1	–	8.3	24.9	–
Rio Grande	–1.1	–4.2	–9.7	–9.9	–11.6	–14.8

[a](–) indicates that no growth center existed in the category.

Source: "Current Population Reports, Population Estimates and Projections," series P-25, no. 461, June 1971, and *County and City Data Book,* 1967, U.S. Department of Commerce/Bureau of the Census

growth centers. This indicates that: (1) counties contiguous to Type I growth centers grew substantially in the manufacturing and service sectors and were thus able to absorb all of the decline in the primary sector; (2) counties contiguous to Type II growth centers had a smaller increase in nonprimary, nonmilitary employment and thus were not able to absorb as much of the decline in the primary sector; and (3) the contiguous RA's fared as well in nonprimary, nonmilitary employment changes but again were not able to absorb as much of the decline in the primary sector as the non-RA counties.

All of the contiguous counties for the Type III EDCs and RCs showed much larger declines in total employment and much smaller increases in nonprimary, nonmilitary employment than the counties contiguous to Type I and Type II growth centers.

Results For Individual Regions

Tables 10-6 and 10-7 also show the median percentage employment changes for each region. For the Appalachia, Ozarks, Tennessee-Green Valley, South Central, Lower Rio Grande, and Southwest regions, all median percentage changes were higher for the Type I growth centers than for the Type II centers; and higher for the Type II centers than for the Type III places.[e]

Three of the remaining four regions each showed results differing slightly from the general pattern. All of the figures for the Great Lakes region were in the expected order except for nonprimary, nonmilitary employment for counties contiguous to the Type II growth centers. These were greater than the corresponding changes for the Type I centers. However, these larger increases in the nonprimary sectors were not able to absorb as much of the decline in the primary sector. Also, counties contiguous to Type III places had a much smaller change in employment than counties contiguous to either Type I or Type II centers. The results for the Great Lakes were therefore consistent with the overall pattern.

The results for the Coastal Plains region were very similar to those for the Great Lakes region. The change in nonprimary, nonmilitary employment for RA counties contiguous to Type II growth centers was larger than the corresponding change for Type I centers. But again, this larger increase was only able to absorb a small portion of the decline in the primary sector. Thus, there was a larger decrease in total employment for RA counties contiguous to Type II centers

---

[e]The New England region also fit this pattern, but it had no Type I growth centers. The median figures for the Type II growth centers were all higher than the median figures for the Type III places. The Terre Haute and Delmarva regions need only brief comment because they are both so small. The Terre Haute region is composed of one modified district and is essentially an SMSA with the addition of three outlying counties. Terre Haute was a Type I growth center because of its large industrial base and the contiguous counties reflect the impact of that base. The Delmarva region consists of one district and it had two Type II growth centers. The counties contiguous to both showed the capacity to absorb the decline in the primary sector.

than for counties contiguous to Type I centers. In addition, employment in counties contiguous to Type III centers declined to a greater extent.

For the Northwest region, contiguous RA counties showed no deviations from the expected pattern. But, all counties contiguous to Type II growth centers had larger increases in total and nonprimary, nonmilitary employment than did counties contiguous to Type I centers. However, both Type I and Type II centers showed larger employment increases than the Type III centers. This situation can be explained. The two Type II centers both had a medium-sized city, but lacked the employment base necessary to be identified as Type I centers. These cities could still have had some impact on their surrounding area, but neither had the desired impact on neighboring RA counties.

The remaining region and only exception was the Far West, but it is easily explained. Three of the four Type II growth centers had much larger employment changes than the Type I center. This was so because all three are contiguous to the Sacramento SMSA and thus are under its influence. Any positive changes in employment can be attributed to the fact that the counties contiguous to the three Type II centers (RCs) are bedroom communities from which people commute to Sacramento. The dominating influence is Sacramento and not the RCs.

In conclusion, the results showed that counties contiguous to Type I growth center counties were better able to absorb the decline in the primary sector than were counties contiguous to those EDCs and RCs classified as Type II or Type III. This was true even when only RA counties were included in the computations.

11 Economic Development for Indian Reservations

Indian Poverty

Of all substantial ethnic populations within the United States, the American Indian, together with the Alaskan native, is the most poorly educated, has the lowest income, suffers from the worst health and highest unemployment.

The total American Indian-Alaskan native population made up only two-fifths of one percent of the 1970 population of the United States. This represents a considerable decrease in percentage of total population since 1890, when the U.S. Census reported that American Indians, Alaskan Indians, Aleuts, and Eskimos comprised nearly 4.4 percent of the total U.S. population. The actual 1970 figures given by the Census Bureau in December 1971 were 793,000 Indians and approximately 35,000 Alaskan Indians, Aleuts, and Eskimos. Of this number, more than 400,000 lived on federal reservations.

The Indian peoples are ethnographically and territorially split into approximately 250 tribal groupings, living on some 200 reservations. In 1964, reservations covered approximately 50 million tribally held acres, and ranged in size from less than one acre to nearly 25,000 square miles. This compares to 140 million Indian-held acres in 1896.

Although the level of median family income for Indians has increased more rapidly than for non-Indians, in 1964 cash income was almost $6,300 for all U.S. males, but only $1,800 for reservation Indians. Three quarters of all Indian families had wage incomes below $3,000; only 10 percent had an annual income of $5,000 or more. Even allowing for the noncash income of the Indian, his standard of living is exceedingly low. Three quarters of all reservation dwellings do not meet minimum standards set by the Department of Housing and Urban Development. More than half are considered irreparable; most have no running water or sanitary facilities.

Indian infant mortality rates are one third higher than the United States average; the death rate for tuberculosis sufferers is four times greater, with the incidence of contraction higher yet, at 7 to 1 in 1965. Death rates from influenza and pneumonia are twice as high for Indians as for the American population as a whole, according to the United States Public Health Service. Rates of syphilitic infection were also twice as high for Indians in 1965.

In educational attainment the Indian is significantly below the national average: median school years completed by Indians was 8.4 in 1960, versus 10.3 for all U.S. males. Even more revealing is the fact that in 1960 only 17.2 percent of the Indian male population had twelve or more years of education, while 39.4 percent of the general United States male population had at least twelve years education. One consequence of this education gap is that the Indian is less well trained and equipped to participate in a technologically advanced economy. This problem, *mutatis mutandi*, is exacerbated by the limited reservation opportunities open to the educated Indian. The result is often that, on the reservation as in other underdeveloped areas of the nation, the younger, better trained residents must leave to find suitable employment. For the Indian, relocation has most often been to the urban centers of the West Coast.

The results of poor health, inadequate housing, and limited education are reflected in the employment patterns of the Indian. In 1960, more than 50 percent of employed male Indians were blue collar workers, with the bulk being nonfarm laborers. In the same year, only 12 percent of rural Indians held white collar jobs, and in the same year half of all reservation males were unemployed. Although this figure had dropped to approximately 37 percent by 1967, it was still almost twelve times higher than the national male unemployment rate, and six times greater than the rate for nonwhites generally. While data are incomplete, it is likely that the reservation unemployment rate has increased since then, as table 11-1 indicates.

Moreover, the simple unemployment figure fails to account for the high rate of underemployment typically found within the reservation economy. Underemployment has been estimated as high as 50 percent. In addition, a substantial differential exists between Indians and non-Indians in labor force participation rates. According to data collected by the Bureau of the Census in 1960 (and not yet available for the 1970 census), 78 percent of Indian males in the prime age group between 25 and 44 years were members of the labor force. Nationally, all males had a labor force participation rate of more than 95 percent for the same age group. The differential was great for the 14- to 24-year-old age bracket as well: 41 percent for Indians, and slightly more than 57 percent for all males. The "true" differential for this group may be even more substantial because the rate of school participation is lower for Indians than the general population, with the Indian "drop out" rate at the high school level twice the national average.

It might well be expected that substantial differences would exist between Indians, considered a typically "rural" minority group, and the U.S. population as a whole, increasingly considered an "urban" group. However, tables 11-2, 11-3, and 11-4 point out how impoverished educationally and economically the rural Indian is even when compared with the total rural population. In 1960, the U.S. Census Bureau defined as rural slightly more than 380,000 Indians, and 54 million of the total population.

Comparing the "modes" for both groups from the data in tables 11-2, 11-3, and 11-4 shows the rural Indian with an annual family income of between $1,000 and $3,000 and a family size of seven or more. For all rural dwellers, however, the mode is a far smaller, two-person family, with an annual income of between $3,000 and $5,000.

Table 11–1

Population and Unemployment Rates for Selected Indian Reservations

Reservation	State	Indian Population	Unemployment Rate
Annette Island (Metlakatla)	Alaska	1,252	No Data
Colorado River	Arizona	1,730	35%
Fort Apache	Arizona	6,230	54%
Gila River	Arizona	7,992	20%
Navajo	Arizona-New Mexico-Utah	127,054	35%
Salt River	Arizona	2,345	12%
San Carlos	Arizona	4,709	46%
Fort Yuma	California	1,243	31%
Red Lake	Minnesota	2,759	39%
Blackfeet	Montana	6,214	44%
Crow	Montana	4,035	32%
Fort Peck	Montana	3,993	41%
Mescalero	New Mexico	1,647	71%
Zuni	New Mexico	4,869	33%
Fort Berthold	North Dakota	2,713	56%
Standing Rock	North/South Dakota	4,712	41%
Crow Creek	South Dakota	1,160	70%
Lower Brule	South Dakota	590	62%
Pine Ridge	South Dakota	11,230	53%
Rosebud	South Dakota	7,069	39%
Uintah and Ouray	Utah	1,455	44%

Source: EDA Indian Desk, "Indian Reservations and Population with Each Regional Area," 1970 Census, Washington, D.C.: U.S. Department of Commerce/Economic Development Administration, January 1972; and BIA Statistics Division, "Indian Population, Labor Force, Unemployment and Underemployment; by State and Reservation: March 1971," Washington, D.C.: U.S. Department of the Interior/Bureau of Indian Affairs, July 1971

Federal Aid

The sickness, unemployment, and poverty which continue to characterize the Indian exist despite massive infusions of federal aid. In recent years, the federal government has spent more than $1,000 per Indian annually on programs designed to assist him. While this is a greater amount than for any other ethnic group, the results to date are not impressive.

One reason for the lack of past success is the vacillation which has characterized the federal-Indian relationship. There has been an attempt to forcibly remove the Indian problem through breaking up tribal lands, and destroying mores and folkways. Relocation and decimation, however, have proved unsuccessful. Alternatively, an overly paternal approach has been employed, with the goal of adapting the Indian to the customs and methods of the larger population, into which it was hoped he would eventually be

Table 11–2

Completed School Years of Indian and Total Rural Population 14 Years Old and Over: 1966

School Years Completed	Rural Indians	Total Rural Population
Grades 1–12:		
None	13.5%	2.1%
1–4 years	13.3%	7.1%
5–8 years	39.0%	36.1%
9–12 years	31.2%	44.6%
College:		
1–3 years	2.3%	6.2%
4 or more	.7%	3.9%
TOTAL	100.0%	100.0%
Total Population 14 Years Old and Older	218,905	36,950,229

Source: U.S. 1960 Census of Population, Series PC (1), PC (2)

Table 11–3

1960 Family Income Distribution of Rural Population

Income	Rural Indian Family Income	Total Rural Population Family Income
Under $1,000	28.0%	9.9%
$ 1,000–$2,999	34.3%	23.6%
$ 3,000–$4,999	19.2%	23.9%
$ 5,000–$6,999	10.2%	20.3%
$ 7,000–$9,999	5.7%	10.8%
$10,000 and over	2.6%	11.5%
TOTAL	100.0%	100.0%
Number of Families	64,361	13,188,351

Source: U.S. 1960 Census of Population, Series PC (1), PC (2)

Table 11–4

1960 Average Family Size of Rural Population

Family Size	Rural Indians	Total U.S. Rural Population
2 Persons	16.9%	30.6%
3 Persons	15.7%	20.3%
4 Persons	14.5%	19.1%
5 Persons	13.8%	13.3%
6 Persons	11.7%	7.9%
7 or More Persons	27.4%	8.8%
TOTAL	100.0%	100.0%
Number of Families	64,361	13,188,355

Source: U.S. 1960 Census of Population, Series PC (1), PC (2)

assimilated. This too has failed, for tribalism and ethnocentrism seem to be dominant forces. Indeed, such consciousness-raising efforts as the recent take-over of San Quentin, and sit-ins at Mount Rushmore suggest an increasing Indian militancy and sense of self-identity.

The various federal agencies with substantial involvement in Indian programs have in the past often been self-serving, paternalistic, and self-centered; histori-cally, they have refused to admit Indian representatives into the decision-making process. Gradually, over the past decade these traits have begun to give way; increasing agency acceptance of the concept of self-determination and increasing Indian employment within Indian-oriented program agencies have both been factors.

EDA's Indian Program

When the Economic Development Administration was created in 1965, special note was taken of the plight of the American Indian and his need for economic advancement. During the legislative hearings, the major suggested limitation on EDA Indian assistance was that minimum population for eligible reservation areas be 1,000. The purpose of this limitation, which was not included in the formal legislation, was to assure some return-to-scale efficiency for agency investment on reservations. Subsequently, approximately half of all 200 state and federal reservations were declared eligible for designation; eligible reserva-tions contained well over half the reservation Indian population.

As noted in chapter 3, fiscal year 1966 was characterized within EDA by the need to commit an entire year's appropriations in eight months. This bureau-cratic crisis was made even more extreme by the fact that the first two of these eight months were consumed in agency organization activities. As a result, approval was given to those projects that could be developed most quickly, and for which planning documents, application forms, and clearance could be completed with minimum delay. These required features, when combined with the scarcity of administrative expertise and grantsmanship talents on reserva-tions, resulted in less than 1 percent of the agency's funds being approved for Indian projects during the 1966 fiscal year.

The $3.2 million approved for reservations in fiscal year 1966 represented an EDA commitment to eighteen projects on thirteen reservations in nine states. Seven public works projects and five business loans, with agency investments of $1.4 million and $1.7 million respectively, were approved, as well as six technical assistance studies with a price tag slightly above $.1 million.[1]

This EDA experience, coupled with that of its predecessor, the Area Redevelopment Administration, convinced the agency that: (1) reservations were not producing a sufficient quantity of good project applications for consideration; and (2) anticipated appropriations would not be sufficient to significantly aid all potential reservation applicants. Consequently, in 1967 EDA began serious development of the Selected Indian Reservation Program (SIRP).

SIRP, which was designed in recognition of the special problems of reservations and the inadequacies of previous federal programs in meeting them, was intended to permit the Economic Development Administration to take a more active partnership role in Indian development.

The program design was to select for special treatment those reservations with significant potential to initiate self-sustaining growth. Beyond selectivity, however, the Selected Indian Reservation Program was intended to precipitate cooperation and coordination between EDA and other federal agencies concerned with programs on reservations. The purpose of this liaison was to achieve concentration of multiagency funds on individual reservations, and create systems to accelerate program delivery. In sum, SIRP represented an attempt to coordinate federal assistance to Indians through a concentrated, accelerated impact program.

Criteria for selecting specific reservations for the SIRP program are threefold:

1. *Community factors*, such as tribal interest in economic development, availability of manpower labor, training programs, and local availability of management skills, both within the tribal community and nearby
2. *Material resource factors*, such as condition of reservation facilities, availability of appropriate raw materials; ongoing industrial activities; and adequate financing capacity: tribal, private, and other agencies
3. *Location factors*, such as propinquity to regional markets, and transportation between the reservation and regional growth centers

The second objective of the Selected Indian Reservation Program—interagency coordination—was achieved through EDA-Office of Economic Opportunity (OEO) contact. Both agencies are legislatively committed to work for the broadest development of low-income, high unemployment areas. Negotiations conducted late in 1967 between the two culminated in an agreement to work together on the Selected Indian Reservation Program. Although no other federal agency has formally joined EDA and OEO, a number have worked on an *ad hoc* basis to bring about community and economic development on specific reservations. These include the Bureau of Indian Affairs, and the Departments of Labor, Housing and Urban Development, and Health, Education, and Welfare.

The first beneficiaries of the EDA SIRP and EDA-OEO coordination were sixteen reservations spread over eight states: in Alaska, Annette Island (Metlakatla); in Arizona, Gila River, Salt River, San Carlos; in Minnesota, Red Lake; in Montana, Blackfeet, Crow; in New Mexico, Mescalero, Zuni; in Arizona, New Mexico and Utah, Navajo; in North Dakota, Fort Bethold; in South Dakota, Crow Creek, Lower Brule, Pine Ridge, Rosebud; and in North and South Dakota, Standing Rock Reservation. Between them, these sixteen reservations have a population of approximately 185,000, with a range from 1,000 residents to more than 120,000. By 1971, the Action List, as the SIRP reservations were later designated, had grown to twenty-one with a total population of more than 200,000 or half of all federal reservation Indians.

Key to the SIRP concept is comprehensive, development-oriented planning. On reservations, as elsewhere, the vehicle for such planning is EDA's requirement for preparation of an Overall Economic Development Program, which must precede project funding. EDA has presumed that only through such planning efforts could a program be laid out with clear indications of community needs that could be met by EDA and other program agencies. The plan, in fact, if well conceived and practical, would make implementation dependent only upon the availability of resources. Truly comprehensive planning would provide an interwoven package of projects, including infrastructure, housing, educational, and health programs existing in a symbiotic relationship. Developers would have clearly indicated for them the federal, state, and local agencies legally capable of funding program elements; and priorities would be obvious.

Thus, SIRP singles out those reservations thought capable of development, demands effective planning, and promises to concentrate funds on them. Table 11-5 presents data on EDA funding to all reservations and to Action List reservations. Only funds obligated since the conception of SIRP are included.

Because of the high agency expectations for the Selected Indian Reservation Program, a decision was made in July 1969 to expand its scope. This was done by creating a Planning List. Reservations placed on the Planning List receive aid in developing the internal capacity to prepare Overall Economic Development Programs. Such assistance includes helping reservations acquire professional staffs to reinforce local capabilities to plan and implement development programs. Planning List designation does not have the same implications for

Table 11–5
EDA – Approved Projects to SIRP (Action List) Reservations:
Fiscal Years 1967–71

Fiscal Year	Total Funds to All Indian Reservations	Funds to SIRP (Action List) Reservations	Percentage of Total to SIRP (Action List) Reservations
1967	$18,220,000	$10,322,000	57%
1968	17,287,797	6,330,367	37%
1969	17,396,158	10,316,005	59%
1970	19,272,064	11,110,062	58%
1971	21,813,183	12,550,000	58%
Totals FY 1967–71	$93,989,202	50,628,434	54%

Source, column 2: Indian Reservation Data as of June 30, 1971, Memorandum, EDA Indian Desk
Source, column 3: EDA Directory of Approved Projects, U.S. Dept. of Commerce, as compiled by Boise Cascade Center for Community Development

agency project assistance as the Action List, to which original SIRP designees were consigned.

Figure 11-1 presents one concept of the alternative approaches for assisting an Indian community.

EDA, as a result of the enabling legislation's directives and agency personnel proclivities, has chosen to support decision making within the community. In its role as a source of funds, it has attempted to provide a high degree of external assistance to Action List reservations. The hope has been that such assistance would permit reservations to achieve tribally defined goals. This approach is depicted in figure 11-1 as Type D. The agency-community relationship vis-a-vis Planning List reservations falls within Type B. EDA assistance has been primarily directed toward community leadership development. The agency goal has been to develop on the reservation the expertise necessary for local problem identification.

Tables 11-6 and 11-7 indicate for fiscal year 1971 the actual EDA approvals to reservations by program type and reservation category. It will be noted that Action List and Planning List members received a proportionately greater share of public works grants and loans, while on "non-selected" reservations, emphasis has been on technical assistance and planning grants.[a]

Locus of Decision Making

	At Agency Level	At Community Level
External Assistance — Low	Type A Use "superior" knowledge of experts; change local customs, habits.	Type B Develop leadership; locals identify problems; formulate goals through self-determination; use community resources to solve problems.
External Assistance — High	Type C Build physical facilities expected to be necessary for development; let community figure out how to use them.	Type D Locals define problems; set own goals. Outside organizations help community to achieve goals.

Figure 11-1. Alternative Approaches to Assistance. *Source:* Adapted from Harvey M. Choldin, reported by Sol Tax and Sam Stanley, "Indian Identity and Economic Development," *Toward Economic Development for Native American Communities*, Washington, D.C.: Government Printing Office, 1969, p. 89

[a] FY 1971 was atypical in the small agency investment in business loans to reservations. In FY 1967, business loans represented 26 percent of all agency dollar approvals to reservations; 12 percent in FY 1968; 3.4 percent in FY 1969; 15.8 percent in FY 1970; and 4 percent in FY 1971.

Table 11–6
EDA Indian Program Expenditures: FY 1971

Reservation Category	Public Works (000)	Business Loans (000)	Technical Assistance (000)	Planning Grants (000)	TOTAL (000)
Action List (21 Reservations)	$10,750	$397	$ 44	$258	$11,450
Planning List (17 Reservations)	3,968	–	16	162	4,147
Nonselected (75 Reservations)	4,542	475	723	479	6,219
TOTAL	$19,259[a]	$872[a]	$783[a]	$900[a]	$21,814[a]

[a]Minor inconsistencies result from rounding.
Source: Indian Reservation Data as of June 30, 1971, Memorandum, EDA Indian Desk

Table 11–7
Percentage of Program Tool Aid by Reservation Category: FY 1971

Reservation Category	Public Works	Business Loans	Technical Assistance	Planning Grants	TOTAL[a]
Action List	94.2%	3.5%	.4%	2.3%	100%
Planning List	95.6%	0%	.4%	3.9%	100%
Nonselected	73.0%	7.6%	11.6%	7.7%	100%

[a]Minor inconsistencies result from rounding.
Source: Indian Reservation Data as of June 30, 1971, Memorandum, EDA Indian Desk

Preliminary Evaluations of EDA Indian Projects and Programs

The first substantial evaluations of EDA impact were primarily project-oriented analyses. Data collected were intended to provide information about the effectiveness of project tools: public works, business loans, technical assistance, and planning grants; little attention was given to specific program types. Consequently, these early efforts did not concentrate on such program categories as growth centers or the Selected Indian Reservation Program. Despite this intentional limitation, a number of individual reservation projects were evaluated. Although no overall account of agency impact on reservations could be determined, a number of intermediate project-oriented findings were possible.

Public Works Evaluation

Boise Cascade Center for Community Development, the consulting firm chosen in 1969 to evaluate the agency's Public Works Program, analyzed through field evaluation a total of 149 EDA projects across the nation. Of this sample, 17 projects were associated with Indian reservations. An EDA task force, using mail and telephone techniques, studied an additional 9. The 26 projects analyzed represented only a small segment of the 209 EDA-approved Indian projects located in the same eleven states. More importantly, the time-since-completion criterion that guided the selection of projects for the general public works evaluation was relaxed for reservation projects. The reason for this relaxation, and consequent diminution of comparability, was the extremely small universe of reservation public works projects completed for at least one year. Of the 26 projects evaluated, 12 were either not fully completed at the time of evaluation, or had been complete for less than one year. This fact must be considered when comparing the results of the reservation subset of public works projects to the universe of evaluated public works projects. The results for these initial evaluations of public works projects on reservations are presented in table 11-8.

The EDA investment-per-direct-job figure of $4,452 was nearly 25 percent higher than the comparable figure for nonreservation public works projects. In addition to the immaturity of reservation projects, however, a significant part of the difference is probably attributable to the higher proportion of total project cost assumed by EDA on the reservations. For the entire sample of public works projects evaluated, the average agency participation rate was found to be 61 percent; for the reservation subset, the figure was 95 percent.

Two other aspects of the Indian public works project analysis also deserve mention. These are, first, the high rate of jobs taken by formerly unemployed

Table 11–8
Indian Public Works Projects Evaluation Results

Category of Analysis	Results
Number of Projects Evaluated	26
Total Cost of Evaluated Projects	$8,177,000
Average Project Cost	$ 314,500
Total EDA Investment	$7,746,000
Average EDA Investment	$ 297,923
EDA Investment as % of Total Project Cost	94.7%
Total Direct Jobs	1,740
EDA Investment Per Direct Job	$ 4,452
% Jobs Taken by Heads of Households	80%
% Jobs to Underemployed, Unemployed, Farm Workers, and New Labor Force Entrants	70%[a]

[a]Based on analysis of projects for which data are available

Source: "A Preliminary Evaluation of Selected Projects on Indian Reservations," (unpublished study, U.S. Department of Commerce/Economic Development Administration, December 1970), pp. 11–13

and underemployed persons, farm workers or new labor force entrants. As table 11-8 indicates, the bulk of jobs created by Indian reservation projects went to new employees, that is, to those previously without substantial employment. The second gratifying result was that, of the more than 1,000 employees for whom data were available, more than 90 percent were Indians.

The high rate of Indian employment in jobs stemming from public works projects is substantially above projections made from data reported to Congress in 1967.[2] Table 11-9 presents the correlations between number of employees and Indian participation noted in the congressional report. No explanation for the unexpectedly high Indian employment rates in firms associated with EDA public works projects on reservations presents itself.

Business Loans Evaluation

In the evaluation of business loans conducted by Booz, Allen & Hamilton, Inc., only three reservation loans were evaluated. Because all three were either for expansion or rebuilding of plants, the subset is distinctly different from the average evaluated business loan. The three loans, all made on Action List reservations, were:

1. A $678,000 loan to Fairchild Semi-Conductor Division, Navajo Indian Reservation, Shiprock, New Mexico, to provide expanded operational facilities for the Semi-Conductor Division of the Fairchild Camera and Instrument Corporation
2. An $184,000 loan to the Red Lake Band of Chippewa Indians, Red Lake Indian Reservation, Redby, Minnesota, to replace a sawmill destroyed by fire
3. A $550,000 loan to Navajo Forest Products Industries, Navajo Indian Reservation, Navajo, New Mexico, for the expansion of an existing lumber mill by the addition of mill-work and cut-stock capability

Table 11-9
Employment Size and Indian Participation

Factory Labor Force Size	Percentage Employees of Indian Descent
1–9 Employees	9%
10–14 Employees	30%
25–49 Employees	72%
50–99 Employees	52%
100 or More Employees	77%

Source: Alan L. Sorkin, "American Indians Industrialize to Combat Poverty" *Monthly Labor Review,* 92, no. 3 (Washington, D.C.: U.S. Government Printing Office, March 1969), p. 19.

The Fairchild plant in Shiprock is one of EDA's prime "success stories." The plant is the largest private Indian employer in the United States and, in 1971, was the largest manufacturer in the state of New Mexico. The loan investigated by Booz, Allen was only one component of a multiproject EDA package. Other related projects were: a second business loan of $463,000; a $153,000 industrial site preparation project; and three sewerage projects with a combined agency investment of $1,906,000. In sum, these six projects from which Fairchild benefits were supported by $3,200,000 in EDA funds.

When evaluated in 1970, 1,225 employees worked at the Fairchild facility. The Booz, Allen field team, based on discussions with plant management as well as other observations, reported that nearly 500 employees had been added by Fairchild following completion of the expansion financed by EDA's $678,000 loan.

Of the total plant labor force at Fairchild, more than 95 percent were Indian; 85 percent were Navajo women employed solely as assemblers at rates averaging $1.82 an hour. The wage rates for men averaged approximately $2.50 an hour. The average combined wage rates for men and women produced an average annual wage of about $4,500, much higher than the median family income of the Navajo, which was estimated to be approximately $1,650 by the Bureau of Indian Affairs in 1970.

The other two business loans evaluated were made directly to Indian groups, and both were oriented toward raw materials—wood products. EDA loans represented 40 percent of the total project cost to replace the Red Lake sawmill and 60 percent of the expansion costs for the Navajo Forest Products Industries millworks.

When EDA approved the business loan to the Red Lake Band of Chippewas, it was expected that sixty-nine jobs would result. The evaluators found that actual employment was far less than predicted; only twenty-two jobs had been created. Nonetheless, the EDA investment represented less than $8,400 per job, and all jobs had been taken by Indians. Furthermore, wages to employees raised their incomes significantly above the average reservation income.

The EDA business loan to Navajo Forest Products, approved in June 1966, allowed expansion of a tribally owned lumber mill. As a result of the loan, approximately seventy-five additional jobs were provided through the plant. The majority of these jobs were of the skilled and unskilled labor type. Approximately 25 percent of the new employees were formerly underemployed or unemployed. The agency's investment per job for this business loan was found to be fairly low, at approximately $6,300.

Technical Assistance and Planning Grants Evaluations

Both technical assistance and planning grants projects can be considered "soft" assistance to recipients. Neither directly results in employment or infrastruture, but they can be significant ingredients in the development process. In studying EDA's Technical Assistance Program, CONSAD Research Corporation looked at five projects intended to benefit Indian reservations. However, for a variety of reasons, a comprehensive analysis of these could not be undertaken.

In four of the cases, technical assistance feasibility studies had been completed, but no decisions had been made about implementation of results. In consequence, it was not possible for CONSAD to draw even tentative conclusions from the reservation subset.

As previously discussed, Batelle Memorial Institute was awarded a contract to conduct evaluations of twenty-six planning grant recipients in February 1970. The major emphasis of the study was on evaluation of development staffs hired with planning grant funds. In evaluating the twenty-six grants, the following reservations were visited: (1) Great Lakes Intertribal Council, composed of ten reservation members; (2) Pine Ridge Reservation; (3) Blackfeet Reservation; (4) Crow and Northern Cheyenne Reservations, which are part of the Big Horn Economic Development Corporation; and (5) Nez Perce Reservations, within the Clearwater Economic Development District. These reservations represent the range of EDA planning grant recipients associated with reservations: multitribe groups; single tribes; and districts containing reservations.

The major finding of the study was that planning grants on Indian reservations tend to be less effective than those made elsewhere. Battelle's findings indicate that major causes of this comparative ineffectiveness are the isolation and economic underdevelopment typifying the reservation community.

Great Lakes Inter-Tribal Council. In the case of the Great Lakes Inter-Tribal Council of Wisconsin, where each of the member reservations has an appointed OEDP committee, the field evaluator felt that the committee form of organization was not particularly useful in helping the Indians to develop their relationships with non-Indians. The committee system had resulted in planning that dealt only with the reservation Indian, rather than the range of relationships between reservations and the non-Indian community.

The development coordinator for the Great Lakes Inter-Tribal Council indicated that there were other problems. One of these was the federal government's reluctance to dispense "seed" money for small projects and high risk projects. Moreover, the Council's two-man staff (the coordinator and his secretary) was too small to serve the widely scattered Wisconsin Indian population.

In discussing the aid received from EDA, the development coordinator expressed satisfaction with the latitude and discretion permitted by the Planning Grant Program. He was concerned, however, by the fact that EDA had not funded any nonplanning projects in the area. As well as other small projects, several applications for industrial parks had been rejected. The coordinator had become convinced that EDA did not want to fund improvements for industrial parks unless the developer could produce a "bird-in-hand" (i.e., an industry committed to locate in the park). He felt this was unfair because most industries are unwilling to commit themselves to locating in an undeveloped park.

Despite the lack of EDA assistance for nonplanning projects, Battelle felt the field coordinator's activities had resulted in substantial job and income benefits for reservation residents. Nonetheless, his future credibility with Indians was questionable, according to Battelle, unless EDA project funds were soon made available.

Blackfeet Reservation. On the Blackfeet Reservation in Montana, EDA planning assistance grants are made to the Tribal Council which, in turn, hires a professional planning staff. Battelle reported that the planning staff had experienced difficulties arising from its relationship with the Tribal Council. Council members automatically serve as members of the Board of Directors of the planning program, and the planning staff is responsible to the Tribal Council for its actions and must coordinate programs with it. The evaluators felt that the lack of continuity in Tribal Council membership had weakened the effectiveness and continuity of the planning program.

On the whole, however, the Blackfeet planning program was judged to be most successful. Since receipt of the first EDA planning grant in 1967, the planning staff had helped raise the Blackfeet's standard of living and assisted in creating new employment opportunities for reservation residents. Among the staff's accomplishments were: (1) acquisition of a Department of Housing and Urban Development (HUD) 701 planning grant for the reservation; (2) obtaining EDA public works assistance to pave streets, build curbs, construct gutters, and install storm sewers in the reservation town of Browning; (3) negotiation of three SBA loans; (4) completion of the backup feasibility, financing, and contract negotiation work necessary to the construction of a forty-unit motel in Browning; and (5) provision of assistance that helped Piegan Products, Inc., a wholly Indian-owned corporation, incorporate and begin operations.

Pine Ridge Reservation. EDA planning grants to the Pine Ridge Reservation in South Dakota are also made directly to the Tribal Council, which recruits the planning staff. Battelle reported that this staff had not been successful in developing industry because of a lack of natural resources on the reservation and difficulty in acquiring local project funds. However, it was also noted that the staff's operations were not well organized, and no noticeable effort had been made to prepare a meaningful development plan.

The relationship between the planning staff and the Tribal Council is similar to that on the Blackfeet Reservation; the Pine Ridge Reservation Tribal Council has been characterized by complete changes of membership every two years. Thus, the staff faces the problem of having to work under a completely new administration, often unfamiliar with the ongoing program.

Nez Perce Reservation. The Clearwater Economic Development Association in Idaho is composed of five counties and the Nez Perce Indian Reservation. Battelle reported that the executive director of the district's planning staff emphasized efforts to improve the Indians' standard of living and to provide them with employment opportunities, but few tangible benefits had resulted.

One project through which the district planning staff was able to aid reservation residents involved acquisition of EDA funds for the Lewis and Clark Vocational Training Center. Another project resulted in the establishment of a small electronics firm on reservation lands, for which the executive director of the planning staff was personally responsible.

Battelle's major criticism of the staff was that it had sought minimal help from outside organizations such as local chambers of commerce, Community Action Program staff members, other local development groups, and the Bureau of Indian Affairs. However, the evaluators complimented the staff on its success in enabling the Indians to initiate an effective dialogue with their non-Indian neighbors.

Crow and Northern Cheyenne Reservations. The Crow and Northern Cheyenne Reservations are joined with Big Horn County to form the Big Horn Economic Development Corporation of Montana. According to Battelle, the four-man staff had focused on the economic development of the reservations, but had been handicapped by long-standing animosities between the two tribes. Even though the organizational structure of the Big Horn Economic Development Corporation provides the opportunity for these tribes to work together, evaluators reported that progress in this direction had been virtually nonexistent. The executive director was forced to work separately with the two tribes. The planning staff's effectiveness was also limited by the manner in which the planners were appointed. The Crow planner and the Northern Cheyenne planner were appointed by their respective tribes, and the district's executive director had no voice in their selection.

The one Crow project completed as a result of the staff's efforts provided telephone service for a remote community on the reservation. In dealing with the Northern Cheyenne tribe, the planning staff had assumed more initiative, including the preparation of an application for an EDA grant to fund an industrial and training facility. The staff was also instrumental in securing a loan from SBA to allow a member of that tribe to start his own small manufacturing operation.

In-House Case Studies

In addition to the initial evaluations of program tools implemented through contracts, an EDA task force independently conducted a series of area case studies. These reports, while exhibiting no rigorous or substantial methodological conformity, were intended to provide a context for the more analytic public works, business loans, technical assistance, and planning grant analyses.

Of the fifteen case studies conducted, four examined EDA-designated Indian reservations. All four—the Navajo, Gila River, Colorado River, and Mescalero Reservations—are Action List reservations. All are coping with the problems of economic underdevelopment: low median income, high rates of unemployment, unskilled labor, lack of capital, etc. However, the evaluators were encouraged by the reservation residents' realization of the efficacy both of planning and federal government programs. The following discussion summarizes the findings of the evaluators, which are presented in more detail in an EDA publication entitled *Summary of Case Studies: Evaluation of EDA Rural Activities in Fifteen Areas.*[3]

Reservation Characteristics. Through their visits to the four reservations, the evaluators acquired the following perception of the characteristics of such places and the problems encountered in attempting to stimulate economic development.

Successful development programs on Indian reservations are achieved only by overcoming a variety of specific impediments. Chief among these is the typical reservation's isolation from most economic activity in the area in which it is located. Dialogue between the reservation and nearby communities is limited. Living conditions on reservations are, by most criteria, substandard. Housing, sanitation, and incomes are all inadequate. Unemployment is high and skill levels of the work force are low.

Opportunities for gainful employment and achieving economic development are minimal. Few Indians, in fact, have had an opportunity to hold meaningful jobs in industry. Given these conditions, it is little wonder that industry has serious misgivings about locating on reservations; it is a high-risk venture.

In general, Indian reservations by themselves do not constitute viable economic units. They lack many of the fundamental necessities for economic development: markets, skilled labor, and raw materials. In addition, the customary two-year changes in tribal government present special problems for development programs.

(1) The new tribal council may not be familiar with the ongoing program and, in fact, may not subscribe to it.
(2) The philosophies, objectives, and priorities of one council sometimes are radically different from those of the previous council. This causes a shift in emphasis of the ongoing program.
(3) The tribe's planning staff has to spend considerable time orienting and educating the new council in planning program matters.[4]

EDA Experience with Reservation Development Programs. The evaluators reported that despite recent efforts to integrate the black community and the white community, little emphasis has been placed on bringing the red man into the economic mainstream of American life. They attributed this partially to the Indian's passivity and the lack of leadership. Moreover, the evaluators stated that prejudices toward the Indian were often stronger than toward the black and would not be quickly removed. It was their opinion that as long as such feelings existed, Indian problems would receive only secondary emphasis and interest; progress toward economic development would be slow. They concluded that the low-level funding provided by EDA and other federal and state agencies would not improve the Indian's situation dramatically in the span of a few years.

The problems of the Indian reservations are massive; so, too, the needs. Through tribal councils, Indian tribes have been active and interested in promoting economic development, but little progress has been made. A general finding of this analysis—reinforced by other evaluations of the agency program on reservations—involved reservation residents' opinion of EDA activities. The evaluators found that EDA generally has a positive local image, relative to that of other federal agencies, because of the feeling that the agency genuinely responds to needs as the residents themselves define them. The case studies indicated the agency has demonstrated a unique capacity to stimulate the development process and provide versatile project financing on reservations.

The most general conclusion of the study was that, where EDA assistance appeared to have been most effective, the success of the program seemed directly attributable to a strong and competent local planning staff and, in particular, the staff's executive director.

Recommendations. From the limited evidence collected in the evaluation, it was not possible for the evaluators to suggest any radical departures from past agency guidelines. On the other hand, the success exhibited by many reservations projects indicated that the basic policies followed had worked well. Consequently, the evaluators presented the following recommendations as suggestions for maximizing project impacts within the EDA program's structure.

It must be recognized that programs on reservations are likely to have a fairly high rate of unsuccessful projects. If funds are awarded only for those projects with a high probability of immediate economic impact, few projects will be funded. Investment in reservation projects is very risky, which is why private capital for such projects has been limited. The goal of federal programs should be to provide that type of capital not available from the private sector. If EDA funds only those projects with a high probability of success, it will simply be providing funds that are likely to displace private capital.

A major obstacle to development and, in particular, to the formation of Indian-owned and operated businesses is the lack of management capability on reservations. This problem has caused applications for large projects to be delayed for long periods of time in EDA regional offices until assurances can be given that outside management will be brought in. The Agency should give

Indians a chance to develop management capability by allowing them to run EDA-funded projects. A large number of small projects should be funded for this purpose, and the Agency should be prepared for an initially high rate of failure. Such projects will not only allow Indians to develop management skills, but also give them a sense of participation, achievement, and responsibility.

During the early stages of development, specialized planning skills are not necessarily required to establish successful minority assistance programs. The main skills needed are ability to communicate with the tribal members, gain the confidence and trust of the group, and communicate the interests and desires of the group to outsiders. The planning program must be flexible enough to adapt to individuals with a variety of personality and cultural characteristics. One of the major difficulties of programs dealing with Indians is that they are often structured to require the Indian to immediately adopt the methods of the non-Indian world. This approach tends to alienate the Indians and, for that reason, is frequently unsuccessful.[5]

Conclusions

The major conclusion to be drawn from these preliminary studies is simply that the problems of reservations are so massive and pervading that any progress in development will be hard won. In consequence, EDA should accept and endure the obvious: reservation programs are likely to have a high rate of unsuccessful projects. If funds were awarded only for projects with a high probability of success, then few projects would be attempted on Indian reservations. Further, limiting assistance to such projects would probably be at the cost of displacing what little private reservation investments would otherwise be made.

EDA Indian Program Evaluation: Round Two

By mid-1970, a substantial data base had been established for project-oriented evaluations. The usual cost-effectiveness ranges for the various program tools within the areas in which EDA works had been identified with a relatively high degree of confidence. Reports on the variety of impacts typifying public works projects, business loans, technical assistance, and planning grants had been made to Assistant Secretary Podesta, high-level staff members, and the respective program offices. These project-based findings, conclusions, and recommendations had also been reported to the Office of Management and Budget and to Congress. Equally important, the EDA staff members charged with evaluation responsibilities had gained experience in the techniques of analysis, and acquired a better understanding of the agency's programs. As a result, plans submitted to the Assistant Secretary for subsequent analyses reflected a move away from purely project-oriented studies toward program-based evaluations. Among those plans approved in late 1970 was a recommendation for evaluation of the agency's Indian effort as a whole, with particular emphasis on the Selected Indian Reservation Program (SIRP).

The Request for Proposal that initiated this effort required potential contractors to propose methodologies that would not only permit accurate assessments of individual reservation project impact, but also outline an approach to systematically integrate such assessments in the broader framework of an analysis of the SIRP itself. Reports on the earlier EDA evaluations, including the separate methodologies used, were open for inspection by the bidders, and material on EDA's Indian involvement was made available. It was anticipated that eighteen man-months would be required to conduct the proposed evaluation.

Twenty contractors submitted proposals in response to the Request for Proposal. A four-man evaluation team from EDA was selected to read all twenty proposals and to score them independently, according to a predetermined Evaluation Guide. After scoring was completed, scores for each individual contractor were totalled and an average score was taken.

The major criteria for evaluation of the proposals were: (1) demonstrated understanding of the EDA Selected Indian Reservation Program; (2) awareness of special problems relevant to Indian reservations in general and to the EDA program in particular; (3) presentation of a specific and detailed methodology to be used in carrying out the four program tool evaluations; (4) proposals for the integration of information and data on program tools into the overview report on the Selected Indian Reservation Program; and (5) availability of qualified personnel for carrying out the evaluations. Most of the proposals submitted were judged to suffer from an inability to extend beyond a series of project reports or case studies to an integral program analysis.

Boise Cascade Center for Community Development received a higher score than those of the other contractors, particularly in presenting the most detailed analytic scheme for integrating data on program tools into a report on the Selected Indian Reservation Program. Its methodology for evaluating the tools themselves—an outgrowth of that developed earlier by Boise Cascade for evaluation of EDA public works projects—also ranked high.

The particular attractiveness of the Boise Cascade proposal was that it included a methodology for weighting primary findings by a "potential score" and an "environmental difficulty factor." In accounting terms, these would permit discounting of individual project impact to a common base, and thus insure the comparability of projects, regardless of type or location. The details of the system proposed by Boise Cascade are laid out in detail in chapter 6.

Boise, in being selected to undertake a major evaluation of EDA's Indian program, was committed to evaluate all approved projects on twelve Action List reservations picked by the agency. These were: Annette Island, Alaska; Fort Apache, Arizona; Salt River, Arizona; San Carlos, Arizona; Red Lake, Minnesota; Blackfeet, Montana; Crow, Montana; Zuni Pueblo, New Mexico; Fort

Berthold, North Dakota; Standing Rock, North Dakota/South Dakota; Rosebud, South Dakota; and Uintah and Ouray, Utah. Table 11-10 shows the number, type, and EDA investment of the projects analyzed.

When the contract for evaluation of EDA's Indian program was first let, an intentional decision was made to exclude the Navajo, Gila River, Mescalero, and Colorado River Reservations from the analysis. These were analyzed as part of the earlier in-house task force study previously described. Since the process of evaluation can be unsettling to the community analyzed, it was judged inappropriate to return to these reservations so soon.

In addition to the problem of reevaluation time factors, the completed projects within the reservations to be examined by Boise were thought to be an adequate sample of the entire program. These reservations' completed projects represented nearly 10 percent of all EDA projects approved on reservations, and more than one quarter of the projects approved on Action List reservations. Further, the twelve reservations to be evaluated contained 10 percent of the total population on federal reservations and almost 25 percent of the Action List population. These figures all increase substantially if the unusually large population of the Navajo reservation (127,000) is excluded from the calculations.

Following development of methodology and field instruments, Boise Cascade initiated a pilot test of its analytic tools on three reservations. These were Annette Island, Red Lake, and the Zuni Reservations.

Table 11-10
Distribution and EDA Investment for Approved Projects

| | Number of Approved Projects | | | | | |
Reservation	PW	BL	TA	PG	Total	Total EDA Investment
Annette Island	4	0	0	0	4	$ 1,621,000
Blackfeet	4	1	1	1	7	3,186,805
Crow	6	2	2	1[a]	11	3,735,900
Fort Apache	4	2	2	1[a]	9	3,698,450
Fort Berthold	4	0	1	1[a]	6	1,553,920
Red Lake	1	2	3	1	7	424,924
Rosebud	6	1	1	1	9	539,141
Salt River	2	0	1	1[a]	4	358,300
San Carlos	4	0	2	1[a]	7	1,584,000
Standing Rock	4	0	0	1[a]	5	1,528,900
Uintah/Ouray	2	0	1	0	3	1,416,780
Zuni Pueblo	5	1	1	1	8	890,221
TOTAL	46	9	15	10	80	$20,538,341

[a]Planning grants support staffs who serve other areas in addition to the reservation. The funds for these grants are not included in the total EDA investment figures.
Source: Boise Cascade Center for Community Development, *Evaluation of EDA's Selected Reservation Program* (Draft), Washington, D.C.: Boise Cascade Center for Community Development, September 1971, vol. I, pp. 34–70

Following the pilot test, which had been closely monitored by agency personnel, meetings were held with EDA representatives to discuss the results. Even though some modifications were introduced into the test instruments because of the field experience and discussions, no major problems emerged. Consequently, with EDA approval, full-scale implementation of the evaluation methodology was begun in March on the remaining nine reservations. All field work was completed by the end of April.

The demands of both EDA officials and Boise Cascade's methodology were for maximum uniformity in criteria and evaluation across all projects and reservations. These requirements together with the dictates of common sense, led Boise to minimize the number of investigators assigned to the analysis. Four was judged to be the minimum number of evaluators capable of conducting the study within the time constraints. Thus, each investigator conducted studies on at least two separate reservations. Further, frequent meetings, both in person and through conference calls, with all other field staff permitted the greatest possible basis for uniformity and cross-comparisons between reservations.

The field report on Red Lake is typical of the individual evaluations conducted by Boise Cascade. Further, the cultural-economic problems reported are similar to those of most other reservations. Chief among these is the internal tension between the desire to maintain the present cultural way of life and values, and the goal of major economic development. All too often, these are perceived as mutually exclusive. And such a perception may be accurate.

A condensed version of Boise Cascade Center for Urban Development's report on the Red Lake Reservation follows.

Red Lake Reservation

The Red Lake Reservation of the Chippewa Tribe is characterized by plentiful natural resources, strong tribal leadership, and considerable federal involvement. Early in the twentieth century, the reservation began to develop its forestry and fishery resources, and close to 300 people are currently gainfully employed (full- or part-time) in businesses based on lumber and fishing.[b] The federal government ment remains the largest employer on the reservation, however, and public subsidy is the largest source of dollars for the Red Lake Reservation.

EDA involvement with the reservation has been rather limited but generally well received. All four program tools have been applied at Red Lake. As a consequence of eight EDA projects, amounting to $203,339 in grants and $221,585 in loans, some income impact has occurred. However, EDA's impact on development potential is by far the most important result to date. There is a feeling among reservation residents that the EDA program is making a meaningful contribution to the economic and social development of the Red Lake Band.

---

[b]As indicated previously, the conditions described in this report are as of April 1971.

Setting and Background

Location. The Red Lake Indian Reservation consists of 636,964 contiguous acres of heavily wooded country in north-central Minnesota. In addition, the Red Lake Band owns scattered tracts of land extending up to the Canadian border, amounting to approximately 156,000 acres. There are three communities located on the reservation: Red Lake and Redby are located on the south shore of the Lower Red Lake, and provide the greatest concentration of population; Ponemah is located on a peninsula between the Upper and Lower Red Lakes. The population of the Red Lake Reservation is nearly 3,700.

The population center nearest to the reservation is Bemidji, a town of 10,000 located 32 miles to the south of the town of Red Lake. Other nearby towns include Blackduck, about 30 miles to the southeast, and Thief River Falls, about 70 miles to the northwest of Red Lake. The Minneapolis-St. Paul metropolitan area is about 200 miles southeast of Red Lake.

The reservation has all-weather north-south and east-west highways running across it; however, these roads are not suitable for heavy truck use, and are not arteries of commerce in northern Minnesota. Secondary roads and bridges are few and of poor quality, and insufficient for full utilization of the reservation's natural resources and recreational opportunities. Although bus and train service are unavailable on the reservation, they are available at Bemidji, Thief River Falls, and Blackduck. Air service is available from both Bemidji and Thief River Falls.

Resources and Economy. The Red Lake Band were known to be thrifty farmers for centuries. Currently, however, only seven families are actively engaged in farming on the reservation. Although sufficient acreage of good farm land is available, the current members of the Band lack the interest, up-to-date knowledge, and capital needed to develop and maintain profitable farm ventures.

The primary resources utilized on the Red Lake Indian Reservation are timber and fish. Agriculture has played a limited role on the reservation in recent years, although the opportunities exist for the cultivation of cranberry marshes, blueberries, and wild rice on a commercial basis, as well as for the expansion of existing agricultural pursuits. In addition, the reservation has a vast recreational potential which has to date been greatly underutilized; some available mineral resources; and a population, eager for employment, which has also been underutilized.

The Red Lake Reservation's timber resources offer a major opportunity for further development. The reservation lands, with the exception of the Northwest Angle (52,000 acres forested by Boise Cascade) are estimated to contain 210 million board feet of saw timber, and over 2 million cords of pulp and other small forest products. The Red Lake Mill, the major business on the reservation, is scheduled to use about 5 million board feet of hard and soft wood per year for each of the next ten years. This is only half the amount the timber lands could support under a sustained yield program. Thus, the reservation has available timber resources to supply the needs of prospective wood-using industries, as well as a mill capable of converting the timber to the finished or semi-finished wood products required by such industries.

Another major resource is fish. Both the Upper and Lower Red Lakes produce a substantial amount of fresh fish for the commercial market, including the walleyed pike and perch. This resource is guarded from harmful exploitation by a yearly quota, fixed by the Secretary of the Interior. Under the present quota, 650,000 pounds of fish were taken out of the lakes by members of the Band in 1970, at a value of approximately $1.5 million. The current fishery operation, conducted by the Red Lake Fisheries Association, is limited to the delivery of walleyed pike and some other species for further processing and marketing by a nontribal group.

The recreation potential of the reservation is undoubtedly vast. The reservation contains beautiful forests and lakes in their natural state, which are ideally situated for development as tourist attractions. Many good trout streams flow on the reservation, several of them stocked by the U.S. Fish and Wildlife Service, and, in cooperation with the U.S. Bureau of Sport Fisheries, the tribe has developed rainbow trout lakes for its own people.

Other tourist resources are guided hunting, trapping and fishing. The reservation contains some of the most famous and coveted hunting and fishing in the country, with large numbers of game, including wild fowl, deer, moose, small game, and game fish. However, about fifteen years ago, a federal dredging operation destroyed one of the country's great natural habitats for fish and wildlife plus one of the best resting grounds for ducks. Dams and other facilities could restore much of the fish wildlife habitat in these areas, thus improving the economy of the reservation. The tribe has developed, with the help of the U.S. Fish and Wildlife Service, two large wildlife areas on the reservation.

Additional attractions include: the nationally famous July 4th Indian Dance Festival that draws participants and spectators from many states and Canada; St. Mary's Mission; and the Indian handcraft products on the reservation.

Other resources capable of fruitful exploitation include agricultural land and minerals. There are 10,000 to 15,000 acres of land on the western edge of the reservation which are suitable for farming and cattle/dairying operations; additional land could be cleared and broken as required. This land is especially good for cranberry marshes and for raising blueberries; it is also suitable for potato and beet crops. All agricultural activity is hampered, however, by the short growing season. Lack of farm training and capital has prevented proper utilization of these land resources.

Mineral resources can only be guessed at pending the completion of more thorough geological studies, but there are preliminary indications of substantial deposits of iron and other ferrous metals, and some copper and nickel deposits.

Permits to explore for these metals are being processed by the tribal council and the federal government. There are also sizable deposits of marl and peat on the reservation, which await possible development.

Until the recent inception of various federal programs, the only sources of income available to tribal residents had been in commercial fishing, a sawmill operation, timber cutting, and, to a very limited extent, agriculture.

The Red Lake Fisheries Association is composed of tribal members who deliver pike and other species of fish for further processing and marketing by a nontribal group. This business has provided income to about 200 persons for a few months of each year. This commercial fishing is confined to Upper and Lower Red Lakes.

The Red Lake Indian Mill at Redby consists of a logging operation, sawmill, and planing mill which employs, on a yearly average, approximately fifty men. However, this source of income and employment had been declining in recent years due to poor market conditions and the obsolescence of the plant. The mill was destroyed by fire in 1965; and the reconstructed plant permits a more economical production of lumber. In addition, new equipment—a timber cant conveyor and a new lumber inspection station—have been installed, and the mill has initiated hauling its own chips by purchasing chip hauling vans. The mill is operated as a tribal venture under the supervision of the Bureau of Indian Affairs (BIA).

The Red Lake Chippewa Cedar Fence Plant, Incorporated, was organized by the tribal council to manage and operate the manufacturing of cedar fence as a tribal enterprise. The plant now employs thirty to thirty-five men, and a $100,000 loan has recently been obtained from SBA for new machinery and working capital.

Seven families are actively engaged in farming and, on an average each owns twenty-one head of dairy cattle and five head of beef cattle. These farm operations produce $9,347 in tribal income and $90,000 in personal income annually.

There are presently 535 male and 336 female members of the Band between the ages of eighteen and sixty-five years. Less than 55 percent of this labor force (457 persons including farmers) is currently regularly employed; and approximately one-half of those regularly employed are Community Action Program workers. Another 25 percent of the labor force derives some earned income from seasonal and temporary work. The remaining members of the community must rely upon relief or welfare payments in order to subsist.

Only a small percentage of the total employable members of the Red Lake Band can be classified as skilled in specialized trades. However, this group of Indians is recognized for having a high degree of manual dexterity and learning trades quickly. Among those presently unemployed, there are approximately eighty-five males and forty females who would properly be classified as skilled or semiskilled.

There are very few places on the reservation to spend the money received from these inflows. The reservation towns of Red Lake and Redby (1,500 and 1,100 people respectively, including outlying tracts) contain only four small general stores and about an equal number of service stations; Ponemay to the north has one store. Major expenditures are made in Bemidji.

Tribal Government. The reservation is governed by a tribal council of eleven persons. The chairman, secretary, and treasurer are elected at large by the reservation members to four-year terms. Two councilmen from each of four districts are elected by the voters of their respective districts for staggered four-year terms. This reservation government is stipulated, and its functions and duties defined, in a constitution and bylaws approved in 1958-59 by the Secretary of the Interior.

The tribal leadership of the Red Lake Reservation is among the most progressive in the country. The tribal council is currently presided over by a strong tribal chairman, who has given new impetus to the concept of developing an economy around tribally-owned resources, and using outside assistance to fund capital improvements and to subsidize tribal living expenses as necessary in the interim. Much of the current activity on the reservation is in fact the direct result of this tribal chairman's efforts.

Community Development. To achieve its economic and social goals for the reservation, the Red Lake Tribal Council has formed an industrial development corporation. For the past nine years, efforts have been made through the Bureau of Indian Affairs and by contact with private individuals to assist industries wishing to locate on the reservation. The corporation intends to serve as the instrument through which the Red Lake Band may invest money for the establishment of plants and facilities for industrial and commercial development on the reservation.

The Bureau of Indian Affairs, in cooperation with the Minnesota State Employment Service, provides assistance in the recruitment of qualified Indian employees to meet prospective companies' staffing needs. The BIA has also provided on-the-job training programs through which qualified enterprises are reimbursed for training eligible Indian workers.

The Department of Labor is active on the reservation, and has various training programs available to help meet the need for vocational and specialized training. One current on-the-job training program, Mini-CEP (Concentrated Employment Program), reimburses the local housing program for training eligible Indian people to be qualified home building workers. SBA has provided loans or loan guarantees for various projects on the reservation.

The Office of Economic Opportunity funds a Community Action Program (CAP) on the reservation at a level of $560,000 for the current fiscal year. The CAP has a staff of sixty.

A Headstart Program is currently funded on the reservation by the U.S. Department of Health, Education, and Welfare. The Red Lake School System, including a six-year accredited high school and two elementary schools with a total student body of 830, is currently funded by Minnesota, the Impacted Areas Program (PL 874) under the Johnson-O'Malley Act, and by Title I funds. The Public Health Service operates a hospital in the town of Red Lake.

The Department of Housing and Urban Development is involved in the successful Mutual Help Housing Program, by which Indians develop "sweat" equity in houses built with sawmill materials, Minnesota Concentrated Action Program-paid and OEO-paid labor, and BIA Superintendent-provided direction. The evolving program has been underway since 1964, with 160 houses built and about thirty men employed at least part time. The tribal council is currently acting as its own developer in this housing effort: the Tribal Housing Authority purchases the completed homes with the help of HUD's Housing Assistance Administration (HAA) funds, and uses subsidized payments from Mutual Help participants to repay HAA.

In addition to the housing available to tribal members through the HUD program, the Red Lake Tribal Credit Program has provided loan funds to members who have built approximately fifty standard homes and renovated many more. Other local sources and federal agencies are now making financial assistance available to tribal members. These include the Veterans Administration, Farmer's Home Administration, and local banks.

State programs currently operating on the Red Lake Reservation, in addition to the school programs, include the Minnesota Concentrated Employment Program and a Green Light Service Program which funds employees in the day care center.

EDA Impact

Table 11-11 outlines the EDA projects on the Red Lake Indian Reservation, including project type, date of approval, and funds obligated by EDA.

Furniture Plant Study and Loan. The technical assistance study approved by EDA in February of 1966 consisted of a $3,000 grant to investigate an applicant for an EDA business loan. The study, conducted by the firm of Ernst and Ernst, investigated the feasibility of establishing a branch plant of Eisen Brothers, Inc., a furniture manufacturer, on the Red Lake Indian Reservation. The operations and financial strength of the Eisen firm were investigated, as well as its commitment to the project. Eisen, by its application for an EDA business loan in 1965, had initiated what would become four years of negotiation regarding the establishment of the furniture plant.

Use of the reservation's timber resources has long been a feature of Red Lake

Table 11-11
EDA Project Activity at Red Lake

Project Type	Date	Funding
Furniture Plant Study (TA)	1966	$ 3,000 (grant)
Saw Mill Rebuilding and Expansion (BL)	1966	184,000 (loan)
Industrial Park (PW)	1967	150,339 (grant)
		37,585 (loan)
Furniture Plant (BL)	1968	Cancelled
Planning Grant	1968	20,000 (grant)
Cedar Fence Plant Accounting Study (TA)	1969	2,500 (grant)
	1970	2,500 (grant)
Forest Products Study (TA)	1970	25,000 (grant)
Timber Study (TA)	1970	Cancelled
TOTAL		$203,339 (grant)
		221,585 (loan)

Source: Boise Cascade Center for Community Development, *Evaluation of EDA's Selected Indian Reservation Program* (Draft), Washington, D.C.: Boise Cascade Center for Community Development, September 1971, vol. II, p. 118

planning. The idea of adding value to the timber through further processing of the wood, while at the same time providing additional reservation jobs, is an attractive one, and has been discussed in the OEDP and other pertinent documents. Thus, the furniture plant was given serious consideration. The Ernst and Ernst study was the first in a long series of studies, meetings and negotiations, leading ultimately to EDA's approval of a $981,500 business loan for the furniture plant in November 1967. However, the Eisen firm subsequently backed out of the project. The firm was unwilling or unable to come up with its share of working capital, despite approval by EDA in November 1967 of a $720,000 working capital loan guarantee. In addition, the tribe was beginning to have misgivings as to whether this was the right firm for the reservation. As a result, the business loan was cancelled, and the furniture manufacturing plant was not located on the reservation.

The technical assistance project appears to have been conceived by EDA in 1965, in response to the application by the Eisen firm for a business loan. The project was approved in 1966. It was EDA who selected Ernst and Ernst to conduct the study; the tribe played a very minimal role in the investigation of the Eisen Brothers Furniture Company, or in the negotiations with the firm.

The report prepared by Ernst and Ernst has never been seen by the tribe. It apparently approved the business loan to the Eisen Brothers Furniture Company, since the business loan negotiations intensified subsequently. The study was completed in 1966.

These projects appear to have had no visible impact on the reservation. Although the business loan was ultimately approved, the Eisen firm located elsewhere, resulting in the loan's cancellation. Intratribal debate over the merits of this firm was often intense, and was one major factor of conflict between the tribal chairman (who supported the firm) and an EDA-funded planner (who did not).

Red Lake Indian Sawmill Business Loan. This project, approved in 1966, consisted of a business loan to rebuild a tribal sawmill which burned down in 1965. The EDA loan consisted of $184,000, 40 percent of the amount needed by the tribe. The remaining 60 percent was supplied by the tribe through insurance proceeds. All other EDA projects at Red Lake related at least indirectly to this mill.

The Red Lake Indian Sawmill is a lumber enterprise consisting of a sawmill and a planing mill covering about three-fourths of an acre of reservation land. Approximately 5 million board feet of pine and hardwood are utilized annually, and about fifty members of the tribe are employed by the operation. It is a tribally developed enterprise, which has operated for forty years under the supervision of the Bureau of Indian Affairs. The mill has played an important role in the economy of the tribe, and has been a focal point of the tribal council's plans for the reservation.

The total cost of rebuilding and enlarging the sawmill after the fire in 1965 was $464,000. Of this amount, EDA contributed 40 percent, or $184,000. The loan was made for fifteen years, at 4.25 percent interest, with EDA maintaining a first lien on the plant constructed with the loan. Working capital was supplied by tribal funds; the exact amount of working capital required is unknown. The remaining 60 percent of the funds required were also supplied by the Red Lake Indian Band. This tribal funding served as a leverage for securing the EDA loan.

At present, there are forty-nine employees at the sawmill. These employees are identified by position and race in table 11-12. An additional thirty employees work on logging crews on the reservation.

At the time of the EDA loan approval, it was expected that sixty-four saved jobs and five new jobs would result from the project. Most of the people now employed at the sawmill were employed there before the fire.

The Red Lake Reservation currently has an application in to EDA for a major improvement and expansion of the mill which would provide further job opportunities, as well as permit the processing of a wider selection of logs and production of cut stock (cut to order) by the mill. The application is for over $800,000 of public works money, to be provided on a 50-50 grant-loan basis.

No measurable indirect benefits have accrued as a result of the EDA loan. The loan did not cause expanded sawmill operation, and it is extremely difficult to accept the proposition that the mill would not have started again in 1966 without $184,000 of EDA money. In view of the stability and long experience of profits of the sawmill, a loan could most likely have been obtained by the reservation from a private bank. The speed with which the loan was approved was, however, of great benefit to the tribe in its period of anxiety, and the rate

Table 11-12
Employment at Red Lake Mill

Position	Indian	Non-Indian
Civil Service Employees (mill manager, purchasing agent, one other)	0	3
Office Employees	1	1
Skilled Employees (foreman, machine operators)	3	4
Semi-Skilled Employees (including log truck drivers)	11	4
Unskilled Employees	21	1
TOTAL	36	13

Source: Boise Cascade Center for Community Development, *Evaluation of EDA's Selected Indian Reservation Program* (Draft), Washington, D.C.: Boise Cascade Center for Community Development, September 1971, vol. II, p. 121

of interest obtained from EDA was favorable when compared against commercial bank rates available.

Although the sawmill has considerable growth potential, this is not directly attributable to the EDA loan, nor has the loan increased the potential value of existing natural resources.

Comparatively rapid receipt of EDA funds for sawmill reconstruction undoubtedly established EDA as a source of financial support for large projects in the minds of the Red Lake Band. Although no private financing sources were tapped as a direct result of the project, the reestablishment of the sawmill provided work opportunities for logging crews who increasingly rely on SBA and Bemidji bank financing for their trucks and equipment. The First National Bank of Bemidji has just over 200 outstanding loans to members of the tribe, in addition to $125,000 invested with an SBA guarantee in the Cedar Fence Plant; many of the loans were for pieces of equipment used in lumbering and fishing.

Redby Industrial Park. The Redby Industrial Park project, approved by EDA in January 1967, consisted of a $150,339 grant by EDA (80 percent of total) and a $37,585 loan (20 percent) for a total EDA contribution of $187,924. This public works project was intended to create an attractive site where outside industrialists could locate wood-related production/processing facilities. The immediate objective of the project was the creation of a water and fire protection system that would benefit the Red Lake Indian Mill, the Red Lake Chippewa Cedar Fence Plant, and the town of Redby; however, the project also prepared industrial sites for the proposed Eisen Brothers furniture plant and for other potential industries.

The tribal council initiated this project. The application for financial assistance was made by the council chairman, who also represented the tribe in the negotiations. The Red Lake Band owns the ninety-seven acre industrial park and the water system which was the main project output. A water commission, reporting to the council, "manages" the water distribution to Redby residents, the sawmill, and cedar fence plant. No other industrial park activities exist to date.

The components of this project include: a 125,000-gallon above-ground storage tank; pump house and pumping mechanism; a water and sewer system for the park and for the town of Redby; improvement and extension of a dirt access road; and clearing and grading of several previously undeveloped sites on the ninety-seven acres. The water distribution system is currently handling over 20,000 gallons of industrial and drinking water per day, serving approximately 100 families in the Redby community, as well as the sawmill and the cedar fence plant. The access road to the industrial site connects with that for the sawmill to form a sort of "U" shape; the industrial site (western) part of the road is seldom used for reaching State Highway 1, but it does increase the accessibility of the sawmill and cedar fence plant. Fire protection is provided at the cedar plant and the new sawmill building (but not for the planing mill) by sprinklers, feasible because of the project's water distribution system. Insurance savings can reasonably be attributed to the project.

As indicated above, there have been numerous beneficiaries from the industrial park project. It has resulted in improved road access for the Red Lake Indian Sawmill, as well as a much improved water supply, increased fire protection, and annual insurance savings of approximately $5,000 for both the sawmill and the cedar fence plant. The Redby community as a whole has benefitted from the new sewer system; water supply is now plentiful, at a cost of only $3.00 to $4.00 per year per home. And the Red Lake Tribal Council has an enhanced interest in, and understanding of, industrial/business development due to their involvement in the development of the industrial park.

No firms have moved into the industrial park to date. A mattress plant in Minnesota has expressed interest in locating in the industrial park, but discussions are not currently active. The only possible job impact attributable to the project is to the members of the water commission. The three members of the commission are Indian; however, their positions are largely honorary (resulting in $450 in salaries since 1967), and these individuals all have other income sources.

Prior to the industrial park development, the infrastructure of the reservation was capable of accommodating some industry; however, available utilities were minimal and existing housing poor. The improvement in utilities and the further availability of industrial sites has certainly made the reservation more attractive for prospective industries.

Little work of real substance is going on to identify and attract viable outside industry to the reservation. The leaders have experienced a certain amount of frustration in their negotiations with private industrialists and the EDA (and BIA and SBA) bureaucracy, but they have learned more about the development potential of the reservation, and are undeniably more familiar with industrial development problems as a result. It remains for this increasing sophistication to be used by the council to attract outside resources to increase job and income opportunities for the Red Lake Band.

Planning Grant. The area planning grant, funded in June 1968 by EDA for $35,900, was to enable the Red Lake Band to employ a full-time professional staff to evaluate the social and economic problems that confront the reservation and to provide overall development planning and implementation of a comprehensive program. Two planners were expected to be hired through the use of EDA planning grant funds. The senior planner was then expected to expand the activity to a professional planning staff of eight, including three trainees, to be funded by EDA, HUD and OEO, with a total planning budget approaching $200,000.

The tribal council hired a young tribal member with no planning experience as executive director of the planning staff. Basic differences in the perception of planning responsibilities and development strategy soon developed between the executive director and tribal council. These differences were exacerbated by tribal politics. The planner wanted to make binding decisions for the tribe. There were also major differences between the executive director and chairman of the tribal council concerning the type of industry to attract to the reservation. The planner, for example, was against the Eisen Brothers project favored by the chairman.

The result of these differences was that the planning staff was not given duties or responsibilities by the council, and carried out activities in spite of, or outside of, the interests of the council. The tribal council decided that the planner was "not the man for the job," and requested that the grant be terminated after nine months, in June 1969. Approximately $20,000 of EDA funds was actually disbursed during this period.

The planning staff submitted a technical assistance proposal for a shopping center feasibility study in January of 1969; it was rejected because shopping centers were then ineligible for EDA financial assistance. A training center proposal never jelled because of difficulty in securing tribal share funds (25 percent of $315,000).

The planning staff did attempt to attract industries and business to Red Lake. Several conversations were held, and a "firm proposal" was secured from a mattress and bedding manufacturer in Minnesota. The council questioned the company's motives, however, and was very hesitant about "selling cheap labor" to an "outside exploiter."

Formalized planning will not work on Red Lake Reservation unless it is done within the context of tribal council hegemony. The council takes its policy-making and care-providing responsibilities (under Constitution and from traditional culture) seriously. It is not clear exactly what was expected of the planner, but it is clear that his stated function ("to provide overall development planning and implementation") was only to be performed insofar as it was consistent with tribal council objectives and priorities.

Cedar Fence Plant Operations Study. The purpose of this technical assistance project was to improve the apparently unprofitable operations of the tribally-owned Red Lake Chippewa Cedar Fence Plant by acquiring management assistance from a local accounting firm. An EDA purchase order for $2,500 was approved for this purpose in October 1969; this was followed by a second purchase order for an additional $2,500 in 1970 to expand the study. An outside accountant (from Thief River Falls) was selected by the tribe to: (1) review operations since the management of the fence plant was taken over by the tribe in 1968; (2) design and install a production record and cost system; and (3) analyze operating deficiencies and recommend corrective measures. The results of this project were less a study than the development of plant organization and management procedures and an accounting information system which would permit improved performance.

The work accomplished under the first purchase order included the following: preliminary review; establishment of cost accounting records; preparation of a reorganization plan; training of a bookkeeper; monitoring of a one-month trial run; preparation of financial statements; and management counselling. Since the work was not completed within the amount of time and money allotted by the first contract, a follow-on was approved in 1970, and it is still underway.

The cedar fence plant is an important part of the tribe's plan to develop its forest resources. It is clearly consistent with that goal, and with the goal of providing jobs for tribal members. Habitant, Inc., the previous operator of the plant, had been prompted by declining production and unsatisfactory profit performance to leave Red Lake in 1968. The tribe took over the plant at that time, and the tribal council has expressed a keen interest in the fate of the operation. In fact, the tribe has invested $29,000 in cash in the plant; the First National Bank of Bemidji has participated with SBA for $125,000 more. Delinquent payments on the note and evident confusion at the plant prompted the call for management assistance by the tribal council. Although the application for the technical assistance grant used some accounting language, the contracting firm was in fact called in to solve whatever operational problems might be discovered.

The tribe selected the accountant to perform the study, and has continued to play an active and supportive role. The tribe initiated the request for a follow-on purchase order when it became apparent that more work was needed.

The project resulted in a report whose value lies not so much in its words as in the activities it describes. The mandate was to provide management and accounting assistance to a stumbling plant; the report simply summarizes the work done in this regard. The work plan described in the report appears sound and well conceived, and the outline of the analysis process and work program is clear. With the funds provided by the second TA grant, the accountant is presently monitoring the program's implementation.

The Red Lake Chippewa Cedar Fence Plant, Inc. provides roughly thirty jobs to members of the Band. However, these jobs cannot be attributed to the EDA technical assistance project. The plant would have undoubtedly been carried by the tribal council as a deficit operation in view of the jobs it provides.

Indian assumption of managerial positions has been encouraged in the plant, but the plant environment is such that the necessary skills are difficult to acquire. The tribal council has gained a greater appreciation of the difficulties inherent in exercising responsibility for an economic enterprise since taking the plant over from the previous owner, and the cooperation extended the accountant in his work indicates a basic appreciation of the importance of competent managerial direction, whether white or Indian. The tribal council is clearly more interested in a profitable venture, with its promise of expanding job opportunities, than in Indian management per se.

The cedar fence plant appears to have good-to-excellent growth prospects based on conversations at the reservation. A Texas company has a long-standing commitment to absorb 50 percent of the firm's production, and the eastern market for a wide variety of cedar cut-stock, posts, and other cedar wood products appears to be expanding. The supply of cedar on the reservation is also vast, with one source claiming that production at present levels is not even keeping pace with timber growth. Any constraint on growth is apparently at the plant itself.

The First National Bank of Bemidji has invested $125,000 in the cedar fence plant. At the time of the field visit, extension of another $100,000 loan was being sought. This additional equipment loan would clearly not have been considered without SBA backing and provision of working capital by BIA. The tribe itself has invested $29,000 of its capital in the cedar fence plant.

The EDA technical assistance resulted in a temporary change in the plant's profit picture. The plant moved from an operating situation which had produced a direct $70,000 loss in a year, or nearly $6,000 per month, to an operation which yielded a $2,050 profit in January 1971.

The improved financial picture, however, has not persisted. Although there is an absence of detailed financial data, information from the bank and the consultant indicates a renewed downward trend. At present, planning concerning the plant is being postponed until a final decision is made about the requested loan from the bank.

Noticeable changes have occurred in the availability of financial assistance to the reservation due to this technical assistance project. The project is largely responsible for the acquisition of $30,000 of working capital from BIA, and will be directly responsible for the receipt of an additional $100,000 from the bank (with an SBA guarantee) for new equipment. The willingness of the tribe to invest more money and management assistance in the plant appears to have strengthened the banking relationship between the Red Lake Band and the First National Bank of Bemidji. Future incremental income flows will probably result from the technical assistance project and from the additional bank and BIA financing.

The Red Lake Tribal Council has been enthusiastic about economic development for a long time. What has changed as a result of this project is its appreciation of the importance of management skills to its business development plans. At least two members of the tribal council admitted that it had been instructive to see the relationship between the management study, the improved performance, the consequent increase in bank/SBA interest, the BIA working capital, and the additional bank financing.

Forest Products Feasibility Study. This project consists of a $25,000 grant made by EDA in May 1970 to determine the feasibility of additional forest industries on the reservation. The contract was awarded to the Mater Engineering Company for a one-year study.

The reservation's forested area is its major natural resource, and shows the greatest potential for development. The forest industry is the major nongovernment employer on the reservation. Presently, the tribe operates a sawmill and cedar post plant. The objective of this technical assistance study is to determine the feasibility of the establishment of additional forest industries in order to fully utilize the reservation's forest resources in creating new, permanent employment. The study is to consider the addition of possible primary processing facilities, e.g., a small saw log mill and complementary manufacturing facilities, such as a dimension stock plant or pallet plant. It is hoped that this study will result in the creation of over 100 new jobs in forest-related industries.

A draft of the study has just been completed. A preliminary review of the part of the report that was made available during the evaluation period suggests a lack of thoroughness and some questionable assumptions. The entire draft was not available for review. It is clear, however, that the study is timely and of potentially high value, although no impact has yet accrued from the project.

Industrial Locations Study. This proposed technical assistance study was approved for $10,000 by EDA in 1970 for the purpose of attempting to find and locate an industry at Red Lake which would be related to the existing timber resources and operations. The study was to be conducted by the consulting firm of Booz, Allen & Hamilton, Inc.

Funding of this project was delayed awaiting completion of the forest products feasibility study. However, since the two studies would be pursuing many of the same objectives, a decision was made to delay and then to cancel this industrial location study.

Conclusions and Recommendations

Red Lake is undergoing a transformation; more and more Indians are supported by some form of welfare. Yet understanding of the fundamentals of viable economic growth is undeniably increasing on the reservation, aided in no small part by the activities of EDA. EDA has provided major inputs to the reservation's economic development activities, and current projects should produce long-term effects. Much remains to be done, however, before heightened understanding of the principles and economics of mutually beneficial business partnerships is gained and used to form policies which will lead to the real economic development allegedly sought by the tribal council.

The major problem on the Red Lake Reservation is the inability of tribal leaders to resolve conflicting priorities of major economic and tourist development, on the one hand, and the desire to preserve tribal culture and reservation resources on the other. An example of the problem can be found in discussions about recreation development. Red Lake has a great deal of recreation potential; much income could be derived from wider use of reservation land for hunting, fishing, boating, and camping. The council professes an interest in such development, but they well know the very real dangers which such policies could lead to for the culturally isolated Band and its homeland. Thus, recreational development is unlikely to occur, despite avowed interest by the Band, as long as it is perceived by tribal members as an insidious threat to their control of the reservation, to the uses to which it is currently put, and to their way of life. Recreational development of Red Lake, whether it is "good" or not, must probably await the development of a cadre of tribal leaders who either feel they can control the form of that development or who are not so acutely aware of their cultural and historical milieu.

A more immediate need is for the council to obtain a better understanding of the realities of business economics. To date, the tribe has been entering negotiations with prospective firms with demands no businessman could accept. A more realistic assessment of incentive and demands is therefore in order. Since the tribal members are clearly opposed to closely supervised production line work, jobs need to be developed in activities which are either less structured (lumbering, craft piece work, modular or prefab housing construction, etc.) or are supervised by competent and motivated outside management.

The establishment of continuing management contracts with nearby management specialists who possess skills in various technologies and demonstrate empathy with Indians and their needs should be given high priority. The relationship between the tribal attorney, consultant-accountant, and the tribe suggests that the Band has much to gain from continual access to competent professionals whose views in development matters will be respected by the tribal council.

Projects which should be given consideration by EDA as the next stage in assisting the reservation include the following: (1) upon review of the timber study, assist the tribe in locating and attracting to the reservation viable business opportunities relating to the timber industry; (2) establish a management grant, analogous to a planning grant, to permit professional management inputs to be made available to the tribe on an ongoing basis, providing qualified management talent can be found; and (3) fund a study of the tourism resources of the reservation which has as its objectives the formulation of an action program for developing the tourist sector of the economy.

Evaluation Results for Twelve Action List Reservations

As noted elsewhere, a substantial "plus" in Boise Cascade's evaluation proposal was the presentation of a weighting system for reducing to a common denominator the evaluation results for individual projects. The proposal acknowledged the primitive stage of the weighting scheme, and this disclaimer was noted by the evaluators of the proposal. It was felt, however, that the agency's need for such an analysis tool warranted further development of the system, even with the accompanying risk of failure.

Coincident with the field work, Boise Cascade analysts continued development of the weighting methodology. As reports from the field became available, they were fed through the system. It was found that considerable skewing of the results occurred because of the use of arbitrary weights. This was most notable in the case of small technical assistance projects. It was found that any technical assistance project with a cost of under $5,000 had a very high ranking, irrespective of its "real" impact.

Constraints of time and money did not permit the necessary adjustments to the weighting methodology. As a result, it was mutually decided by the contractor and EDA not to base conclusions on the scoring system.[c]

Program Tool Evaluation—Public Works

Of the four program tools used on the twelve reservations, public works projects represented the largest EDA investment. In this respect, the evaluated Selected

---

[c]Additional information is available in Boise Cascade Center for Community Development's *Evaluation of EDA's Selected Indian Reservation Program* (Draft), Washington, D.C.: Boise Cascade Center for Community Development, September 1971, vol. I.

Indian Reservation Program reservations are akin to all areas in which EDA works. Public works funds have, in fact, accounted for approximately two-thirds of all agency expenditures. On the reservations, slightly less than half of the projects were public works, but these grants and loans represented more than 85 percent of the investments made. The forty-six public works projects represented $17.2 million in approved grants and loans, with the bulk, $14.2 million, in grants.

The forty-six projects represent only thirty-seven separate development packages, because many consist of more than one project. Of the thirty-seven, only eighteen development packages were physically complete at the time of the field work. In six cases, actual construction had not even begun. The remaining thirteen development packages were in varying stages of construction.

Through the eighteen completed project packages, just over 200 jobs had been located which were judged attributable to EDA financial participation. Eighty-five percent of these jobs had been taken by Indians. The total income generated by these projects was approximately $1.4 million, of which more than $1 million was Indian wages. In nearly every case, the wages from the EDA-attributable job provided the recipient with an income considerably above the respective tribal family average.

The approved public works projects were found to be components of twelve community service efforts, nine infrastructure units, nine tourism complexes, and seven industrial parks. Boise Cascade's analysis indicated that neither the community service nor the infrastructure project groups had any important impact in directly providing jobs. Nonetheless, their impact upon broader aspects of economic development and community improvement was without exception significant. Assistance such as road improvement was providing important community benefits and probably substantial, although unmeasurable, indirect economic benefits as well. Other project packages in this category included facilities used for vocational and other forms of training. Again, although it is difficult to assign precise economic value to these kinds of impact, Boise analysts believed the resultant benefits were high. In fact, it was noted that over time these might prove to be the most beneficial types of projects.

The tourism complexes included the most costly projects. None had been completed long enough to be adequately assessed in terms of operating experience. On the other hand, several of the developments were judged unlikely to be financially successful. The reason for this was, in part, because of their apparently excessive size and cost in relation to expected demand. There was reason to believe that several of the facilities, in order to break even, would require a level of tourism far above that predicted. In at least one other case, the total outlay the development represented was so great compared with the capacity of the facility produced, that it was effectively priced out of the probable market.

Two other situations observed by the analysts decreased the probability of success for the tourism projects. In no case did tribal citizens possess the training or experience that would permit indigenous management. As a result, all the tourism developments seemed likely to require external management and entrepreneurial skills, but few contacts had been established with professionals who might oversee the facilities. Secondly, in all cases justification of the project was based on the assumption that the facility would share equitably in the national tourist boom. Without substantial—and, for many of the out-of-the-way facilities, extraordinary—promotion, this assumption will probably not hold. Despite this, few Indian groups had even initiated adequate promotion campaigns.

Despite the doubts raised by analysis of the tourism programs, all the reservations were enthusiastic and optimistic about their potential. In total, the nine complexes, representing $10.7 million in EDA grants and loans, were expected to result in about 400 jobs and $2 million in annual wages. If they are successful, the indirect dollar impact, generated through arts and crafts sales and so forth, might also be significant.

Only one of the seven evaluated industrial parks on the reservations was occupied as of spring 1971. And the one occupant of that park had also received an EDA business loan. Even in this case, the future of the firm, a carpet mill, was uncertain. Industrial parks on two other reservations were believed to have firm commitments to locate from one industry apiece. In fact, an in-house industrial parks study initiated by EDA in July 1971 revealed that one of these commitments materialized during the summer of 1971, but the other had not been realized as of September 1971.

Overall, Boise found the investment per job for public works grants and loans to be very high: substantially over $30,000. Moreover, at the time of the evaluation, the rate of return on this investment, in terms of wages generated, had been fairly low. However, this must be weighted against the considerable infrastructure improvement and the development potential generated by these projects. While they did not appear cost-effective at the time of evaluation, it is difficult to conceive of a comprehensive Indian development program without substantial inputs to infrastructure.

Business Loans

The dollar value of business loans on the evaluated reservations, as in the EDA program generally, was second only to public works projects. Even so, only nine business loans had been approved on the twelve reservations. Three of these loan approvals were later withdrawn because the recipients decided not to locate on the reservations. A fourth loan was no longer outstanding at the time of the field work because the original recipient, a sawmill operation, had been taken over by the U.S. Plywood Corporation, which immediately liquidated the obligation.

The five loans outstanding in early 1971 represented an EDA investment of more than $2.5 million and had resulted in 234 jobs. Of the jobs stemming from the agency loans, about one-third were saved jobs, the consequence of EDA financial assistance in rebuilding of the Red Lake sawmill. The 79 saved jobs were found to consist of 49 at the mill and an additional thirty forest workers, mostly loggers. It is interesting to note the increase in employment over the one-year span separating the Booz, Allen & Hamilton, Inc. and Boise Cascade field work.[d] Only twenty-two mill employees were counted by Booz, Allen, less than half the work force reported by Boise Cascade.

As was noted in the Boise Cascade report on that reservation, the Red Lake mill might well have reopened eventually without EDA assistance. Another third of the business loan jobs on reservations were found at the unstable Crow Reservation carpet mill, which had also benefited from EDA funding of the industrial park on which it was located.

Although the EDA investment per job of approximately $10,000 for business loans was much smaller than that for public works projects, the evaluators concluded that loans had not been particularly effective on the reservations examined. Business loans had not contributed substantially to expanding or strengthening the economies of these reservations.

One reason for the lack of business loan impact seems simply to be the low demand level. The Small Business Administration provides loans of $350,000 and less. Thus, EDA is not the only supplying agency for loans of this size. The major advantage EDA loans offer is their low interest rates. The business subsidy this represents is intended to make location within EDA-qualified areas more attractive. In the case of most reservations, however, the diseconomies caused by their poor locations, lack of skilled labor, distance from markets, and limited natural resources outweigh the incentive provided by interest rate subsidies. Furthermore, even if the agency were permitted to markedly increase such incentives, the possibility is great that incompetent entrepreneurs, unqualified to meet the demands of commercial credit institutions, would be the major applicants. The probable high failure rate of such marginal operations would probably prove discouraging to the community. No case was found of a sound prospect that failed to materialize because of inadequate financing.

Technical Assistance

EDA had approved funding of fifteen distinct technical assistance projects on the twelve evaluated reservations. In total, these represented an agency cost of less than $348,000; almost half were for $3,000 or less. In nine cases, the Boise Cascade team felt that technical assistance studies had not resulted in impact of any kind.

[d]Booz, Allen evaluated this project in the spring of 1970 as part of the examination of EDA's Business Loan Program.

Only one set of interrelated technical assistance studies led to any job impact. These were two natural resource feasibility reports for the Fort Apache Reservation. The feasibility studies, which documented the supply of timber needed to justify expansion of the tribal timber operation and construction of a mill for small logs, resulted in a tribal application to EDA for a $1.1 million business loan for constructing and equipping the facility. The mill was under construction at the time of evaluation, and it was anticipated that seventy-five jobs would be created upon completion.

During the course of the evaluation, several difficulties were observed with respect to technical assistance projects. The most important of these was the fact that the Indian community itself was infrequently involved either in setting the scope of the studies or in their implementation. Two consequences were apparent: first, the assumptions guiding the work definition sometimes had no basis in either the real or perceived needs of the community. Second, and consequently, the recommendations and data flowing from technical assistance were neither compatible with nor adequately linked to an overall development effort. Most were responses to particular *ad hoc* problems, rather than attempts to provide information with more long-range value. Even in those studies that should have proved useful to the tribal community, the Indians' exclusion from project development activities led to a lack of interest in the results.

A last consequence of the apparent lack of Indian involvement was that the learning experience the projects themselves might have provided was lost. Instead of exposing Indians to planning methods, all too many of the technical assistance projects were presented to the tribes as a *fait accompli*.

Despite such severe criticism of reservation technical assistance projects generally, Boise Cascade evaluators reported that several did serve as development vehicles. This was particularly true on the Fort Apache Reservation, as noted above. Further, in the Red Lake case, a conscious attempt was made to use the technical assistance project as a method for transferring technical skills and experience to the tribe.

Planning Grants

Ten of the twelve reservations investigated under the Boise Cascade contact were or had been recipients of EDA-funded planning assistance. The exceptions, while not beneficiaries of agency planning funds, were receiving the same type of assistance from the Office of Economic Opportunity.

As was the case with the planning grants examined earlier by Battelle Memorial Institutes, the reservations received EDA planning assistance through: (1) direct reservation-specific funding; (2) the Indian Development District of Arizona; or (3) the economic development districts in which they were located. Further, the kinds of efforts found at the reservation level were diverse, some placing emphasis on planning, and others on project development.

The thread most common to all the efforts examined was the absence of the type and degree of sophisticated development planning the Selected Indian Reservation Program is theoretically dependent on. None of the reservations analyzed had a planning program based on comprehensive analyses of problems and priorities, identification of potential funding sources, and detailed development strategies.

Instead, a major problem faced by the planner on the reservation, as elsewhere, is the demand for paper products. Too often the result has been that so much of the planner's time is devoted to meeting the administrative and procedural requirements of funding agencies that not enough is available for development planning per se. Furthermore, the attempt to construct detailed master plans for development may be both more difficult and irrelevant on the reservation than elsewhere.

The urban planner is frequently in a position to call upon a multitude of experts to aid him in each aspect of a master plan's development. Further, the community with which he deals usually has a degree of infrastructure and economic sophistication that allows the interrelation of its various aspects in a long-term, overall development plan. None of these capacities exists at the reservation level. The planner is isolated from supporting skills and technical help. Development of all sectors of the economy is at such a low level that few interrelationships exist. Consequently, given the pervasive needs of the tribal communities, comprehensive planning goals may not be an adequate base line.

Because of the problems of the reservation, Boise Cascade analysts stipulated that the most useful planning approach might well be the sector- and project-specific method, rather than the master plan. Instead of dealing with broad community objectives in such abstract terms as "more jobs," sector-specific planning concerns itself with breaking planning down into the areas of particular concern. Thus, development of the forest-based resources of the Red Lake Reservation would constitute one major planning sector on that reservation. Another could well be concerned with the specific housing needs of the community, and a third directed to the development potential of tourism.

This kind of sector-specific planning would also dovetail with recommendations regarding technical assistance projects. Such planning would give guidance to the outside expert on the assumptions that should underlie his study. Increased potential for Indian involvement in study conduct would also exist. The major goal, however, of sector-specific planning is to provide an action-oriented structure for detailing a series of development strategies, each keyed to understandable and manageable problems. The evaluators noted that to maintain the action orientation of such planning, each sectoral strategy should be assigned a series of short-term goals and results, to be met within a realistic time-frame.

In summary, Boise Cascade analysts concluded that the type of planning likely to have the greatest impact within the reservation context would be sectionally defined, with primary emphasis on resources, projects, and performance. Such an approach would lead to a series of limited, loosely coordinated plans, rather than to one highly integrated but unrealistic master plan.

These findings on the planning program should not be construed as negative. Indeed, the planning grant was usually found to have the greatest long-term potential for reservation development. When consideration is given to the minimal investments which have been made, planning grants' cost effectiveness becomes even more apparent. The sectoral approach is emphasized merely as a means by which to realize the potential of the program.

Additional Evaluation Efforts

As was noted previously, a conscious decision was made to eliminate from the second round of evaluation three of the original Action List members: the Mescalero Apache, Navajo, and Gila River Reservations. Approximately $20 million of EDA funds had been approved for projects on these three reservations. This represents about 50 percent of all agency commitments to the Action List reservations. Furthermore, projects actually completed amount to more than $11 million, approximately equal to the dollar investment made in the twelve evaluated reservations.

As a consequence of the disproportionate investment made on the Mescalero Apache, Gila River, and Navajo Reservations, it is statistically possible that figures such as investment per job, etc., found for the twelve studied reservations may not typify the Selected Indian Reservation Program as a whole. Because of this, a decision was made by the agency to expand the Boise Cascade contract to include the remaining three original Action List reservations, as well as the Pine Ridge and Lower Brule/Crow Creek Reservations. This expansion was made possible by the fact that the report on the twelve reservations was not received by EDA until late in 1971. Consequently, the time elapsed between the original task force evaluation and the Boise Cascade visits would be considerable. Thus, the original cause for exclusion no longer pertained.

Field work at the Navajo, Mescalero Apache, Gila River, Pine Ridge, and Lower Brule/Crow Creek Reservations did not begin until the last month of 1971, and was not completed until well into 1972. Consequently, the entire study is not reflected here, but no significant changes are expected.

The Future

When compared with the impact of Economic Development Administration investments elsewhere in the United States, the results on reservations are not encouraging. Clearly, measures such as investment per job and absolute numbers of new jobs derived as a result of agency reservation funding do not lead to sanguine conclusions. Most of EDA's program tools have been, in absolute terms, more effective off the reservation than on.

Despite this, it would be inappropriate to view the impact of the EDA's Indian program in such a limited manner. Table 11-13 offers a useful perspective by showing the total number of firms established on Indian reservations between 1957 and 1968. Although the figures imply that neither the federal government nor the private sector has been successful in generating industrial employment on reservations, they also indicate that EDA's assistance has been involved in a significant portion of the limited industrial development that has occurred.

Through its Selected Indian Reservation Program, EDA has sought to single out those reservations with the greatest potential for development. The agency has attempted to concentrate substantial project funds on the SIRP reservations generally, and the Action List particularly. In terms of the absolute number of eligible reservation areas, this has been achieved. If, however, the measure of concentration used is EDA dollars per capita, then Action List reservations have not received concentrated funding. As reference to table 11-5 indicates, just about 50 percent of all funding has been approved for Action List reservations, but those reservations, in turn, contain approximately half of the entire reservation population.

Both political necessity and the realities of potential investment opportunities

Table 11-13
Summary of Plants Established on Indian Reservations, and
Labor Force: 1957-68

Fiscal Year	Number of Plants			Labor Force	
	Established	Closed Down	Operating at End of Year	Indian	Non–Indian
1957-59	4	1	3	391	171
1960	3	0	6	525	256
1961	4	0	10	702	505
1962	5	1	14	887	600
1963	6	2	18	1,395	1,719
1964	14	7	25	1,668	2,286
1965	21	6	40	2,011	2,479
1966	21	4	57	3,044	3,224
1967	23	3	77	3,730	3,666
1968	36	1	114	4,112	4,775
TOTAL	137	25			

Source: U.S. Bureau of Indian Affairs, unpublished tabulations, as presented by Alan L. Sorkin, "Trends in Employment Earnings of American Indians" in Toward Economic Development for Native American Communities, A Compendium of Papers Submitted to the Subcommittee on Economy in Government of the Joint Economic Committee, Congress of the United States, vol. 1, part I: Development Prospects and Problems, (Washington, D.C.: U.S. Government Printing Office, 1969), p. 112.

indicate that limiting EDA investments to Selected Indian Reservation Program members is unrealistic. There is little evidence that viable SIRP reservation project proposals representing substantial employment impact potential have failed to gain approval because of EDA investment commitments to other reservations.

In comparing EDA projects on reservations in the Selected Indian Reservation Program (or agency investments on other reservations) with projects in other types of designated areas, due weight must be given to the difficulties which exist. These problems—barriers to reservation development—are overwhelming, even on reservations with the greatest relative potential. And the costs of improvement are correspondingly high.

The reader, like the policy maker, must decide on grounds other than relative cost effectiveness whether the benefits obtained to date through government investments have been worthwhile. It is up to the reader and the political apparatus to make the tradeoffs between the costs necessary for reservation development and the needs of reservation residents.

Anthropological studies both of the Indian and primitive societies elsewhere demonstrate that developmental change cannot be limited to economic factors. Social and cultural changes are inevitable by products. As discussed earlier, EDA accepts the necessity of placing decision-making responsibilities at the community level. Moreover, other funding agencies are adopting similar postures. As a result, the burden is placed squarely upon the Indian, who must grapple with the difficult problem of improving economic conditions without sacrificing cultural values.

12 Evaluation of EDA's Training-Related Projects

Background

EDA has funded numerous training-related projects to prepare unemployed and unskilled residents of depressed areas for available jobs. In many cases these projects are linked with other EDA projects to form an integrated program for alleviating unemployment. An example is the agency's program in the Chicago Stockyards area briefly described in appendix A. There, EDA funded the development of an industrial park, provided business loans to five firms to locate in the park, and supplied funds for a skill center to train local residents for the jobs that would become available.

In the past, EDA has been involved with training-related projects in three ways:

1. Provision of public works grants for the construction of skill centers. EDA provides construction funds for the development of skill centers. On the average, this has amounted to $10 million per year for ten projects
2. Provision of administrative grants for training organizations. The Technical Assistance Program provides grants to local and national organizations to administer training programs. Prime examples of these are Opportunities Industrialization Centers
3. Direction of Department of Labor (DOL) funds. Under Section 241 of the Manpower Development and Training Act, DOL is authorized to provide up to $22 million annually for the purpose of training the unemployed and underemployed residents of EDA-designated redevelopment areas. EDA has responsibility for stimulating, reviewing, and recommending applications for the expenditure of these funds.

In the case of public works grants, EDA has a set of rigorous funding criteria. To obtain funds for a skill center, the community must lack an adequate training facility for unemployed adults. In other words, the proposed school should not function as a vocational high school, but should serve unemployed adults and unemployed youths who are no longer in school. The school should also have definite plans for recruitment and transportation of trainees, and identifiable sources for operating funds.

The evaluation described in this chapter refers only to the first two types of training-related projects. These are the projects that directly involve EDA funds.

333

The evaluation consisted of a sample of eight skill centers and three technical assistance training grants. Table 12-1 shows the location of these projects. All of the projects shared the objective of training the under- and unemployed to prepare them for available jobs.

The evaluation was conducted by Development Associates, Inc., a private consulting firm. It is described in detail in a report to EDA entitled *An Evaluation of EDA Training Related Projects.*[1]

Methodology

One of the intentions of the evaluation was to address four basic questions: (1) What is the size of the trainee population? (2) What are the socioeconomic characteristics of the trainees? (3) What are the effects of the training on the individual? (4) What are the effects of the project on the businesses in the area?

Answers to these questions were obtained by developing interview questionnaires and applying them to a sample of trainees and other people in the communities. In total, for the eleven projects, 401 trainees, 102 project administrators, 84 businessmen, and 101 community residents were interviewed. It was estimated that 10,650 students were enrolled in adult vocational courses in these schools during a typical year. Thus, approximately a 4 percent sample of trainees was used. The four basic questions were answered by extrapolating from the sample.

In addition to answering these questions, a method of comparing projects was derived. From an examination of the objectives of these projects, four criteria were chosen for ranking projects. These criteria reflected the funding intentions of EDA, which were that the school was to be primarily devoted to training unemployed adults and aiding them in finding suitable employment. The criteria are: (1) number of trainees from EDA's target population as a percentage of the

Table 12-1
Location of Projects Evaluated

EDA-Sponsored Skill Centers	*EDA-Sponsored Training Organizations*
San Diego, California	San Jose, California
Fayetteville, Arkansas	Wardell, Missouri
Shawnee, Oklahoma	Montgomery, Alabama
Fayette, Mississippi	
Fall River, Massachusetts	
Camden, New Jersey	
Wilson, North Carolina	
Harlingen, Texas	
Gila River Indian Reservation, Arizona	

total enrollment in the school. EDA's target population was defined as the trainees previously unemployed, on welfare, or disadvantaged according to OEO poverty guidelines; (2) percentage of trainees from the EDA target group that were placed or upgraded as a result of training; (3) percentage change in trainee income attributable to the training; and (4) percent of trainees reporting a change in socioeconomic status as a result of training.

Projects were ranked on the basis of these four criteria, and an overall ranking was derived by weighting the individual ranks equally. Results of this procedure are discussed below.

Findings

Size of Trainee Population

Table 12-2 shows the size of the trainee population by project. Overall, the eleven projects served 10,657 adult vocational students out of a total enrollment of 14,765, or a ratio of 72.2 percent. Further, EDA's target group made up 47.1 percent of the total enrollment. Table 12-2 identifies three schools that are apparently failing to recruit from EDA's target group. However, six schools are serving a large percentage of the target group.

In general, five of the eleven projects studied served substantial numbers of high school students, and in all but one case were part of a local or statewide system of vocational-technical schools whose primary emphasis was high school vocational education. In four of the five cases, Fayette excepted, the schools were clearly not adhering to the funding criteria specified by EDA. Specifically, while the schools had relatively easy access to EDA's target areas and most were located in areas lacking adequate training facilities, all of the schools' primary emphasis was on daytime, high school students.

Socioeconomic Characteristics of Trainees

Program participant characteristics for each project are shown in table 12-3. The age, education, and family size of trainees had small variances. On the average, program participants were about thirty years old, had eleven years of previous education, and a family of four. Table 12-3 also indicates some outliers. These include the three projects serving almost totally white students in areas with substantial numbers of unemployed minorities. The two projects training a high percentage of females are also outliers.

Table 12-2
Size of Trainee Population

Measurement Categories	Total	San Diego	Harlingen	Shawnee	Fayetteville	Wilson	Fall River	Fayette	Camden	San Jose	Montgomery	Bootheel
One-Year Adult Vocational Enrollment[a]	10,657	1,847	1,020	832	250	4,228	726	175	461	447	447	224
% of Adult Enrollment Classified as EDA Target Group[b]	65.3%	84.6%	86.4%	46.4%	29.3%	61.4%	26.6%	86.3%	40.5%	76.7%	86.8%	87.5%
Estimated Target Group Enrollment	6,957	1,563	881	386	73	2,596	193	151	187	343	388	196
Total Year Enrollment[c]	14,765	1,847	1,020	1,178	1,404	4,989	1,617	251	1,341	447	447	224
Estimated % of Total Enrollment Classified as EDA Target Group	47.1%	84.6%	86.4%	32.8%	5.1%	52.0%	11.9%	60.2%	13.9%	76.7%	86.8%	87.5%

[a]The sample was drawn only from adults taking vocational courses during one year (normally 1969). High school students and adults taking nonvocational courses were eliminated from the sample universe. This was done because, by definition, high school students and adults taking nonvocational courses are not EDA's target groups and could not be assisted in the way intended by EDA. This does not assume those eliminated from the sample were not helped, just that they were not helped in accordance with EDA's objectives.

[b]Based on sample

[c]Based on figures provided by each program and adjusted to 12 months where necessary. Figures include all students for the sample year.

Source: Development Associates, Inc., *An Evaluation of EDA Training Related Projects*, Washington, D.C.: Development Associates, Inc., December 1971, vol. IV-14

Table 12-3
Program Participant Characteristics by Project

Participant Characteristics	San Diego	Harlingen	Shawnee	Fayetteville	Wilson	Fall River	Fayette	Camden	San Jose	Montgomery	Bootheel
											Project Location
Average Age	31.8%	27.4%	32.5%	31.7%	30.2%	30.5%	27.7%	31.5%	33.5%	27.8%	29.1%
Percentage Male	38.5%	75.0%	53.6%	75.6%	59.1%	53.3%	47.7%	21.6%	50.0%	13.1%	66.6%
Percentage White	50.0%	2.2%	92.9%	100%	75.0%	100%	0	5.4%	27.0%	2.6%	16.7%
Percentage Black	23.0%	0	0	0	25.0%	0	100%	83.8%	10.0%	97.4%	83.3%
Percentage Mexican-American	23.0%	97.8%	3.6%	0	0	0	0	0	53.0%	0	0
Percentage Other	4.0%	0	3.6%	0	0	0	0	10.8%	10.0%	0	0
Average Education (Year)	10.8	7.7	11.9	11.8	12.1	11.7	10.4	11.3	11.0	11.1	9.1
Average Family Size	3.9	5.0	3.1	3.9	4.0	3.3	6.8	3.9	3.9	4.9	6.4

Source: Development Associates, Inc., *An Evaluation of EDA Training Related Projects,* Washington, D.C.: Development Associates, Inc., December 1971, vol. I, p. IV-2

Effects of Training the Individual

Three areas of impact in the individual were examined. These were the training's impact on: (1) obtaining a job; (2) receiving increased income; and (3) experiencing an improved life style.

Job Placement/Upgrading. Table 12-4 shows the record of each project in placing and upgrading its adult enrollment and EDA's target group. Table 12-5 shows these results broken down according to the previous employment status of the trainee.

Overall, it was estimated that approximately 67 percent of the EDA target population participating in the training programs, or about 4,770 people, were either placed in jobs or upgraded.

The values in table 12-5 might be interpreted as probabilities. For example, an unemployed person enrolling in a training program in the San Diego Skill Center will have a probability of 0.71 of being placed in a job, whereas a person on welfare before training in the same school will have a probability of 0.69 of finding a job.

Income Changes. Before and after trainee incomes are presented in table 12-6. Substantial increases in income were experienced by trainees in most programs. Seven of the eleven projects assisted the trainees in securing average income increases of over $1,000. The average increase for all projects was $1,412 or approximately 50 percent above trainees' previous incomes.

Four projects assisted participants to raise their incomes above the OEO poverty guidelines for a family of four.[a] However, for three projects, the average pretraining incomes were already above that level.

Socioeconomic Impact. Trainees were asked if, as a result of their training, their lives had improved in any of five socioeconomic areas: housing, health, transportation, food consumption, and personal savings. This is a subjective measure, but to some extent it demonstrates the degree to which trainees believed the quality of their lives had improved. It also indicates to some degree the significance of any rise in income.

Table 12-7 gives the results for this category of individual impact. In general, it was found that the greater the increase in income, the greater the overall improvement in the socioeconomic areas. Improvements in housing and personal savings were perceived most often by the trainees, while improvements in the health area were least frequently perceived.

Effects of Project on Creation of Jobs

One question addressed by the evaluation was whether the training project helped create or retain jobs in the area where it was located. This question was

---

[a]At the time of this evaluation, the OEO poverty guideline for a family of four was $3,800 per annum.

Table 12-4
Job Placement/Upgrading by Project

Measurement Categories	Total	Project Location										
		San Diego	Harlingen	Shawnee	Fayetteville	Wilson	Fall River	Fayette	Camden	San Jose	Montgomery	Bootheel
One-Year Adult Vocational Enrollment	10,657	1,847	1,020	832	250	4,228	726	175	461	447	447	224
Percentage of Adult Enrollment Classified as EDA Target Group	65.3%	84.6%	86.4%	46.4%	29.3%	61.4%	26.6%	86.3%	40.5%	76.7%	86.8%	87.5%
Estimated Target Group Enrollment	6,957	1,563	881	386	73	2,596	193	151	187	343	388	196
Percentage Target Group Placed	42.3%	63.6%	26.3%	23.1%	50.0%	22.2%	58.3%	13.2%	26.7%	100%	39.4%	42.9%
Estimated Number of Target Group Placed	2,690	994	232	89	37	575	113	20	50	393	153	84
Percentage Target Group Upgraded	38.6%	4.5%	50.0%	23.1%	33.3%	48.1%	33.3%	5.2%	13.3%	0	18.2%	19.0%
Estimated Number of Target Group Upgraded	2,078	70	441	89	24	1,249	64	8	25	0	71	37
Percentage Target Group Placed or Upgraded	80.9%	68.1%	76.3%	46.2%	83.3%	70.3%	91.6%	18.4%	40.0%	100%	57.6%	61.9%

Source: Development Associates, Inc., *An Evaluation of EDA Training Related Projects*, Washington, D.C.: Development Associates, Inc., December 1971, vol. I, p IV–14

Table 12-5
EDA Target Group Job Placement/Upgrading by Project and Previous Status of Trainee

Measurement Categories	Project Location											Means for all Projects	
	San Diego	Harlingen	Shawnee	Fayetteville	Wilson	Fall River	Fayette	Camden	San Jose	Montgomery	Boot-heel	Unweighted	Weighted[a]
Percentage Sample Unemployed before Training	26.9%	18.2%	28.6%	19.5%	22.7%	17.7%	61.4%	24.3%	30.0%	36.8%	33.3%	29.0%	28.8%
Percentage Unemployed Placed	71.4%	100%	37.5%	75.0%	60.0%	87.5%	22.0%	33.3%	100%	85.7%	87.5%	69.1%	67.8%
Percentage Sample on Welfare before Training	50.0%	4.5%	0	0	0	0	0	10.8%	46.6%	7.9%	25.0%	13.2%	16.2%
Percentage on Welfare Placed	69.2%	100%	0	0	0	0	0	25.0%	100%	33.3%	33.3%	24.6%	26.7%
Sample Disadvantaged before Training	7.7%	63.6%	17.9%	9.8%	38.6%	8.8%	25.0%	5.4%	0	42.1%	29.2%	22.6%	29.9%
Percentage Disadvantaged Upgraded	50.0%	67.9%	60.0%	100%	76.5%	100%	18.0%	100%	0	37.5%	57.1%	60.6%	66.8%

[a]For an explanation of the weighted mean, see Table 12-6.

Source: Development Associates, Inc., *An Evaluation of EDA Training Related Projects*, Washington, D.C.: Development Associates, Inc., December 1971, vol. I, p. IV-12

Table 12-6
Income Changes by Project[a]

Projects (Cities)	Mean Income Before Training ($)	Mean Income After Training ($)	Mean Increase or Decrease ($)	Percentage Increase or Decrease
San Diego	$ 2,064	$ 3,997	$ 1,933	93.7%
Harlingen	2,597	3,604	1,007	38.8%
Shawnee	3,130	3,772	642	20.5%
Fayetteville	4,233	5,017	784	18.5%
Wilson	2,738	5,032	2,294	83.8%
Fall River	5,203	7,378	2,175	41.8%
Fayette	1,001	841	(160)[b]	(15%)[b]
Camden	4,178	4,547	369	8.8%
San Jose	1,904	6,059	4,155	218.2%
Montgomery	1,782	2,793	1,011	56.7%
Bootheel	2,048	3,366	1,318	64.4%
TOTAL	$30,878	$46,406	$15,528	—
OVERALL MEAN	$ 2,807	$ 4,219	$ 1,412	50.3%
WEIGHTED MEANS[c]	$ 2,782	$ 4,597	$ 1,815	65.2%

[a]Based on a sample of 401 participants in the 11 programs listed. It is estimated that this represents a group of 10,657 participants.

[b]Approximately

[c]The weighted mean is derived by multiplying the unweighted means by the weight for each program. The weight is calculated by dividing the sum of the adult vocational enrollment for all programs into the enrollment for each program.

Source: Development Associates, Inc., *An Evaluation of EDA Training Related Projects*, Washington, D.C.: Development Associates, Inc., December 1971, vol. I, p. IV-10

analyzed by asking local businessmen if the training had any effect on their decision to locate, expand, or remain in the area.

For the most part, the training programs had no influence on location decisions. However, in one project, Harlingen, numerous businesses in an EDA-funded industrial park indicated that the training program was a major consideration in location decisions.

The generally negative response with respect to this type of impact might be explained by the fact that many employers' work forces were much larger than the number of trainees at the schools. San Diego and San Jose were typical examples of this situation. Also, a number of the schools were in competition with other training institutions in the area. This was true in San Jose, San Diego, Shawnee, Montgomery, and Camden. A third factor is that the nationwide recession had resulted in a glutted manpower pool in many of the areas under study.

Comparison of Projects

The eleven projects evaluated were ranked according to the four criteria discussed earlier. The criteria are presented with the resulting rankings in table 12-8.

Table 12-7
Percentage of Trainees Reporting Improvement in Five Socioeconomic Areas

Measurement Categories	Project Location										
	San Diego	Harlin-gen	Shawnee	Fayette-ville	Wilson	Fall River	Fayette	Camden	San Jose	Mont-gomery	Bootheel
Percentage Reporting Improvement After Training In:											
Housing	26.9%	29.5%	3.5%	14.6%	29.5%	13.3%	31.8%	8.1%	50.0%	26.3%	33.3%
Health	30.8%	45.5%	3.5%	9.8%	25.0%	0	25.0%	5.4%	23.0%	5.3%	20.8%
Transportation	23.1%	43.2%	3.5%	9.8%	29.5%	11.1%	11.4%	5.4%	46.0%	5.3%	37.5%
Food Consumption	19.2%	18.2%	3.5%	9.8%	27.3%	0	20.5%	2.7%	60.0%	21.0%	29.1%
Personal Savings	19.2%	36.4%	28.6%	19.5%	50.0%	22.2%	18.2%	13.5%	33.3%	36.8%	29.1%

Source: Development Associates, Inc., An Evaluation of EDA Training Related Projects, Washington, D.C.: Development Associates, Inc., December 1971, vol. I, p. IV-12

Table 12-8
Project Comparison Rankings

Ranking Criteria	Project Ranking										
	San Diego	Harlin-gen	Shawnee	Fayette-ville	Wilson	Fall River	Fayette	Camden	San Jose	Mont-gomery	Bootheel
Percentage of All Enrollees EDA Target Group	4	3	8	11	7	10	6	9	5	2	1
Percentage EDA Target Group Placed or Upgraded	6	4	9	3	6	2	11	10	1	8	5
Post-training Income Increase	4	7	9	8	2	3	11	10	1	6	5
Average Percentage of Socioeconomic Improvement	5	2	10	8	3	9	6	11	1	7	4
TOTAL SCORE	19	16	36	30	18	24	34	40	8	23	15
OVERALL RANKINGS	5	3	10	8	4	7	9	11	1	6	2

Source: Development Associates, Inc., *An Evaluation of EDA Training Related Projects*, Washington, D.C.: Development Associates, Inc., December 1971, Vol. I, p. IV–16

The top six programs accounted for most of the impact for all eleven projects. Specifically, these six projects contained: (1) 86 percent of the EDA target group enrollment; (2) 88.5 percent of the EDA target group participants placed; and (3) 89.9 percent of the EDA target group participants upgraded. All of the top six programs assisted their participants to increase their incomes by over $1,000 per annum.

Conclusions

Based on the findings presented above, several conclusions were developed regarding the effectiveness of training-related projects:

1. *Projects that required EDA funds at early stages of development were more effective*

   In these cases, the agency was able to exert influence on the formation of the programs. Most of the low-ranked projects were expansions of existing programs. The effect in these cases was such that the EDA project became more like the existing high school program than a significant new program devoted to the unemployed and underemployed

2. *Projects that involved EDA funds for administration were more effective (in terms of the four project comparison criteria) than those funded for construction and equipment improvement*

   A basic difference between EDA's Office of Public Works and the Office of Technical Assistance is in the type of funding each can provide. Because of the terms of EDA legislation, the Office of Public Works can only provide funds to projects for construction and equipment needs, while the Office of Technical Assistance has a wide latitude in the projects it funds. This includes the ability to fund a training facility's operations and to provide aid in areas not eligible on the basis of EDA designation criteria. This latitude is significant in that all three of the technical assistance projects studied were among the top six in effectiveness, and furthermore, all had received a substantial proportion of their operating funds from EDA. On the other hand, only three of the eight public works projects evaluated were among the top six

   In the three technical assistance projects, EDA had exercised considerably more authority over the projects through the annual refunding process. While these projects were not monitored any more closely than public works projects, the annual review process required for refunding had the effect of tying project operations more closely to EDA funding objectives

3. *Projects with staffs who were willing and able to provide a wide and flexible range of supportive services to participants were the most effective*

The six best-rated projects had staffs who perceived training as just one means to an end, i.e., job placement, and were prepared and willing to provide whatever support a participant needed to be successful with a job. In some cases, this meant legal assistance, ranging from extended payment of debts, arranging for glasses or other health needs, and in general, working to help the participant overcome any problems that would prevent successful employment

In several of the six projects, counselors and/or follow-up staff were assigned specific supportive services responsibility. In others, however, teachers were responsible. It is significant that in all six cases, staff members clearly understood that their role was to assist each participant to secure and hold the best possible job. This meant that the staff actively sought to learn of participants' problems so they could help resolve them

While the other five projects provided supportive service assistance, such aid did not receive the priority given it by the six top-ranked projects. Rather, staff for these five projects viewed their role as one of training and tended to provide supportive assistance only when the need was visible or vocal

4. *Active support and cooperation from employers is essential to project success*

While all projects received support from businesses in terms of providing jobs for participants and participating on the projects' Advisory Boards or Boards of Directors, only the top six ranked programs received support in the form of cash or in-kind contributions. Development Associates evaluators felt that this additional indication of support suggested a positive, qualitative difference as business is unlikely to provide such support to a project with which it is not deeply involved. Since this depth of support was only found in the top six ranked projects, it would appear that one reason for these projects' greater effectiveness was the additional business support.

5. *Projects with a balance of funding from multiple sources were more effective in serving and assisting the EDA target group*

The six most effective projects all received the bulk of their funds from state and federal sources. While they also received local support, that support was never large enough to govern project policy. In addition, the six projects all received sufficient support to insure their ability to operate near capacity. Four of the five less effective projects, on the other hand, were heavily dependent on local funds for support; moreover, local priorities required a heavy focus on high school students.

13 Prognosis for the Future

Extension and Modification of EDA's Program

During the spring and summer of 1971, Congress considered EDA's future. The deliberations were complicated by President Nixon's January 1971 proposal to implement a program of revenue sharing. The purpose of this program was to distribute funds for certain types of programs directly to state governments. EDA's program was among those recommended for administration at the state level rather than the federal level.

At hearings held in March by the Special Subcommittee on Economic Development Programs of the House Committee on Public Works, EDA officials supported this position. Testifying for the Department of Commerce, they advocated only a one-year extension of the EDA legislation. The purpose of this extension was to facilitate a smooth transition from EDA's program to revenue sharing. In response to questions from subcommittee members, agency officials discussed the problems associated with EDA's designation criteria and possible solutions.

EDA's representatives at these hearings also testified against the $2 billion accelerated public works program under consideration. This program, which was a revitalization of the APW Act passed in 1962, provided for public works funds to be invested in (1) EDA-designated areas and (2) other places that were economically depressed but did not meet EDA designation criteria.[a] Such areas would not be required to show evidence of local planning.

Despite the opposition of the administration and EDA officials, Congress passed a bill (S.575) containing both the $2 billion accelerated public works program and the two-year extension of EDA's legislation.[b] This bill, which received the overwhelming approval of both branches, was sent to the President on June 15. Fourteen days later it was vetoed. In a message to the Senate explaining his action, the President stated that because construction projects

---

[a] Nondesignated places eligible for these funds were: those areas which the Secretary of Labor designates each month as having been areas of substantial unemployment for at least six of the preceding twelve months; and those areas which the Secretary of Labor designated each month as areas having an average rate of unemployment of Vietnam veterans at least 25 percent above the national average rate of all unemployment for three consecutive months or more during the preceding twelve-month period.

[b] The bill also included provisions for the Appalachian Regional Commission and the five regional commissions established under authority contained in the Public Works and Economic Development Act of 1965.

have long lead times, "spending under this bill would not become fully effective for at least 18 months, at which time further stimulation would be unnecessary and inflationary."[1]

Other reasons for the President's veto included the administration's belief that the program would have little effect in reducing joblessness among those groups with high unemployment: Vietnam veterans, unskilled young people, and other persons unemployed because of lack of training or opportunity.

Determined to pass authorizing legislation for EDA and the regional commissions before the scheduled August adjournment date, members of both the Senate and House Committees on Public Works turned their attention to structuring a new bill. To eliminate the necessity of a House-Senate conference, a decision was made to prepare identical bills in both chambers. Approximately three weeks after the President's veto, the Senate passed S.2317, which was amended and passed by the House on July 28. Two days later, the Senate agreed to the House amendment and the bill was sent to the President, who signed it into law on August 5.

In addition to extending EDA's authorization through June 30, 1973, the portion of the legislation concerning EDA—the Public Works and Economic Development Act Amendments of 1971—introduced a modified version of the Accelerated Public Works Program. The amendments required that between 25 and 35 percent of all appropriations for EDA public works grants be invested in newly designated special areas. These areas were to be communities or neighborhoods with (1) large concentrations of low-income persons, (2) substantial out-migration (rural areas), (3) substantial unemployment, or (4) an actual or threatened abrupt rise of unemployment.

As was the case with places designated under the APW Act of 1962, these special areas are not required to show evidence of local planning through the preparation of Overall Economic Development Programs. Such areas also differ from redevelopment areas with respect to the types of projects funded. Projects in these areas (public works impact projects—PWIP) are to provide immediate useful work to unemployed and underemployed area residents, and can receive 100 percent grants if the local or state government has exhausted its taxing and borrowing capacity for such purposes.

Although Congress provided general criteria for identifying places eligible for these types of projects, the responsibility for developing specific guidelines for area designation and program implementation lay with agency officials. Assistant Secretary Podesta delegated these tasks to the Office of Public Works and the Office of Planning and Program Support. By the end of September, personnel in these offices had completed their assignments.

Between August 5 when the amendments to EDA's Act were signed into law and the end of September, Podesta made a decision to use the PWIP authority to demonstrate what could be accomplished through a program of this type. Although the agency had supported the Nixon Administration in testifying against such a program, Podesta and his staff felt its implementation should be regarded as a learning experience. Their position was that funding the best possible PWIP projects and collecting hard data on their results would permit for the first time an objective measure of the impact generated by a program of this type. Such knowledge would clearly be useful to Congress and the administration in their continuing efforts to develop effective tools for stimulating economic development.

In addition to introducing the PWIP Program, the August amendments to EDA's legislation altered several other provisions of the act. In every case these modifications were beneficial to residents of depressed areas, and in most cases, they were based on EDA's legislative proposal. Places designated as redevelopment areas were assured of at least three years' eligibility. Previously, areas that had been designated for only one year were subject to de-designation if they failed to meet the standards of the annual review. The amendments also extended eligibility to areas with a median family income between 40 and 50 percent of the national median. Such areas could not be designated under the 40 percent ceiling set by the original legislation. In addition, eligibility was extended to areas where the percentage of persons employed had declined significantly during the preceding ten-year period. The only major EDA recommendation not legislated by Congress was the reduction in the number of redevelopment areas necessary to form a district.

EDA's Program and the Role of Evaluation

During the six years that have elapsed since the passage of the Public Works and Economic Development Act, the EDA program has experienced considerable success. Thousands of jobs have been created for the residents of distressed areas, and numerous economic development institutions have been born as a result of EDA influence and encouragement. In addition, agency activities have stimulated community discussions of economic needs and objectives, as well as development projects, in towns with no history of collective effort.

In these and other instances, EDA's impact is obvious. However, agency officials continue to emphasize the importance of improving the program's effectiveness. A small percentage of the firms that received EDA business loans have failed. A few public works projects have had little or no economic impact. Some technical assistance funds have been expended without visible results. Although the experience of developers here and abroad suggests that unproductive projects are common in programs of EDA's nature, agency administrators emphasize the need to learn from failures and prevent their recurrence.

Program evaluation is one tool EDA has used to analyze the results of agency investments and to identify which types of projects are most successful in generating jobs and income for EDA's target population. Under the best circumstances, translation of evaluation findings and recommendations into policy guidelines is a complex endeavor. This is so even for agencies with a single clientele group. For an agency like the Economic Development Administration, however, the problem is intensified. EDA policy makers must be responsive to a wide range of groups and individuals. These include community leaders for a diverse group of local areas, linked only by underemployment, unemployment, or other chronic economic difficulties. Other pressure and clientele groups include various state departments concerned with economic development, state governors' offices, and congressional representatives and delegations. Each of these, appropriately, represents special interest demands. Also significant are Congress as a whole, whose legislative intent EDA policy makers must attempt to comprehend and carry out, and the Office of the President, as represented by the Office of Management and Budget.

All these forces contend for the attention of the policy maker, and to all he must at least appear responsive. Thus, although the recommendations of evaluation are frequently apolitical, they have very real political consequences, which the policy maker must consider.

Acknowledgment of these forces does much to explain why many of the recommendations stemming from EDA evaluation efforts have been neither quickly nor fully realized in policy changes; also, why such conclusions and recommendations often do not win the full support and acceptance of operating officials and policy makers. Nevertheless, it is the unapologetic contention of this volume's authors that the interchange of ideas, findings, and conclusions stimulated by the evaluation exercise has been fruitful and productive. Rarely do evaluations result in dramatic policy reversals; more often in small and individually insignificant movements. Cumulatively, however, the result is a pattern of incremental change and improvement.

Finally, despite their doubts about the scope and import of recommendations stemming from evaluation, agency officials continue to need—and support—program analysis.

At this time, the course of EDA's future cannot be accurately charted. It is clear that economic distress will continue to plague millions of Americans in rural and urban areas throughout the country. Past experience indicates that without guidance and financial assistance residents of depressed areas cannot reverse the economic trends of a decade or more. On the basis of these factors, it seems obvious that the federal government will continue to assist residents of depressed areas in their struggles to develop viable economies.

The evaluations of EDA's impact described in this book have concluded that in most instances the agency has been successful in locating jobs, generating income, and stimulating the development process in economically depressed areas. Moreover, EDA's program has escaped the controversy surrounding some federal aid programs because it does not represent a "welfare approach" to combating unemployment and underemployment. However, despite EDA's success, the agency's future role in assisting residents of depressed areas will depend on the actions of Congress and the administration, and these could vary from substantially increasing the agency's budget to eliminating EDA's program and distributing revenue for development efforts directly to the states.

Appendixes

Appendix A: Pilot Test of Methodology for Evaluating EDA's Urban Program

The following data were taken from an EDA document entitled *Evaluation of EDA's Urban Program: Pilot Test in Chicago, Illinois.*[1] The document presents the results of the pilot test of the methodology structured for evaluating agency activities in urban areas. The area covered by the pilot test is shown in figure A-1. The material that appears below is a summary of the evaluators' findings and recommendations, as well as the tentative issues suggested by the April 1971 study.

Chicago Program Summary

Introduction

Through June 30, 1970, EDA's projects in large urban areas amounted to $145 million, about 11 percent of the agency's total program funds. Consequently, procedures for systematically evaluating urban investments were needed. The methodology had to consider the unique economic and political conditions of each city as well as compare similar types of projects in different cities. This report presents the results of the pilot test of such a methodology in Chicago, Illinois.

The depressed part of Chicago is roughly the central third of the city. EDA has designated two redevelopment areas within Mid-Chicago: the Stockyards Redevelopment Area (1967), because of a sudden rise in unemployment, and the Midwest Impact Area (1970), under the special impact provision. Approved agency funding, totaling $18.4 million at the end of Fiscal Year 1970, can be divided into three major parts:

1. support for the Mayor's Committee for Economic and Cultural Development, to plan and implement programs for the entire Mid-Chicago area;
2. redevelopment efforts focused on the Stockyards, where most of EDA's existing projects are located; and
3. activities in the Midwest Impact Area, where several major projects are currently being planned.

Table A-1 summarizes the objectives for Mid-Chicago's development and the progress toward achieving them in each designated area.

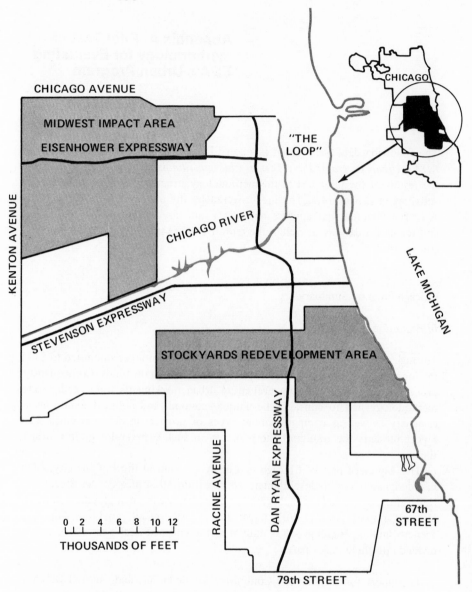

Figure A-1. Mid-Chicago

Table A-1
Status of Mid-Chicago Efforts

	Status	
Objective	*Stockyards Redevelopment Area*	*Midwest Impact Area*
Increase the total number of jobs	3,159 direct jobs[a] are expected to be created or saved.	6,350-7, 350 direct jobs are expected to be created or saved by the proposed Special Impact Program.
Focus on companies with high entry-level wages and advancement possibilities	Most employees[a] make $7,500 to $8,000 per year, according to employers.	Many of the new jobs are expected to meet these criteria. Community ownership of some projects may help. Also, recent training activities have helped prepare the labor force.
Improve the tax base by increasing private investment	Total capital investment[a] exceeds $15 million.	Annual tax revenues are expected to be increased by more than $2 million.
Stop income leakages from the area	Little has been accomplished so far, but the proposed shopping center could have an impact.	Community shopping centers will enable more goods to be purchased locally. Assistance to minority contractors and a proposed housing factory could also reduce income leakages.
Increase incomes of poverty level residents	Most of the surveyed employees reported income increases; many had previously been unemployed.	New employment opportunities could have significant impact on incomes of community residents.

[a]Includes only firms in the Ashland Industrial District or firms with an EDA business loan

Source: Mary Toborg, *et al.*, *Evaluation of EDA's Urban Program: Pilot Test in Chicago, Illinois,* Washington, D.C.: U.S. Department of Commerce/Economic Development Administration, April 1971, Vol. I, pp, 1-5

Mayor's Committee for Economic and Cultural Development

The Mayor's Committee received funds from the Area Redevelopment Administration for a major study of Mid-Chicago. This study, completed in 1966, proposed short- and long-run programs for alleviating the area's economic distress. EDA provided $616,000 for staff to implement these proposals through the Mid-Chicago Economic Development Project. Four major programs were developed. These are discussed below.

Industrial Conservation. The top priority of the industrial conservation program was to retain existing manufacturing firms within Mid-Chicago. This was accomplished by:

1. helping more than 400 individual companies solve site and manpower problems; and
2. forming six "industrial councils" to work with community organizations on area-wide problems.

Industrial Development. The industrial development program was designed to stimulate industrial growth in Mid-Chicago by developing under-utilized parcels of land. The major activity was redevelopment of the Stockyards square mile. This was considered an important key to economic development in Mid-Chicago.

Commercial Development. In the short-run, the commercial development program has helped individual minority entrepreneurs prepare loan applications and supporting documentation. Twelve loans, totaling $705,000, have been approved. The long-run emphasis of the program is to assist groups of entrepreneurs, by establishing community-oriented shopping centers. Three centers are now being planned.

Manpower Program. Manpower activities link employment creation under the other programs with training and placement of local residents. The program has included working with placement agencies, disseminating training information, and planning the Chicago Skill Center in the Stockyards Redevelopment Area.

Stockyards Redevelopment Area

The Stockyards square mile had several advantages for industry, including:

1. A central location, well served by expressways and railroads.
2. Proximity to a labor supply.
3. Availability of large tracts of industrially zoned land.

However, the lack of adequate roads within the Stockyards hindered redevelopment efforts. Consequently, EDA approved $4,866,000 in public works funds for one-and-a-half miles of access roads and related utilities within the Stockyards area. As a result, the Ashland Industrial District is being developed on land abandoned by the meat-packers. The District is currently half filled, with four firms employing 465 people. When fully operational, these firms are expected to provide 1,200 jobs. Ashland's developers agreed that only high-density employers will locate in the District. This is important, because the Stockyards area is a desirable location for warehousing operations, which do not employ many people. Employment densities at the Ashland Industrial District are expected to exceed 40 workers per acre.

When completely filled, the District is expected to provide employment for

2,450 people. EDA has generated additional employment opportunities at five firms which received business loans and located in the Stockyards area. One of these is located in the Ashland Industrial District. Altogether, EDA's public works and business loan investments of $10,903,000 within the Stockyards square mile are expected to create or save 3,159 direct jobs. The resulting investment per direct job of $3,451 is substantially less than EDA's nationwide average. Moreover, when estimated indirect employment is included, based on a multiplier of 1.3, the investment per job is $1,500.

A major EDA project currently under construction is the $6.4 million Chicago Skill Center. Expected to open in 1972, the Center is designed to link employment creation with jobs for the target population. The Center will utilize electronic teaching devices and emphasize "programmed learning." It will be operated by Chicago City College and have a capacity of 1,200 trainees.

Until the permanent center opens, limited training is being done at an interim facility. The first class of about 120 trainees will graduate in the summer of 1971.

EDA-funded studies for the Stockyards Redevelopment Area established the feasibility of the Chicago Skill Center and determined that a synthetic carpet mill was not feasible. Two studies now underway are an analysis of the potential of a proposed shopping center in the Stockyards Redevelopment Area and an assessment of the effect of ethnic ties on out-migration from urban neighborhoods.

Midwest Impact Area

The Midwest Impact Area was designated in October 1970 under the special impact criterion. Special impact programs are designed to arrest "tendencies toward dependency, chronic unemployment, and rising community tensions." In the Midwest Impact Area, such programs will be developed by an OEDP Committee representing four groups:

1. The Mayor's Committee for Economic and Cultural Development.
2. The North Lawndale Economic Development Corporation, a community-controlled group.
3. The East Garfield Park Joint Planning Committee, another community organization.
4. The Industrial Council of the Northwest Community, a group of local employers.

The major projects endorsed by the OEDP Committee are:

1. Construction of a large shopping center in the North Lawndale area and, later, of a similar one in the east Garfield Park area.

2. Industrial redevelopment of the Lawndale site to be vacated by the International Harvester Company.
3. Development of a Superblock to help retain existing industry in the area served by the Industrial Council of the Northwest Community.
4. Industrial development of the Northwest Center for Industry in the Garfield Park area.

These projects are expected to create or save between 5,350 and 6,350 jobs. Development of smaller, scattered sites should generate an additional 1,000 jobs.

Shopping Center. The top priority project for the Midwest Impact Area is development of a shopping center at the intersection of Roosevelt Road and Kedzie Avenue in Lawndale. This center will replace more than 200,000 square feet of commercial space, which was destroyed by civil disorders in 1968. The Office of Economic Opportunity (OEO) approved a $1.2 million grant to the North Lawndale Economic Development Corporation (NLEDC) for preliminary planning and site acquisition.

When completed, the shopping center is expected to employ 250 people, largely local residents. In addition, most stores will be minority-owned; consumers will be able to purchase better merchandise locally; and the physical appearance of the area will be improved.

International Harvester Site. The International Harvester Company will stop production at its tractor works on the outskirts of Lawndale by 1972. The North Lawndale Economic Development Corporation (NLEDC) plans to purchase and redevelop the 92-acre site. The preliminary plans for the area envision mixed land use, including residences, manufacturing firms, and commercial facilities. However, these plans are tentative, and the area may ultimately be developed primarily for industrial use.

The NLEDC received an OEO grant of $1.4 million for seed money for this project. After redevelopment, the International Harvester site is expected to employ 2,600 people.

Superblock. The Industrial Council of the Northwest Community has developed a plan for redesigning nine regular city blocks into one Superblock. The center block will be cleared and converted to a functional service core, containing warehousing, shipping-receiving, parking, and service facilities for the firms in the other eight blocks. Access to the area will be controlled. The Superblock is expected to save or create between 1,000 and 2,000 jobs.

Northwest Center for Industry. The 48-acre Northwest Center for Industry is being developed entirely with private capital. It is part of the Life Insurance Program on Urban Problems, a program of investment in central city areas by life insurance companies. An estimated 1,500 jobs will be located at the Center.

Problems. The redevelopment program for the Midwest Impact Area faces several problems, including the following.

Site acquisition. The shopping center site must be assembled from small parcels of land; the terms of sale of the International Harvester site must be negotiated; and a location for the Superblock must be selected.

Relocation of residents. Both the shopping center and Superblock projects will probably require some relocation of residents.

Relocation of jobs. Some of the expected employment will be relocated from other sites in the Midwest Impact Area. Although such employment is saved for the area, it does not provide new employment opportunities.

Assurance that local residents benefit from the projects. Special surveys in 1968-69 indicated that there were more jobs than labor force members in the Midwest Impact Area. However, its unemployment rate was more than twice the national average. The existence of a substantial number of jobs in the area had not solved its unemployment problems. Most jobs located in the area are held by nonresidents. Consequently, special efforts will be needed to insure that new employment opportunities are channeled to local residents and that saved employment also benefits them.

Past Projects. Three technical assistance projects had been approved for the Midwest Impact Area prior to its designation. EDA provided $153,000 for assistance to the United Builders Association, a group of 52 minority construction contractors. Member contractors have been assisted in acquiring loans, obtaining bonds, preparing bids, and improving their business procedures. As a result, the contractors have increased their annual sales by an estimated $1.3 million and their employment by 114 people.

The Opportunities Industrialization Center (OIC) received $175,000 to support its training activities. At first, these efforts focused on pre-vocational training, which is designed to provide basic skills and information needed for any job. Later, emphasis shifted to skills training for specific jobs. The pre-vocational approach did not result in long-run income benefits for the trainees. Some could not obtain jobs at substantially higher wages than they received before the training program; others obtained jobs which did not use their training; and still others are now unemployed. The more recent emphasis on training for specific jobs, however, seems to be considerably more effective. Graduates reported obtaining jobs which used their skills and realizing significant income gains.

A final project, approved for $24,000, provided management assistance to a small bakery. However, the bakery's management was uncooperative, and operations were not improved.

Other Programs in Mid-Chicago

The effect that EDA's investments will have in Mid-Chicago depends, to some extent, upon the other activities within the area. Consequently, economic development programs of other government agencies and private groups were identified and analyzed. The major conclusion of the analysis is that EDA's investments do not duplicate those of other groups.

Most other organizations emphasize training, social service, or health and welfare programs. They do not focus on employment creation, industrial location, and similar economic development efforts. In some cases, however, programs of other groups complement EDA's activities. For example, the Model Cities Administration has established a $1.5 million equity capital fund to assist minority entrepreneurs.

Recommendations

There are two major recommendations concerning EDA's activities in Chicago.

EDA should continue to support Mid-Chicago development efforts. Existing investments have achieved high levels of impact. However, further investments will be needed to reduce the excessive unemployment rates in designated areas. These investments should include continued support for local groups working to alleviate economic distress as well as continued assistance for projects which generate employment for area residents.

EDA should insure that projects in the Midwest Impact Area will benefit local residents. Most of the jobs currently located in the Midwest Impact Area are held by non-residents. Therefore, it is particularly important to channel new jobs to target group members and to insure that saved employment also benefits them. Community ownership will help achieve this goal for two of the proposed projects, the shopping center and the redevelopment of the International Harvester site. The Superblock project, primarily designed to save employment for the area, can also benefit local residents—if they hold most of the jobs to be saved. This should be EDA's first concern, after a specific site has been proposed.

Issues

Five tentative issues were suggested by the pilot test in Chicago. These will receive further consideration as the urban evaluation continues.

Need for Employment Opportunities

Although many ghetto areas contain only a few jobs, some have substantial concentrations of business. For example, the Midwest Impact Area in Chicago has more jobs than labor force members. Although many ghetto residents need jobs, EDA cannot assume that new jobs created in target areas will go to residents of the area.

Meaning of Ghetto Designation

The meaning of designation in an urban context is sometimes unclear. The designated area frequently houses only part of a city's poor and unemployed people. Therefore, workers who commute into the designated area may have socioeconomic characteristics resembling those of local residents.

Sometimes, a question arises as to how EDA should weigh benefits for nonresidents against those for residents of the designated area. If only benefits for special impact area residents were counted, assistance to people living a few hundred feet away would be excluded. On the other hand, if benefits for unemployed nonresidents were included, the meaning of designation would be unclear: it would delineate the boundaries for location of public works and business loan projects, but it would not delineate the real target group.

Effects of Training

A recent study[2] demonstrated that blacks in urban slums have achieved educational levels comparable to those of whites in the same neighborhood. In spite of this, ghetto blacks continue to lag behind ghetto whites in terms of earnings, unemployment rates, and job status. For example, white workers living in urban slums earned, on the average, well over twice as much per extra year of schooling as nonwhites.

While this analysis focused largely on the effects of formal schooling, the conclusions probably apply to training programs, which are another form of education. Several studies have documented that graduation from a training program often makes no long-term difference in a person's economic status. In many cases, he will still be unable to find work. Some writers have referred to this as "training to be unemployed," with the only benefit being the stipend received during training.

The evaluation of the training programs of the Opportunities Industrialization Center confirms these views. Some trainees could not obtain jobs at substantially higher wages than they received before the training program; others obtained jobs which did not use their training; and still others are now unemployed.

Apparently, training alone is an inadequate response to the problems facing ghetto blacks. Efforts to increase the demand for their labor seem to be more needed than attempts to change or upgrade their skills.

Need for Better Coordination

The need for better coordination seems to pervade all government programs. Based on the analysis of Chicago, improved coordination appears to be needed both among the various Federal agencies and within EDA. A mechanism for better coordination among Federal agencies may be required from an organization such as the Office of Management and Budget. However, it is possible that a "lead agency" approach to coordination could be implemented effectively.

Within EDA, at least four different offices must be consulted to determine Agency activity within any given city. It is even difficult to determine which EDA employees visited a city within the last few months, and whom they interviewed on what subjects. This problem could be mitigated by the establishment of "city desks" with the incumbents responsible for the activities in those cities.

EDA's Role

The definition of EDA's role in specific matters depends partly on the general strategy which is endorsed. This strategy could consist largely of response to local initiatives. If the problems to be solved are basically local ones, perhaps Federal agencies should become involved only when asked to do so.

On the other hand, EDA could initiate activities, in cooperation with local groups, and make an active commitment to their successful implementation. Such a strategy would reflect a belief that the problems are national ones, even though they are concentrated in specific localities.

The strategy adopted could affect the Agency's policies in a number of ways. Two examples are EDA's relationship to local development groups and the Agency's contribution to project development. If the problems are national ones, Federal funding of an organization should imply a Federal commitment to helping the group resolve these problems. It would then be in the national interest to support the groups with management assistance or other forms of aid, if needed. This approach can be compared with that of funding a group, watching what it does, and then deciding whether to fund it again.

EDA currently does not accept any institutional responsibility for project development. Usually, projects are developed at the local level and submitted to

EDA for approval. However, if the problems are viewed as national ones, perhaps EDA should make efforts to help local groups develop projects for resolving these problems. At a minimum, EDA could provide information to various groups about projects which have been successfully implemented in different places.

Appendix B: Estimation of Indirect Jobs

The economic base concept is central to the development of indirect job multipliers. This concept states that cities, towns, or other urban places are, to different degrees, viable economic areas which are capable of providing themselves with goods and services as well as providing some goods and services to other areas.[a] Most economic base studies have used industrial employment data as a proxy for the goods and services produced within the area. Cities are also divided into population groups since economic theory has traditionally implied that the larger the city, the larger the number of specialities that can be supported and the more self-contained (viable) the city can be. In sum, the economic base concept is a static model which attempts to: (1) describe the employment structures of different size cities; and (2) by comparing cities, determine how viable they are.

To illustrate the economic base concept, assume that there are only three *non-basic* industries—food production (F), clothing production (C), and entertainment (E); also assume that there are only six cities—three cities (X, Y, and Z) with populations between 25,000 and 100,000, and three cities (R, S, and T) with populations between 300,000 and 800,000. The following five-step procedure is used to describe the employment structures of these cities.[b]

First, compute employment ratios for each industry by dividing the number employed within the industry by the city's total employment; secondly, array these values by city size as in table B-1.

Thirdly, determine the smallest value for each industry by city group and designate these values as minimum requirements for cities in their respective groups. These are arranged in table B-2 and are assumed to be the internal (nonbasic) component of a city's employment within each industry.

Fourth, by summing each group's values in table B-2, the gross internal (nonbasic) component of a city's employment is derived. Thus the sum of values in Group I equals 0.40 and in Group II equals 0.50. By subtracting each value

[a]Goods and services consumed within the city are called "internal" or "nonbasic"; those goods and services not consumed within the city are designated as "exports" or "basic." These terms are used by E.L. Ullman and M.F. Dacey in their article, "The Minimum Requirements Approach to the Urban Economic Base," *PPRSA*, Vol. 6, 1960. For additional information, see I. Morrissett, "The Economic Structure of American Cities," *PPRSA*, Vol. 4, 1958, and G. Alexanderson, *The Industrial Structure of American Cities, A Geographic Study of Urban Economy in the U.S.*, London, 1965.

[b]The first four steps were performed by Ullman and Dacey in their paper, "The Minimum Requirements Approach to the Urban Economic Base." The fifth step was taken to produce the numbers in table 6-3.

Table B-1
Employment Structures for Cities of Varying Sizes

City Group	Industry Food (F)	Clothing (C)	Entertainment (E)
Group I Cities			
City X	0.30	0.20	0.10
City Y	0.50	0.10	0.15
City Z	0.20	0.25	0.10
Group II Cities			
City R	0.50	0.05	0.45
City S	0.20	0.25	0.55
City T	0.10	0.30	0.35

Table B-2
Minimum Percentage Employed in Cities of Varying Size Classes,
Three-Industry Classification

Industry	F	C	E	Total
Group I	.20	0.10	0.10	0.40
Group II	0.10	0.05	0.35	0.50

from one (1), the basic or export employment for each group is derived. For Group I, the basic employment value is 0.60; for Group II, the basic value is 0.50.

Fifth, by forming ratios of the two values (external employment/internal employment) for the two groups, the indirect job multiplier is obtained. Thus:

Group I Cities (0.40/0.60) = .7
Group II Cities (0.50/0.50) = 1

The ratio .4/.6 for Group I means that for each export job located in the city, .7 indirect jobs must also be created. A similar interpretation holds for Group II values; for every export job located in the city, one indirect job must be created.

Appendix C: Detailed Findings of the Growth Center Identification System

This appendix presents the detailed findings of the implementation of the Growth Center Identification System by region and county. The following data are given in tables C-1 through C-13 for each county examined: (1) percentage change in employment in seven major sectors between 1950 and 1960; (2) ratio of nonbasic employment to total employment in 1960; (3) ratio of manufacturing employment to total employment in 1960; and (4) percentage change in population between 1960 and 1970. For each county, these data were compared with the corresponding regional figures presented in table 9-4 to determine a center's ranking. In addition, the population of the city or town designated as the growth center is provided.

The underlined figures in the tables were the deciding factors in determining a county's ranking (Type I, Type II, or Type III). Distance from redevelopment areas was also considered in determining a county's ranking.

Table C-1
New England Region

Center Status	City Population 1970	Employment Change 1950–60	Ratio of Non-Basic Empl. to Total Empl. 1960	Ratio of Mfg. Empl. to Total Empl. 1960	Change in County Population 1960–70
Economic Development Centers					
Type I					
None					
Type II					
Fall River (Bristol), Mass.	96,898	*4.6%*	*.44*	.51	11.5%
Taunton (Bristol), Mass.	43,756	*4.6%*	*.44*	.51	11.5%
Rome-Utica (Oneida), N.Y.	141,759	16.7%	.60	.32	*2.9%*
Type III					
Amsterdam (Montgo-mery), N.Y.	25,524	*– 14.2%*	*.45*	.45	*– 2.4%*
Bangor-Brewer (Pen-obscot), Me.	42,468	26.4%	.54	*.28*	*– 0.8%*
Newport (Orleans), Vt.	4,664	16.2%	.46	*.22*	*0.0%*
St. Johns-bury-Lyndon (Caledonia), Vt.	12,144	*2.3%*	.54	*.25*	*0.0%*
Redevelopment Centers					
Type I					
None					
Type II					
Glens Falls (Warren), N.Y.	17,223	14.0%	.66	*.30*	12.3%
New Bedford (Bristol), Mass.	101,771	*–4.6%*	*.44*	.51	11.5%

Table C-1 (Cont.)

Center Status	City Population 1970	Employment Change 1950–60	Ratio of Non-Basic Empl. to Total Empl. 1960	Ratio of Mfg. Empl. to Total Empl. 1960	Change in County Population 1960–70
Type III					
Berlin (Coos), N.H.	15,256	*9.8%*	*.47*	.46	*– 7.7%*
Masenna (St. Lawrence), N.Y.	14,042	17.0%	.59	.22	0.7%
Ogdensburg (St. Lawrence), N.Y.	14,552	17.0%	.59	.22	0.7%
Plattsburg (Clinton), N.Y.	18,715	30.6%	.52	.15	0.3%
St. Albans (Franklin), Vt.	3,270	*3.6%*	*.45*	.20	*6.1%*
Watertown (Jefferson), N.Y.	30,787	*9.4%*	*.59*	.24	0.8%
Additional Growth Centers					
Type I					
None					
Type II					
Burlington (Chittendon), Vt.	38,633	19.6%	.68	*.20*	33.2%
Over 250,000					
Boston, Mass.	628,215	20.9%	.60	.33	*5.2%*

Table C-2
Delmarva Region: Economic Development Centers

Center Status	City Population 1970	Employment Change 1950–60	Ratio of Non-Basic Empl. to Total Empl. 1960	Ratio of Mfg. Empl. to Total Empl. 1960	Change in County Population 1960–70
Type I					
None					
Type II					
Dover (Kent), Del.	17,488	49.0%	.46	.17	24.7%
Salisbury (Wicomico), Md.	15,252	31.4%	.58	.28	10.6%
Type III					
None					

Table C-3
Terre Haute Region: Economic Development Centers

Center Status	City Population 1970	Employment Change 1950–60	Ratio of Non-Basic Empl. to Total Empl. 1960	Ratio of Mfg. Empl. to Total Empl. 1960	Change in County Population 1960–70
Type I					
Terre Haute (Vigo), Ind.	70,286	4.0%	.61	.27	5.6%
Type II					
None					
Type III					
None					

Table C–4
Appalachian Region

Center Status	City Population 1970	Employment Change 1950–60	Ratio of Non-Basic Empl. to Total Empl. 1960	Ratio of Mfg. Empl. to Total Empl. 1960	Change in County Population 1960–70
Economic Development Centers					
Type I					
Bristol-Kingsport (Sullivan), Tenn.	52,002	27.3%	.50	.40	11.6%
Gainesville (Hall), Ga.	15,459	38.6%	.50	.38	19.4%
Knoxville (Knox), Tenn.	174,587	20.7%	.65	.32	10.3%
Marietta (Washington), Ohio	16,861	36.6%	.58	.30	10.6%
Martinsburg-Charlestown (Berkeley, Jefferson), W. Va.	17,649	*13.4%*	.50	.32	9.9%
McMinnville (Warren), Tenn.	10,662	33.1%	.45	.32	16.8%
Morristown (Hamblen), Tenn.	20,318	68.6%	.47	.41	16.9%
Toccoa (Stephans), Ga.	6,971	25.4%	.48	.46	10.5%
Type II					
Athens (Athens), Ohio	23, 310	46.2%	.72	*.16*	16.8%
Campbellsville (Taylor), Ky.	7,598	*−12.4%*	.53	*.13*	5.2%
Cookeville (Putnam), Tenn.	14,270	40.3%	.55	*.28*	21.4%
Crossville (Cumberland), Tenn.	5,381	36.1%	.49	*.23*	8.4%
Johnson City (Washington), Tenn.	33,770	*17.6%*	.59	*.26*	14.0%

Table C–4 (Cont.)

Center Status	City Population 1970	Employment Change 1950–60	Ratio of Non-Basic Empl. to Total Empl. 1960	Ratio of Mfg. Empl. to Total Empl. 1960	Change in County Population 1960–70
Type III					
Ashland (Boyd), Ky.	29,245	*14.7%*	.55	.36	*0.4%*
Alcoa-Mary-ville (Blount), Tenn.	63,744	*18.4%*	.53	.37	10.8%
Chillicothe (Ross), Ohio	24,842	19.5%	.54	*.31*	*0.0%*
Huntingdon (Huntingdon), Pa.	6,871	*14.1%*	.51	.31	*–0.9%*
Johnstown (Cambria), Pa.	42,065	*10.9%*	.48	.37	*–8.1%*
Martin's Ferry-Bellaire (Belmont), Ohio	80,917	*6.4%*	.52	*.29*	*–3.5%*
Magisterial Districts of Powell & Taylor (Scott), Va.	5,492	19.8%	*.39*	*.26*	*–5.6%*
Oak Ridge (Anderson, Roane), Tenn.	28,319	*8.5%*	.48	.45	*0.0%*
Portsmouth (Scioto), Ohio	27,633	*4.1%*	.52	.37	*–8.6%*
Somerset (Pulaski), Ky.	10,436	*17.7%*	.47	*.17*	*2.4%*
Redevelopment Centers					
Type I					
None					
Type II					
Somerset (Somerset), Pa.	6,163	34.1%	.54	.24	*–1.8%*
Type III					
Hazard (Perry), Ky.	5,459	*11.8%*	.56	*.05*	*–26.4%*

Table C-4 (Cont.)

Center Status	City Population 1970	Employment Change 1950-60	Ratio of Non-Basic Empl. to Total Empl. 1960	Ratio of Mfg. Empl. to Total Empl. 1960	Change in County Population 1960-70
Pikesville (Pike), Ky.	4,576	13.4%	.49	.06	-10.6%
Prestonburg-Paintsville (Floyd-Johnson), Ky.	7,290	10.5%	.48	.03	-12.9%
Bedford (Bedford), Pa.	3,160	25.3%	.52	.21	-0.2%
Lebanon (Russell), Va.	2,272	68.4%	.37	.07	-6.7%
Richlands (Tazewell), Va.	4,843	29.5%	.51	.12	-11.1%
Beckley (Raleigh), W. Va.	19,884	11.8%	.59	.10	-10.0%
Bluefield-Princeton (Mercer), W. Va.	23,174	3.8%	.64	.13	-7.3%
Keyser (Mineral), W. Va.	6,586	15.5%	.40	.30	3.4%
Moorefield (Hardy), W. Va.	2,124	22.1%	.44	.23	4.9%
Williamson (Mingo), W. Va.	5,831	-5.1%	.51	.06	-17.5%
Additional Growth Centers					
Type I					
Chattanooga (Hamilton), Tenn.	119,082	13.1%	.61	.33	6.9%
Over 250,000					
Cincinnati Ohio	452,524	15.1%	.59	.36	19.0%

Table C–5
Ozarks Region

Center Status	City Population 1970	Employment Change 1950–60	Ratio of Non-Basic Empl. to Total Empl. 1960	Ratio of Mfg. Empl. to Total Empl. 1960	Change in County Population 1960–70
Economic Development Centers					
Type I					
Conway (Faulkner), Ark.	15,510	49.9%	.60	.21	29.9%
Fayetteville-Springdale (Wash.), Ark.	47,512	46.3%	.62	.19	38.7%
Fort Smith-Van Buren (Sebastian), Ark.	71,175	*15.1%*	.67	.25	18.8%
Harrison (Boone), Ark.	7,239	33.8%	.60	.22	18.3%
Little Rock-N. Little Rock (Pulaski), Ark.	192,523	23.9%	.70	.17	18.2%
Russellville-Dardanelle (Pope, Yell), Ark.	15,047	34.0%	.57	.26	29.3%
Springfield (Greene), Mo.	120,096	35.0%	.66	.22	21.1%
Type II					
Hot Springs (Garland), Ark.	35,631	*-3.5%*	.78	*.15*	15.9%
Mena (Polk), Ark.	4,530	*18.0%*	.47	.38	11.0%
Mountain Home (Baxter), Ark.	3,936	*-16.1%*	.67	*.10*	54.1%
Claremore (Rogers), Okla.	9,084	40.0%	.62	*.15*	37.9%
Duncan (Stephans), Okla.	19,718	48.6%	.56	.21	-5.5%
Sapulpa-Bristow (Creek), Okla.	19,812	*15.2%*	.57	*.22*	12.4%

Table C–5 (Cont.)

Center Status	City Population 1970	Employment Change 1950-60	Ratio of Non-Basic Empl. to Total Empl. 1960	Ratio of Mfg. Empl. to Total Empl. 1960	Change in County Population 1960-70
Type II (cont.)					
Stillwater (Payne), Okla.	31,126	*3.3%*	.75	.09	14.5%
Type III					
El Dorado (Union), Ark.	25,283	*6.5%*	.59	.27	*-8.3%*
Newport (Jackson), Ark.	7,725	*14.7%*	*.51*	*.13*	*-10.5%*
Texarkana (Miller), Ark.	21,682	*9.3%*	.69	*.16*	5.4%
Poplar Bluff (Butler), Mo.	16,653	*19.8%*	.63	*.13*	*-3.3%*
West Plains (Howell), Mo.	6,893	38.8%	*.53*	.25	6.8%
Ada (Pontotoc), Okla.	14,859	*11.2%*	.70	*.14*	*-0.8%*
Ardmore (Carter), Okla.	20,881	*18.7%*	.67	*.08*	*-4.3%*
Chickasha (Grady), Okla.	14,194	*15.1%*	.63	*.11*	*-0.8%*
Durant (Bryan), Okla.	11,118	*18.7%*	.65	*.10*	5.4%
Shawnee (Pottawatomie), Okla.	25,075	*15.0%*	.71	*.13*	4.0%
Vinita (Craig), Okla.	5,847	22.1%	.66	*.10*	*-9.7%*
Redevelopment Centers					
Type I					
None					
Type II					
Batesville (Independence), Ark.	7,209	*10.5%*	*.53*	.20	13.3%
Searcy (White), Ark.	9,040	43.7%	.56	.20	*-4.8%*
McAlester (Pittsburgh), Okla.	18,802	-1.8%	.68	*.13*	9.2%

Table C–5 (Cont.)

Center Status	City Population 1970	Employment Change 1950–60	Ratio of Non-Basic Empl. to Total Empl. 1960	Ratio of Mfg. Empl. to Total Empl. 1960	Change in County Population 1960–70
Type III					
Brinkley (Monroe), Ark.	5,275	*13.0%*	*.47*	*.14*	*– 9.6%*
Hope (Hempstead), Ark.	8,810	*– 4.0%*	*.52*	*.22*	*– 1.8%*
Malvern (Hot Spring), Ark.	8,739	*8.8%*	*.50*	*.37*	*0.3%*
Muskogee (Muskogee), Okla.	37,331	*5.0%*	*.71*	*.15*	*– 3.8%*
		Additional Growth Centers			
Type I					
None					
Type II					
Joplin (Jasper, Newton), Mo.	39,256	43.5%	*.52*	*.28*	9.3%
Lawton (Comanche), Okla.	74,470	51.0%	*.41*	*.03*	19.1%
Over 250,000					
Oklahoma City (Oklahoma), Okla.	366,481	34.4%	.78	*.13*	19.9%
Tulsa (Tulsa), Okla.	331,638	36.0%	.65	.22	16.1%

Table C–6
Tennessee-Green Valley Region

Center Status	City Population 1970	Employment Change 1950–60	Ratio of Non-Basic Empl. to Total Empl. 1960	Ratio of Mfg. Empl. to Total Empl. 1960	Change in County Population 1960–70
Economic Development Centers					
Type I					
Jonesboro (Craighead), Ark.	27,050	34.9%	.53	.20	10.1%
Bowling Green (Warren), Ky.	36,253	31.2%	.60	.18	26.2%
Type II					
Carbondale (Jackson), Ill.	22,582	43.5%	.72	*.12*	30.5%
Elizabethtown Radcliffe-Vine-Grove (Hardin), Ky.	22,616	52.8%	*.21*	*.03*	15.7%
Type III					
Glasgow (Barren), Ky.	11,301	29.8%	.50	*.13*	*1.3%*
Hopkinsville (Christian), Ky.	21,250	30.6%	*.36*	*.08*	*– 1.2%*
Madisonville (Hopkins), Ky.	15,332	31.8%	.53	*.09*	*– 0.8%*
Dexter-Bloomfield (Stoddard), Mo.	7,608	*21.2%*	*42*	.20	*– 12.6%*
Sikeston (Scott), Mo.	14,699	*6.7%*	.52	.24	*1.5%*
Redevelopment Centers					
Type I					
None					
Type II					
None					
Type III					
Forrest City (St. Francis), Ark.	12,521	26.0%	*.48*	*.11*	*– 7.5%*

Table C-6 (Cont.)

Center Status	City Population 1970	Employment Change 1950-60	Ratio of Non-Basic Empl. to Total Empl. 1960	Ratio of Mfg. Empl. to Total Empl. 1960	Change in County Population 1960-70
Type III (Cont.)					
Harrisburg (Saline), Ill.	9,461	-6.4%	.62	.11	-1.9%
Batesville (Panola), Miss.	3,796	39.4%	.42	.12	-6.8%
Clarksdale (Coahoma), Miss.	21,673	12.9%	.50	.10	-12.5%
New Madrid (New Madrid), Mo.	2,719	-0.3%	.41	.09	-25.3%
Additional Growth Centers					
Type I					
Murray (Calloway), Ky.	13,537	40.5%	.61	.19	32.0%
Lexington (Fayette), Ky.	108,137	23.4%	.51	.28	32.2%
Owensboro (Daviess), Ky.	50,329	35.3%	.54	.31	12.6%
Corinth (Alcorn), Miss.	11,581	23.5%	.51	.27	7.5%
Jackson (Madison), Tenn.	39,996	11.3%	.61	.19	8.4%
Union City (Obion), Tenn.	11,925	23.8%	.53	.22	11.1%
Cape Girardeau (Cape Girardeau), Mo.	31,282	17.2%	.59	.24	17.4%
Type II					
Paducah (McCracken), Ky.	31,627	23.4%	.62	.24	1.7%
Clarksville (Montgomery), Tenn.	31,719	32.2%	.42	.12	12.7%
Over 250,000					
Louisville, Ky.	361,472	16.2%	.60	.32	13.8%

Table C–6 (Cont.)

Center Status	City Population 1970	Employment Change 1950–60	Ratio of Non-Basic Empl. to Total Empl. 1960	Ratio of Mfg. Empl. to Total Empl. 1960	Change in County Population 1960–70
Over 250,000 (Cont.)					
Memphis, Tenn.	623,530	*21.6%*	.67	.24	15.2%
Nashville, Tenn.	447,877	24.2%	.70	.23	12.0%

Table C–7
Great Lakes Region

Center Status	City Population 1970	Employment Change 1950–60	Ratio of Non-Basic Empl. to Total Empl. 1960	Ratio of Mfg. Empl. to Total Empl. 1960	Change in County Population 1960–70
Economic Development Centers					
Type I					
Bay City-Midland-Saginaw (Bay, Midland, Saginaw), Mich.	174,369	27.5%	.50	.43	14.8%
Type II					
Tawas City-East Tawas (Iosco), Mich.	3,950	43.9%	.54	*.14*	50.9%
Type III					
Ontonagon-White Pine (Ontonagon), Mich.	2,402	*– 2.7%*	*.43*	*.15*	*– 0.3%*
Duluth (St. Louis), Minn.	100,578	*– 0.9%*	.59	*.13*	*– 4.7%*
Redevelopment Centers					
Type I					
None					
Type II					
Alpena (Alpena), Mich.	13,661	54.8%	.52	.39	*7.5%*
Marquette-Negaunee-Ispeming (Marquette), Mich.	34,854	*10.4%*	.53	*.13*	15.2%
Traverse City (Grand Traverse), Mich.	17,687	25.4%	.70	*.19*	17.0%
Type III					
Escanaba-Gladstone (Delta), Mich.	20,413	*18.9%*	.54	.28	*4.7%*

Table C-7 (Cont.)

Center Status	City Population 1970	Employment Change 1950-60	Ratio of Non-Basic Empl. to Total Empl. 1960	Ratio of Mfg. Empl. to Total Empl. 1960	Change in County Population 1960-70
Houghton (Houghton), Mich.	6,052	-3.1%	.63	.12	-2.8%
Iron Mountain-Kingsford-Norway (Dickinson), Mich.	16,862	5.1%	.62	.28	-0.7%
Iron River (Iron), Mich.	2,667	4.9%	.53	.06	-19.6%
Ironwood-Bessemer Wakefield (Gogebic), Mich.	13,814	-11.0%	.52	.15	-15.2%
Newberry (Luce), Mich.	2,330	12.0%	.85	.12	-13.3%
St. Ignace (Mackinac), Mich.	2,889	25.2%	.72	.08	-11.0%
Sault-Ste. Marie (Chippewa), Mich.	14,812	-3.9%	.59	.09	-0.7%
Additional Growth Centers					
Type I					
Grand Rapids (Kent), Mich.	195,892	18.9%	.56	.37	13.2%
Grayling (Crawford), Mich.	2,092	54.2%	.69	.26	30.4%
Type II					
St. Cloud (Stearns), Minn.	36,691	31.6%	.55	.18	18.7%
Mt. Pleasant (Isabella), Mich.	19,961	79.1%	.64	.19	26.2%
Over 250,000					
Minneapolis-St. Paul, Minn.	744,380	21.9%	.68	.26	21.8%

Table C-8
Coastal Plains Region

Center Status	City Population 1970	Employment Change 1950-60	Ratio of Non-Basic Empl. to Total Empl. 1960	Ratio of Mfg. Empl. to Total Empl. 1960	Change in County Population 1960-70
Economic Development Centers					
Type I					
Dothan (Dale, Houston), Ala.	36,733	40.5%	.60	.20	33.9%
Athens (Clarke), Ga.	44,342	29.6%	.70	.22	43.7%
Brunswick (Glynn), Ga.	19,585	44.9%	.59	.25	20.4%
Carrollton (Carroll), Ga.	13,520	29.3%	.47	.41	24.6%
Wilmington (New Hanover, Brunswick), N. C.	46,169	48.5%	.50	.22	16.5%
Aiken-N. Augusta, (Aiken), S. C.	26,319	74.1%	.48	.40	12.3%
Greenwood (Greenwood), S. C.	21,069	*7.1%*	.48	.46	12.0%
Type II					
Panama City (Bay), Fla.	32,096	49.3%	.59	*.11*	12.1%
Albany (Dougherty), Ga.	72,623	53.9%	.62	*.13*	18.4%
Augusta (Richmond), Ga.	59,864	*8.7%*	.54	*.17*	19.8%
Dublin-East Dublin, (Laurens), Ga.	17,129	41.5%	.57	.23	*1.3%*
Hinesville (Liberty), Ga.	4,115	38.6%	*.38*	*.13*	21.3%
Milledgeville, (Baldwin), Ga.	11,601	34.7%	.74	.20	*0.5%*
Tifton (Tift), Ga.	12,179	*24.8%*	.58	*.16*	16.2%

Table C–8 (Cont.)

Center Status	City Population 1970	Employment Change 1950–60	Ratio of Non-Basic Empl. to Total Empl. 1960	Ratio of Mfg. Empl. to Total Empl. 1960	Change in County Population 1960–70
Type II (Cont.)					
Valdosta (Lowndes), Ga.	32,303	47.0%	.55	.20	*11.9%*
Waycross (Ware), Ga.	18,996	30.9%	.55	.20	*– 2.0%*
Fayetteville (Cumberland), N. C.	53,510	41.1%	*.38*	*.07*	*42.9%*
Kinston (Lenoir), N. C.	22,309	41.9%	.58	.20	*– 0.1%*
Florence-Darlington (Florence-Darlington), S. C.	32,987	35.4%	.54	.20	*4.1%*
Type III					
Montgomery (Montgomery), Ala.	133,386	*18.6%*	.70	*.12*	*0.0%*
Marianna (Jackson), Fla.	6,741	47.5%	.65	*.11*	*–4.9%*
Americus (Sumter), Ga.	16,091	*19.9%*	.57	.21	*9.2%*
Bainbridge (Decatur), Ga.	10,887	*25.4%*	.49	*.17*	*–11.5%*
La Grange (Troup), Ga.	23,301	*– 7.8%*	.47	.47	*– 5.8%*
Columbus (Muscogee), Ga.	154,168	*13.8%*	.50	*.18*	*5.5%*
Swainsboro (Emanuel), Ga.	7,325	46.8%	*.44*	.24	*2.1%*
Goldsboro (Wayne), N. C.	26,810	31.4%	.51	*.12*	*4.1%*
Newbern (Craven), N. C.	14,660	*24.4%*	*.44*	*.12*	*6.4%*
Washington (Beaufort), N. C.	8,961	*10.2%*	.53	*.16*	*– 0.1%*
Williamston (Martin), N. C.	6,570	*27.5%*	*.45*	*.14*	*– 8.9%*

Table C-8 (Cont.)

Center Status	City Population 1970	Employment Change 1950–60	Ratio of Non-Basic Empl. to Total Empl. 1960	Ratio of Mfg. Empl. to Total Empl. 1960	Change in County Population 1960–70
Redevelopment Centers					
Type III					
Greenville (Butler), Ala.	8,033	7.3%	.49	.30	– 10.4%
Troy (Pike), Ala.	11,482	23.2%	.58	.13	– 3.7%
Greenville (Pitt), N. C.	29,063	6.2%	.47	.17	5.7%
Orangeburg (Orangeburg), S. C.	13,252	47.5%	.52	.20	1.8%
Additional Growth Centers					
Type I					
Charleston (Charleston, Berkeley), S. C.	66,945	56.4%	.46	.30	19.4%
Type II					
Gainesville (Alachua), Fla.	64,510	58.9%	.80	.09	41.4%
Columbia (Richland), S. C.	133,542	22.3%	.61	.09	16.9%
Jacksonville (Onslow), N. C.	16,021	90.6%	.24	.01	19.6%
Tallahassee (Leon), Fla.	71,897	57.4%	.86	.07	38.8%
Pensacola (Escambia), Fla.	59,507	70.2%	.64	.18	18.1%
Over 250,000					
Atlanta, Ga.	496,973	37.9%	.68	.20	36.6%

Table C–9
South Central Region

Center Status	City Population 1970	Employment Change 1950–60	Ratio of Non-Basic Empl. to Total Empl. 1960	Ratio of Mfg. Empl. to Total Empl. 1960	Change in County Population 1960–70
		Economic Development Centers			
Type I					
Baton Rouge (E. Baton Rouge), La.	165,963	43.2%	.75	.21	24.0%
Nacogdoches-Lufkin-Diboll (Nacogdoches, Angelena), Tex.	69,147	*13.1%*	.59	.21	26.3%
Type II					
Pine Bluff-Sheridan (Jefferson), Ark.	59,869	36.5%	.59	.22	*4.9%*
Jackson (Hinds), Miss.	153,968	36.3%	.76	*.15*	14.9%
Pascagoula (Jackson), Miss.	27,264	112.8%	*.50*	.41	58.5%
Bryan-College Station (Brazos), Tex.	49,672	34.5%	.79	*.08*	29.1%
Killeen-Temple (Bell), Tex.	32,645	36.2%	*.44*	*.07*	32.3%
Lafayette-New Iberia (Lafayette), La.	99,055	69.8%	.70	*.08*	29.6%
Monroe-West Monroe (Ouachita), La.	71,242	31.5%	.75	*.17*	13.5%
Type III					
Shreveport-Bossier City (Caddo, Bossier), La.	223,659	30.8%	.75	*.12*	*4.4%*
Hattiesburg (Forrest), Miss.	38,277	*25.9%*	.73	.18	*9.7*
Grenada (Grenada), Miss.	9,944	*28.7%*	*.58*	.24	*7.8%*

Table C–9 (Cont.)

Center Status	City Population 1970	Employment Change 1950–60	Ratio of Non-Basic Empl. to Total Empl. 1960	Ratio of Mfg. Empl. to Total Empl. 1960	Change in County Population 1960–70
Type III (Cont.)					
Meridian (Lauderdale), Miss.	45,083	10.8%	.71	.18	0.0%
Natchez (Adams), Miss.	19,704	9.9%	.66	.23	–1.2%
Vicksburg (Warren), Miss.	25,478	8.4%	.69	.19	6.6%
Texarkana (Miller), Tex.	29,393	1.9%	.65	.22	10.5%
Waco (McLennan), Tex.	92,600	20.3%	.67	.18	–1.7%
Crosset-Hamburg, (Ashley), Ark.	9,293	15.8%	.40	.39	3.1%
Forest (Scott), Miss.	4,085	30.8%	.44	.21	0.9%
McComb (Pike), Miss.	11,969	17.5%	.57	.22	–9.4%
Marshall (Harrison), Tex.	22,666	12.9%	.61	.26	–1.7%
Northeast Texas Municipal Water District (Cass Camp, Morris, Up-shaw), Tex.	63,222	9.3%	.59	.23	5.6%
Sulphur Springs (Hopkins), Tex.	10,447	13.8%	.55	.15	11.4%

Redevelopment Centers

Type I

None

Type II

None

Table C–9 (Cont.)

Center Status	City Population 1970	Employment Change 1950–60	Ratio of Non-Basic Empl. to Total Empl. 1960	Ratio of Mfg. Empl. to Total Empl. 1960	Change in County Population 1960–70
Type III					
Alexandria-Pineville (Rapids), La.	50,508	*26.5%*	.70	*.10*	*6.0%*
Natchitoches (Natchitoches), La.	15,974	35.1%	.68	*.10*	*–1.2%*
Opelousas (St. Landry), La.	20,121	34.6%	.59	*.05*	*–1.4%*
Cleveland (Boliva), Miss.	13,327	*25.5%*	*.44*	*.08*	*–9.3%*
Greenville (Washington) Miss.	39,648	38.6%	.56	*.15*	*–10.2%*
Greenwood (LeFlore), Miss.	22,400	*11.2%*	.58	*.07*	*–10.7%*
Jefferson (Marion), Tex.	2,703	*–11.3%*	.59	.21	*5.8%*
Additional Growth Centers					
Type I					
Tupelo (Lee), Miss.	20,471	54.6%	.53	.29	13.7%
Sherman (Grayson), Tex.	28,352	*16.3%*	.58	.19	13.9%
Type II					
Beaumont-Port Arthur-Orange (Orange, Jefferson), Tex.	196,383	49.5%	.55	.33	*17.9%*
Columbus (Lowndes), Miss.	25,795	41.0%	.54	.20	6.6%
Over 250,000					
Dallas, Tex.	836,121	47.5%	.69	.23	39.5%

Table C-10
Northwest Region

Center Status	City Population 1970	Employment Change 1950-60	Ratio to Non-Basic Empl. to Total Empl. 1970	Ratio of Mfg. Empl. to Total Empl. 1960	Change in County Population 1960-70
Economic Development Centers					
Type I					
Lewiston (Nez Perce), Idaho	26,068	24.0%	.60	.25	12.2%
Type II					
None					
Type III					
Hardin (Big Horn), Mont.	2,733	*15.3%*	*.51*	*.05*	*0.5%*
Havre (Hill), Mont.	10,558	29.1%	.60	*.03*	*-6.9%*
Redevelopment Centers					
Type I					
None					
Type II					
None					
Type III					
Butte-Anaconda (Silver Bow, Deer Lodge), Mont.	33,139	*-2.0%*	*.46*	*.39*	*-11.4%*
Colville (Stevens), Wash.	3,742	*16.2%*	*.46*	.20	*-2.7%*
Additional Growth Centers					
Type I					
Coeur D'Alene (Kootenai), Idaho	16,228	26.5%	.61	.26	19.5%

Table C-10 (Cont.)

Center Status	City Population 1970	Employment Change 1950–60	Ratio of Non-Basic Empl. to Total Empl. 1960	Ratio of Mfg. Empl. to Total Empl. 1960	Change in County Population 1960–70
Type I (Cont.)					
Billings (Yellowstone), Mont.	61,581	46.9%	.70	.13	10.6%
Missoula (Missoula), Mont.	29,497	31.6%	.69	.16	30.5%
Type II					
Boise (Ada), Idaho	74,990	38.3%	.78	*.10*	20.1%
Bozeman (Gallatin), Mont.	18,670	32.7%	.70	*.09*	24.8%

Table C-11
Far West Region

Center Status	City Population 1970	Employment Change 1950–60	Ratio of Non-Basic Empl. to Total Empl. 1960	Ratio of Mfg. Empl. to Total Empl. 1960	Change in County Population 1960–70
Economic Development Centers					
None					
Redevelopment Centers					
Type I					
None					
Type II					
Grass Valley-Auburn (Nevada, Placer), Calif.	11,615	45.0%	.70	*.15*	33.0%
South Lake Tahoe (El Dorado), Calif.	11,998	118.6%	.72	*.18*	49.1%
Type III					
None					
Additional Growth Centers					
Type I					
Medford (Jackson), Ore.	28,454	33.1%	.64	.23	27.8%
Type II					
Takoma (Pierce), Wash.	154,581	*21.5%*	*.54*	*.18*	27.8%
Redding (Shasta), Calif.	16,365	67.4%	.69	*.19*	30.6%
Over 250,000					
Portland, Ore.	382,619	42.8%	.62	.23	20.9%
Sacramento, Calif.	257,860	87.4%	.71	*.16*	25.6%
Seattle, Wash.	530,831	32.9%	.63	.28	23.7%

Table C-12
Southwest Region

Center Status	City Population 1970	Employment Change 1950-60	Ratio of Non-Basic Empl. to Total Empl. 1960	Ratio of Mfg. Empl. to Total Empl. 1960	Change in County Population 1960-70
Economic Development Centers					
Type I					
None					
Type II					
Santa Fe (Santa Fe), N. Mex.	41,167	*25.0%*	.89	*.06*	19.5%
Type III					
Alamosa (Alamosa), Colo.	6,985	*10.0%*	.72	*.06*	*14.2%*
Pueblo (Pueblo), Colo.	97,453	*29.6%*	.56	.34	*- 0.4%*
Trinidad (Las Animas), Colo.	9,901	*- 15.4%*	.57	.04	*- 21.2%*
Delta City (Millard), Utah	1,610	*16.7%*	.53	.03	*- 11.2%*
Redevelopment Centers					
Type I					
None					
Type II					
None					
Type III					
Las Vegas (San Miguel), N. Mex.	7,528	*19.4%*	.75	.05	*- 6.5%*
Moab (Grand), Utah	4,793	196.6%	.43	.03	5.4%
Price (Carbon), Utah	6,213	*16.5%*	.52	.03	*- 26.0%*
Richfield (Sevier), Utah	4,471	*9.7%*	.59	.15	*- 4.4%*

Table C–12 (Cont.)

Center Status	City Population 1970	Employment Change 1950-60	Ratio of Non-Basic Empl. to Total Empl. 1960	Ratio of Mfg. Empl. to Total Empl. 1960	Change in County Population 1960-70
Additional Growth Centers					
Type I					
Provo-Orem (Utah), Utah	78,860	49.8%	.63	.27	28.8%
Salt Lake City (Salt Lake), Utah	175,885	43.2%	.70	.17	19.7%
Type II					
Albuquerque (Bernalillo), N. Mex.	243,751	93.7%	.77	.09	20.4%
Colorado Springs (El Paso), Colo.	135,060	78.2%	.62	.07	64.2%
Type III					
None					

Table C–13
Rio Grande Region

Center Status	City Population 1970	Employment Change 1950–60	Ratio of Non-Basic Empl. to Total Empl. 1960	Ratio of Mfg. Empl. to Total Empl. 1960	Change in County Population 1960–70
Economic Development Centers					
Type I					
Victoria (Victoria), Tex.	39,349	54.9%	.68	.13	15.7%
Type II					
None					
Type III					
Corpus Christi-Aransas Pass (Nueces, Aransas), Tex.	207,175	30.6%	.68	.13	7.8%
McAllen (Hidalgo), Tex.	36,761	35.2%	.58	.08	0.3%
Redevelopment Centers					
Type I					
None					
Type II					
Del Rio (Val Verde), Tex.	20,928	39.5%	.49	.06	12.3%
Laredo (Webb), Tex.	65,491	16.0%	.66	.06	12.5%
Brownsville-Harlingen (Cameron), Tex.	85,085	28.6%	.60	.11	-7.1%
Uvalde (Uvalde), Tex.	10,403	23.0%	.64	.08	-1.2%
Additional Growth Centers					
Type I					
None					

Table C–13 (Cont.)

Center Status	City Population 1970	Employment Change 1950–60	Ratio of Non-Basic Empl. to Total Empl. 1960	Ratio of Mfg. Empl. to Total Empl. 1960	Change in County Population 1960–70
Type II					
Eagle Pass (Maverick), Tex.	15,277	38.5%	.63	.07	24.7%
Over 250,000					
San Antonio (Bexar), Tex.	650,188	31.5%	.68	.09	20.9%

Appendix D

The following table presents absolute migration data for all EDC, RC, non-EDC/non-RC counties by region and district. The data sources are Current Population Reports, Population Estimates and Projections, series P-25, no. 461 (June 28, 1971), U. S. Department of Commerce, Bureau of the Census.

Table D-1

Absolute Migration by Region, District — EDC and RC Counties, Non-EDC, Non-RC Counties: 1960-70

Regions and Districts	EDC Counties	RC Counties	Non-EDC and Non-RC Counties	Total Regions and Districts
New England	− 29,623	− 34,889	42,594	− 21,918
Pride	− 17,299	None	− 6,714	− 24,013
Southeastern	14,522	None	52,975	67,497
New Hampshire-Vermont	− 3,226	− 5,892	6,112	− 3,006
Black River-St. Lawrence	None	− 17,003	− 6,992	− 23,995
Eastern Adirondack	None	− 11,994	− 3,300	− 15,294
Mohawk Valley	− 23,620	None	513	− 23,107
Delmarva	4,487	None	− 10,878	− 6,391
Appalachia	− 62,952	−105,901	−404,474	− 573,327
Georgia Mountains	1,492	None	2,284	3,776
Big Sandy	None	− 31,759	− 5,497	− 37,256
Fivco	− 5,302	None	− 6,776	− 12,078
Kentucky River	None	− 14,953	− 25,975	− 40,928
Lake Cumberland	2,838	None	− 15,695	− 12,857
Buckeye Hills-Hocking Valley	− 532	None	− 9,333	− 9,865
Ohio Valley	− 19,909	None	− 15,964	− 35,873
Turnpike	− 30,826	− 9,555	− 9,890	− 50,271
East Tennessee	− 10,582	None	− 14,280	− 24,862
First Tennessee-Valley	− 797	None	− 4,499	− 5,296
Upper Cumberland	3,892	None	− 9,257	− 5,365
Cumberland Plateau	None	− 13,028	− 17,216	− 30,244
Lenowisco	− 3,583	None	− 18,299	− 21,882
Southern West Virginia	None	− 33,897	− 76,135	− 110,032
Upper Potomac	357	− 2,709	− 3,115	− 5,467
Northeastern	None	None	− 27,619	− 27,619
Northern Tier	None	None	− 3,504	− 3,504

Table D-1 (Cont.)

Regions and Districts	EDC Counties	RC Counties	Non-EDC and Non-RC Counties	Total Regions and Districts
Cumberland Valley	None	None	− 46,115	− 46,115
Gateway	None	None	− 730	− 730
South Central	None	None	− 10,173	− 10,173
Southeast	None	None	− 12,534	− 12,534
District 2	None	None	− 20,990	− 20,990
District 4	None	None	− 9,221	− 9,221
District 5	None	None	− 22,951	− 22,951
North Central	None	None	− 20,990	− 20,990
Ozarks	50,753	− 5,865	− 16,774	28,114
Central	11,956	− 4,042	− 2,433	5,481
North Central	− 4,555	5,218	546	1,209
Northwest	21,232	None	11,342	32,574
Southwest	− 10,707	− 1,293	− 9,689	− 21,689
West Central	12,850	− 1,386	− 1,146	10,318
Western	6,580	None	947	7,527
Lakes Country	15,952	None	10,326	26,278
Ozark Foothills	− 2,423	None	1,048	− 1,375
South Central Ozark	684	None	− 3,444	− 2,760
Central	4,050	None	− 6,652	− 2,602
Eastern	None	− 5,688	9,007	3,319
Kiamichi	None	1,326	1,380	2,706
NECO	4,509	None	1,672	6,181
SODA	− 4,076	None	− 5,308	− 9,384
South Central	− 5,299	None	− 10,947	− 16,246
Mid-America	None	None	− 13,423	− 13,423
Tennessee-Green Valley	− 11,023	− 41,263	−132,429	− 184,715
East Arkansas	− 601	− 9,881	− 71,135	− 81,617
Greater Egypt	8,348	None	− 253	8,095
Southeastern	23,792	None	− 44,828	− 21,036
Lower Savannah	− 1,496	− 9,046	− 11,629	− 22,171
Pee Dee	− 13,969	None	− 24,266	− 38,235
Upper Savannah	− 155	None	− 12,654	− 12,809
North Central	None	None	− 1,470	− 1,470
Albemarle	None	None	− 8,192	− 8,192
Santee Wateree	None	None	− 29,895	− 29,895
Waccamaw	None	None	− 30,202	− 30,202
South Central	− 36,672	− 77,574	−204,620	− 318,866
Southeast	− 11,333	None	− 18,140	− 29,473
Capital	12,167	None	3,480	15,647
Evangeline	1,194	− 15,802	− 16,307	− 30,915
Kisatchie-Delta	None	− 7,860	20,343	12,483
North Delta	− 3,606	None	− 34,377	− 37,983
Northwest	− 27,578	− 4,175	− 15,108	− 46,861
Central	− 1,975	None	− 24,264	− 26,239
East Central	− 10,456	None	− 18,275	− 28,731

Table D-1 (Cont.)

Regions and Districts	EDC Counties	RC Counties	Non-EDC and Non-RC Counties	Total Regions and Districts
North Central	− 1,173	73,004	− 17,050	− 31,227
South Delta	None	− 36,822	− 29,153	− 65,975
Southern	17,448	None	− 24,346	− 6,898
Southwest	− 12,711	None	− 18,013	− 30,724
Brazos Valley	4,662	None	− 6,953	− 2,291
Central	− 10,046	None	− 3,911	− 13,957
Southeastern Illinois	None	117	− 2,682	− 2,565
Barren River	5,178	None	− 3,128	2,050
Lincoln Trail	− 5,355	None	− 11,141	− 16,496
Pennyrile	− 9,457	None	− 4,447	− 13,904
North Delta	None	− 19,615	− 22,221	− 41,836
Bootheel	− 9,136	− 11,884	− 30,173	− 51,193
Green River	None	None	− 1,839	− 1,839
Purchase	None	None	3,323	3,323
Mid-Cumberland	None	None	31,527	31,527
Tennessee Valley	None	None	− 6,596	− 6,596
Southwest	None	None	− 13,664	− 13,664
Great Lakes	− 28,343	− 21,267	554	− 49,056
Central Upper Peninsula	337	− 2,575	− 3,733	− 6,171
East Central	− 317	None	9,041	8,724
Eastern Upper Peninsula	None	− 10,444	None	− 10,444
Northeast	None	− 1,830	3,964	2,134
Northwest	None	2,293	5,848	8,141
Western Upper Peninsula	− 768	− 8,711	34	− 9,445
Arrowhead	− 27,595	None	− 13,668	− 41,263
Grand Rapids-Muskegon	None	None	3,003	3,003
Region 2	None	None	− 3,137	− 3,137
Region 5	None	None	− 9,423	− 9,423
Northwestern	None	None	8,825	8,825
Coastal Plains	− 76,606	− 23,920	−332,796	− 433,322
Central	− 21,299	− 8,999	− 12,037	− 42,335
Southeast	13,455	None	− 10,969	2,486
Northwest Florida	− 8,265	None	− 2,156	− 10,421
Central Savannah River	8,636	None	− 19,408	− 10,772
Chattahoochee-Flint	− 2,838	None	− 8,906	− 11,744
Coastal Area	416	None	− 2,400	− 1,984
Coastal Plain	− 3,341	None	− 10,539	− 13,880
Heart of Georgia	− 3,827	None	− 11,019	− 14,846
Lower Chattahoochee Valley	− 26,045	None	1,946	− 24,099
Middle Flint	− 1,291	None	− 11,172	− 12,463
Northeast Georgia	12,594	None	− 1,774	10,820

Table D-1 (Cont.)

Regions and Districts	EDC Counties	RC Counties	Non-EDC and Non-RC Counties	Total Regions and Districts
Oconee	− 3,374	None	− 9,902	− 13,276
Slash Pine	− 4,970	None	− 10,282	− 15,252
Southwest	− 8,853	None	− 29,740	− 38,593
Mid-East	− 9,190	− 5,875	− 9,673	− 24,738
Neuse River	− 26,586	None	− 21,629	− 48,215
Deep East	10,034	None	− 2,693	7,341
North East	− 3,299	89	− 4,477	− 7,687
Golden Triangle	None	None	− 18,938	− 18,938
Northeast	None	None	− 10,867	− 10,867
North Central	None	None	34,429	34,429
Northwest	− 5,057	− 13,326	− 13,733	− 32,116
Clearwater	484	None	− 1,196	− 712
Bear Paw	− 3,746	None	− 4,789	− 8,535
Big Horn	− 1,795	None	164	− 1,631
Inter-County	None	− 11,853	683	− 11,170
Trico	None	− 1,473	− 2,035	− 3,508
Northern Idaho	None	None	− 992	− 992
Southwestern	None	None	− 2,767	− 2,767
Upper Columbia	None	None	− 2,801	− 2,801
Far West	None	30,971	251,062	282,033
Sierra	None	30,971	15	30,986
North Coast	None	None	− 19,275	− 19,275
Superior	None	None	5,809	5,809
District Eight	None	None	18,653	18,653
Central Puget Sound	None	None	229,340	229,340
South Puget Sound	None	None	22,187	22,187
Mid-Columbia	None	None	− 5,667	− 5,667
Southwest	− 22,588	− 15,146	− 35,844	− 73,578
Southern	− 19,763	None	− 16,020	− 35,783
North Central	− 1,202	− 5,612	− 12,993	− 19,807
Six-County	− 1,623	− 1,206	− 2,084	− 4,913
Southeastern	None	− 8,328	− 3,613	− 11,941
Southwest	None	None	− 1,134	− 1,134
Rio Grande	− 80,984	− 66,534	− 75,392	− 222,910
Coastal Bend	− 34,952	None	− 46,801	− 81,753
Lower Rio Grande Valley	− 46,032	− 48,529	8,701	− 103,262
Middle Rio Grande Valley	None	− 6,497	− 13,591	− 20,088
South	None	− 11,508	− 6,299	− 17,807
NATIONAL TOTALS	−932,790	−298,608	−374,714	−1,606,112

Notes

Notes

Chapter 4
Program Maturation (October 1966 to January 1969)

1. Ross D. Davis, "Planning for Growth," *Economic Development* (Washington, D.C.: U.S. Department of Commerce/Economic Development Administration, February 1967), vol. 4, no. 2, p. 1.
2. Ibid.
3. Ross D. Davis, "Summary of EDA Mission and Objectives, and Preparation of Office Planning Documents," Economic Development Administration Memorandum, December 30, 1966.
4. Economic Opportunity Amendments of 1967, P.L. 90-222, December 23, 1967.
5. Independent Study Board, *Regional Effects of Government Procurement and Related Policies* (Washington, D.C.: U.S. Department of Commerce/Economic Development Administration, 1967), p. ix.

Chapter 5
The Republican Tenure (February 1969 to September 1971)

1. J.W. Van Gorkom, Chairman, National Public Advisory Committee on Regional Economic Development, Letter to the Honorable Maurice H. Stans, Secretary of Commerce, January 6, 1971.
2. Richard M. Nixon, "1970 State of the Union Message," (Washington, D.C.: U.S. Government Printing Office, 1970).

Chapter 6
Evaluation Approach

1. Public Works and Economic Development Act, Sec. 401(a), 79 Stat. 560 (1965).
2. For a description of the history of per capita personal income by region since 1840, see Hugh O. Nourse, *Regional Economics* (New York: McGraw-Hill, 1968), pp. 145-49. The general conclusion is that the variation in personal income by region is converging to the national average over time. The Advisory Commission on Intergovernmental Relations in its report, *Urban and Rural America: Policies for Future Growth*, April 1968, provides a discussion of the following six growth measures at the regional level over the time period 1950-66: (1) percentage change in per capita income; (2) absolute change in per

capita income; (3) percentage change in population; (4) absolute change in population; (5) percentage change in total income; and (6) absolute change in total income.

3. For a much more detailed description of these secondary measures and their statistical relationship to the primary measures for Office of Business Economics Regions, see the forthcoming thesis of James Sample, "A Study of Economic Development Process Elements and Stages," The American University, 1972.

Chapter 7
Summary of Initial Results and Conclusions

1. Boise Cascade Center for Community Development, *An Evaluation of EDA Public Works Projects* (Washington, D.C.: Boise Cascade Urban Development Corporation, August 1970), vol. 1.

2. *The Economic Development Administration's Public Works Program—An Evaluation* (Washington, D.C.: U.S. Department of Commerce/Economic Development Administration, July 1970), vol. 1.

3. Steven Frank and Joseph W. Noah, *Analysis of the Costs of EDA's Public Works Program* (Washington, D.C.: U.S. Department of Commerce/Economic Development Administration, September 1971).

4. Booz, Allen & Hamilton, Inc., *An Evaluation of the Business Loan Program of the Economic Development Administration* (Washington, D.C.: Booz, Allen & Hamilton, Inc., July 1970), parts I, II, and III.

5. Chilton Research Services, *Multiple Job Shifts Associated with EDA Business Loans* (Philadelphia, Pa.: Chilton Research Services, June 1970).

6. CONSAD Research Corporation, *An Analysis of Economic Development Administration Technical Assistance Projects Activities and Impacts* (Pittsburgh, Pa.: CONSAD Research Corporation, July 1970).

7. Battelle Memorial Institute, *Evaluation of Economic Development Administration Planning Grants* (Columbus, Ohio: Battelle Memorial Institute, May 1970).

Chapter 8
Growth Centers: The Wave of the Future

1. See, for example, Niles M. Hansen, "A Growth Center Strategy for the United States," *Review of Regional Studies* (1969): 161-73; and Brian J.L. Berry, *Potential Growth Centers and Growth Center Potentials in the Upper Great Lakes Region*, a report to the Upper Great Lakes Regional Commission, October 19, 1968.

2. Francois Perroux, "Economic Space: Theory and Applications," *Quarterly Journal of Economics* (February 1950), pp. 90-97.

3. Reported in "Program Evaluation: The Economic Development Administration Growth Center Strategy," (unpublished report, U.S. Department of Commerce/Economic Development Administration, 1972).

4. Lyndon B. Johnson, "Presidential Message on Area and Regional Economic Development," March 25, 1965.

5. Expanded descriptions of these case studies can be found in "Detailed Case Studies of the EDA Growth Center Evaluation" (unpublished report, U.S. Department of Commerce/Economic Development Administration, 1972).

Chapter 9
A Growth Center Identification System

1. See, for example, N. Dann Milne, "Selecting Growth Centers," Economic Development Administration Office of Economic Research Discussion Paper no. 6, April 1970; and Niles M. Hansen, "Criteria for a Growth Center Policy," Economic Development Administration Office of Economic Research Discussion Paper no. 9, September 1970.

2. Donald J. Bogue and Calvin L. Beale, *Economic Areas of the United States* (New York: The Free Press of Glencoe, Inc., April 1961), p. xiiv.

3. Ibid.

4. For a more detailed discussion, see U.S. Department of Commerce Office of Business Economics, Regional Economics Division, *OBE Economic Areas of the United States* (Washington, D.C.: U.S. Department of Commerce/Office of Business Economics, September 1967).

5. For some contributions to the literature on economic base theory, see Irving Morrissett, "The Economic Structure of American Cities," presented at the Regional Science Association Meeting and published in *Papers and Proceedings of the Regional Science Association (1958)*, vol. 4; Edward L. Ullman and Michael F. Dacey, "The Minimum Requirements Approach to the Urban Economic Base," ibid. (1960), vol. 6; and Charles L. Leven, "The Economic Base and Regional Growth," *Research and Education for Regional and Area Development* (Ames, Iowa: Iowa State University Center for Agricultural and Economic Development, Iowa State University Press, 1971).

6. Harvey S. Perloff, et al., *Regions, Resources and Economic Growth* (Lincoln, Nebraska: University of Nebraska Press, 1960), p. 462. In addition to Perloff's view, Ullman and Dacey, p. 189, have empirically determined that manufacturing employment is generally the largest export component of most cities.

7. For a discussion of the roles of the basic and nonbasic sectors in the development process, see Charles M. Tiebout, "The Community Economic Base

Study," *Supplementary Paper No. 16*, Committee for Economic Development. For a discussion of policy implications and the role of the nonbasic sector in the development process, see Charles M. Tiebout and Theodore Lane, "The Local Service Sector in Relation to Economic Growth," *Research and Education for Regional and Area Development* (Ames, Iowa State University Center for Agricultural and Economic Development, Iowa State University Press, 1971).

8. See Perloff, et al.; Victor R. Fuchs, *Changes in Location of Manufacturing in the United States Since 1929* (New Haven, Connecticut: Yale University Press, 1962); George H. Borts and Jerome L. Stein, *Economic Growth in a Free Market* (New York: Columbia University Press, 1964); and Edgar S. Dunn, Jr. "A Statistical and Analytical Technique for Regional Analysis," *Papers and Proceedings of the Regional Science Association*, 1960, vol. 6. For criticisms see David B. Houston, "The Shift and Share Analysis of Regional Growth: A Critique," *The Southern Economic Journal* (April 1967), pp. 577-81, and rejoinder by Lowell D. Ashby, "The Shift and Share Analysis: A Reply," *The Southern Economic Journal* (January 1968), pp. 423-25.

9. The measurement of economic growth is discussed in some detail in the Advisory Commission on Intergovernmental Relations' report entitled *Urban and Rural America; Policies for Future Growth* (Washington, D.C.: Advisory Commission on Intergovernmental Relations, April 1968), A-32, pp. 30-53. See also Harvey S. Perloff, "Problems of Assessing Regional Economic Progress," National Bureau of Economic Research, *Studies in Income and Wealth* (Princeton: Princeton University Press, 1957), vol. 21, pp. 35-62.

Chapter 10
Supporting Analysis for the GCIS

1. "Program Evaluation: The Economic Development Administration Growth Center Strategy," pp. 155-66.

Chapter 11
Economic Development for Indian Reservations

1. "EDA Indian Reservation Data as of June 30, 1971," Economic Development Administration Memorandum.

2. Reported in Alan L. Sorkin, "American Indians Industrialize to Combat Poverty," *Monthly Labor Review*, 92, no. 3 (March 1969): p. 19.

3. Washington, D.C.: U.S. Department of Commerce/Economic Development Administration, n.d., pp. 32-37.

4. Ibid., pp. 34-35.

5. Ibid., pp. 36-37.

Chapter 12
Evaluation of EDA's Training-Related Projects

1. Washington, D.C.: Development Associates, Inc., December 1971.

Chapter 13
Prognosis for the Future

1. Richard M. Nixon, Message to the Senate of the United States, June 29, 1971.

Appendix A

1. Mary Toborg, et al., *Evaluation of EDA's Urban Program: Pilot Test in Chicago, Illinois* (Washington, D.C.: U.S. Department of Commerce/Economic Development Administration, April 1971), vol. 1, pp. I-1-I-14.

2. Bennett Harrison, "Education and Underemployment in the Urban Ghetto," in *The Political Economy of Urban Problems*, ed. David Gordon (Lexington, Massachusetts: D.C. Heath and Company, 1971).

Index

About the Authors

Raymond H. Milkman is currently the Director of Evaluation of the White House's Special Action Office For Drug Abuse Prevention. He was the Assistant Director for Program Analysis at the Economic Development Administration when the data for this book were compiled. Mr. Milkman's specialty is operations research. He lectured in statistics for a number of years at the Johns Hopkins University.

Christopher Bladen is the Chief of the Special Studies Branch of the Economic Development Administration. He was previously associated with Syracuse University. Mr. Bladen's specialty is in program analysis and research. He is coauthor of *Alliance in International Politics.*

Beverly Lyford is on the staff of the Assistant Director for Program Analysis in the Economic Development Administration. Her principal areas of interest are policy analysis and congressional affairs. Ms. Lyford has concentrated on analyses of economic growth center strategies and on an analysis of the Economic Development Administration's policy evolution in helping to prepare this book.

Howard L. Walton is the Deputy Director for Evaluation of the White House's Special Action Office For Drug Abuse Prevention. He is a mathematician with special interest in program evaluation methodology development. Mr. Walton was formerly the Deputy Assistant Director for Program Analysis at the Economic Development Administration. He now teaches at the University of Virginia.